Criminal Law

ASPEN PUBLISHERS

Criminal Law

THE BASICS

Second Edition

FRANK AUGUST SCHUBERT

Northeastern University, Emeritus

Wolters Kluwer

Law & Business

AUSTIN   BOSTON   CHICAGO   NEW YORK   THE NETHERLANDS

Aspen Publishers
Attn: Permissions Department
76 Ninth Avenue, 7th Floor
New York, NY 10011-5201

To contact Customer Care, e-mail customer.service@aspenpublishers.com, call 1-800-234-1660, fax 1-800-901-9075, or mail correspondence to:

Aspen Publishers
Attn: Order Department
PO Box 990
Frederick, MD 21705

Printed in the United States of America.

1 2 3 4 5 6 7 8 9 0

ISBN 978-0-7355-8418-1

Library of Congress Cataloging-in-Publication Data

Schubert, Frank A.
  Criminal law : the basics/Frank August Schubert.—2nd ed.
    p. cm.
  Includes index.
  ISBN 978-0-7355-8418-1
1. Criminal law—United States. 2. Criminal law—United States—Cases. I. Title.
  KF9218.S38 2010
  345.73-dc22

                                                                2010011490

About Wolters Kluwer Law & Business

Wolters Kluwer Law & Business is a leading provider of research information and workflow solutions in key specialty areas. The strengths of the individual brands of Aspen Publishers, CCH, Kluwer Law International and Loislaw are aligned within Wolters Kluwer Law & Business to provide comprehensive, in-depth solutions and expert-authored content for the legal, professional and education markets.

CCH was founded in 1913 and has served more than four generations of business professionals and their clients. The CCH products in the Wolters Kluwer Law & Business group are highly regarded electronic and print resources for legal, securities, antitrust and trade regulation, government contracting, banking, pension, payroll, employment and labor, and healthcare reimbursement and compliance professionals.

Aspen Publishers is a leading information provider for attorneys, business professionals and law students. Written by preeminent authorities, Aspen products offer analytical and practical information in a range of specialty practice areas from securities law and intellectual property to mergers and acquisitions and pension/benefits. Aspen's trusted legal education resources provide professors and students with high-quality, up-to-date and effective resources for successful instruction and study in all areas of the law.

Kluwer Law International supplies the global business community with comprehensive English-language international legal information. Legal practitioners, corporate counsel and business executives around the world rely on the Kluwer Law International journals, loose-leafs, books and electronic products for authoritative information in many areas of international legal practice.

Loislaw is a premier provider of digitized legal content to small law firm practitioners of various specializations. Loislaw provides attorneys with the ability to quickly and efficiently find the necessary legal information they need, when and where they need it, by facilitating access to primary law as well as state-specific law, records, forms and treatises.

Wolters Kluwer Law & Business, a unit of Wolters Kluwer, is headquartered in New York and Riverwoods, Illinois. Wolters Kluwer is a leading multinational publisher and information services company.

TO WALLACE W. SHERWOOD, ESQ.,

A WONDERFUL LAWYER, EDUCATOR, AND FRIEND

SUMMARY OF CONTENTS

CHAPTER 1

Introduction to Criminal Law

CHAPTER 2

Constitutional Limitations on the Definition and Punishment of Criminal Offenses

---

C H A P T E R 3
General Principles of Criminal Liability

CHAPTER 4

Complicity and Vicarious Liability

Criminal Defenses

CHAPTER 6

Crimes Against Persons

CHAPTER 7

Crimes Against Property and Habitation

Inchoate Crimes and Derivative Crime

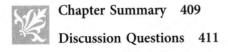

Appendix A: Reading and Understanding the *Lopez* Case   413

Appendix B: Procedural Considerations   419

This textbook is intended for undergraduate students enrolled in a one-semester introductory course in criminal law. It is an outgrowth of my over 40-year career interest in criminal law as a law student, practitioner (police administration and prosecutor), college professor, and author. My objective has been to write a focused, understandable, and concise exposition on the basic principles of criminal law. The text introduces students to the most important concepts in an interesting, intellectually challenging subject and explains how our democracy uses law to respond to the problem of crime in our society.

Back in 1980, when I was new to teaching criminal law, I required my students to read every chapter in a 700-page textbook that was overstuffed with information. After teaching the course a few times, I discovered, to my chagrin, that many students were not focusing on learning what I thought was the crux of the course. Instead of concentrating on learning the basic concepts, they were trying to memorize bits of information and "black letter rules." Many students confessed that they were overwhelmed by the seeming complexity of the topics, intimidated by the legal jargon, and exhausted by the lengthy reading assignments.

It was obvious that if I wanted students to learn "the important things," I had to be willing to trade breadth of coverage for increased understanding. I had to focus on teaching the basic conceptual building blocks of criminal law. My response was to cut the amount of required reading, reduce the amount of information that students were expected to learn, and insist that students really understand what was being taught. My shift in emphasis resulted in my having more time to better explain concepts. The class atmosphere was more relaxed and students actually began to ask questions. My students began reporting on their teacher/course evaluations that they were learning more and that the course was more interesting than they had anticipated. The university even gave me an award for teaching excellence.

This textbook consists of eight chapters. The first five chapters establish a sound foundation for the discussion of substantive offenses that follows. The substantive offenses discussed in the final three chapters give students an ample opportunity to apply the foundational concepts they have learned in earlier chapters as they learn about specific criminal offenses. Chapters 6 and 7 focus on crimes against persons (homicide, assault and battery, rape and sexual assault, kidnapping, and false imprisonment), and crimes against property and habitation (larceny, embezzlement, false pretenses, theft, robbery, extortion, forgery, burglary, arson, and trespassing). Chapter 8 addresses inchoate and derivative crimes (solicitation, attempt, conspiracy, and RICCO offenses).

Underlying Themes

The text emphasizes two underlying themes: the common law heritage that has so influenced criminal law in this country and the importance of federalism in our republic. Few students are aware of the common law's significant role in the development of American criminal law. Many enter the course expecting to study "the criminal law" and are surprised to learn that there are actually fifty-one sets of "criminal laws" in this country. While almost all students are aware of the U.S. Supreme Court and the existence of federal courts, few know anything about the constitutional boundaries that theoretically distinguish federal and state jurisdiction. This text helps to clarify, albeit at a basic level, some of the issues and implications of these themes.

Use of Cases

The text relies primarily on carefully edited appellate opinions coupled with brief, textual expositions to explain relevant principles. Once students learn how to read cases, they will find that they are better able to understand the underlying legal principles because these principles are presented within the context of a real dispute.

Instructors will find that cases work well in the classroom and can be used to teach both substantive and procedural law. By systematically guiding students through each case, instructors can help students understand the "what" of each case, as well as the more important question, the "why." If an instructor manipulates the facts of the cases, other questions and issues will arise and students will learn how to reason from example to example. This process naturally encourages class participation and the ultimate goal—learning. The cases have been carefully selected for their "teachability." Statutes are often included so that students understand that it is the legislature and not the courts that primarily defines what is criminal and determines the sentencing options.

Website

In the interest of saving space in the printed text, supplemental materials—including cases, text, statutes, and dissenting/concurring opinions that are too long to include in the printed text—are available on the textbook's website. The website materials will be periodically updated to reflect current developments in criminal law.

Textbook Resources

In the interest of saving space in the printed text, supplemental materials—including cases, text, statutes, and dissenting/concurring opinions that are too long to include in the printed text—are available on the textbook's companion website at **www.aspenlawschool.com/schubert_criminallaw/**. The website provides additional resources for students and instructors, including:

- Study aids to help students master the key concepts for this course. Visit the site to access interactive StudyMate exercises such as flash cards, matching, fill-in-the-blank, and crosswords. These activities are also available for download to an iPod or other hand-held device.
- Instructor resources to accompany the text, including additional cases.
- Links to helpful websites and updates.

The website materials will be periodically updated to reflect current developments in criminal law.

Criminal Law: The Basics comes packaged with four months of prepaid access to Loislaw's online legal research database, at http://www.loislawschool.com/.

Blackboard and eCollege course materials are also available to supplement this text. This online courseware is designed to streamline the teaching of the course, providing valuable resources from the book in an accessible electronic format.

Lastly, instructor resources to accompany this text include a comprehensive Instructor's Manual, Test Bank, and PowerPoint slides. All of these materials are available on a CD-ROM or for download from our companion website.

This textbook would not have been possible without the valuable contributions of numerous individuals. I would like to thank the following reviewers, whose suggestions and insightful commentary helped to shape the content of the second edition of this book: Marisol Abuin, Berkeley College; Frank Butler, La Salle University; Janine Ferraro, Nassau Community College; Peter Collins, Washington State University; Ivy Kempf, Peirce College; Nikole Knight, Bronx Community College; Michael Stevenson, University of Toledo; and Jennifer Walsh, Azusa Pacific University.

The dedicated professionals at Aspen Publishers also significantly improved the manuscript. Special thanks go to Betsy Kenny and Troy Froebe.

This edition is dedicated to my former colleague for 25 years at Northeastern University, Professor Wallace Sherwood. His dedication to law and the teaching of criminal law have benefited Northeastern students for over 35 years.

Finally, I wish to thank two special people in my family who have directly assisted me in writing this book. First, thanks go to my daughter Tracy for her work in proofreading the text. I am very proud that my daughter has so directly contributed to the completion of this project. As always, I thank my wife Barbara, who has constantly encouraged and supported my writing endeavors. Her suggestions, insight, and perspective have greatly influenced my thinking, writing, and teaching for over three decades.

It has been my experience that while undergraduate students find the study of criminal law to be fascinating, many attempting to read judicial opinions for the first time find the legal jargon and the formalistic language used by appellate court judges intimidating. The following suggestions are offered to help you overcome this barrier. The most important task is to strengthen your vocabulary skills. A good technique for ensuring long-term retention of newly acquired vocabulary is to develop a "personal dictionary" that you can refer to and periodically revise. Basically, at first you need to look up every word with which you are unfamiliar. Many of these words will be included in the glossary at the back of this textbook. You can find most nontechnical words in a standard English dictionary. For legal jargon, you can either buy a paperback version of a legal dictionary or use an online legal dictionary (one good source is *www.Findlaw.com*). If you systematically look up unfamiliar words, record them in a personal dictionary, and revise and review the dictionary's contents from time to time, your vocabulary skills will improve. As vocabulary skills strengthen, you'll need less time to read and understand the cases and you'll begin to experience a "learning dividend." That is, you'll discover that you can read and understand not only this and other textbooks but also newspaper and magazine articles that contain legal terms. If you make the commitment to strengthen your vocabulary skills, you are likely to jump the vocabulary hurdle by the third or fourth week. The learning dividend will continue to pay off for a lifetime.

Criminal Law

Introduction to Criminal Law

CHAPTER OUTLINE

1

Criminal Law

Although there is no commonly accepted definition of law, it is possible to identify probably the two primary features of American criminal law. Firstly, the respected English philosopher H. L. A. Hart once observed, "The most prominent general feature of law at all times and places is that its existence means that certain kinds of human conduct are no longer optional, but are in some sense obligatory."[1] Secondly, as Henry M. Hart famously noted,[2] convicted persons are formally branded as deserving of societal contempt. The consequences of being stigmatized as an "ex-con" often last a lifetime. This stigma works best when the public agrees with and strongly supports laws which declare specified conduct as criminal. This is certainly the case with laws that punish those who harm others such as murderers, rapists, robbers, and sexual predators. But the stigma can backfire if government attaches the criminal label to conduct prohibited by laws that are widely viewed as unjust. Martin Luther King, Rosa Parks, Representative John Lewis, and countless others were arrested during the 1950s and 1960s for protesting racial segregation in this country. Certainly no ex-con stigma has attached to these civil rights heroes in part because of the "justness" of their cause, but also because they responded non-violently to even brutal attacks by the "law enforcers."[3]

Sometimes it has been politically advantageous to be arrested. During the week of Thanksgiving in 1984, some three dozen people participated in well-choreographed and orchestrated "celebrity arrests of the day" for illegally protesting against apartheid outside the South African Embassy in Washington, D.C. Some of those arrested were politicians who found it helpful in their campaigns to be able to claim that their misdemeanor convictions proved the depth of their commitment to changing the South African government's racist policies.

Approximately 14 states have concluded (to varying degrees) that criminalizing the possession of small amounts of marijuana is not good public policy and have reclassified such possession as a civil rather than a criminal offense. The significance of this decriminalization is that it makes offenders only subject to a civil fine and eliminates the risk of imprisonment and a criminal record, at least for a first offense. States have great flexibility in defining what conduct to criminalize so long as those decisions conform to basic state and federal constitutional requirements.

Lawmaking in America

The process of deciding what conduct is criminalized and which governmental apparatus is responsible for enacting criminal laws in America is heavily influenced by structural and cultural considerations that require special attention in an introductory criminal law course.

One of the most important structural influences on lawmaking was the founder's decision that the country would feature the federal form of government. The most important cultural influence on American lawmaking was the acceptance in most of the country of the **common law** tradition. For some, the following discussion will simply be a review of topics that have been previously mastered. For others, it will introduce important concepts that are essential to an understanding of substantive criminal law.

The Federal Form of Government

The decision that this country would have a federal form of government was pivotal to our future. Under **federalism**, governmental power is disbursed and not concentrated in one all-powerful national government. The national and state governments are sovereign and complete with executive, legislative, and judicial branches. In the United States, some power is delegated to the national government, but in theory the remaining power is either retained by the states or by the people. The founder's decision to adopt federalism was certainly influenced by the serious problems encountered between 1781 and 1788 when our country experimented with the Articles of Confederation. The confederation model featured an extremely weak national government and powerful states that wouldn't collaborate with one another and often refused to comply with treaties negotiated by the national government. Some of the biggest problems confronting the national government under the Articles were its inability to regulate commerce, impose and collect taxes, enact national laws, and operate national courts. These failures were the catalyst for replacing the Articles with a new constitution.

The Police Power of the States

It is important to remember at the outset of this discussion that the original colonies (which became American states in 1781 upon adoption of the Articles of Confederation) were fully functioning governmental units under the British monarchs prior to the Revolutionary War and sovereign governments prior to the ratification of our Constitution in 1788. Among the most important powers exercised by the original colonies was what is called the **police power**. This term refers to the right of the sovereign states to exercise broad legislative powers for the purpose of protecting the public health, safety, welfare, and morals. The original colonies never relinquished the police power to the national government and thus retained the right to continue exercising this power after the colonies became states.[4] That is why each of the state governments today has the constitutional right to enact and enforce criminal laws (subject to limitations contained in the U.S. Constitution).

The Source of the Federal Government's Lawmaking Power

The sole source of the national government's powers is the U.S. Constitution. The Constitution expressly grants specific legislative powers to the federal government in **Article I, Section 8** of the Constitution (as supplemented by the 13th, 14th, 15th, 23rd, 24th, and 26th Amendments).[5] When Congress wants to enact a criminal statute based on an implicit grant of power (i.e., a power not expressly authorized in Article 1) it often seeks shelter in the Constitution's Commerce and Necessary and Proper Clauses (see Article I, Section 8, Clauses 3 and 18). Congress first claims that the statute it has created is necessary to remedy some specified problem. It then claims that the problem identified is substantially harmful to interstate commerce. A good example of this scenario is a famous 1964 case, *Heart of Atlanta Motel v. United States*, 379 U.S. 241 (1964). In that case, Congress wanted to stamp out racial discrimination in public accommodations in this country. It included a provision to that affect in the Civil Rights Act of 1964. The motel, which only accepted bookings from whites, said that Congress had no constitutional right to require it to accept bookings from non-whites. The U.S. Supreme Court sided with Congress, asserting that only permitting whites to stay at the motel could "substantially" and "adversely" affect interstate commerce. (Students can read this case on Loislaw and online by searching for *Heart of Atlanta Motel v. United States*). Later on in this chapter readers will learn more about the federal government's right to criminalize conduct that directly and indirectly affect matters of federal concern.

Federal and State Jurisdiction Can Overlap

It is common for a single criminal act to simultaneously violate federal and state criminal laws. Thus each sovereign can declare in its **statutes** that it is a crime to rob a bank. The federal government will provide in the **U.S. Code** that it is a crime to rob a federally insured bank. The states will prohibit bank robbery in their state statutes. And if state law permits, it will be constitutionally permissible for a person who robs one federally insured bank to be prosecuted twice for this robbery. There would be no double jeopardy problem because each sovereign is prosecuting the offender once. The state is acting pursuant to the police power, and the federal government is proceeding pursuant to its Article 1 powers in the federal Constitution. There will be more discussion about this later on in the textbook.

The distribution of power between the state and federal governments, while theoretically distinct, often turns out to be ambiguous in practice. This ambiguity can create friction between the federal and state government as to who had jurisdiction. One source of friction is when Congress attempts to legislate in an area that arguably is beyond the scope of its Article 1, Section 8 powers. When turf disputes like this arise, the U.S. Supreme Court is sometimes called upon to decide whether Congress was "out of bounds." Beginning in 1937 during the Great Depression and lasting for almost 60 years, the Court had a policy of deferring to the Congress in jurisdictional disputes if its legislation targeted a problem that, although only minimally impacting interstate commerce on main street in small towns, could have a substantial impact on commerce when viewed from the broader, national perspective (i.e., like in *Heart of Atlanta Motel*).

That changed, however, in 1995 when the Supreme Court decided *United States v. Lopez*, (514 U.S. 549 (1995)). Congress, said the Court, was not constitutionally permitted to enact a criminal statute making it a federal crime for a person to possess a firearm in a school zone. The Court rejected the government's claim that the statute and commerce were sufficiently connected to permit federal jurisdiction.

Internet Tip

Additional materials for each chapter that augment the textual discussion can be found on the textbook's website. The Chapter 1 portion of the website, for example, contains the Gun-Free School Zone statute from the U.S. Code, as well as additional text relating to federalism and the police power.

The Chapter 1 materials also include a more detailed discussion of federalism, the historical evolution of the Commerce Clause, and an edited version of *United States v. Lopez*.

Ten years later, however, in the case of *Gonzales v. Raich*, 545 U.S. 1 (2005), the U.S. Supreme Court ruled that Congress did have the right under the **Commerce Clause** to prohibit California and eight other states from statutorily permitting the instate cultivation and use of marijuana for medicinal purposes. Justice O'Connor wrote a dissenting opinion in which she explained why she believed that the states had the right to enact such statutes. (Students can read the majority and dissenting opinion online through Loislaw.) Justice O'Connor wrote in dissent and argued on behalf of preserving state sovereignty.

Justice Sandra Day O'Connor, dissenting

We enforce the "outer limits" of Congress' Commerce Clause authority not for their own sake, but to protect historic spheres of state sovereignty from excessive federal encroachment and thereby to maintain the distribution of power fundamental to our federalist system of government. . . . One of federalism's chief virtues, of course, is that it promotes innovation by allowing for the possibility that "a single courageous State may, if its citizens choose, serve as a laboratory; and try novel social and economic experiments without risk to the rest of the country." . . .

This case exemplifies the role of States as laboratories. The States' core police powers have always included authority to define criminal law and to protect the health, safety, and welfare of their citizens. . . . Exercising those powers, California (by ballot initiative and then by legislative codification) has come to its own conclusion about the difficult and sensitive question of whether marijuana should be available to relieve severe pain and suffering. Today the Court sanctions an application of the federal Controlled Substances Act that extinguishes that experiment, without any proof that the personal cultivation, possession, and use of marijuana for medicinal purposes, if economic activity in the first place, has a substantial effect on interstate commerce and is therefore an appropriate subject of federal regulation. In so doing, the Court announces a rule that gives Congress a perverse incentive to legislate broadly pursuant to the Commerce Clause—nestling questionable assertions of its authority into comprehensive regulatory schemes—rather than with precision. That rule and the result it produces in this case are irreconcilable with our decisions in *Lopez, supra*. . . . Accordingly I dissent. . . .

AUTHOR'S COMMENTARY

It is important to note that although *Gonzales v. Raich* remains the law of the land, and the federal government has a legal right to prosecute, federal enforcement policy with respect to the targeting of individuals who use marijuana for medicinal purposes has changed dramatically under the Obama administration. In October 2009, Attorney General Holder promulgated enforcement guidelines which provided that federal resources should not be focused on individuals who reside in one of the approximately 13 states that authorize the use of marijuana for medicinal purposes if the individuals exercising this right are fully compliant with that state's law. The Attorney General emphasized that this is an exception and that the Department of Justice remains fully committed to otherwise enforcing the federal laws prohibiting the illegal distribution and sale of marijuana.

Because of federalism, state governments, within constitutional limits, have experimented and developed unique responses to public problems, and they can innovate without having to obtain permission from other states or from the national government. Examples include Nebraska's adoption of its unicameral legislature (a single house state legislature); California's "three strikes" sentencing law; Colorado's "make my day" self defense law; Oregon's and Washington's enactment of assisted-suicide laws; Vermont's and New Hampshire's legislatively enacted same-sex marriage laws and the judicial recognition of same-sex marriages in Massachusetts, Connecticut, and Iowa; and Louisiana's decision to permit juries to convict defendants in criminal cases where 9 out of 12 jurors are convinced of the defendant's guilt beyond a reasonable doubt.

It is very important that students reading this textbook understand that because of federalism we do not have a "national" criminal law applicable at the state level of government. Although the federal government enforces the federal criminal statutes nationwide, each state determines for itself what constitutes a burglary, robbery, or arson, etc., and how offenders should be sentenced. Thus state laws often differ. Readers are encouraged to use Loislaw and discover the extent to which the criminal statutes in neighboring states differ from corresponding laws in the reader's home state.

The Supremacy Clause and the Tenth Amendment

The founding fathers were aware that federalism would inevitably produce jurisdictional conflicts between the national government and the states. Their response was the Tenth Amendment to the Constitution and Article VI's **Supremacy Clause**. The Tenth Amendment provides that "powers not delegated to the United States by the Constitution . . . are reserved to the states . . . or to the people." The Supremacy Clause provides, in general, that state laws are invalid if they frustrate or are contrary to congressional objectives in a subject area that is appropriately within the federal domain. In cases of conflicts between federal and state laws, courts consider the nature of the subject matter, any vital national interests that may be involved, the need for uniformity between state and federal laws, and the expressed or implied intent of Congress.[6]

 Internet Tip

For a discussion of jurisdictional friction between the federal and state governments as a consequence of the increasing overlapping of responsibility for crimes that have traditionally been the responsibility of the states, please see the website for the text.

Having examined the most important structural considerations of American criminal law we turn to the historical considerations.

The Common Law Tradition

You may recall from your study of American history that most of the colonists who settled along the eastern seaboard of what is now the United States in the early 1600s were English. These settlers brought with them the English language, English culture, and the distinguishing characteristic of the seventeenth-century English legal tradition, the common law.

Although the antecedents of the common law go back to Anglo-Saxon times, histories of the common law often highlight the contributions of William the Conqueror's fourth son, Henry I (monarch from 1100 to 1135) and Henry II (monarch from 1154 to 1189 and Henry I's grandson). One of Henry I's most important innovations was the requirement that members of his council (the Curia Regis) ride circuit throughout England listening to pleas and supervising the local courts. Henry II is credited with professionalizing the judges (choosing as judges members of his council who had ridden circuit) and institutionalizing a national court system. During his reign, the Court of Common Pleas (courts by that same name exist today in Ohio, South Carolina, and Delaware) was established, which started a process that ultimately resulted in the king's courts replacing the communal courts (which had generally applied the local, customary law of the region) and the feudal law practiced in the courts of the barons. Because the king's courts applied the same body of law throughout England (a system based on precedent), the law applied in the king's courts became known as the common law. By approximately 1400, the national court system and the common law were supreme.

Obviously, the inhabitants in England's North American colonies were greatly influenced by the common law. The colonists' understanding of the common law was greatly enhanced by the publication in 1765 of the immensely popular **Commentaries on the Laws of England**, a collection of lectures on English common law written by Sir William Blackstone. It is said that prospective lawyers—down to and including Abraham Lincoln—read Blackstone as part of their legal training. If you are interested in perusing Blackstone, look for it on the shelves of your college library. These early Americans, however, often modified or rejected Blackstone's rules whenever they were found to be unworkable or undesirable.

Following the American Revolution there was considerable public backlash against things English, and many states began replacing the traditional reliance on judge-made law with written statutes enacted by the state's legislature. Many of these statutes contained provisions similar to the principles of the English common law, but they were now more acceptable, having been "Americanized" through their transformation into statutory form.

The common law was known for its often inflexible and complex procedures as well as its substantive law. Growing dissatisfaction with common law procedures in the late 1840s resulted in a movement for fundamental legal reforms.[7] Contract law, for example, gradually replaced the old writ of assumpsit, and the fault-based concept of tort law eventually replaced the venerable thirteenth-century writ of trespass on the case. Collections of statutes, called **codes**, began to appear. The codes were essentially collections of statutes that related to a particular topic (such as property law, criminal law, and civil procedure). They are not, however, always comprehensive compilations and important details are often found in supplementing regulations.[8]

Reformers also encouraged a shift away from the technicalities and vagaries of the old common law writ system and toward standardized rules of civil procedure. The momentum for reform increased in the aftermath of the Civil War as the country experienced massive population growth and rapid industrialization. Reformers during the late 1800s and early 1900s (some of whom called themselves "progressives") organized to refocus the nation's priorities on the problems of middle- and lower-class people.

The first half of the twentieth century brought a major depression bookended between two world wars. All these events led to yet further public demand for social, economic, and political as well as legal change. Interest groups formed and lobbied for legal reforms favoring organized labor, civil rights, and the women's and environmental movements, often expanding on themes raised by the progressives.

Yet, despite all these changes, many traditional common law principles have survived to the present, although sometimes in modified form. Today, all federal and state courts turn to the common law when determining the meaning of constitutional rights, judicial doctrines, and statutes. As we proceed through the chapters of this text, readers will see examples illustrating how the common law continues to influence American law in the twenty-first century.

Common Law and Criminal Codes

Table 1.1 illustrates what have come to be known as the **common law crimes**. Most common law offenses were originally defined as criminal by judges rather than by legislatures. Although, after 1812 federal criminal prosecutions could not be based on violations of the common law,[9] the movement at the state level to replace common law crimes with legislatively enacted criminal codes (statutes) occurred during the late 1850s.

Today, crimes are primarily defined by statute. Statutes are generally organized into what are called criminal codes. Figures 1.1 and 1.2 illustrate the difference between judge-made criminal law and legislatively enacted criminal codes. The current Massachusetts assault statute is illustrative of the common law approach (see Figure 1.1). Notice that the statute defines how a person convicted

TABLE 1.1 COMMON LAW CRIMES

Felonies	Misdemeanors
Arson	Assault
Burglary	Battery
Larceny	Corrupting morals
Manslaughter	Disturbing the peace
Murder	False imprisonment
Rape	Libel
Robbery	Perjury

Figure 1.1. Massachusetts General Law Chapter 265:13A

> **Assault or assault and battery; punishment**
> Section 13A. Whoever commits an assault or an assault and battery upon another shall be punished by imprisonment for not more than two and one half years in a house of correction or by a fine of not more than five hundred dollars.
> A summons may be issued instead of a warrant for the arrest of any person upon a complaint for a violation of any provision of this section if in the judgment of the court or justice reviewing the complaint there is reason to believe that he will appear upon a summons.

of assault can be punished but does not define the elements that must be proven for conviction of the crime—that determination is addressed in opinions handed down by the judges of the Massachusetts Supreme Judicial Court.

The Massachusetts Supreme Judicial Court explained in a leading 1962 assault case that "with respect to the crime of assault, . . . the Legislature has prescribed the penalty for the crime but has not defined the crime itself. . . . For the definition of the crime of assault, resort must be had to the common law."[10] Thus the elements of the crime are to be found in the case law, rather than in the statutes.

The imprecision of the common law was one of the motivating factors that led reformers such as the authors of the **Model Penal Code**[11] to call for the abolition of common law crimes. But some states have partially resisted the change. In Massachusetts, for example, the Governor's Committee on Law Enforcement and the Administration of Criminal Justice, which in 1972 was chaired by the state's attorney general, unsuccessfully urged the state legislature to adopt a state penal code that was based on the recommendations of the Model Penal Code. This

Figure 1.2. Proposed Criminal Code of Massachusetts Chapter 265 Part 3. Assault (not adopted)

Section 6. Assault in the First Degree

A person is guilty of assault in the first degree, a class B felony, if he:

(a) intentionally causes serious bodily injury to another person;

(b) intentionally causes serious bodily injury to another person with a dangerous weapon;

(c) knowingly or recklessly causes serious bodily injury to another person under circumstances manifesting extreme indifference to the value of human life; or

(d) knowingly or recklessly causes serious bodily injury to another person with a dangerous weapon.

Section 7. Assault in the Second Degree (omitted in the interests of space)

Section 8. Assault in the Third Degree (omitted in the interests of space)

---

proposal would have replaced the common law crimes with the following statute. Excerpts from the proposed assault statute can be seen in Figure 1.2.[12]

Notice that the proposed statute in Figure 1.2 not only defines the elements of assault, it also determines the range of penalties that can be imposed on a convicted person (class B felony).

Because the preceding discussion made reference to the Model Penal Code, it is appropriate at this time to explain what that code is and why it is important.

The Model Penal Code

Model codes are sets of proposed laws in a given subject area that are prepared as a resource for lawmakers and law reformers. They are not law unless and until they become enacted into law by a lawmaking body such as a state legislature. The Model Penal Code, for example, was written primarily by legal scholars, judges, and lawyers interested in assisting criminal law reform in this nation in the 1950s. Law reformers were frustrated with the common law's inconsistencies, ambiguities, and backward-looking tendencies. The authors developed this model code in order to present a comprehensive set of statutory alternatives to the criminal law approaches that had been unchanged in many states for over 100 years. The major headings of the Model Penal Code can be seen in Table 1.2.

Many jurisdictions have been influenced by the Model Penal Code, and from time to time readers will find portions of its contents reprinted in this text. The proposed (but not adopted) Criminal Code of Massachusetts chapter relating to assault, which is depicted in Figure 1.2, was based on the Model Penal Code.

Having almost completed our discussion of the structural and historical foundations of American law making, it is time to prepare to read the textbook's first

TABLE 1.2	MAJOR HEADINGS OF THE MODEL PENAL CODE

Part 1 General Provisions	Part II Definition of Specific Crimes
Article 1. Preliminary	Offenses involving danger to the person
Article 2. General principles of liability	Offenses against property
Article 3. General principles of justification	Offenses against the family
Article 4. Responsibility	Offenses against public administration
Article 5. Inchoate crimes	Offenses against public order and decency
Article 6. Authorized disposition of offenders	

Model Penal Code, copyright 1985 by The American Law Institute. All rights reserved. Reprinted with permission.

case, a case in which a criminal defendant challenges his common law based prosecution. Before reading the first case, however, readers may want to develop their reading and/or briefing skills.

Reading, Briefing, and Understanding the First Case

This textbook relies on edited case reports to illustrate the legal principles being discussed. It is common for students reading a case report for the first time to have difficulty understanding the material. The author has placed tips on reading and briefing cases and a sample brief of *United States v. Lopez* in the appendix to this textbook. Interested readers should consider looking at this material and perhaps take a second look at the Author's Note to Students that follows the Preface to this text. Students who are required by their instructors to brief case reports will find these materials and suggestions especially helpful.

As readers will see in the first case, prosecutors will occasionally charge a defendant with a common law offense where no appropriate statutory crime exists (this option is only available, however, in those states which have not abolished all common law crimes).

Criminal defense attorneys frequently move to dismiss common law charges against their clients, claiming that no such common law offense has been recognized in that state. This happened in South Carolina in 1980 with respect to a common law crime known as **misprision of felony**. Under the common law of England, a person who knew about the commission of a felony had a legal duty to notify authorities. Whether misprision of a felony should be recognized as a common law crime in South Carolina was put before that state's highest court.

STATE v. ISAAC E. CARSON
262 S.E.2d 918
Supreme Court of South Carolina
February 19, 1980

AUTHOR'S INTRODUCTION

Isaac Carson was prosecuted for misprision of a felony in the aftermath of a murder and armed robbery. The police alleged that Carson had not been truthful with them about whether he had witnessed the commission of the two crimes. They further alleged that Carson had committed misprision by withholding information from the police concerning his knowledge about the commission of the crimes. Carson, subsequent to his arrest, admitted that he had been present at the scene and provided information that exonerated him from any possible criminal liability as an aider and/or abettor of the perpetrators. Carson was tried and convicted of misprision and sentenced to three years imprisonment. Carson appealed to the South Carolina Supreme Court. On appeal, Carson claimed that the trial court should have granted his motion for a directed verdict of acquittal. Carson argued that misprision of felony prosecutions were prohibited by the federal and state constitutional protections against self-incrimination.

It is important to note that Carson had been charged with common law misprision of felony because there was no such statutory crime in that state. Amazingly, Isaac Carson was the only person to be tried for misprision of felony in South Carolina since 1712 (you can find this historical nugget on Loislaw on page 627 of the following case, *State v. McAteer*, 333 S.C. 615, 627 (Ct. App. 1998)).

Although the South Carolina Code of Laws did not include a misprision of felony statute, that state's law code did include the following highly relevant statute (see Figure 1-3).

Figure 1.3. South Carolina Code of Laws 14-1-50

§ 14-1-50. Common law of England shall continue in effect.

All, and every part, of the common law of England, where it is not altered by the Code or inconsistent with the Constitution or laws of this State, is hereby continued in full force and effect in the same manner as before the adoption of this section.

OPINION OF THE COURT

GREGORY, Justice:

. . . The offense of misprision of felony is a part of the common law of England and of this country as well. . . . It is also recognized by statute in the federal law [18 U.S.C. § 4.] . . . and in certain jurisdictions wherein it is punishable as a misdemeanor.

Appellant and the state are in agreement with the following description of the common law offense:

> It is described as a criminal neglect either to prevent a felony from being committed or to bring the offender to justice after its commission, but without such previous concert with, or subsequent assistance of, him as will make the concealer an accessory before or after the fact. . . .
>
> Under the federal and state statutes embodying the offense, mere silence or failure to come forward is not enough to constitute misprision; there must be some positive act of concealment of the felony. . . .

It cannot be seriously questioned that the offense, cognizable at common law, exists in this state. Section 14-1-50, Code of Laws of South Carolina (1976). . . .

Appellant argues against our recognition of the offense on the grounds it has lain dormant for so long and is without precedent in this state. However, this argument was not raised in the court below and . . . is therefore improperly before us for the first time on appeal. . . . We note, however, that had such an argument been raised and preserved, it would yet be unpersuasive. It is clear that the common law will not be impliedly changed, but only by clear and unambiguous legislative enactment will the settled rules of common law be eroded. . . . The General Assembly has neither enacted, modified nor repealed the common law offense of misprision of felony.

Appellant contends the offense by its very nature conflicts with his privilege against self-incrimination. We disagree. While it is true the privilege sometimes works to bar prosecution for misprision, this is only when the statements concealed would incriminate the defendant as an accessory or principal in the protected felony. . . .

Here, there is no particular conflict with the proscription against self-incrimination shown. Appellant deliberately concealed important information when police first questioned him which, when later disclosed, fully exculpates appellant from the crimes he witnessed. The argument that his arrest demonstrates he was in an incriminating position overlooks the reason for his arrest. Appellant created a reasonable and probable cause to believe he was involved in the crimes by concealing information and denying he was present in the face of independent evidence obtained . . . by the police that appellant was at the scene of the crimes. In fact, appellant was neither a principal nor an accessory before or after the fact, but merely a witness who concealed valuable information from the investigating officers. That in itself constitutes the common law offense of misprision of felony.

The judgment of the lower court is accordingly affirmed.

CASE QUESTIONS

1. Why did the South Carolina Supreme Court recognize misprision of a felony as a common law defense?

2. South Carolina is the only state that continues to recognize the common law crime misprision of felony. Does that fact influence how you feel about South Carolina's continued support of this common law crime?

AUTHOR'S COMMENTARY

The federal government and South Dakota are currently the only remaining American jurisdictions that by statute permit misprision of felony prosecutions (see Figure 1-4). But federal prosecutors charge persons with violating the federal misprision statute in federal district courts located in all 50 states. It is very ironic that there are many instances in which attorneys plead guilty to federal misprision charges in states which don't even recognize misprision of felony as a crime. These accused attorneys, if convicted, may subsequently face disciplinary sanctions from a regulatory board, which can include the revocation or suspension of their licenses to practice law. They have, after all, been convicted of a felony. (Readers can see this for themselves by going to Loislaw and searching "all state cases" for the words "misprision of felony").

Figure 1.4. Surviving Misprision Statutes

South Dakota Misprision Statute

22-11-12. Any person who, having knowledge, which is not privileged, of the commission of a felony, conceals the felony, or does not immediately disclose the felony, including the name of the perpetrator, if known, and all of the other relevant known facts, to the proper authorities, is guilty of misprision of a felony. Misprision of a felony is a Class 1 misdemeanor

United States Code Title 18 Section 4

Sec. 4. Misprision of felony

Whoever, having knowledge of the actual commission of a felony cognizable by a court of the United States, conceals and does not as soon as possible make known the same to some judge or other person in civil or military authority under the United States, shall be fined under this title or imprisoned not more than three years, or both.

Having completed the discussion of common law crimes, we now address what lawmakers have to consider when determining what conduct should be classified as criminal.

Deciding What Conduct Is Deemed Criminal

The determination of whether particular conduct should be classified as criminal involves a balancing of two competing, fundamental priorities. On the one hand, Americans expect government to protect them from crime. They want laws in place that criminalize conduct that threatens or injures their physical well-being, wrongfully disrupts public order, violates their property, or infringes on their privacy rights. On the other hand, Americans don't want to live in a police state. They want freedom from unwarranted governmental interference, and they want their civil liberties protected. But the process of determining where the rights of society end and the rights of the individual begin never ends. As social values and priorities change over time, the balance between these competing interests also shifts. Learning to view criminal law as flexible and evolving rather than as a catalogue of inflexible rules is central to the study of criminal law.[13]

Although this text concentrates on society's legal response to crime, it is important to emphasize that government agencies are only secondarily responsible for preventing crime. Parents are expected to raise their children to be "law-abiding citizens." Churches, mosques, and synagogues are counted on to teach their members about the norms of acceptable behavior. Schools are similarly expected to teach youth about ethical conduct and society's rules, along with English, math, and science. Similarly, youth sports organizations have a responsibility to teach good sportsmanship as well as the rules of soccer or basketball.

Nor does society exclusively rely on government agencies to resolve disputes stemming from conduct that would be classified as criminal were it brought to the attention of public authorities. Many disputes involving "criminal" conduct are resolved privately within families, neighborhoods, and by the memberships of various formal and informal organizations. Nevertheless, there are times when government intervention is necessary. At such times, democratic societies need substantive laws that define criminal offenses and procedural laws for determining whether a criminally accused person is guilty as charged.

Today, the public's elected state and federal legislators have primary responsibility for determining what types of conduct will be defined as criminal. Given the complexity of our modern society, the law of crimes has been rapidly expanding at both the federal and state levels. But government's legal authority to criminalize conduct is not unlimited, as we will see in Chapter 2. It is constrained by our written constitutions, which protect each person's fundamental substantive and procedural rights.

Civil and Criminal Law

It is likely that students studying criminal law know little about either civil law or criminal law. It is important in a criminal law course that students have at least a minimal understanding about how these two branches of American law differ. In some respects they are very similar. The federal government and the 50 state governments all have established laws and judicial systems governing how people should behave in their personal and business dealings with one another. Following the English tradition, we have some laws which are collectively known as criminal laws, and that which is not criminal is classified as "civil law." The civil law is primarily intended to address the needs of individual litigants. It provides disputing parties (and occasionally governments) with legal remedies and an impartial judicial process for judicially resolving private disputes. The relief most often requested by civil plaintiffs is a judicial determination that the defendant pay the plaintiff money damages. The plaintiff wants to be compensated by the defendant for having allegedly harmed the plaintiff personally, damaged the plaintiff's property, or harmed the plaintiff by breaching a contract. The civil courts provide a neutral forum in which adverse parties each have their say. Detailed rules of civil procedure and **rules of evidence** establish a roadmap for the conduct of the dispute, and the federal and state constitutions guarantee that the proceedings will conform to the requirements of fundamental due process.

State civil courts have jurisdiction over most non-criminal disputes. There are some actions (bankruptcy, for example) that are exclusively the jurisdiction of federal courts. The U.S. District Courts are the federal trial courts. The district courts exercise both civil and criminal jurisdiction. One or more of the district courts is found in every state. Federal courts apply the **Federal Rules of Civil Procedure** to federal civil trials, and the **Federal Rules of Criminal Procedure** to federal criminal trials. The states apply comparable state procedural rules in state civil and criminal actions. Federal subject matter jurisdiction in civil actions is limited to federal questions (claims based on the federal constitution, treaties, or federal statutes) and where diversity jurisdiction exists (usually suits between citizens from different states where the amount in controversy exceeds $75,000). A party to a civil lawsuit is normally responsible for paying for the expenses it has incurred in bringing/defending the suit, including investigative costs and attorney fees. A prevailing party in a civil action is awarded a judgment by the court, which is normally enforceable throughout the country because of the

Full Faith and Credit Clause of the U.S. Constitution (see Article IV, Section 1 of the Constitution).

Students can search online for the Federal Rules of Criminal Procedure, the Federal Rules of Civil Procedure, and the corresponding state rules applicable in any of the 50 states. Check out the procedural rules from your state to see how the civil and criminal procedural rules differ.

Some Interesting Differences Between Civil Law and Criminal Law

There are many differences between civil actions and criminal prosecutions in this country. Because of space limitations what follows is only a partial list:

1. The plaintiff in **criminal cases** is the government. Because criminal cases are brought on behalf of the society as a whole, federal prosecution cases are captioned "United States" v. (defendant). In state prosecutions the caption varies by jurisdiction. The most common are "State" v. (defendant), "People" v. (defendant), or "Commonwealth" v. (defendant). In civil cases the caption will normally contain the last names of the opposing parties—"Ortiz v. Chang."
2. At the beginning of a criminal prosecution the defendant is presumed to be innocent of the charges. Defendants do not have any advantage in civil cases as the parties are on an equal footing.
3. The government in a criminal case is constitutionally required to prove its case by the highest level burden of proof. To convict the defendant the prosecutor must prove guilt "beyond a reasonable doubt." To prevail in most civil cases the plaintiff need only prove its claims by a preponderance of the evidence—the lowest level burden of proof.
4. Indigent criminal defendants have a constitutional right to appointed counsel in any case which could result, upon conviction, in the defendant being sentenced to incarceration. There is no equivalent right to appointed counsel for indigent people in civil actions. Indigent parties who cannot afford a lawyer and who attempt to represent themselves are seriously disadvantaged in cases in which the other party has retained counsel.
5. Prosecutors have to disclose some of their evidence to defendants, typically including confessions obtained from the defendant, physical evidence, exculpatory evidence, and reports of scientific tests. Criminal defendants are

minimally obligated to provide information to prosecutors (examples include a defendant's claim of incompetency or a defendant's claim of self-defense, alibi, or insanity). In civil lawsuits the law provides for broad discovery rights. Each party is legally required to disclose to the opposing party most of what it knows about the relevant facts. Each party can require the other to answer questions under oath (at a deposition) and produce relevant documents for copying and examination.

6. A criminal defendant has a Fifth Amendment right to refuse to give any testimony. A civil defendant has no such right. Of course, any witness at a civil or criminal trial has a Fifth Amendment right to refuse to answer any question, the answer to which might have some tendency to incriminate him/her criminally.

7. In a criminal action, the government is in charge of the case and makes strategic decisions. The victim has no right to decide on the amount of resources devoted to investigating the case, whether an experienced or inexperienced prosecutor will be assigned, what charges are filed, and whether a felony charge will be reduced to a misdemeanor in exchange for the defendant's agreement to plead guilty to a misdemeanor. The prosecutor will also decide what sentencing recommendation is made to the court in the sentencing phase of a criminal trial. The extent to which police and prosecutors discuss any of these matters with victims varies greatly. The plaintiff/victim in a civil action has total control of the case. He/she/it is responsible for investigating the facts, selecting an attorney, and paying for the costs associated with bringing the suit (filing fees, costs of serving documents, retaining expert witnesses, and otherwise discovering the facts of the case). The plaintiff also decides whether to accept a defendant's settlement offer or demand a trial.

8. It is important to emphasize that one allegedly wrongful act can result in separate criminal and civil actions against the defendant. Victims of crime are not parties to the criminal action and are not awarded money damages at the conclusion of a criminal trial. A defendant in a criminal case can be civilly sued irrespective of whether the criminal case resulted in a conviction or acquittal. For example, if a person is convicted of criminal damage to property the victim of that crime can file a **civil suit** against the criminal defendant for the purpose of recovering compensatory damages. These actions are separate and serve different purposes—justice for the harm caused to society and justice for the harm sustained by the individual victim.[14]

9. Other procedural rights that are unique to criminal cases include the right to a speedy trial, grand jury indictments (sometimes), preliminary hearings, the privilege against self-incrimination, restrictions on the admission of evidence obtained contrary to constitutional requirements, and at least one taxpayer-financed appeal.

10. Lastly, criminal sentences are also more severe than the relief awarded in civil actions, ranging from death to incarceration, probation, community service, and/or a fine.

The following case of *Katko v. Briney* illustrates the principle that civil suits and criminal suits are independent of each other. It involves a civil suit for money damages brought by a civil plaintiff who was convicted of larceny for stealing the civil defendant's property.

KATKO v. BRINEY
183 N.W.2d 657
Supreme Court of Iowa
February 9, 1971

AUTHOR'S INTRODUCTION

Katko and a friend, acting without permission and ignoring the posted "no trespassing" signs, broke into Briney's boarded-up and uninhabited old farmhouse in order to look for antique jars and bottles. When Katko attempted to open the door to the north bedroom, a spring gun discharged, "blowing away" much of his right leg. No warning was given that a spring gun was rigged up within the north bedroom. Katko was hospitalized for 40 days, was in a cast for one year, and wore a brace for an additional year. His leg was permanently deformed and shortened, and he experienced considerable pain. He also sustained money damages for medical care and loss of earnings resulting from his injuries.

Katko pleaded guilty to larceny and was given a $50 fine and 60 days in jail. He filed a civil suit against Briney, the owner of the farmhouse, to recover compensatory and punitive damages for his injuries. The case was tried by a jury, which returned a plaintiff's verdict. The trial court entered judgment on the verdict, and Briney appealed to the state supreme court. Briney objected to the trial judge's **jury instructions**. The trial court had instructed the jury that "the only time when . . . setting a 'spring gun' . . . is justified would be when [a] trespasser was committing a felony of violence punishable by death, or [was] . . . endangering human life by his act." The defendant, Briney, urged the court to rule that "the law permits use of a spring gun in a dwelling or warehouse for the purpose of preventing the unlawful entry of a burglar or thief." The Iowa Supreme Court's resolution of this dispute follows.

EXCERPT FROM THE CASE

Chief Justice MOORE:

The primary issue presented here is whether an owner may protect personal property in an unoccupied boarded-up farmhouse against trespassers and thieves by a spring gun capable of inflicting death or serious injury. . . .

The overwhelming weight of authority, both textbook and case law, supports the trial court's statement of the applicable principles of law. Prosser on Torts . . . states that

> the law has always placed a higher value upon human safety than upon mere rights in property. [I]t is the accepted rule that there is no privilege to use any force calculated to cause death or serious bodily injury to repel the threat to land or chattels, unless there is also such a threat to the defendant's personal safety as to justify a self-defense. . . . [S]pring guns and other man-killing devices are not justifiable against a mere trespasser, or even a petty thief. They are privileged only against those upon whom the landowner, if he were present in person, would be free to inflict injury of the same kind.

Restatement of Torts, § 85, page 180, states that

> the value of human life and limbs, not only to the individual concerned but also to society, so outweighs the interest of a possessor of land in excluding from it those whom he is not willing to admit thereto that a possessor of land has, as is stated in § 79, no privilege to use force intended or likely to cause death or serious harm against another whom the possessor sees about to enter his premises or meddle with his chattel, unless the intrusion threatens death or serious bodily harm to the occupiers or users of the premises. . . . A possessor of land cannot do indirectly and by a mechanical device that which, were he present, he could not do immediately and in person. Therefore, he cannot gain a privilege to install, for the purpose of protecting his land from intrusions harmless to the lives and limbs of the occupiers or users of it, a mechanical device whose only purpose is to inflict death or serious harm upon such as may intrude, by giving notice of his intention to inflict, by mechanical means and indirectly, harm which he could not, even after request, inflict directly were he present . . .

In Hooker v. Miller, 37 Iowa 613, we held defendant vineyard owner liable for damages resulting from a spring gun shot although plaintiff was a trespasser and there to steal grapes. At pages 614, 615, this statement is made: "This court has held that a mere trespass against property other than a dwelling is not a sufficient justification to authorize the use of a deadly weapon by the owner in its defense; and that if death results in such a case it will be murder, though the killing be actually necessary to prevent the trespass." . . . At page 617 this court said: "[T]respassers and other inconsiderable violators of the law are not to be visited by barbarous punishments or prevented by inhuman inflictions of bodily injuries."

The facts in Allison v. Fiscus, 156 Ohio 120, decided in 1951, are very similar to the case at bar. There plaintiff's right to damages was recognized for injuries received when he feloniously broke a door latch and started to enter defendant's warehouse with intent to steal. As he entered, a trap of two sticks of dynamite buried under the doorway by defendant owner was set off and plaintiff seriously injured. The court held the question whether a particular trap was justified as a use of reasonable and necessary force against a trespasser engaged in the commission of a felony should have been submitted to the jury. The Ohio Supreme Court recognized the plaintiff's right to recover punitive or exemplary damages in addition to compensatory damages. . . .

In United Zinc & Chemical Co. v. Britt, 258 U.S. 268, 275, the Court states: "The liability for spring guns and mantraps arises from the fact that the defendant has . . . expected the trespasser and prepared an injury that is no more justified than if he had held the gun and fired it."

In addition to civil liability many jurisdictions hold a landowner criminally liable for serious injuries or homicide caused by spring guns or other set devices. . . .

In Wisconsin, Oregon, and England the use of spring guns and similar devices is specifically made unlawful by statute. . . .

The legal principles stated by the trial court in instructions 2, 5 and 6 are well established and supported by the authorities cited and quoted supra. There is no merit in defendants' objections and exceptions thereto. Defendants' various motions based on the same reasons stated in exceptions to instructions were properly overruled. . . .

Affirmed.

CASE QUESTIONS

1. Why did the Iowa Supreme Court quote from Prosser and the Restatement of Torts when explaining its rationale for prohibiting the use of spring guns under the circumstances of this case?

2. Does the supreme court of any other state have the legal obligation to follow the precedent established in Iowa?

3. What is the rationale for prohibiting the use of spring guns under circumstance like those in this case?

AUTHOR'S COMMENTARY

We see in this civil case that Katko, the plaintiff, had been previously charged, convicted, and sentenced for violating the criminal laws of the state. The victim of the crime, Briney, was subsequently sued by Katko in a civil action for money damages. Katko accused Briney of having violated a civil duty owed by an owner of an unoccupied farmhouse to a trespasser like Katko. Briney was alleged to have used excessive force against the plaintiff in defense of his property. Ultimately, the Iowa Supreme Court agreed and affirmed the award of a civil judgment in favor of Katko. The fact that Katko was convicted of criminal wrongdoing in a parallel case stemming from the same incident was no bar to the civil action. Civil and criminal actions serve different purposes, with the imposition of punishment constituting one of the most obvious distinguishing characteristics of criminal law.

Having completed the discussion of how civil laws and criminal laws differ, we briefly consider how criminal offenses are classified.

Classification of Offenses—Felonies and Misdemeanors

Crimes carrying penalties of incarceration for one year or more, or for incarceration in a state prison, are generally classified as **felonies**. Crimes classified as felonies include murder, manslaughter, theft, arson, rape, burglary, possession of controlled substances with intent to distribute, and robbery. Less serious offenses such as simple assaults, disturbing the peace, disorderly conduct, public intoxication, and possession of small amounts of a controlled substance are classified as **misdemeanors** and are punished with fines and county jail sentences of less than one year.

The introductory discussion to this point has primarily focused on state-based criminal law and little attention was given to federal criminal law outside of the discussion of federalism. What follows now is a brief overview of federal substantive criminal law.

Federal Criminal Law

Although federal criminal statutes have existed since the 1860s, the great expansion of federal influence in the area of criminal law occurred during the second half of the twentieth century. In 1948, most federal criminal statutes were found in Title 18 of the United States Code (18 U.S.C.). Unfortunately, Title 18 is not organized in the manner of modern penal codes (see Table 1.2). Rather, it is an alphabetical compilation of laws devoid of the conceptual integration of purpose and theory common to modern criminal codes. Efforts to enact a modern federal criminal code have been unsuccessful despite serious attempts in the late 1960s and early 1970s.

The federal crimes most prosecuted in U.S. District Courts in 2008 included robbery, fraud, forgery, drug trafficking, and immigration offenses. But most criminal cases are litigated in state and not federal courts. Bureau of Justice statistics indicate that only 6 percent of all adult felons convicted in the United States in 2004 were prosecuted in federal court.

Federal criminal jurisdiction is classified based on whether the federal interest being protected is direct or indirect. We next briefly examine each of these categories.

Direct Federal Interests

Congress has enacted many statutes criminalizing conduct involving interests that are direct matters of federal concern. These interests include offenses such as treason, assaults on federal officers, the theft of federal property or money, counterfeiting currency or postage stamps, bribery of federal officers, mail fraud, and federal tax fraud.

Congress has also authorized federal jurisdiction for criminal offenses committed within federal parks, courthouses, military installations, and post offices (federal enclaves). Title 18 U.S.C. Section 13(a) permits federal prosecutions of people who commit acts or omissions on federal enclaves that, although not prohibited by federal statute, would be criminal acts according to the law of the state in which the federal enclave is situated. Prior to Congress's enactment of a sexual abuse statute in 1986, for example, a federal prosecution could have been maintained if the accused's conduct in a post office would have constituted a violation of that state's sexual abuse statute.

Indirect Federal Interests

Although the federal government, unlike the states, does not have a general police power and is theoretically a government with limited, enumerated powers, federal statutes often criminalize conduct that is already a violation of state criminal law.

Many federal statutes criminalize conduct that is only indirectly a matter of federal concern and for which federal jurisdiction is loosely hinged on Article 1, Section 8's Commerce Clause. The Gun-Free School Zones Act, previously mentioned in conjunction with the *United States v. Lopez* case, is an example. Congress evidently concluded that state statutes criminalizing the possession of guns in school zones were inadequate and that a federal statute was required. The U.S. Supreme Court, however, concluded that Congress had overstepped its bounds and had no constitutional right to legislate.

In some instances, the federal and state governments have overlapping jurisdiction, which can produce tension between the federal and state levels of government. The constitutional implications of dual federal-state criminal jurisdiction was one of the concerns addressed by the U.S. Supreme Court in its decision in *Lopez*. The majority was concerned that further expansion of federal jurisdiction under the Commerce Clause could lead de facto to a quasi-federal police power, which the majority feared could reduce federalism to a legal fiction.

However, our history provides scenarios where the existence of dual federal and state criminal jurisdiction has proven very beneficial. U.S. Attorneys have often initiated prosecutions based on federal civil rights laws where local police departments have been unable or unwilling to rigorously enforce comparable state laws. It is also clear that federal prosecutions based on federal statutes have significantly contributed by rooting out pervasive governmental corruption.

If prosecutors are successful in obtaining a conviction, the focus of a criminal trial shifts to determining the appropriate sentence to be imposed on the convicted defendant. In order to understand this process it is necessary that we next consider the purposes of punishment.

The Purposes of Punishment

Although death was the sentence for persons convicted of most of the original common law crimes,[15] modern judges are often provided with other sentencing options, including incarceration, fines, probation (often with a condition imposed requiring restitution to the victim), and community service. Legislatures also commonly provide grading systems to staircase sentences so that they are in some sense proportionate to the seriousness of the offense. It is common for the sentencing options to reflect the full gamut of the traditional justifications for punishment—**retribution**, **deterrence**, **incapacitation**, and **rehabilitation**.

A person convicted of first-degree murder, for example, might receive a retributive sentence of death; a second-degree murderer might receive a long sentence of incarceration primarily for purposes of retribution (punishment for punishment's sake) and incapacitation (a person in prison cannot harm society) and partially for rehabilitation (probation, treatment, and parole); and a person convicted of vehicular homicide or involuntary manslaughter might receive a lesser term of incarceration imposed primarily to deter the public at large (general deterrence) and partially for incapacitative and retributive reasons (because although the offender never intended to kill in the first place, someone's loved one was nevertheless killed, and if no incarceration is imposed it might appear that the defendant did not receive his just desserts).

Retribution

Retribution essentially amounts to punishment for punishment's sake. One underlying argument supporting retribution is the notion that a criminal offender "deserves" harmful consequences for having committed a crime. A second argument is that society needs to express its contempt for those who commit crimes, and citizens need to see that their institutions are "doing something" to those who harm society by breaking the criminal laws.

Three U.S. Supreme Court justices explained their reasons for allowing states to impose capital punishment for retribution purposes in the following excerpt from the case of *Gregg v. Georgia*.

GREGG v. GEORGIA
428 U.S. 153
U.S. Supreme Court
July 2, 1976

EXCERPT FROM THE CASE

Justices STEWART, POWELL, and STEVENS:

In part, capital punishment is an expression of society's moral outrage at particularly offensive conduct. This function may be unappealing to many, but it is essential in an ordered society that asks its citizens to rely on legal processes rather than self-help to vindicate their wrongs.

The instinct for retribution is part of the nature of man, and channeling that instinct in the administration of criminal justice serves an important purpose in promoting the stability of a society governed by law. When people begin to believe that organized society is unwilling or unable to impose upon criminal offenders the punishment they "deserve" there are sown the seeds of anarchy—of self-help, vigilante justice, and lynch law. Furman v. Georgia, . . . (Stewart, J., concurring).

Retribution is no longer the dominant objective of the criminal law, . . . but neither is it a forbidden objective nor one inconsistent with our respect for the dignity of men. . . . Indeed, the decision that capital punishment may be the appropriate sanction in extreme cases is an expression of the community's belief that certain crimes are themselves so grievous an affront to humanity that the only adequate response may be the penalty of death.

CASE QUESTION

How do Justices Stewart, Powell, and Stevens explain their support for permitting states to utilize capital punishment in murder cases?

AUTHOR'S COMMENTARY

Because people differ in their views about the goals of punishment, there is constant tension between proponents of retribution and proponents of rehabilitation. These debates often become politicized, with retributionists accusing their rehabilitation-oriented opponents of being soft on crime, because there can be no justice unless the criminal offender receives "what he or she has coming." Those favoring rehabilitation parry and riposte by condemning their critics for their inability to see that "an eye for an eye" doesn't really provide any long-term benefits to society.

General and Specific Deterrence

Some punishments are imposed on convicted persons to generally deter other members of society from committing crimes (**general deterrence**). When other people learn how offenders have been sentenced, they will remain law abiding because of a desire not to suffer the same fate. When punishment is imposed to convince an existing offender not to commit future crimes, the sentence is an instrument of **specific deterrence**. In this instance the premise is that sentences should be structured so that convicted offenders, after weighing the gains derived from criminal conduct against the pains of the likely sanction, will decide not to recidivate.

Incapacitation

Incapacitation aims to remove dangerous offenders from society. Sometimes this means that the offender forfeits his or her life, but usually it means that the person is sentenced to a term of incarceration. When someone is incarcerated, the length of the term is roughly proportionate to the extent that a particular offender is believed to pose a future threat to the public or deserves to be excluded from society because of past deeds. Many legislatures have taken this approach one step further by enacting so-called "three strikes" laws that result in the imposition of life sentences on recidivists. This approach is often applied mechanically and substitutes the convicted person's number of convictions for an individualized assessment of the person's dangerousness. The theory behind such laws is that persons who are "career criminals" deserve to be permanently removed from society. You can see how persons convicted of selected felonies in 2002 in state courts were sentenced in Table 1.3.

Rehabilitation

Traditionally, juveniles and many first offenders are often placed on some form of probation, which may be coupled with requirements that the offender participate in counseling, attend a special school program, perform community service, take job training, or attend a boot camp. The hope is that these "treatments" will enable

| TABLE 1.3 | DISTRIBUTION OF TYPES OF FELONY SENTENCES IMPOSED IN STATE COURTS BY OFFENSE 2002 |

Most serious conviction offense	Total	Percent of felons sentenced to—			
		Incarceration			
		Total	Prison	Jail	Probation
All offenses	100%	69%	41%	28%	31%
Violent offenses	100%	77%	52%	25%	23%
Murder[a]	100	95	91	4	5
Sexual assault[b]	100	82	59	23	18
Rape	100	89	67	22	11
Other sexual assault	100	78	55	23	22
Robbery	100	86	71	15	14
Aggravated assault	100	71	42	29	29
Other violent[c]	100	77	42	35	23
Property offenses	100%	66%	38%	28%	34%
Burglary	100	72	46	26	28
Larceny[d]	100	67	36	31	33
Motor vehicle theft	100	76	37	39	24
Fraud[e]	100	59	31	28	41
Drug offenses	100%	66%	39%	27%	34%
Possession	100	62	34	28	38
Trafficking	100	68	42	26	32
Weapon offenses	100%	73%	45%	28%	27%
Other offenses[f]	100%	70%	35%	35%	30%

Note: For persons receiving a combination of sentences, the sentence designation came from the most severe penalty imposed—prison being the most severe, followed by jail, then probation. Prison includes death sentences. Felons receiving a sentence other than incarceration or probation are classified under "probation." This table is based on an estimated 1,047,931 cases.
[a]Includes nonnegligent manslaughter.
[b]Includes rape.
[c]Includes offenses such as negligent manslaughter and kidnaping.
[d]Includes motor vehicle theft.
[e]Includes forgery and embezzlement.
[f]Composed of nonviolent offenses such as receiving stolen property and vandalism.
Source: U.S. Bureau of Justice Statistics, Estimated number of felony convictions in State courts, 2002, Table 2, December 2004.

offenders to turn their lives around. Treatment programs also exist within prisons, and proponents of rehabilitation argue that since most prisoners will ultimately be released back to society, it is desirable that prisoners participate in programs that will lead to their successful reintegration.

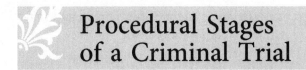

Procedural Stages of a Criminal Trial

Introductory criminal law students should have some understanding of the procedural stages of a criminal trial. Familiarity with procedure not only improves understanding when students read case reports, it also builds confidence. An understanding of basic procedure also helps students understand substantive criminal law as they grapple with motions for directed verdict, the difference between burdens of production and persuasion, the role of presumptions, when defenses are raised, etc.

Undoubtedly, readers of this textbook come to the introductory study of criminal law with widely divergent backgrounds. Some will be very acquainted with the interrelationship between trial procedures and substantive law, and others will know little, if anything, about these matters.

Therefore, readers who believe a procedural review would be of benefit will find a Procedural Primer in an Appendix at the back of this textbook.

Chapter Summary

The introductory chapter to any textbook exists to prepare students for the substantive discussion that follows in subsequent chapters. It provides readers who come to the study of criminal law with varying backgrounds with baseline information that constitutes the intellectual foundation for the remainder of the textbook. This chapter has focused on our nation's common law heritage, federalism, the purposes of punishment, and a procedural overview of the trial of a criminal case. We began with a discussion of our nation's common law tradition.

Our Nation's Common Law Heritage

Because England won the French and Indian War (1754-1763), England's North American colonies remained English. This insured the retention of the English language, culture, and legal system in the colonies rather than those of France.

The foundation of the English legal system was the common law, a legal system in which judges, and not legislative bodies, primarily determined what society considered to be criminal. Even today, federal and state judges make reference to the common law and to important English documents, such as the Magna Carta, and cite the authoritative writings of such respected English legal authorities as Edward Coke (early 1600s) and William Blackstone (1765). Although there are few states today that continue to recognize some common law crimes, all federal crimes and most state crimes are statutory and not judge made.

Because of widely understood inadequacies with the common law, reformers sought an alternative approach to criminal law. The Model Penal Code was developed in the 1950s to meet that need. It provided state legislators with a modern, cohesive, rational alternative to the irrational and often ambiguous common law crimes. The code was a comprehensive collection of proposed statutes and was produced by acknowledged experts and scholars. Legislators took notice, and many states, after careful study, adopted all or portions of the Model Penal Code. Readers will learn more about the Modern Penal Code in the chapters that follow.

The United States Has a Federal Form of Government

The importance of our federal form of government (federalism) was also emphasized in Chapter 1.

Readers learned that the states were complete, sovereign governments prior to the enactment of the U.S. Constitution. As sovereigns, states were entitled to exercise what is known as the police power, the right to enact legislation to protect the public health, welfare, safety, and morals. Because each state, within Constitutional limitations, has the right to enact criminal laws, state criminal laws can and often do differ. Yes, conduct that is criminal in one state can be lawful in another. Because of federalism we have 51 sovereign jurisdictions declaring and enforcing criminal laws in the United States. That is why we study criminal law principles in this textbook instead of a unitary "American Criminal Law"—it doesn't exist.

Like the states, the federal government is also sovereign. The U.S. Constitution, which was ratified by the states, authorized the creation of a national government. It defined the executive, legislative, and judicial branches of government and provided each branch with specified powers. The federal government has no police power. Congress derives all of its lawmaking power, either directly or indirectly, from the Constitution. Congress has the right to enact criminal laws that protect federal interests, both direct and indirect. It is common for federal and state crimes to overlap. For example, robbing a federally insured bank violates both state and federal statutes, and if state law permits, both federal and state prosecutors can bring charges against the perpetrator. Because the founders were aware that in a federal system it was inevitable that there would be jurisdictional conflict, they included Article VI in the Constitution. This article provides that no state can enact legislation that contradicts with a federal law that is appropriately in the federal domain. This means, for example, that when Congress passes legislation pursuant to its authority to regulate interstate commerce, no conflicting law can be enacted by any state. The drafters of the Bill of Rights also emphasized in the Tenth

Amendment that powers not delegated to the federal government "are reserved to the states . . . or to the people.

The Purposes of Punishment

Everything that precedes the sentencing phase of a criminal prosecution is intended to ensure that only persons deserving of punishment are subject to that sanction. There are four traditionally approved theories for punishing convicted offenders; retribution (offenders deserve to be punished), deterrence (offenders should be punished to deter others and to deter the offender from reoffending), incapacitation (the offender needs to be removed from society), and rehabilitation (the offender is placed on probation and required to complete educational, vocational, or another type of program to help turn his/her life around).

Procedural Considerations

The chapter ended with a review of trial procedures.

 ## Discussion Questions

1. A prosecutor used **peremptory challenges** to exclude the only two black jurors on the panel of a criminal defendant who was also black. The prosecutor, in seeking to justify his actions on nondiscriminatory grounds, explained that he disliked the way the jurors looked and emphasized that one excluded juror's hair was "unkempt" and that both excluded jurors wore facial hair. Do you believe that this explanation constituted a racially neutral reason for the juror exclusions?

Purkett v. Elem, 514 U.S. 765 (1995)

2. Should prosecutors be forbidden to exclude all members of a jury, solely because of their gender?

J.E.B. v. Alabama, 511 U.S. 127 (1994)

3. Assume that a prosecutor is trying a case against a woman defendant and that the prosecutor would prefer to replace the only two members of the jury panel who happen to be women. Assume further that both female jurors are nursing students. Should the prosecutor be entitled to defend against allegations of gender

discrimination in his use of peremptory challenges on the grounds that he was merely challenging nurses?

J.E.B. v. Alabama, 511 U.S. 127 (1994)

4. Should a juvenile, charged with juvenile delinquency, have a constitutional right to a **jury trial**?

McKiever v. Pennsylvania, 403 U.S. 528 (1971)

5. Arguments can be made both supporting and opposing the expansive use of jury trial in criminal cases. What arguments can you make on both sides of the question? Two justices debated this question in the 1968 case of *Duncan v. Louisiana*, with Justice White supporting an expansion of the right to jury trial in his majority opinion and Justice Harlan arguing to the contrary in his dissent.

Duncan v. Louisiana, 391 U.S. 145 (1968)

NOTES

1. H.L.A. Hart, *The Concept of Law* (Oxford: Clarendon Press, 1961), p. 6.
2. "[W]hat distinguishes a criminal from a civil sanction and all that distinguishes it . . . is the judgment of community condemnation which accompanies and justifies its imposition." Henry M. Hart, Jr. "The Aims of the Criminal Law," 23 *Law & Contemporary Problems*, 401 (1958).
3. John Lewis said ". . . Growing up in the rural South, you learned . . . [getting arrested] was not the thing to do. To go to jail was to bring shame and disgrace on the family. But for me it was like being involved in a holy crusade, it became a badge of honor." In H. Hampton & S. Fayer, *Voices of Freedom* (New York: Bantam Books, 1990), p. 58.
4. See the the U.S. Constitution's Tenth Amendment.
5. Section 2 of the Twenty-sixth Amendment provides that "the Congress shall have the power to enforce this article by appropriate legislation."
6. This topic is called "preemption" and is quite complicated. In some instances Congress explicitly preempts subject matter by legislation. In other instances it so dominates a subject area that a reviewing court rules that Congress has preempted the field by implication.
7. The merger of the equitable and common law courts has been omitted in the interest of saving space.
8. It is common, for example, for legislative bodies to delegate authority to regulatory agencies to promulgate administrative rules that are enforceable to the same extent as statutes. These administrative rules are normally collected in publications specifically intended for this purpose. Such rules are not housed in the criminal code along with the statutes.
9. *United States v. Hudson & Goodwin*, 11 U.S. 32 (1812).
10. *Commonwealth v. Slaney*, 185 N.E.2d 919 (Mass. 1962).
11. The Model Penal Code was developed by the commission on Uniform State Laws and the American Law Institute. It is a collection of suggestions for reforming criminal law.

In particular, the authors intended to replace common law crimes with modern, comprehensive statutes. The final draft of this proposed code was approved in 1962.

12. The Massachusetts Criminal Law Revision Commission, *Proposed Criminal Code of Massachusetts* (Rochester: The Lawyers Co-Operative Publishing Co., 1972), pp. 98-99.

13. As Gardner put it, "Criminal law is a study of the authority of government to regulate conduct within constitutional limitations so that maximum freedoms and liberties may be enjoyed by all." See T. Gardner, *Criminal Law Principles and Cases*, 4th ed. (St. Paul: West Publishing, 1989).

14. It is important to note that a witness in a civil action cannot be required to answer questions at either a civil or criminal trial that would have any tendency to incriminate him or her criminally. But a former criminal defendant can be required to testify at a subsequent civil trial if the testimony given does not expose that person to self-incrimination. Thus once an accused is acquitted or convicted in a criminal trial, the double jeopardy clause of the U.S. Constitution's Fifth Amendment protects him or her from any further criminal prosecution (except for perjury) relating to the same offense as the first prosecution. The acquitted criminal defendant could be required to testify at a subsequent civil action about matters that would have been self-incriminating in the criminal trial because governmental prosecutors would be constitutionally barred from bringing any subsequent criminal action.

15. Mayhem is the exception—the penalty for maiming another was mutilation.

Constitutional Limitations on the Definition and Punishment of Criminal Offenses

Obviously, the U.S. Constitution, as interpreted by the U.S. Supreme Court, establishes a "constitutional floor" for state legislatures. If the U.S. Supreme Court rules that laws prohibiting inter-racial marriage violate the federal constitution, no state can by state law contradict that ruling. However, if the U.S. Supreme Court rules that states are not required by the federal constitution to require that defendants in criminal cases tried to a jury be convicted by a unanimous vote of the jurors, no "constitutional ceiling" is established. States are free to decide as a matter of state law that unanimous verdicts not are required for conviction in that state. This is just another example of federalism at work. It is why Oregon and Washington are able to permit physician-assisted suicides and why Michigan can make such assistance a crime.

In Chapter 2 we learn about how the federal constitution sometimes explicitly, and at other times implicitly, establishes a "constitutional floor" for legislatures as they define crimes and punish offenders.

We will focus on the following constitutionally based controls:

1. Prohibitions against bills of attainder and *ex post facto* laws
2. Due process limitations
3. Equal protection limitations
4. Cruel and unusual punishment limitations

As we discuss each of these topics in turn, we begin with one of the oldest express constitutional limitations on federal and state legislative bodies, prohibitions against bills of attainder and *ex post facto* laws.

Prohibitions Against Bills of Attainder and *Ex Post Facto* Laws

A **bill of attainder** is a law passed by a legislative body that declares a criminally accused person to be guilty and imposes **capital punishment**. The U.S. Constitution expressly prohibits the Congress and state legislatures from passing such legislation in Article I, Sections 9 and 10. The founding fathers were familiar with the British Parliament's use of this device to deny specially targeted individuals (who were often accused of treason) the right to a trial conducted by the judiciary. This prohibition ensures that the judiciary is responsible for conducting criminal trials.

When a legislative body criminalizes conduct that was not criminal at the time that the conduct occurred or retroactively "changes the punishment, and inflicts a greater punishment" than was authorized by law when the act was committed, it has enacted an ***ex post facto*** law. *Ex post facto* laws have long been disfavored.

Sir William Blackstone, who opposed such laws, expressed his opposition to them in Volume 1 of his *Commentaries on the Laws* (1753). Blackstone's influence was recognized in the famous early U.S. Supreme Court case of *Calder v. Bull*, 3 U.S. 386 (1798).[10]

Internet Tip

Readers interested in a fascinating case study of *ex post facto* in which a convicted sex offender loses an *ex post facto* claim in the U.S. Supreme Court, but ultimately prevails in the Alaska Supreme Court, can find an edited version of *Doe v. State*, 189 P.3d 999 (2008), in the Chapter 2 portion of the website. Because of the twists and turns this case takes as it winds it way through the federal and state judicial systems, additional citations have been provided for each of the judicial steps along the way. This will enable the interested reader to access these cases on Loislaw.

Doe was convicted of molesting one of his minor children in 1985 and was sentenced to 12 years of incarceration. Alaska enacted its registration act, the Alaska Sex Offender Registration Act (ASORA), in 1994. Doe finished completing his sentence, parole, and probation in 1995. Doe filed suit against the state in 1994 challenging ASORA was as to him an *ex post facto* law under Article 1, Section 9, Clause 3 and the **Fourteenth Amendment Due Process Clause** of the U.S. Constitution. The U.S. District Court ruled that Doe had to register as required by the statute but that the state could not publicly disclose Doe's personal information. Note that Doe's suit was initially brought as "Rowe" in the District Court (see *Rowe v. Burton*, 884 F. Supp. 1372 (D. Alaska 1994). The state appealed to the U.S. Court of Appeals (see *Doe I v. Otte*, 259 F.3d 979 (9th Cir. 2001)), which ruled that the ASORA was an *ex post facto* law if applied to Doe/Rowe. The Ninth Circuit affirmed the district court as to the public dissemination of information and additionally enjoined the state from requiring Doe to register as a sex offender. The state petitioned the U.S. Supreme Court, which completely reversed the Court of Appeals (see *Smith v. Doe*, 538 U.S. 84 (2003)).

Doe's response to the U.S. Supreme Court loss was to file a new suit in a state trial court claiming that ASORA was an *ex post facto* law as applied to him and therefore a violation of Article I, Section 15 of the Alaska Constitution. After the trial court ruled in favor of the state, Doe appealed to the Alaska Supreme Court. Many readers will at this point be thinking "how can Doe bring a second *ex post facto* lawsuit against Alaska after having lost in the U.S. Supreme Court?" The answer lies in federalism. Doe's claim in the first suit was based on his rights under the federal constitution. The U.S. Supreme Court is the final arbiter of the

(continued)

meaning of the U.S. Constitution. It does not have the final say with respect to the meaning of the Alaska Constitution. The Alaska Supreme Court has the final say. . . . It is true that the Alaska Supreme Court cannot establish a standard that provides less rights than are required under the federal constitution (because of the U.S. Constitution's supremacy clause (see Article 6, Section 2)). It can, however, and did interpret the state's constitution as providing more protections for persons in Doe's situation than exist under the federal constitution.

Due Process Limitations

The Fifth Amendment to the U.S. Constitution was adopted in 1791 as part of the Bill of Rights. One of its clauses, the famous Due Process Clause, provides that no person shall be "deprived of life, liberty or property without due process of law." This clause can be traced to the 1776 constitutions of Maryland and North Carolina, and is historically linked to the Magna Carta of 1215.

Because the **Fifth Amendment**'s due process requirement was intended to apply only to the federal government, the states had the right to ignore its terms as they saw fit. This situation did not begin to change until 1891, when the Fourteenth Amendment, containing a Due Process Clause, was ratified by the states and added to the Constitution. Thereafter, case after case was brought to the U.S. Supreme Court as individuals sought to convince the Court that they were entitled to judicial relief for Fourteenth Amendment due process violations committed by state government agencies. The Due Process Clauses of the Fifth and Fourteenth Amendments are shown in Figure 2.1.

In general terms, the Due Process Clauses protect individuals from unfair treatment by government. Due process claims must involve alleged governmental deprivation of an individual's life, liberty, or property, but courts have defined these

Figure 2.1. Due Process Clauses of the Fifth and Fourteenth Amendments

The Fifth Amendment Due Process Clause
     No person shall . . . be deprived of life, liberty, or property without due process of law. . . .

The Fourteenth Amendment Due Process Clause
     [N]or shall any state deprive any person of life, liberty, or property, without due process of law. . . .

terms flexibly. For example, the U.S. Supreme Court ruled that when a student is suspended from a public school, the student's property right to a public education and liberty interest in having a "good reputation" are put in jeopardy, qualifying the student to make a due process claim.[1]

Government acts in many forums, and some governmental agencies, are not well known or understood. The Congress, state legislatures, and city councils will be on most people's lists of government agencies, along with the FBI and state and local policing entities, but numerous other agencies are less obvious, such as public schools and colleges; municipal libraries; public housing authorities; public park boards; administrative boards licensing barbers, lawyers, doctors, and hairdressers; the Immigration and Naturalization Service; the Internal Revenue Service; public turnpike authorities; and so on. As government agencies, all are obligated to respect the substantive and procedural due process rights of individuals.

Substantive Due Process

Substantive law is the part of the law that creates and defines legal rights and duties. When the content of a statute, ordinance, or library rule is the instrument of government unfairness, as contrasted with the procedures used to implement the law, a claim can be made that the law violates **substantive due process**. When the claim is made that the content of a law is either too vague or overly broad, the substantive due process problem is one of insufficient precision.

Precision

It is incumbent on legislative bodies to write laws, particularly criminal laws, so that they clearly distinguish the conduct that is forbidden from that which is not. If the content of such laws is ambiguous or criminalizes constitutionally protected conduct, it creates problems for citizens who wish to be law abiding but can't figure out what constitutes a violation. It also creates enforcement problems for police officers in that they have difficulty determining whom to arrest. This situation leads to an overabundance of uncontrolled police discretion and can easily result in arbitrary police decision making.

For over 50 years the U.S. Supreme Court has ruled that due process requires that legislatures write our laws so that they are precise. They cannot be either too vague or overly broad.

Vagueness

For most of the last 30 years the Supreme Court has generally required that legislative bodies define criminal offenses so that they are not too vague. This has traditionally meant that laws must be written "with sufficient definiteness that ordinary people can understand what conduct is prohibited and in a manner that does not encourage arbitrary and discriminatory enforcement."[2] However, since 1974, the Court has emphasized that the need to control police arbitrariness[3] is of greater importance than the need to provide notice to citizens. This problem is illustrated in this recently decided case before the U.S. Court of Appeals for the Sixth Circuit.

UNITED STATES v. LONNIE RAY DAVIS
No. 07-1964
United States Court of Appeals, Sixth Circuit
December 19, 2008

AUTHOR'S INTRODUCTION

Lonnie R. Davis was driving his car at about 2:10 A.M. when stopped by Officer Griffin. The officer suspected that Davis might be violating a Michigan statute that makes it illegal to operate a motor vehicle which has an object hanging from the rearview mirror that impairs the driver's vision. The officer had observed Davis operating a motor vehicle with a "Tweety Bird" air freshening device hanging from the mirror post. Believing that the "Tweety Bird" device was obstructing Davis's vision, Officer Griffin stopped Davis's vehicle, and Davis was arrested when he was unable to produce an operator's license. A search incident to this arrest yielded a loaded pistol, a stun gun, cash, an open pint bottle of cognac, and 24 grams of cocaine base. Davis, a previously convicted felon, was charged with illegal possession of the pistol and with possession of the cocaine base with intent to distribute. He pled guilty and was sentenced to prison for 15 years, 8 months.

EXCERPT FROM THE CASE

Boyce F. MARTIN, Jr., Circuit Judge.
    Lonnie Ray Davis challenges his convictions for being a felon in possession of a firearm and possession of cocaine base with intent to distribute. He argues that the evidence used to convict him was obtained through a search conducted without probable cause. . . .

II

The sole justification for the stop was the officer's belief that the four-inch Tweety Bird doll hanging from Davis's rearview mirror violated MICH. COMP. LAWS § 257.709(1)(c). The difficulty of this case lies in the ambiguity of this provision. . . . This law does not ban all dangling objects; rather, it bans only ornaments that "obstruct the vision of the driver of the vehicle." Yet the statute does not specify to what degree the driver's vision must be obstructed or for how long. This leaves an undefined category of dangling ornaments that arguably violate the statute—one that could be very large depending upon how individual law enforcement officials interpret it—because the statute itself provides no additional guidance to govern enforcement. This is problematic for two reasons. First, the breadth of discretion it delegates to law enforcement: legislatures have a constitutional duty to set out "minimum guidelines to govern law enforcement," *Kolender v. Lawson*, 461 U.S. 352, 358 (1983), but here no such neutral, objective standards are set forth. Second, the discretion delegated to law enforcement by this statute has a potentially far-reaching application in practice. Objects hung from rearview mirrors are legal in Michigan and are indeed quite common. Many vehicles on the road today have something hanging from the rearview mirror, whether it be an air freshener, a parking pass, fuzzy dice, or a rosary. And many organizations, both public and private, either encourage or require their use. . . . Because of this, many vehicles on the road may violate the obstruction law, but the statute itself provides no guidance either to motorists or police as to which ones do. It is simply up to the officer on the street to decide. We believe that the Constitution requires more of Michigan's legislature.

In *Kolender v. Lawson*, the Supreme Court struck down as void for vagueness a San Diego ordinance that required individuals on the street to provide "credible and reliable" identification when requested by an investigating police officer because the ordinance failed to provide "minimal guidelines to govern law enforcement." . . . In doing so, the Court explained the concerns animating the vagueness doctrine at length: "[T]he void-for-vagueness doctrine requires that a penal statute define the criminal offense with sufficient definiteness that ordinary people can understand what conduct is prohibited and in a manner that does not encourage arbitrary and discriminatory enforcement." . . . The Court continued:

> Although the doctrine focuses both on actual notice to citizens and arbitrary enforcement, we have recognized recently that the more important aspect of the vagueness doctrine "is not actual notice, but the other principal element of the doctrine-the requirement that a legislature establish minimal guidelines to govern law enforcement." Where the legislature fails to provide such minimal guidelines, a criminal statute may permit "a standardless sweep [that] allows policemen, prosecutors, and juries to pursue their personal predilections."

. . . Likewise, in *City of Chicago v. Morales*, 527 U.S. 41 (1999), the Court struck down a Chicago ordinance that prohibited "criminal street gang members" from "loitering" with others in a public place, on the grounds that it gave "absolute discretion to police officers to determine what activities constitute[d] loitering." . . . This ordinance, the Court explained, was "impermissibly vague" even though it "d[id] not reach a substantial amount of constitutionally protected conduct" because it "fail[ed] to establish standards for the police and public that are sufficient to guard against the arbitrary deprivation of liberty interests." . . .

As the Supreme Court observed in *Kolender* and *Morales*, the failure to provide objective standards to govern enforcement of a law is effectively a delegation of lawmaking power to the individuals that enforce it. Put a different way, a vague statute "necessarily entrusts lawmaking to the moment-to-moment judgment of the policeman on his beat." . . . Such a delegation is dangerous because it lends itself to the sort of arbitrary, pretextual, and discriminatory enforcement that is inimical to individual liberty and the rule of law:

> The rule of law signifies the constraint of arbitrariness in the exercise of government power. In the context of the penal law, it means that the agencies of official coercion should, to the extent feasible, be guided by rules—that is, by openly acknowledged, relatively stable, and generally applicable statements of proscribed conduct. The evils to be retarded are caprice and whim, the misuse of government power for private ends, and the unacknowledged reliance on illegitimate criteria of selection. The values to be advanced are regularity and evenhandedness in the administration of justice and accountability in the use of government power.

John C. Jeffries, Jr., Legality, Vagueness, and the Construction of Penal Statutes, 71 Va. L. Rev. 189, 212 (1985). This concern for excessive delegation is distinct from the related doctrines of insufficient notice and overbreadth. . . . Unlike the similar doctrines of insufficient notice and overbreadth, the "arbitrary enforcement" branch of vagueness doctrine is not primarily concerned with the effect of a law on the conduct of regulated parties. Rather, it is focused on the conduct of regulators—specifically, unguided discretion within the process of lawmaking and law enforcement. . . .

We believe the concerns animating the Supreme Court's decisions in *Kolender* and *Morales* apply equally to the case at hand. *Morales* identified three factors that made the Chicago ordinance particularly suspect. First, the ordinance contained no criteria or clear standards to guide enforcement. Second, it covered a substantial amount of innocent conduct unrelated to the purposes of the statute. Third, because of the statute's breadth, it invited subjective judgments by officers and did nothing to discourage arbitrary and biased judgments in the field. . . . Here, as noted above, the Michigan statute provides almost no standard for determining whether a given ornament obstructs the vision of the driver; it thus "necessarily entrusts lawmaking to the moment-to-moment judgment of the policeman on his beat." . . . Further, the application of the statute is broad: a simple look around when driving confirms that many vehicles on the road have something hanging from their rearview mirror or suspended from their windshield, and few of these "obstruct" the driver's vision in any material way—certainly not enough to impair their ability to operate their vehicles. . . . The sense in which such dangling ornaments "obstruct" drivers' vision is not related to the safety purpose of the statute.

In sum, then, the lack of minimal law enforcement standards provided by the statute, combined with the prevalence of dangling ornaments in vehicles—which is not discouraged by the State of Michigan—gives law enforcement officers authority to engage in a "standardless sweep" of most of the vehicles on the road. This is precisely the infirmity the Supreme Court identified in the statutes struck down in *Kolender* and *Morales*. And, as those cases make clear, it is not an answer to say that one can avoid potential liability by refraining from using a dangling ornament: liability in *Kolender* could have been avoided by refraining from "loiter[ing] or wander[ing] upon the streets . . . without apparent reason"; likewise, liability in Morales could have been avoided by refraining from "loitering." As the *Morales* Court explained, this objection misses the point:

> That the ordinance does not apply to people who are moving—that is, to activity that would not constitute loitering under any possible definition of the term—does not even address the question of how much discretion the police enjoy in deciding which stationary persons to disperse under the ordinance.

. . . Again, the problem in *Kolender* and *Morales* was the degree of discretion delegated to law enforcement officials—that is, the lack of objective standards supplied by the legislature to govern enforcement. Broad applicability simply compounds that concern. Because the statute at issue here suffers the same infirmity as those at issue in *Kolender* and *Morales*, it should suffer the same fate.

Finally, we note that the rule of law concerns underlying the vagueness doctrine are even stronger in the Fourth Amendment context. . . . If courts cannot review the motives of law enforcement officers after the fact, it is crucial that they review the breadth of discretionary authority police receive from legislatures at the outset. The alternative is a broad abdication of the judicial duty to enforce the Fourth Amendment's prohibition on unreasonable searches and seizures at a time when this duty is more important than ever. . . .

Fortunately for the state of Michigan, this is not a case where further precision is either impossible or impractical. . . . Michigan could ban all dangling ornaments (with or without enumerated exceptions), explain in detail what kind of obstruction the statute does not allow, or provide other objective criteria to constrain the discretionary authority of those charged with enforcing the law. Because the current statute lacks these qualities, we hold that it is unconstitutionally vague.

CASE QUESTIONS

1. The Sixth Circuit expressed concern about the scope of police discretion in this case. What was it that was problematic?

2. What, according to the U.S. Supreme Court, are the two principal elements of the **vagueness** doctrine? Is one more important than the other?

3. What could the Michigan legislature do to correct the problem with this law?

Internet Tip

The preceding excerpted opinion was edited to focus on the vagueness issue and omitted the courts discussion relating to whether the evidence found by the officer while making a search incident to arrest should have been excluded at trial. Readers can read the omitted portion of the case on Loislaw. The Chapter 2 materials included on the textbook's website also include an edited version of a major vagueness case, *Chicago v. Morales*, 527 U.S. 41 (1999), which the U.S. Supreme Court decided in 1999.

AUTHOR'S COMMENTARY

After reading this case, you can better understand how difficult it is to write a criminal statute. If the drafters of a criminal law define the crime with great specificity, potential offenders will be able to argue that the law, by its terms, does not prohibit the acts they are accused of committing (thus they can get around the law). If, however, the law is written in general terms, criminally accused individuals can challenge the statute's constitutionality by alleging vagueness and—the topic we are about to discuss—**overbreadth**.

Overbreadth

Legislation suffers from overbreadth "if in its reach it prohibits constitutionally protected conduct. . . . The crucial question . . . is whether the ordinance sweeps within its prohibitions what may not be punished."[4] Due process requires that statutes be narrowly focused on prohibitable conduct.[5] An ordinance, for example, cannot be written so broadly that it could be used to arrest not only disorderly persons but also someone who is engaged in conduct that is protected by the First Amendment.

Internet Tip

Students wishing to learn more about overbreadth should read *Arab-American Anti-Discrimination Committee v. City of Dearborn*, 418 F.3d 600 (6th Cir. 2005). This is a case about whether the City of Dearborn, Michigan, had the right to enforce a municipal ordinance and thereby deny 200 Arab Americans the right to protest against "the reported movement of Israeli soldiers into Palestine." This case can be accessed on Loislaw.

The Right to Privacy

The U.S. Supreme Court has also recognized that substantive due process is violated when the content of a law infringes on an individual's liberty interests and invades a privacy right protected by the Due Process Clauses. When invasion of privacy occurs, the problem is not that a government's procedures are unfair or that the language is too imprecise; rather, a statute or ordinance wrongfully purports to allow the government to decide matters that rightfully should be decided by each individual.

Although the federal Constitution does not contain an explicit **privacy rights** article similar to those seen in Figure 2.2, the Supreme Court has ruled that limited privacy rights are implicit in the federal Constitution. The Court ruled it is found in the Fifth and Fourteenth Amendments' Due Process Clauses, which guarantee due process with respect to life, liberty, and property. It is also implicit in the First Amendment, which explicitly protects the right to religious freedom as well as the freedoms of speech, press, and assembly and other Amendments as discussed in the next case, *Griswold v. Connecticut*.

The Supreme Court has established a two-tier test for determining whether a particular law has infringed on a privacy right protected by the Due Process Clauses. The higher tier protects the rights that are found in the First Amendment and other privacy rights found by the Court to be fundamental and constitutionally deserving of protection because they are "implicit in the concept of ordered liberty." Privacy rights that have been recognized as fundamental are generally associated with the

Figure 2.2. Excerpts from the Alaska and Florida Constitutions

---

Alaska Constitution
Article I, Section 22
    The right of the people to privacy is recognized and shall not be infringed. The legislature shall implement this section.

Florida Constitution
Article I, Section 23
    Every natural person has the right to be let alone and free from governmental intrusion into the person's private life except as otherwise provided herein. This section shall not be construed to limit the public's right of access to public records and meetings as provided by law.

---

most intimate of personal interests such as marriage, procreation, education, child rearing, and family relationships. The Court has made it theoretically possible for government to override a right which has been deemed "fundamental," but it must meet a very high burden to be successful[6] The U.S. Supreme Court has also recognized that government can also violate a protected privacy right where a state abuses the police power. Government has no right to enact laws that have no rational connection to the public health, welfare, or safety (this is called the "rational basis" test). The problem here is that the law is arbitrary. Government is intruding on the rights of individuals to make their own decisions where a law has no rational basis to a legitimate governmental purpose.

    The Supreme Court first recognized the existence of a limited, federally protected privacy right in the 1965 case of *Griswold v. Connecticut.*

GRISWOLD v. CONNECTICUT
381 U.S. 479
U.S. Supreme Court
June 7, 1965

AUTHOR'S INTRODUCTION

In *Griswold*, the defendants were criminally prosecuted by the State of Connecticut for having provided married couples with information about birth control, a violation of state law. The defendants challenged the constitutionality of the statutes. They claimed that they, and not the state, were entitled to make the decision about whether to practice contraception. They also claimed that this "right" was protected conduct under the Fourteenth Amendment Due Process Clause.

EXCERPT FROM THE CASE

Justice DOUGLAS delivered the opinion of the Court.

... Coming to the merits, we are met with a wide range of questions that implicate the Due Process Clause of the Fourteenth Amendment.... We do not sit as a super-legislature to determine the wisdom, need, and propriety of laws that touch economic problems, business affairs, or social conditions. This law, however, operates directly on an intimate relation of husband and wife and their physician's role in one aspect of that relation.

The association of people is not mentioned in the Constitution nor in the Bill of Rights. The right to educate a child in a school of the parents' choice—whether public or private or parochial—is also not mentioned. Nor is the right to study any particular subject or any foreign language. Yet the First Amendment has been construed to include certain of those rights.

... Without those peripheral rights the specific rights [in the Bill of Rights] would be less secure. ...

[The] specific guarantees in the Bill of Rights have penumbras [shadows], formed by emanations from those guarantees that help give them life and substance. ... Various guarantees create zones of privacy. The right of association contained in the penumbra of the First Amendment is one, ... the Third Amendment in its prohibition against the quartering of soldiers "in any house" in time of peace without the consent of the owner is another facet of that privacy. The Fourth Amendment explicitly affirms the "right of the people to be secure in their persons, houses, papers, and effects, against unreasonable searches and seizures." The Fifth Amendment in its Self-Incrimination Clause enables the citizen to create a zone of privacy which government may not force him to surrender to his detriment. The Ninth Amendment provides: "The enumeration in the Constitution, of certain rights, shall not be construed to deny or disparage others retained by the people."

The present case, then, concerns a relationship lying within the zone of Privacy created by several fundamental constitutional guarantees. And it concerns a law which, in forbidding the use of contraceptives rather than regulating their manufacture or sale, seeks to achieve its goals by means having a maximum destructive impact upon that relationship. Such a law cannot stand in light of the familiar principle, so often applied by Court, that a "governmental purpose to control or prevent activities constitutionally subject to state regulation may not be achieved by means which sweep unnecessarily broadly and thereby invade the area of protected freedoms."

... Would we allow the police to search the sacred precincts of marital bedrooms for telltale signs of the use of contraceptives? The very idea is repulsive to the notions of privacy surrounding the marriage relationship.

We deal with a right of privacy older than the Bill of Rights—older than our political parties, older than our school system. Marriage is a coming together for better or for worse, hopefully enduring, and intimate to the degree of being sacred. It is an association that promotes a way of life, not causes; a harmony in living, not political faiths; a bilateral loyalty, not commercial or social projects. Yet it is an association for as noble a purpose as any involved in our prior decisions.

Reversed.

CASE QUESTIONS

1. What does Justice Douglas mean when he says that the rights specifically mentioned in the Bill of Rights have "penumbras"?

2. Do you think that it makes any significant difference that a privacy right is explicitly established by constitutional provision rather than by judicial implication (as was done in *Griswold*)?

AUTHOR'S COMMENTARY

The Supreme Court in *Griswold*, emphasized the fact that it was addressing the privacy right of married people to use contraceptives within the marital bedroom. But the *Griswold* case began an exploration of privacy rights that has continued to this day, particularly with respect to procreation, abortion, and private adult sexuality. The *Griswold* case was followed by subsequent decisions that expanded individual privacy rights to make reproductive decisions to unmarried adults in *Eisenstadt v. Baird*, 405 U.S. 438 (1972), to pregnant women in *Roe v. Wade*, 410 U.S. 113 (1973), and the right of children under 16 to have access to non-medical contraception in *Carey v. Population Services International*, 431 U.S. 678 (1977). However, the Court has also limited the rights of low-income women to exercise personal rights by refusing to require the government to pay for their abortions, *Harris v. McRae*, 448 U.S. 297 (1980), and until recently had refused to recognize constitutional protections for the privacy rights of homosexuals.

In 2003, the Supreme Court agreed to reconsider one of its earlier decisions, the 1986 case of *Bowers v. Hardwick*, 478 U.S. 186. The *Bowers* decision had permitted states, including Texas, to make it a crime for adult homosexuals to consensually engage in sodomy in the privacy of their homes.

The petitioners in the following case, Lawrence and Garner, argued that the Texas "deviate intercourse" statute, which was the legal justification for their criminal prosecutions, violated their rights under the Equal Protection and Due Process Clauses of the Fourteenth Amendment to the U.S. Constitution.

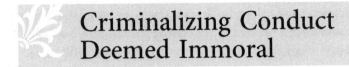

Criminalizing Conduct Deemed Immoral

LAWRENCE v. TEXAS
539 U.S. 558
U.S. Supreme Court
June 26, 2003

AUTHOR'S INTRODUCTION

John G. Lawrence and Tyron Garner were prosecuted and convicted of violating the Texas deviate sexual intercourse statute. Both men appealed claiming that the statute was unconstitutional because it violated their rights to privacy. They argued that as consenting adults they had a constitutionally protected right under the **Fourteenth Amendment's Equal Protection** and Due Process Clauses to engage in sodomy within their apartment.

EXCERPT FROM THE CASE

Justice KENNEDY delivered the opinion of the Court.

Liberty protects the person from unwarranted government intrusions into a dwelling or other private places. In our tradition the State is not omnipresent in the home. And there are other spheres of our lives and existence, outside the home, where the State should not be a dominant presence. Freedom extends beyond spatial bounds. Liberty presumes an autonomy of self that includes freedom of thought, belief, expression, and certain intimate conduct. The instant case involves liberty of the person both in its spatial and more transcendent dimensions.

I

The question before the Court is the validity of a Texas statute making it a crime for two persons of the same sex to engage in certain intimate sexual conduct.

In Houston, Texas, officers of the Harris County Police Department were dispatched to a private residence in response to a reported weapons disturbance. They entered an apartment where one of the petitioners, John Geddes Lawrence, resided. The right of the police to enter does not seem to have been questioned. The officers observed Lawrence and another man, Tyron Garner, engaging in a sexual act. The two petitioners were arrested, held in custody over night, and charged and convicted before a Justice of the Peace.

The complaints described their crime as "deviate sexual intercourse, namely anal sex, with a member of the same sex (man)." . . . The applicable state law is Tex. Penal Code Ann. § 21.06(a) (2003). It provides: "A person commits an offense if he engages in deviate sexual intercourse with another individual of the same sex." The statute defines "[d]eviate sexual intercourse" as follows:

> (A) any contact between any part of the genitals of one person and the mouth or anus of another person; or (B) the penetration of the genitals or the anus of another person with an object. § 21.01(1).

The petitioners exercised their right to a trial de novo in Harris County Criminal Court. They challenged the statute as a violation of the Equal Protection Clause of the Fourteenth Amendment and of a like provision of the Texas Constitution. . . . Those contentions were rejected. The petitioners, having entered a plea of nolo contendere, were each fined $200 and assessed court costs of $141.25. . . .

The Court of Appeals for the Texas Fourteenth District considered the petitioners' federal constitutional arguments under both the Equal Protection and Due Process Clauses of the Fourteenth Amendment. After hearing the case en banc the court, in a divided opinion, rejected the constitutional arguments and affirmed the convictions. . . . The majority opinion indicates that the Court of Appeals considered our decision in *Bowers v. Hardwick*, 478 U. S. 186 (1986), to be controlling on the federal due process aspect of the case. *Bowers* then being authoritative, this was proper. . . .

The petitioners were adults at the time of the alleged offense. Their conduct was in private and consensual.

II

We conclude the case should be resolved by determining whether the petitioners were free as adults to engage in the private conduct in the exercise of their liberty under the Due Process Clause of the Fourteenth Amendment to the Constitution. . . .

There are broad statements of the substantive reach of liberty under the Due Process Clause in earlier cases . . . , but the most pertinent beginning point is our decision in *Griswold v. Connecticut*, 381 U. S. 479 (1965).

In *Griswold* the Court invalidated a state law prohibiting the use of drugs or devices of contraception and counseling or aiding and abetting the use of contraceptives. The Court described the protected interest as a right to privacy and placed emphasis on the marriage relation and the protected space of the marital bedroom. . . .

After *Griswold* it was established that the right to make certain decisions regarding sexual conduct extends beyond the marital relationship. In

Eisenstadt v. Baird, 405 U. S. 438 (1972), the Court invalidated a law prohibiting the distribution of contraceptives to unmarried persons. The case was decided under the Equal Protection Clause, . . . but with respect to unmarried persons, the Court went on to state the fundamental proposition that the law impaired the exercise of their personal rights. . . . It quoted from the statement of the Court of Appeals finding the law to be in conflict with fundamental human rights, and it followed with this statement of its own:

> It is true that in *Griswold* the right of privacy in question inhered in the marital relationship. . . . If the right of privacy means anything, it is the right of the individual, married or single, to be free from unwarranted governmental intrusion into matters so fundamentally affecting a person as the decision whether to bear or beget a child. . . .

The opinions in *Griswold* and *Eisenstadt* were part of the background for the decision in *Roe v. Wade*, 410 U. S. 113 (1973). As is well known, the case involved a challenge to the Texas law prohibiting abortions, but the laws of other States were affected as well. Although the Court held the woman's rights were not absolute, her right to elect an abortion did have real and substantial protection as an exercise of her liberty under the Due Process Clause. The Court cited cases that protect spatial freedom and cases that go well beyond it. *Roe* recognized the right of a woman to make certain fundamental decisions affecting her destiny and confirmed once more that the protection of liberty under the Due Process Clause has a substantive dimension of fundamental significance in defining the rights of the person.

In *Carey v. Population Services Int'l*, 431 U. S. 678 (1977), the Court confronted a New York law forbidding sale or distribution of contraceptive devices to persons under 16 years of age. Although there was no single opinion for the Court, the law was invalidated. Both *Eisenstadt* and *Carey*, as well as the holding and rationale in *Roe*, confirmed that the reasoning of *Griswold*, could not be confined to the protection of rights of married adults. This was the state of the law with respect to some of the most relevant cases when the Court considered *Bowers v. Hardwick*.

The facts in *Bowers* had some similarities to the instant case. A police officer, whose right to enter seems not to have been in question, observed *Hardwick*, in his own bedroom, engaging in intimate sexual conduct with another adult male. The conduct was in violation of a Georgia statute making it a criminal offense to engage in sodomy. One difference between the two cases is that the Georgia statute prohibited the conduct whether or not the participants were of the same sex, while the Texas statute, as we have seen, applies only to participants of the same sex. Hardwick was not prosecuted, but he brought an action in federal court to declare the state statute invalid. He alleged he was a practicing homosexual and that the criminal prohibition violated rights guaranteed to him by the Constitution. The Court, in an opinion by Justice White, sustained the Georgia law. Chief Justice

Burger and Justice Powell joined the opinion of the Court and filed separate, concurring opinions. Four Justices dissented. . . .

The Court began its substantive discussion in *Bowers* as follows: "The issue
presented is whether the Federal Constitution confers a fundamental right upon
homosexuals to engage in sodomy and hence invalidates the laws of the many States
that still make such conduct illegal and have done so for a very long time." . . . That
statement, we now conclude, discloses the Court's own failure to appreciate the
extent of the liberty at stake. To say that the issue in *Bowers* was simply the right to
engage in certain sexual conduct demeans the claim the individual put forward, just
as it would demean a married couple were it to be said marriage is simply about the
right to have sexual intercourse. The laws involved in *Bowers* and here are, to be
sure, statutes that purport to do no more than prohibit a particular sexual act. Their
penalties and purposes, though, have more far-reaching consequences, touching
upon the most private human conduct, sexual behavior, and in the most private of
places, the home. The statutes do seek to control a personal relationship that,
whether or not entitled to formal recognition in the law, is within the liberty of
persons to choose without being punished as criminals.

This, as a general rule, should counsel against attempts by the State, or a court,
to define the meaning of the relationship or to set its boundaries absent injury to a
person or abuse of an institution the law protects. It suffices for us to acknowledge
that adults may choose to enter upon this relationship in the confines of their homes
and their own private lives and still retain their dignity as free persons. When
sexuality finds overt expression in intimate conduct with another person, the conduct can be but one element in a personal bond that is more enduring. The liberty
protected by the Constitution allows homosexual persons the right to make this
choice.

Having misapprehended the claim of liberty there presented to it, and thus
stating the claim to be whether there is a fundamental right to engage in consensual
sodomy, the *Bowers* Court said: "Proscriptions against that conduct have ancient
roots." . . . In academic writings, and in many of the scholarly amicus briefs filed to
assist the Court in this case, there are fundamental criticisms of the historical
premises relied upon by the majority and concurring opinions in *Bowers*. . . . We
need not enter this debate in the attempt to reach a definitive historical judgment,
but the following considerations counsel against adopting the definitive conclusions
upon which *Bowers* placed such reliance.

At the outset it should be noted that there is no longstanding history in this
country of laws directed at homosexual conduct as a distinct matter. Beginning in
colonial times there were prohibitions of sodomy derived from the English criminal
laws passed in the first instance by the Reformation Parliament of 1533. The English
prohibition was understood to include relations between men and women as well as
relations between men and men. . . . Nineteenth-century commentators similarly

read American sodomy, buggery, and crime-against-nature statutes as criminalizing certain relations between men and women and between men and men. . . . The absence of legal prohibitions focusing on homosexual conduct may be explained in part by noting that according to some scholars the concept of the homosexual as a distinct category of person did not emerge until the late 19th century. . . . Thus early American sodomy laws were not directed at homosexuals as such but instead sought to prohibit nonprocreative sexual activity more generally. This does not suggest approval of homosexual conduct. It does tend to show that this particular form of conduct was not thought of as a separate category from like conduct between heterosexual persons.

Laws prohibiting sodomy do not seem to have been enforced against consenting adults acting in private. . . . Instead of targeting relations between consenting adults in private, 19th-century sodomy prosecutions typically involved relations between men and minor girls or minor boys, relations between adults involving force, relations between adults implicating disparity in status, or relations between men and animals. . . .

The policy of punishing consenting adults for private acts was not much discussed in the early legal literature. We can infer that one reason for this was the very private nature of the conduct. Despite the absence of prosecutions, there may have been periods in which there was public criticism of homosexuals as such and an insistence that the criminal laws be enforced to discourage their practices. But far from possessing "ancient roots". . . . American laws targeting same-sex couples did not develop until the last third of the 20th century. The reported decisions concerning the prosecution of consensual, homosexual sodomy between adults for the years 1880-1995 are not always clear in the details, but a significant number involved conduct in a public place. . . .

It was not until the 1970s that any State singled out same-sex relations for criminal prosecution, and only nine States have done so. . . . Post-*Bowers* even some of these States did not adhere to the policy of suppressing homosexual conduct. Over the course of the last decades, States with same-sex prohibitions have moved toward abolishing them. . . .

In summary, the historical grounds relied upon in *Bowers* are more complex than the majority opinion and the concurring opinion by Chief Justice Burger indicate. Their historical premises are not without doubt and, at the very least, are overstated.

It must be acknowledged, of course, that the Court in *Bowers* was making the broader point that for centuries there have been powerful voices to condemn homosexual conduct as immoral. The condemnation has been shaped by religious beliefs, conceptions of right and acceptable behavior, and respect for the traditional family. For many persons these are not trivial concerns but profound and deep convictions accepted as ethical and moral principles to which they aspire and which thus determine the course of their lives. These considerations do not answer the question before us, however. The issue is whether the majority may use the power of the State to enforce these views on the whole society through operation of the criminal law. "Our obligation is to define the liberty of all, not to mandate our own moral code." . . .

In all events we think that our laws and traditions in the past half century are of most relevance here. These references show an emerging awareness that liberty gives substantial protection to adult persons in deciding how to conduct their private lives in matters pertaining to sex. "[H]istory and tradition are the starting point but not in all cases the ending point of the substantive due process inquiry." . . .

This emerging recognition should have been apparent when *Bowers* was decided. In 1955 the American Law Institute promulgated the Model Penal Code and made clear that it did not recommend or provide for "criminal penalties for consensual sexual relations conducted in private." . . . It justified its decision on three grounds: (1) The prohibitions undermined respect for the law by penalizing conduct many people engaged in; (2) the statutes regulated private conduct not harmful to others; and (3) the laws were arbitrarily enforced and thus invited the danger of blackmail. . . . In 1961 Illinois changed its laws to conform to the Model Penal Code. Other States soon followed. . . .

Of even more importance, almost five years before *Bowers* was decided the European Court of Human Rights considered a case with parallels to *Bowers* and to today's case. An adult male resident in Northern Ireland alleged he was a practicing homosexual who desired to engage in consensual homosexual conduct. The laws of Northern Ireland forbade him that right. He alleged that he had been questioned, his home had been searched, and he feared criminal prosecution. The court held that the laws proscribing the conduct were invalid under the European Convention on Human Rights. . . . Authoritative in all countries that are members of the Council of Europe (21 nations then, 45 nations now), the decision is at odds with the premise in *Bowers* that the claim put forward was insubstantial in our Western civilization.

In our own constitutional system the deficiencies in *Bowers* became even more apparent in the years following its announcement. The 25 States with laws prohibiting the relevant conduct referenced in the *Bowers* decision are reduced now to 13, of which 4 enforce their laws only against homosexual conduct. In those States where sodomy is still proscribed, whether for same-sex or heterosexual conduct, there is a pattern of nonenforcement with respect to consenting adults acting in private. The State of Texas admitted in 1994 that as of that date it had not prosecuted anyone under those circumstances. . . .

Equality of treatment and the due process right to demand respect for conduct protected by the substantive guarantee of liberty are linked in important respects, and a decision on the latter point advances both interests. If protected conduct is made criminal and the law which does so remains unexamined for its substantive validity, its stigma might remain even if it were not enforceable as drawn for equal protection reasons. When homosexual conduct is made criminal by the law of the State, that declaration in and of itself is an invitation to subject homosexual persons to discrimination both in the public and in the private spheres. The central holding of *Bowers* has been brought in question by this case, and it should be addressed. Its continuance as precedent demeans the lives of homosexual persons.

The stigma this criminal statute imposes, moreover, is not trivial. The offense, to be sure, is but a class C misdemeanor, a minor offense in the Texas legal system. Still, it remains a criminal offense with all that imports for the dignity of the persons charged. The petitioners will bear on their record the history of their criminal convictions. . . . We are advised that if Texas convicted an adult for private, consensual homosexual conduct under the statute here in question the convicted person would come within the registration laws of a least four States were he or she to be subject to their jurisdiction. . . . This underscores the consequential nature of the punishment and the state-sponsored condemnation attendant to the criminal prohibition. Furthermore, the Texas criminal conviction carries with it the other collateral consequences always following a conviction, such as notations on job application forms, to mention but one example. . . .

In the United States criticism of *Bowers* has been substantial and continuing, disapproving of its reasoning in all respects, not just as to its historical assumptions. . . . The courts of five different States have declined to follow it in interpreting provisions in their own state constitutions parallel to the Due Process Clause of the Fourteenth Amendment. . . .

To the extent *Bowers* relied on values we share with a wider civilization, it should be noted that the reasoning and holding in *Bowers* have been rejected elsewhere. The European Court of Human Rights has followed not *Bowers* but its own decision in *Dudgeon v. United Kingdom*. . . . Other nations, too, have taken action consistent with an affirmation of the protected right of homosexual adults to engage in intimate, consensual conduct. . . . The right the petitioners seek in this case has been accepted as an integral part of human freedom in many other countries. There has been no showing that in this country the governmental interest in circumscribing personal choice is somehow more legitimate or urgent. . . .

The rationale of *Bowers* does not withstand careful analysis. In his dissenting opinion in *Bowers* Justice Stevens came to these conclusions:

> Our prior cases make two propositions abundantly clear. First, the fact that the governing majority in a State has traditionally viewed a particular practice as immoral is not a sufficient reason for upholding a law prohibiting the practice; neither history nor tradition could save a law prohibiting miscegenation from constitutional attack. Second, individual decisions by married persons, concerning the intimacies of their

physical relationship, even when not intended to produce offspring, are a form of "liberty" protected by the Due Process Clause of the Fourteenth Amendment. Moreover, this protection extends to intimate choices by unmarried as well as married persons. . . .

Justice Stevens' analysis, in our view, should have been controlling in *Bowers* and should control here.

Bowers was not correct when it was decided, and it is not correct today. It ought not to remain binding precedent. *Bowers v. Hardwick* should be and now is overruled.

The present case does not involve minors. It does not involve persons who might be injured or coerced or who are situated in relationships where consent might not easily be refused. It does not involve public conduct or prostitution. It does not involve whether the government must give formal recognition to any relationship that homosexual persons seek to enter. The case does involve two adults who, with full and mutual consent from each other, engaged in sexual practices common to a homosexual lifestyle. The petitioners are entitled to respect for their private lives. The State cannot demean their existence or control their destiny by making their private sexual conduct a crime. Their right to liberty under the Due Process Clause gives them the full right to engage in their conduct without intervention of the government. "It is a promise of the Constitution that there is a realm of personal liberty which the government may not enter." . . .

The Texas statute furthers no legitimate state interest which can justify its intrusion into the personal and private life of the individual. Had those who drew and ratified the Due Process Clauses of the Fifth Amendment or the Fourteenth Amendment known the components of liberty in its manifold possibilities, they might have been more specific. They did not presume to have this insight. They knew times can blind us to certain truths and later generations can see that laws once thought necessary and proper in fact serve only to oppress. As the Constitution endures, persons in every generation can invoke its principles in their own search for greater freedom.

The judgment of the Court of Appeals for the Texas Fourteenth District is reversed, and the case is remanded for further proceedings not inconsistent with this opinion.

It is so ordered.

CASE QUESTIONS

1. On which constitutional provision did Justice Kennedy rely in deciding the *Lawrence* case? Explain his reasoning in your own words.

2. Why did Justice Kennedy disagree with Texas's claim that its statute merely criminalized morally inappropriate sexual conduct?

3. How did Justice Kennedy justify his conclusion that an implicit constitutional right of privacy had been violated in this case, given the fact that the term "liberty" is not explicitly defined in the Constitution?

AUTHOR'S COMMENTARY

One of the most interesting and enduring debates surrounding the question of constitutionally protected privacy rights involves whether it is constitutional for states to use the criminal law to impose majoritarian moral views upon those who reject the prevailing moral norms.

The legislative branches of the state governments are primarily charged with protecting the public health, welfare, safety, and morals pursuant to the exercise of the police power. But this interest can also be viewed as intruding on legitimate privacy rights of individuals. Courts are often asked to engage in constitutional line drawing, as we just saw in *Lawrence v. Texas*.

The task of drawing lines is somewhat easier where there is broad agreement in society that specified conduct is both criminal and immoral. Examples include crimes such as murder, rape, arson, and assault with a deadly weapon. It is not easy where there is widespread disagreement as to whether given conduct is immoral or as to the extent to which conduct thought to be immoral by political majorities can be made criminal.

Although Justice Kennedy, writing for the Court in *Lawrence*, made it clear that his opinion had nothing to do with same-sex marriages, his point-by-point refutation of the *Bowers'* Court's rationale for continuing to criminalize sodomy prosecutions will surely be cited by those advocating further expansion of the liberty rights of homosexuals.

 Internet Tip

The state supreme courts had been deciding cases involving facts that were similar to those in *Lawrence* for many years. These cases involved constitutional challenges based on the federal and/or state constitutions. In some of these cases, the judges debated in their opinions whether state "deviate" sexual practices statutes were constitutionally permissible exercises of the police power or the improper imposition of majoritarian moral views which infringed on the rights of individuals. You can find edited excerpts from two of these cases, *Pennsylvania v. Bonadio*, 415 A.2d 47 (1987), and *Kentucky v. Wesson*,

(continued)

842 S.W.2D 487 (1992), in the materials included within the Chapter 2 portion of the textbook's website. The judges in these cases engage in a debate over the philosophy of John Locke.

Procedural Due Process

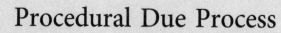

Government has to use fair procedures in judicial proceedings when it is attempting to deprive a person of "life, liberty or property." This means that the targeted person must be allowed the full benefit of all procedural rights protected by the Due Process Clauses of our Constitution.

The most basic requirement of procedural due process is that government provide every person with *notice* of any charges that have been brought against him or her and a *fair hearing* at which the accused person has the right to defend against the charges. Government should not be able to manipulate the process by which justice is carried out in order to control the outcome of a given case. The U.S. Supreme Court has made it clear that the requirements of due process vary with the circumstances of each case. Due process, it has ruled, does not require that a public board of education provide a misbehaving student whom it wishes to suspend from school with the same degree of procedural protections that are mandatory when a criminal defendant is prosecuted for committing a crime. In a school suspension case, said the Court, there was no need for trial-type procedures, lawyers, cross examination, and so on. Due process is satisfied, said the Court, if the accused student receives some kind of notice and some kind of a hearing.[7]

As you may be aware, the U.S. Constitution's Bill of Rights contains many procedural protections for criminally accused persons.[8] We have already seen that when enacted and ratified by the states, the Bill of Rights applied only to the federal government. This means that states were not required by the federal Constitution to provide the same rights in state proceedings as would be required in federal prosecutions and trials. The U.S. Supreme Court, in a series of cases stretching back to 1884,[9] decided that most of these procedural protections were basic to our society and should be binding on the states as a matter of federal law (in legal jargon, one would say that these rights have been *incorporated* into the Fourteenth Amendment Due Process Clause). Thus while an indigent defendant on trial for a crime punishable by a sentence of imprisonment in a federal trial has a Sixth Amendment right to appointed counsel, a similarly situated state criminal defendant's right to appointed counsel is based on the Fourteenth Amendment's Due Process Clause.

JASON C. SMITH v. STATE OF IDAHO

Docket No. 33254
Supreme Court of Idaho
February 10, 2009

AUTHOR'S INTRODUCTION

You may be familiar with a statute popularly known as **"Megan's Law."** Versions of this statute, which originated in New Jersey, have been enacted by all 50 states as well as the federal government (42 U.S.C. 1407). "Megan's Law" statutes require that convicted sex offenders register with a state or local agency and provide for the collection and dissemination of personal information about registrants to the general public. Many states provide this information to the public via the internet.

Jason Smith, the appellant in the following case, was a convicted sexual offender. He was convicted three times for rape and admitted to a fourth rape (for which he was never prosecuted). Three of his victims were male and one was female. His victims ranged in age from 5 to 15 years of age. Under Idaho law, before a convicted sexual offender can be released from incarceration back into the community, the Idaho Sexual Offender Classification Board has to determine whether the offender should be classified as a violent sexual predator. The Board ruled that Smith deserved to be classified as a violent sexual predator. Smith appealed the Board's decision to the district court. After the district court affirmed the Board, Smith appealed again, this time to the Idaho Supreme Court.

EXCERPT FROM THE CASE

HORTON, Justice.

Jason Smith was incarcerated for the 1998 rape of a fifteen-year-old girl. Prior to his release, he was referred to the Sexual Offender Classification Board (the Board or SOCB) to determine whether he should be classified as a violent sexual predator (VSP). The Board classified Smith as a VSP. Smith sought judicial review of that decision. After conducting an evidentiary hearing, the district court upheld the Board's decision. We conclude Smith's designation was not constitutionally sound and, therefore, reverse and remand with instructions to vacate Smith's designation as a VSP. . . .

ANALYSIS

. . . We begin by acknowledging the obvious: Smith's history of violent deviant sexual behavior is such that the Board's designation as a VSP may well be warranted. The important question presented by this appeal, however, is not whether he deserves that label. Rather, the question that is the focal point of this Court's inquiry is whether the State of Idaho has labeled Smith as a VSP in a fashion that comports with his constitutional right to due process. . . .

A. THE STATUTORY FRAMEWORK FOR VSP DESIGNATION IN IDAHO PRESENTS SIGNIFICANT CONSTITUTIONAL SHORTCOMINGS

1. The Statutory Framework

Designation as a VSP is based on the provisions of Idaho's Sexual Offender Registration Notification and Community Right to Know Act (the Act or SOR Act). . . . Only offenders convicted of certain specified crimes are eligible for designation as VSPs. . . . The Board is charged with the duty of considering for VSP designation those inmates scheduled for release who have been referred by the department of correction or the parole commission. . . . Smith was such an inmate. . . . A VSP designation is based upon the Board's determination that the offender continues to "pose a high risk of committing an offense or engaging in predatory sexual conduct." . . . The Board's rules provide that "[a] sexual offender shall be designated as a VSP if his risk of re-offending sexually or threat of violence is of sufficient concern to warrant the designation for the safety of the community." . . . In reaching this decision, the Board is required to "assess how biological, psychological, and situational factors, may cause or contribute to the offender's sexual behavior." . . . Once the Board determines whether to designate the offender as a VSP, it must make written findings that include a risk assessment of the offender, the reasons upon which the risk assessment is based, the Board's determination whether the offender should be designated, and the reasons upon which the determination is based. . . .

Apart from submitting to a mandatory . . . psychosexual evaluation . . . , the offender has no opportunity to provide input to the Board. "The Board and the evaluator conducting the psychosexual evaluation may have access to and may review all obtainable records on the sexual offender to conduct the VSP designation assessment." . . . The offender is not given notice of the information being considered by the Board, much less an opportunity to be heard as to the reliability of that information. If the Board determines that the offender is to be designated as a VSP, the offender is notified of the Board's decision by way of a copy of the Board's written findings. . . .

If the Board makes a VSP designation, the offender has 14 days from receipt of the notice to seek judicial review. . . . An offender designated a VSP is only entitled to challenge the designation on two grounds:

> (a) The offender may introduce evidence that the calculation that led to the designation as a violent sexual predator was incorrectly performed either because of a factual error, because the offender disputes a prior offense, because the variable factors were

improperly determined, or for similar reasons; . . . and (b) The offender may introduce evidence at the hearing that the designation as a violent sexual predator does not properly encapsulate the specific case, i.e., the offender may maintain that the case falls outside the typical case of this kind and, therefore, that the offender should not be designated as a violent sexual predator. . . .

The scope of judicial review is limited to "a summary, in camera review proceeding, in which the court decides only whether to affirm or reverse the board's designation of the offender as a violent sexual predator." . . . Thus, the Act contemplates that judicial review will ordinarily occur without the offender having the opportunity to address the basis of the Board's decision. The Act does provide that "[w]here the proof, whether in the form of reliable hearsay, affidavits, or offers of live testimony, creates a genuine issue of material fact as to whether the offender is a violent sexual predator, the court should convene a fact-finding hearing and permit live testimony." . . . At the hearing, the State bears the burden of presenting a prima facie case justifying the Board's designation. . . . Despite this threshold burden of production, the offender ultimately bears the burden of proof, . . . provides that "[t]he court shall affirm the board's determination unless persuaded by a preponderance of the evidence that it does not conform to the law or the guidelines."

2. The Constitutional Shortcomings

The oddity lies herein: while both parties may introduce evidence, neither party is provided with the record utilized by the Board to make its determination, except for a written summary of information relied upon by the Board and documents that are available to the parties by other means. . . . All records that contain witness or victim names or statements, reports prepared in making parole determinations, or other "confidential" records are withheld from disclosure to the offender, his attorney, and even the prosecutor, and are available only to the district court for the purpose of reviewing the Board's determination. . . . The rules of evidence do not apply. . . .

In our view, there are significant constitutional shortcomings in the statutory procedure as a result of the lack of procedural due process afforded an offender. "Where a person's good name, reputation, honor, or integrity is at stake because of what the government is doing to him, notice and an opportunity to be heard are essential." *Wisconsin v. Constantineau*, 400 U.S. 433, 437 (1971). "[C]ertainly where the State attaches 'a badge of infamy' to the citizen, due process comes into play." . . . We take it as a given that the label of "violent sexual predator" is a "badge of infamy" that necessitates due process protections. The high court of New York has recognized that an individual's

private interest, his liberty interest in not being stigmatized as a sexually violent predator, is substantial. The ramifications of being classified and having that information disseminated fall squarely within those cases that recognize a liberty interest where there is some stigma to one's good name, reputation or integrity, coupled with some more "tangible" interest that is affected or a legal right that is altered. More than "name calling by public officials," the sexually violent predator label "is a determination of status" that can have a considerable adverse impact on an individual's ability to live in a community and obtain or maintain employment. . . .

Idaho provides a computerized sex offender registry that is accessible to the public via the Internet complete with photos of all sex offenders, along with their personal information including name, address, date of birth, and offense history. . . . Furthermore, there is a special link for those sex offenders designated as VSPs. This Court has recognized "the fact that registration brings notoriety to a person convicted of a sexual offense . . . prolong[s] the stigma attached to such convictions." . . .

Designation as a VSP results in consequences beyond simply requiring the designee to register as a sex offender. Sex offenders need only update their information and photographs in the registry annually, while VSPs must do so every ninety days. . . . Non-VSP offenders may petition a court for relief from the duty to register after a period of ten years. . . . On the other hand, a VSP has no right to such relief. Thus, for an offender designated as a VSP, the scarlet letters are indelible.

While the duty to register as a sex offender is triggered simply by reason of conviction for a specified crime, classification as a VSP is based upon a factual determination of probable future conduct, i.e., that the offender poses a high risk of committing an offense or engaging in predatory sexual conduct. . . . This distinguishes Idaho's VSP system from a sex offender registry based solely on the fact of conviction of a predicate offense. As to the latter, the United States Supreme Court has concluded that sex offender registration laws do not violate the offender's procedural due process rights, noting the offender "has already had a procedurally safeguarded opportunity to contest" the charge. *Conn. Dep't of Pub. Safety v. Doe*, 538 U.S. 1, 7 (2003); . . . In reaching this conclusion, the Supreme Court emphasized that Connecticut's registry requirement is "based on the fact of previous conviction, not the fact of current dangerousness . . . [i]ndeed, the public registry explicitly states that officials have not determined that any registrant is currently dangerous." . . .

Under *Constantineau* and its progeny, procedural due process is a constitutional prerequisite to the state's ability to designate an individual a VSP. "Only when the whole proceedings leading to the pinning of an unsavory label on a person are aired can oppressive results be prevented." . . . This Court has stated:

Procedural due process basically requires that a person, whose protected rights are being adjudicated, is afforded an opportunity to be heard in a timely manner. There must be notice and the opportunity to be heard must occur at a meaningful time and in a meaningful manner. . . .

In spite of the existence of well-established standards of procedural due process, Idaho's statutory scheme for VSP designation minimizes, at every turn, the possibility that an offender has the constitutionally required notice and opportunity to be heard. The offender is not provided notice or opportunity to be heard before the Board. At the district court level, the offender is provided only a summary of the information considered by the Board, presenting little meaningful opportunity to respond to specific information considered by the Board. The offender is given his first opportunity to be heard only if he can persuade the district court that there is a genuine issue of material fact whether he is a VSP. In the event that the offender clears this threshold hurdle, he then bears the burden of disproving the propriety of the designation, all the while being denied access to many of the documents upon which the designation may have been based. . . .

We do not question the legitimate state interest in identifying those offenders who pose a high risk of reoffending or engaging in predatory sexual conduct. However, the United States Constitution prohibits the state from doing so without affording the offender due process. In our view, Idaho's statutory scheme violates an offender's right to procedural due process by failing to provide notice and an opportunity to be heard at a meaningful time and in a meaningful manner and by placing the burden of proof on the offender . . . at the only hearing in which he is permitted to appear. . . .

CONCLUSION

When information upon which the VSP designation is based is withheld from an offender it cannot be said that there is either notice or a meaningful opportunity to be heard. The procedures afforded by the statute must comport with constitutional standards of procedural due process.

> [F]airness can rarely be obtained by secret, one-sided determination of facts decisive of rights . . . [s]ecrecy is not congenial to truth-seeking and self-righteousness gives too slender an assurance of rightness. No better instrument has been devised for arriving at truth than to give a person in jeopardy of serious loss notice of the case against him and opportunity to meet it. . . .

The statutory scheme for VSP designation is constitutionally infirm. The district court did not succeed in fashioning an *ad hoc* remedy to the invalid statute. Until Smith has the benefit of his constitutional right to notice and an opportunity to be heard, the State may not designate him as a VSP. Accordingly, we reverse the decision of the district court and remand this matter to the district court with direction to vacate Smith's designation as a VSP.

Justices BURDICK and J. JONES, concur.

INTRODUCTION TO THE DISSENT

Two justices dissented in the *Smith* case in an opinion written by Justice Jones. The dissenters thought it was unnecessary for the Court to reach the constitutional issues. Smith's due process objections were waived because they had been properly raised at trial.

EXCERPT FROM JUSTICE JONES'S DISSENT

Although I am sympathetic to the due process analysis made by the majority and I fully agree that the statutory scheme is questionable as to its constitutionality, I am also mindful that this case is not one which is appropriate for judicial review. The ultimate reality is that despite constitutional infirmities in the statutes, Smith was not affected or prejudiced by them. . . . Smith did not request disclosure [of information upon which the VSP designation was based]. I cannot speculate how the district court would have reacted in light of such a request; therefore, it is inappropriate for this Court to assume that . . . the district court would have ultimately refused disclosure. For the foregoing reasons, I would affirm the decision of the district court.

Chief Justice EISMANN concurs in the dissent.

CASE QUESTIONS

1. Assume that you are a member of the Idaho legislature and you are seeking reelection. Your opponent is running television commercials in which you are accused of being soft on crime. How would you explain to your constituents why convicted sex offenders should be entitled to procedural due process?

2. In your opinion, how should the Idaho legislature amend its statute so that it will satisfy the requirements of procedural due process?

3. To what extent should the Idaho Supreme Court consider the potential real-life repercussions of its due process ruling when making its decision?

AUTHOR'S COMMENTARY

Questions about who is entitled to procedural due process and the availability of the writ of habeas corpus have been very much in the news in recent years.

The Padilla Cases

The U.S. Supreme Court has twice declined to address the merits of procedural due process in a case involving Jose Padilla. Padilla's cases have raised profound questions regarding the procedural due process rights of Americans in the era of "the war on terror." Padilla, an American citizen who was initially arrested in 2002, was suspected (but not charged) by the U.S. Justice Department with being involved in a dirty bomb conspiracy. President Bush declared Padilla to be an "enemy combatant" and had him transferred from civil courts to a military brig. The President claimed the right to detain him until the end of the "war on terror." Padilla was kept isolated and denied access to the courts for two years. A lawsuit challenging the government's right to detain Padilla (a petition for a writ of habeas corpus) worked its way through the federal judiciary, and a petition was filed asking the U.S. Supreme Court to rule on whether the U.S. Constitution provided American citizens who had been declared by the President to be enemy combatants with any procedural due process rights. The Court twice declined to decide the merits of the case based on legal technicalities. The first time the Court decided that Padilla's petition had been filed in the wrong state. The second time the Court refused to grant certiorari (i.e., declined to hear the case).

Justice Ginsburg took the unusual step of writing a dissent from the denial of certiorari. She wrote:

> Does the President have authority to imprison indefinitely a United States citizen arrested on United State soil distant from a zone of combat, based on an Executive declaration that the citizen was, at the time of his arrest, an "enemy combatant"? It is a question the Court heard, and should have decided, two years ago. . . . Nothing the Government has yet done purports to retract the assertion of Executive power Padilla protests.

You can read the Opinion of the Court and Justice Ginsburg's dissent on Padilla's petition for writ of certiorari (*Padilla v. Hanft*, 126 S. Ct. 1649 (2006)) on Loislaw.

The Guantanamo Bay Detainees

The question as to whether alleged enemy combatants at the Guantanamo Bay detention center are constitutionally protected has also received considerable attention. Congress, in the Military Commissions Act (2006), prohibited the federal civil courts from hearing habeas petitions filed by "enemy combatants" detained in Guantanamo.

In *Boumediene v. Bush*, 553 U.S. ___ (2008), the U.S. Supreme Court, by a 5-4 margin, found the MCA statute to be unconstitutional. The Court's majority concluded that Congress's attempt to limit detainees to significantly inferior alternate procedures (spelled out in the Detainee Treatment Act of 2005) in lieu of the right to petition for habeas corpus in a federal court was totally inadequate. The justices ruled that detainees in Guantanamo had a constitutionally protected right to petition for habeas corpus in a federal district court. Interested readers can read this case on Loislaw.

Equal Protection Limitations

The fact that the Fourteenth Amendment to the U.S. Constitution contains an Equal Protection Clause is often obscured by the prominence of its more famous counterpart, the Due Process Clause. Although the meaning of the term "equal protection" is ambiguous, the U.S. Supreme Court has interpreted the clause very narrowly. The Court has rejected the notion that the clause guarantees equal outcomes, because to do so would infringe on the powers of the Congress and state legislatures. Thus the members of one race cannot prove a violation of equal protection rights by alleging that members of their group have not benefitted from a law to the same extent as the members of some other race. Instead, the justices have limited its scope to focusing on how laws are unequally applied. They limit its scope to situations where a law targets (in legalese "establishes a classification scheme") one group of people (in legalese "similarly situated individuals") and either denies group members their fundamental rights or singles out the group members for unfavorable treatment when the disfavored group is compared to other groups. For example, groupings based on race, national origin, or the fact that a person is not a citizen (alienage), have been labeled as "suspect classes."

The Equal Protection Clause is only explicitly found in the Fourteenth Amendment and therefore applies to the states but not the federal government. But the U.S. Supreme Court has ruled that the equal protection of the laws is implicit in the meaning of due process and therefore an "equal protection" challenge to a federal law would allege a violation of the Fifth Amendment Due Process Clause.

As readers will see in the case of *Loving v. Virginia*, which follows, the Supreme Court subjects inherently suspect classifications to "strict scrutiny." This means that for the challenged law to be sustained government will have to prove that no adequate non-discriminatory alternative exists and that there is a "compelling" governmental interest which requires that the group be singled out for discriminatory treatment.

Internet Tip

California Governor Schwarzenegger learned how difficult it is to satisfy the compelling interest test in the case of *Video Software Dealers Association v. Arnold Schwarzenegger*, 556 F.3d 950 (2009). California sought to make it a civil offense for anyone to sell or rent violent video games like *Grand Theft Auto* to any minor. Interested readers can find this case via Loislaw.

Attempts to broaden the scope of equal protection in order to redress economic discrimination in this country, for example, have been unsuccessful. Were the Court to pursue that path, it would find itself constantly in conflict with the political branches of government over public policy in a virtually unlimited number of extremely complicated and controversial subject areas (such as school funding, equal access to health care, and housing—matters better decided by the legislative and executive branches of government).

One of the most famous equal protection and due process cases is excerpted below: *Loving v. Virginia*. This case tested the constitutionality of a Virginia **miscegenation statute**, a state law that made it a felony for Richard Loving, a white man, and Mildred Jeter, a black woman, to marry one another. The legendary Chief Justice Earl Warren picks up the story in his opinion for the Court. This is a case every American should read.

LOVING v. COMMONWEALTH OF VIRGINIA
388 U. S. I
U.S. Supreme Court
June 12, 1967

EXCERPT FROM THE CASE

Chief Justice WARREN delivered the opinion of the Court.

This case presents a constitutional question never addressed by this Court: whether a statutory scheme adopted by the State of Virginia to prevent marriages between persons solely on the basis of racial classifications violates the Equal Protection and Due Process Clauses of the Fourteenth Amendment. . . .

In June 1958, two residents of Virginia, Mildred Jeter, a Negro woman, and Richard Loving, a white man, were married in the District of Columbia pursuant to its laws. Shortly after their marriage, the Lovings returned to Virginia and established their marital abode in Caroline County. At the October Term, 1958, of the Circuit Court of Caroline County, a grand jury issued an indictment charging the Lovings with violating Virginia's ban on interracial marriages. On January 6, 1959, the Lovings pleaded guilty to the charge and were sentenced to one year in jail; however, the trial judge suspended the sentence for a period of 25 years on the condition that the Lovings leave the State and not return to Virginia together for 25 years. He stated in an opinion that:

> Almighty God created the races white, black, yellow, malay and red, and he placed them on separate continents. And but for the interference with his arrangement there would be no cause for such marriages. The fact that he separated the races shows that he did not intend for the races to mix. . . .

The two statutes under which appellants were convicted and sentenced are part of a comprehensive statutory scheme aimed at prohibiting and punishing interracial marriages. The Lovings were convicted of violating § 20-58 of the Virginia Code:

> *Leaving State to evade law.*—If any white person and colored person shall go out of this State, for the purpose of being married, and with the intention of returning, and be married out of it, and afterwards return to and reside in it, cohabiting as man and wife, they shall be punished as provided in § 20-59.

Section 20-59, which defines the penalty for miscegenation, provides:

> *Punishment for marriage.*—If any white person intermarry with a colored person, or any colored person intermarry with a white person, he shall be guilty of a felony and shall be punished by confinement in the penitentiary for not less than one nor more than five years. . . .

Virginia is now one of 16 States which prohibit and punish marriages on the basis of racial classifications. Penalties for miscegenation arose as an incident to slavery and have been common in Virginia since the colonial period. The present statutory scheme dates from the adoption of the Racial Integrity Act of 1924, passed during the period of extreme nativism which followed the end of the First World War. The central features of this Act, and current Virginia law, are the absolute prohibition of a "white person" marrying other than another "white person," a prohibition against issuing marriage licenses until the issuing official is satisfied that the applicants' statements as to their race are correct, certificates of "racial composition" to be kept by both local and state registrars, and the carrying forward of earlier prohibitions against racial intermarriage. . . .

In upholding the constitutionality of these provisions in the decision below, the Supreme Court of Appeals of Virginia referred to [a 1955 decision in which it] concluded that the State's legitimate purposes were "to preserve the racial integrity of its citizens," and to prevent "the corruption of blood," "a mongrel breed of citizens," and "the obliteration of racial pride," obviously an endorsement of the doctrine of White Supremacy. . . .

While the state court is no doubt correct in asserting that marriage is a social relation subject to the State's police power, . . . the State does not contend in its argument before this Court that its powers to regulate marriage are unlimited notwithstanding the commands of the Fourteenth Amendment. . . . Instead, the State argues that the meaning of the Equal Protection Clause, as illuminated by the statements of the Framers, is only that state penal laws containing an interracial element as part of the definition of the offense must apply equally to whites and Negroes in the sense that members of each race are punished to the same degree. Thus, the State contends that, because its miscegenation statutes punish equally both the white and the Negro participants in an interracial marriage, these statutes, despite their reliance on racial classifications, do not constitute an invidious discrimination based upon race. . . .

In the case at bar, we deal with statutes containing racial classifications, and the fact of equal application does not immunize the statute from the very heavy burden of justification which the Fourteenth Amendment has traditionally required of state statutes drawn according to race. . . .

There can be no question but that Virginia's miscegenation statutes rest solely upon distinctions drawn according to race. The statutes proscribe generally accepted conduct if engaged in by members of different races. . . . At the very least, the Equal Protection Clause demands that racial classifications especially suspect in criminal statutes, be subjected to the "most rigid scrutiny," . . . and, if they are ever to be upheld, they must be shown to be necessary to the accomplishment of some permissible state objective, independent of the racial discrimination which it was the object of the Fourteenth Amendment to eliminate. Indeed, two members of this Court have already stated that they "cannot conceive of a valid legislative purpose . . . which makes the color of a person's skin the test of whether his conduct is a criminal offense." . . .

There is patently no legitimate overriding purpose independent of invidious racial discrimination which justifies this classification. The fact that Virginia prohibits only interracial marriages involving white persons demonstrates that the racial classifications must stand on their own justification, as measures designed to maintain White Supremacy. We have consistently denied the constitutionality of measures which restrict the rights of citizens on account of race. There can be no doubt that restricting the freedom to marry solely because of racial classifications violates the central meaning of the Equal Protection Clause.

These statutes also deprive the Lovings of liberty without due process of law in violation of the Due Process Clause of the Fourteenth Amendment. The freedom to marry has long been recognized as one of the vital personal rights essential to the orderly pursuit of happiness by free men.

Marriage is one of the "basic civil rights of man," fundamental to our very existence and survival. . . . To deny this fundamental freedom on so unsupportable a basis as the racial classifications embodied in these statutes, classifications so directly subversive of the principle of equality at the heart of the Fourteenth Amendment, is surely to deprive all the State's citizens of liberty without due process of law. The Fourteenth Amendment requires that the freedom of choice to marry not be restricted by invidious racial discriminations. Under our Constitution, the freedom to marry or not marry a person of another race resides with the individual and cannot be infringed by the State.

These convictions must be reversed. It is so ordered.

Reversed.

CASE QUESTIONS

1. Why, according to the U.S. Supreme Court, does Virginia's miscegenation statute violate the Equal Protection Clause?

2. Why does the U.S. Supreme Court conclude that this statute violated the Fourteenth Amendment's Due Process Clause?

3. What does the U.S. Supreme Court say about statutory classification schemes based on race?

AUTHOR'S COMMENTARY

The *Loving* case came into prominence once again in the aftermath of the Supreme Court's decision in *Lawrence v. Texas*, 539 U.S. 55 (2003). Proponents of same-sex marriages have used many of the same arguments that the Supreme Court included in its rationale in the *Loving* decision.

Cruel and Unusual Punishment

The constitutional prohibition against the infliction of **"cruel and unusual punishments"** in the **Eighth Amendment** traces its history to the English Bill of Rights of 1689. Although when it was adopted the Eighth Amendment only limited the federal government, this is no longer the case. The U.S. Supreme Court has held that the prohibition is included within the meaning of "due process" and is "incorporated" (made part of) the Fourteenth Amendment's Due Process Clause.[11] This means that it is binding on the states as well as the federal government. "Cruel and unusual punishment" has been interpreted as the imposition of **barbaric punishments,** and to some extent, punishments deemed to be disproportionate to the crime.[12]

Barbaric Punishments

The U.S. Supreme Court has repeatedly rejected claims that capital punishment is inherently barbaric and a cruel and unusual punishment.[13] At the present time, 35 states support and 15 states prohibit capital punishment. Since 2000, two states have reversed their previous positions and abolished capital punishment by statute, New Jersey (2007) and New Mexico (2009), and New York's statute was declared unconstitutional in 2004 for procedural reasons by that state's highest court. But punishment methods that feature torture or that are otherwise inherently inhumane—such as whipping, burning at the stake, beheading, branding, and keel-hauling—are undoubtedly impermissible in our society. In recent years many states have changed their preferred method of execution, replacing such traditional methods as hanging, the use of firing squads, gas chambers, and electrocution, with death by lethal injection. The motivation for change has often been the belief that lethal injection is a more humane method of carrying out the sentence. Some states have resisted this argument. A death-row prisoner sentenced to be executed in Florida's electric chair asked the U.S. Supreme Court to rule that this method of execution was cruel and unusual. Shortly after the Court agreed to decide the case, Florida changed its law to permit condemned prisoners to choose lethal injection instead of electrocution. The Court then declared that the issue was moot (there was no longer any dispute between the parties for it to decide) and declined to take the case.

Arguments on both sides of the question of whether the death penalty amounts to cruel and unusual punishment under the Eighth and Fourteenth Amendments were made by justices of the U.S. Supreme Court in *Gregg v. Georgia.*

GREGG v. GEORGIA
428 U.S. 153
U.S. Supreme Court
July 2, 1976

AUTHOR'S INTRODUCTION

Justices Stewart, Powell, and Stevens contended that sentencing a convicted murderer to death is constitutionally permissible. They supported their position with several historically based arguments. They noted, for example, that capital punishment had been an acceptable punishment in both England and the United States for hundreds of years and that state courts were sentencing people to death throughout the period of time when the Constitution and the Eighth Amendment were adopted and ratified. The Constitution itself implicitly approved of the death penalty in the Fifth Amendment ("No person shall be held to answer for a capital, or otherwise infamous crime unless on a presentment or indictment of a Grand Jury" . . .), and the First Congress even enacted laws providing for capital punishment.

These three justices also argued that capital punishment serves two utilitarian objectives: it is an appropriate expression of society's need for retribution (so that an enraged citizenry doesn't form lynch mobs and take the law into their own hands) and it deters others from committing heinous offenses.

EXCERPT FROM THE CASE

Justices STEWART, POWELL, and STEVENS concurring.

. . . In sum, we cannot say that the judgment of the Georgia Legislature that capital punishment may be necessary in some cases is clearly wrong. Considerations of federalism, as well as respect for the ability of a legislature to evaluate, in terms of its particular State, the moral consensus concerning the death penalty and its social utility as a sanction, require us to conclude, in the absence of more convincing evidence, that the infliction of death as a punishment for murder is not without justification and thus is not unconstitutionally severe. . . .

We hold that the death penalty is not a form of punishment that may never be imposed, regardless of the circumstances of the offense, regardless of the character of the offender, and regardless of the procedure followed in reaching the decision to impose it. . . .

AUTHOR'S INTRODUCTION

Justice Brennan in dissent argued that capital punishment is morally impermissible. He maintained that our societal morality has matured to the point that punishments that are incompatible with human dignity, which to him would include the death penalty, are cruel and unusual under the Eighth and Fourteenth Amendments.

EXCERPT FROM THE CASE

Justice BRENNAN, dissenting.

In *Furman v. Georgia*, I said:

> From the beginning of our Nation, the punishment of death has stirred acute public controversy. Although pragmatic arguments for and against the punishment have been frequently advanced, this longstanding and heated controversy cannot be explained solely as the result of differences over the practical wisdom of a particular government policy. At bottom, the battle has been waged on moral grounds. . . . In the United States, as in other nations of the western world, "the struggle about this punishment has been one between ancient and deeply rooted beliefs in retribution, atonement or vengeance on the one hand, and, on the other, beliefs in the personal value and dignity of the common man that were born of the democratic movement of the eighteenth century, as well as beliefs in the scientific approach to an understanding of the motive forces of human conduct, which are the result of the growth of the sciences of behavior during the nineteenth and twentieth centuries." . . . It is this essentially moral conflict that forms the backdrop for the past changes in and the present operation of our system of imposing death as a punishment for crime. . . .
>
> Death for whatever crime and under all circumstances "is truly an awesome punishment. The calculated killing of a human being by the State involves, by its very nature, a denial of the executed person's humanity. . . . An executed person has indeed 'lost the right to have rights.'" Death is not only an unusually severe punishment, unusual in its pain, in its finality, and in its enormity, but it serves no penal purpose more effectively than a less severe punishment; therefore the principle inherent in the Clause that prohibits pointless infliction of excessive punishment when less severe punishment can adequately achieve the same purposes invalidates the punishment. . . .

The fatal constitutional infirmity in the punishment of death is that it treats "members of the human race as non-humans, as objects to be toyed with and discarded. [It is] thus inconsistent with the fundamental premise of the Clause that even the vilest criminal remains a human being possessed of common human dignity.".. As such it is a penalty that "subjects the individual to a fate forbidden by the principle of civilized treatment guaranteed by the [Clause]." I therefore would hold, on that ground alone, that death is today a cruel and unusual punishment prohibited by the Clause." . . .

AUTHOR'S INTRODUCTION

Justice Marshall also dissented in *Gregg*. He maintained that it is morally untenable to defend capital punishment in terms of deterrence and retribution. Life imprisonment without parole, argued Marshall, would be an equally effective deterrent. Marshall also dismissed the argument that retribution is morally good on the grounds that it is incompatible with fundamental human dignity, which he believed was at the core of the Eighth Amendment.

EXCERPT FROM THE CASE

Justice MARSHALL, dissenting.

The concept of retribution is a multi-faceted one, and any discussion of its role in the criminal law must be undertaken with caution. On one level, it can be said that the notion of retribution or reprobation is the basis of our insistence that only those who have broken the law be punished, and in this sense the notion is quite obviously central to a just system of criminal sanctions. But our recognition that retribution plays a crucial role in determining who may be punished by no means requires approval of retribution as a general justification for punishment. It is the question whether retribution can provide moral justification for punishment—in particular, capital punishment—that we must consider.

My Brothers Stewart, Powell, and Stevens offer the following explanation of the retributive justification for capital punishment:

> The instinct for retribution is part of the nature of man, and channeling that instinct in the administration of criminal justice serves as important purpose in promoting the stability of a society governed . . . by law. When people begin to believe that organized society is unwilling or unable to impose upon criminal offenders the punishment they "deserve," then there are sown the seeds of anarchy—of self-help, vigilante justice, and lynch law. . . .

This statement is wholly inadequate to justify the death penalty. As my Brother Brennan stated . . . "[t]here is no evidence whatever that utilization of imprisonment rather than death encourages private blood feuds and other disorders." . . . It simply defies belief to suggest that the death penalty is necessary to prevent the American people from taking the law into their own hands. . . .

There remains for consideration, however, what might be termed the purely retributive justification for the death penalty—that the death penalty is appropriate, not because of its beneficial effect on society, but because the taking of the murderer's life is itself morally good. Some of the language of the opinion of my Brothers Stewart, Powell, and Stevens . . . appears positively to embrace this notion of retribution for its own sake as a justification for capital punishment. . . .

Of course, it may be that these statements are intended as no more than observations as to the popular demands that it is thought must be responded to in order to prevent anarchy. But the implication of the statements appears to me to be quite different—namely, that society's judgment that the murderer "deserves" death must be respected . . . because it is appropriate that society make the judgment and carry it out. It is this . . . notion, in particular, that I consider to be fundamentally at odds with the Eighth Amendment. . . . The mere fact that the community demands the murderer's life in return for the evil he has done cannot sustain the death penalty, for as Justices Stewart, Powell, and Stevens remind us, "the Eighth Amendment demands more than that a challenged punishment be acceptable to contemporary society." . . . To be sustained under the Eighth Amendment, the death penalty must "compor[t] with the basic concept of human dignity at the core of the Amendment," the objective in imposing it must be "[consistent] with our respect for the dignity of [other] men." Under these standards, the taking of life "because the wrongdoer deserves it" surely must fall, for such a punishment has as its very basis the total denial of the wrongdoer's dignity and worth.

The death penalty, unnecessary to promote the goal of deterrence or to further any legitimate notion of retribution, is an excessive penalty forbidden by the Eighth and Fourteenth Amendments. I respectfully dissent from the Court's judgment upholding the sentences of death imposed upon the petitioners in these cases. . . .

CASE QUESTIONS

1. Why did Stewart, Powell, and Stevens conclude that states are entitled to make the decision regarding whether to provide for capital punishment?

2. Justice Brennan's dissent focused on the morality of capital punishment. What was the essence of his position?

3. Justice Marshall took issue with Stewart, Stevens, and Powell. Where, in his estimation, did they err?

AUTHOR'S COMMENTARY

Although a few U.S. Supreme Court justices have been adamant that the death penalty is inherently a cruel and unusual punishment and prohibited by the Eighth Amendment, justices adhering to these views have never constituted a majority on the court. In 1972, the U.S. Supreme Court did suspend the use of capital punishment because it became convinced that the procedures for determining which individuals should be put to death were discriminatory. The Court's ruling in *Furman v. Georgia* resulted in several states revising their procedures in an effort to remedy the Court's objections. Their revised procedures were reviewed favorably by the Court in 1976 (in the *Gregg* case), and once again the states were constitutionally permitted to impose capital punishment.

Disproportionate Punishments

The U.S. Supreme Court has been inconsistent in its rulings about the extent to which the Eighth Amendment requires that convicted defendants receive sentences proportionate to the crimes they commit. In 1977, *Coker v. Georgia* was before the Court for decision. Coker, a convicted rapist of an adult woman, had been sentenced to death pursuant to a Georgia statute. Coker maintained that the imposition of capital punishment upon a rapist who did not kill his victim would be a **disproportionate penalty** under the Eighth Amendment. The Supreme Court agreed. The Court expanded the scope of its disproportionality doctrine in 1983 when it decided *Solem v. Helm*.[14] In *Solem* it adopted a three-prong test that became the standard commonly applied by lower courts in cases involving proportionality issues. The three *Solem* factors can be seen in Table 2.1.

TABLE 2.1   *SOLEM v. HELM* FACTORS

1. Is the harshness of the sentence proportionate to the severity of the offense?
2. Is the offender being punished as harshly as, or more harshly than, other offenders who have been convicted of more serious offenses within the same jurisdiction?
3. How do other jurisdictions punish offenders for this crime?

In 1991, the Court revisited the question of whether the Eighth Amendment requires lower courts to follow the *Solem* proportionality formula in the case of *Harmelin v. Michigan.*

HARMELIN v. MICHIGAN
501 U.S. 957
U.S. Supreme Court
June 27, 1991

AUTHOR'S INTRODUCTION

The defendant/petitioner was convicted by a Michigan trial court of possessing 672 grams of cocaine, for which he received a mandatory life sentence without possibility of parole. He argued on appeal that a life sentence for this crime was disproportionate to the seriousness of the crime and that the state statute in question should have permitted the trial judge to consider Harmelin's particular circumstances when determining the sentence. He concluded that his rights under the Eighth and Fourteenth Amendments had been violated.

EXCERPT FROM THE CASE

Justice SCALIA announced the judgment of the Court and delivered the opinion of the Court with respect to Part IV. . . .

IV

It is true that petitioner's sentence is unique in that it is the second most severe known to the law; but life imprisonment with possibility of parole is also unique in that it is the third most severe. And if petitioner's sentence forecloses some "flexible techniques" for later reducing his sentence, it does not foreclose all of them, since there remain the possibilities of retroactive legislative reduction and executive clemency. In some cases, moreover, there will be negligible difference between life without parole and other sentences of imprisonment—for example, a life sentence with eligibility for parole after 20 years, or even a lengthy term sentence without eligibility for parole, given to a 65-year-old man. But even where the difference is the greatest, it cannot be compared with death. We have drawn the line of required individualized sentencing at capital cases, and see no basis for extending it further.

The judgment of the Michigan Court of Appeals is Affirmed.

AUTHOR'S INTRODUCTION

Justice Scalia, in addition to announcing the Court's judgment and its rationale (above), also wrote another opinion in which he explained his own views regarding proportionality. He disputed the contention that England's cruel and unusual punishment jurisprudence included a protection against disproportionality. Justice Scalia also suggested that the First Congress had enacted several criminal penalties that would undoubtedly be thought to be disproportionate when viewed through modern eyes.

EXCERPT FROM THE CASE

Justice SCALIA delivered an opinion with which CHIEF JUSTICE REHNQUIST joined.

We may think that the First Congress punished with clear disproportionality when it provided up to seven years in prison and up to $1,000 in fines for "cut[ting] off the ear or ears, . . . cut[ting] out or disabl[ing] the tongue, . . . put[ting] out an eye . . . with intention to maim or disfigure," but provided the death penalty for "run[ning] away with [a] ship or vessel, or any goods or merchandise to the value of fifty dollars." . . . But then perhaps the citizens of 1791 would think that today's

Congress punishes with clear disproportionality when it sanctions "assault by . . . wounding" with up to six months in prison, . . . unauthorized reproduction of the "Smokey Bear" character or name with the same penalty, . . . offering to barter a migratory bird with up to 10 years in prison, . . . and purloining a "key suited to any lock adopted by the Post Office Department" with a prison term of up to 10 years. . . . Perhaps both we and they would be right, but the point is there are no textual or historical standards for saying so. . . .

III

In *Coker v. Georgia* . . . the Court held that, because of disproportionality, it was a violation of the Cruel and Unusual Punishments Clause to impose capital punishment for rape of an adult woman . . . as part of our death penalty jurisprudence, rather than a generalizable aspect of Eighth Amendment law. We think that is an accurate explanation, and we reassert it. Proportionality review is one of several respects in which we have held that "death is different," and have imposed protections that the Constitution nowhere else provides. . . . We would leave it there, but will not extend it further. . . .

AUTHOR'S INTRODUCTION

Justices White, Blackmun, and Stevens dissented in an opinion authored by Justice White. They emphasized that our modern society is very different from the one inhabited by the founders in the late 1700s. They pointed out that the *Solem* formula had worked well in practice and that courts had rarely found sentences to be unconstitutionally disproportionate.

EXCERPT FROM THE CASE

Justice WHITE, with whom Justice BLACKMUN and Justice STEVENS join, dissenting.

The Court . . . has recognized that a punishment may violate the Eighth Amendment if it is contrary to the "evolving standards of decency that mark the progress of a maturing society." . . . In evaluating a punishment under [the *Solem v. Helm*] test, "we have looked not to our own conceptions of decency, but to those of modern American society as a whole" in determining what standards have "evolved." . . .

Contrary to Justice Scalia's suggestion, the *Solem* analysis has worked well in practice. Courts appear to have had little difficulty applying the analysis to a given sentence, and application of the test by numerous state and federal appellate courts has resulted in a mere handful of sentences being declared unconstitutional. Thus, it is clear that reviewing courts have not baldly substituted their own subjective moral values for those of the legislature. Instead, courts have demonstrated that they are "capable of applying the Eighth Amendment to disproportionate noncapital sentences with a high degree of sensitivity to principles of federalism and state autonomy." *Solem* is wholly consistent with this approach, and when properly applied, its analysis affords "substantial deference to the broad authority that legislatures necessarily possess in determining the types and limits of punishments for crimes, as well as to the discretion that trial courts possess in sentencing convicted criminals," and will only rarely result in a sentence failing constitutional muster. The fact that this is one of those rare instances is no reason to abandon the analysis. . . .

To be constitutionally proportionate, punishment must be tailored to a defendant's personal responsibility and moral guilt. . . .

Application of *Solem's* proportionality analysis leaves no doubt that the Michigan statute at issue fails constitutional muster. The statutorily mandated penalty of life without possibility of parole for possession of narcotics is unconstitutionally disproportionate in that it violates the Eighth Amendment's prohibition against cruel and unusual punishment.

Consequently, I would reverse the decision of the Michigan Court of Appeals.

CASE QUESTIONS

1. What exactly did the majority of justices agree upon in *Harmelin?*

2. Why did Justice Scalia, in an opinion joined by Chief Justice Rehnquist, reject the use of disproportionality review of sentences not involving capital punishment?

3. Why did Justices White, Blackmun, and Stevens dissent?

AUTHOR'S COMMENTARY

Justices Scalia and Rehnquist were unable to persuade a majority of the Court to agree with them that the Eighth Amendment only requires proportionality between the sentence imposed and the severity of the crime in cases involving the death penalty. Justice Kennedy wrote an opinion that was joined by Justices O'Connor and Souter which concluded that while the Eighth Amendment does require a limited proportionality review in noncapital cases, no reasonable inference of disproportionality was permissible in *Harmelin* given the facts of that case. An edited version of Justice Kennedy's concurring opinion in *Harmelin* can be found on the website.

The Michigan Supreme Court, when confronted in a second drug case (*People v. Bullock*) with the proportionality issue, concluded that sentencing persons found to have possessed 650 grams or more of a mixture of drugs containing cocaine to a mandatory sentence of life imprisonment without parole amounted to cruel or unusual punishment in violation of the Michigan Constitution. The Court rejected the arguments made in *Harmelin* by U.S. Supreme Court Justices Scalia and Kennedy because they found Justice White's (dissenting) opinion in *Harmelin* to be more persuasive.[15]

Internet Tip

An edited version of *People v. Bullock*, 485 N.W.2d 866 (1992), can be found in the Chapter 2 portion of the website.

ATKINS v. COMMONWEALTH OF VIRGINIA
536 U.S. 304
U.S. Supreme Court
June 20, 2002

AUTHOR'S INTRODUCTION

The Court indicated its continuing support for proportionality review in capital murder cases in *Atkins v. Virginia*. This was the case in which the Court decided to revisit an issue it had previously decided back in 1989 (*Penry v. Lynaugh*, 492 U.S. 302) as to whether executing the mentally retarded constituted cruel and unusual punishment as that term is used in the Eighth Amendment.

EXCERPT FROM THE CASE

Justice STEVENS delivered the opinion of the Court.

Those mentally retarded persons who meet the law's requirements for criminal responsibility should be tried and punished when they commit crimes. Because of their disabilities in areas of reasoning, judgment, and control of their impulses, however, they do not act with the level of moral culpability that characterizes the most serious adult criminal conduct. Moreover, their impairments can jeopardize the reliability and fairness of capital proceedings against mentally retarded defendants. Presumably for these reasons, in the 13 years since we decided *Penry v. Lynaugh*, 492 U.S. 302 (1989), the American public, legislators, scholars, and judges have deliberated over the question of whether the death penalty should ever be imposed on a mentally retarded criminal. The consensus reflected in those deliberations informs our answer to the question presented by this case: whether such executions are cruel and unusual punishments prohibited by the Eighth Amendment to the Federal Constitution.

I

Petitioner, Daryl Renard Atkins, was convicted of abduction, armed robbery, and capital murder, and sentenced to death. At approximately midnight on August 16, 1996, Atkins and William Jones, armed with a semiautomatic handgun, abducted Eric Nesbitt, robbed him of the money on his person, drove him to an automated teller machine in his pickup truck where cameras recorded their withdrawal of additional cash, then took him to an isolated location where he was shot eight times and killed.

... In the penalty phase, the defense relied on one witness, Dr. Evan Nelson, a forensic psychologist who had evaluated Atkins before trial and concluded that he was mildly mentally retarded. His conclusion was based on interviews with people who knew Atkins, a review of school and court records, and the administration of a standard intelligence test which indicated that Atkins had a full scale IQ of 59.

The jury sentenced Atkins to death. . . . The Supreme Court of Virginia affirmed the imposition of the death penalty. . . . Atkins did not argue before the Virginia Supreme Court that his sentence was disproportionate to penalties imposed for similar crimes in Virginia, but he did contend that he is mentally retarded and thus cannot be sentenced to death. . . . The majority of the state court rejected this contention. . . .

The Court was not willing to commute Atkins sentence of death to life imprisonment merely because of his IQ score. . . .

Because of the gravity of the concerns expressed by the dissenters, and in light of the dramatic shift in the state legislative landscape that has occurred in the past 13 years, we granted *certiorari* to revisit the issue that we first addressed in the *Penry* case.

II

The Eighth Amendment succinctly prohibits excessive sanctions. It provides: Excessive bail shall not be required, nor excessive fines imposed, nor cruel and unusual punishments inflicted. In *Weems v. United States*, 217 U.S. 349 (1910), we held that a punishment of 12 years jailed in irons at hard and painful labor for the crime of falsifying records was excessive. We explained that it is a precept of justice that punishment for crime should be graduated and proportioned to the offense. . . . We have repeatedly applied this proportionality precept in later cases interpreting the Eighth Amendment. . . . Thus, even though imprisonment for ninety days is not, in the abstract, a punishment which is either cruel or unusual, it may not be imposed as a penalty for the status of narcotic addiction, *Robinson v. California*, . . . (1962), because such a sanction would be excessive. As Justice Stewart explained in *Robinson:* "Even one day in prison would be a cruel and unusual punishment for the crime of having a common cold." . . .

A claim that punishment is excessive is judged not by the standards that prevailed . . . when the Bill of Rights was adopted, but rather by those that currently prevail. As Chief Justice Warren explained . . . "The basic concept underlying the Eighth Amendment is nothing less than the dignity of man. The Amendment must draw its meaning from the evolving standards of decency that mark the progress of a maturing society." . . .

Proportionality review . . . should be informed by objective factors to the maximum possible extent. . . . We have pinpointed that the clearest and most reliable objective evidence of contemporary values is the legislation enacted by the country's legislatures. . . . Relying in part on such legislative evidence, we have held that death is an impermissibly excessive punishment for the rape of an adult woman, *Coker v. Georgia*, 433 U.S. 584, . . . (1977), or for a defendant who neither took life, attempted to take life, nor intended to take life, *Enmund v. Florida*, 458 U.S. 782 . . . (1982). . . .

We also acknowledged in *Coker* that the objective evidence, though of great importance, did not wholly determine the controversy, for the Constitution contemplates that in the end our own judgment will be brought to bear on the question of the acceptability of the death penalty under the Eighth Amendment. . . .

For example, in *Enmund*, we concluded by expressing our own judgment about the issue:

> For purposes of imposing the death penalty, Enmund's criminal culpability must be limited to his participation in the robbery, and his punishment must be tailored to his personal responsibility and moral guilt. Putting Enmund to death to avenge two killings that he did not commit and had no intention of committing or causing does not measurably contribute to the retributive end of ensuring that the criminal gets his just deserts. This is the judgment of most of the legislatures that have recently addressed the matter, and we have no reason to disagree with that judgment for purposes of construing and applying the Eighth Amendment. . . .

Thus, in cases involving a consensus, our own judgment is brought to bear, . . . by asking whether there is reason to disagree with the judgment reached by the citizenry and its legislators.

Guided by our approach in these cases, we shall first review the judgment of legislatures that have addressed the suitability of imposing the death penalty on the mentally retarded and then consider reasons for agreeing or disagreeing with their judgment.

III

The parties have not called our attention to any state legislative consideration of the suitability of imposing the death penalty on mentally retarded offenders prior to 1986. In that year, the public reaction to the execution of a mentally retarded murderer in Georgia [Jeremy Bowden] ... apparently led to the enactment of the first state statute prohibiting such executions. ... In 1988, when Congress enacted legislation reinstating the federal death penalty, it expressly provided that a sentence of death shall not be carried out upon a person who is mentally retarded. In 1989, Maryland enacted a similar prohibition. ... It was in that year that we decided *Penry*, and concluded that those two state enactments, even when added to the 14 States that have rejected capital punishment completely, do not provide sufficient evidence at present of a national consensus. ...

Much has changed since then. Responding to the national attention received by the Bowden execution and our decision in *Penry*, state legislatures across the country began to address the issue. In 1990 Kentucky and Tennessee enacted statutes similar to those in Georgia and Maryland, as did New Mexico in 1991, and Arkansas, Colorado, Washington, Indiana, and Kansas in 1993 and 1994. ... In 1995, when New York reinstated its death penalty, it emulated the Federal Government by expressly exempting the mentally retarded. ... Nebraska followed suit in 1998. ... There appear to have been no similar enactments during the next two years, but in 2000 and 2001 ... South Dakota, Arizona, Connecticut, Florida, Missouri, and North Carolina joined the procession. ... The Texas Legislature unanimously adopted a similar bill, ... and bills have passed at least one house in other States, including Virginia and Nevada. ...

It is not so much the number of these States that is significant, but the consistency of the direction of change. ... Given the well-known fact that anti-crime legislation is far more popular than legislation providing protections for persons guilty of violent crime, the large number of States prohibiting the execution of mentally retarded persons (and the complete absence of States passing legislation reinstating the power to conduct such executions) provides powerful evidence that today our society views mentally retarded offenders as categorically less culpable than the average criminal. The evidence carries even greater force when it is noted that the legislatures that have addressed the issue have voted overwhelmingly in favor of the prohibition. ... Moreover, even in those States that allow the execution of mentally retarded offenders, the practice is uncommon. Some States, for example New Hampshire and New Jersey, continue to authorize executions, but none have been carried out in decades. Thus there is little need to pursue legislation barring the execution of the mentally retarded in those States. And it appears that even among those States that regularly execute offenders and that have no prohibition with regard to the mentally retarded, only five have executed offenders possessing a known IQ less than 70 since we decided *Penry*. ... The practice, therefore, has become truly unusual, and it is fair to say that a national consensus has developed against it. . . .

To the extent there is serious disagreement about the execution of mentally retarded offenders, it is in determining which offenders are in fact retarded. In this case, for instance, the Commonwealth of Virginia disputes that Atkins suffers from mental retardation. Not all people who claim to be mentally retarded will be so impaired as to fall within the range of mentally retarded offenders about whom there is a national consensus. . . . [W]e leave to the State[s] the task of developing appropriate ways to enforce the constitutional restriction upon its execution of sentences. . . .

IV

This consensus unquestionably reflects widespread judgment about the relative culpability of mentally retarded offenders, and the relationship between mental retardation and the penological purposes served by the death penalty. Additionally, it suggests that some characteristics of mental retardation undermine the strength of the procedural protections that our capital jurisprudence steadfastly guards.

. . . [C]linical definitions of mental retardation require not only sub-average intellectual functioning, but also significant limitations in adaptive skills such as communication, self-care, and self-direction that became manifest before age 18. . . . Mentally retarded persons frequently know the difference between right and wrong and are competent to stand trial. Because of their impairments, however, by definition they have diminished capacities to understand and process information, to communicate, to abstract from mistakes and learn from experience, to engage in logical reasoning, to control impulses, and to understand the reactions of others. . . . There is no evidence that they are more likely to engage in criminal conduct than others, but there is abundant evidence that they often act on impulse rather than pursuant to a premeditated plan, and that in group settings they are followers rather than leaders. . . . Their deficiencies do not warrant an exemption from criminal sanctions, but they do diminish their personal culpability.

In light of these deficiencies, our death penalty jurisprudence provides two reasons consistent with the legislative consensus that the mentally retarded should be categorically excluded from execution. First, there is a serious question as to whether either justification that we have recognized as a basis for the death penalty applies to mentally retarded offenders. *Gregg v. Georgia* . . . identified retribution and deterrence of capital crimes by prospective offenders as the social purposes served by the death penalty. Unless the imposition of the death penalty on a mentally retarded person measurably contributes to one or both of these goals, it is nothing more than the purposeless and needless imposition of pain and suffering, and hence an unconstitutional punishment. . . .

With respect to retribution, the interest in seeing that the offender gets his just deserts, the severity of the appropriate punishment necessarily depends on the culpability of the offender. Since *Gregg,* our jurisprudence has consistently confined the imposition of the death penalty to a narrow category of the most serious crimes. For example, in *Godfrey v. Georgia* . . . (1980), we set aside a death sentence because the petitioner's crimes did not reflect a consciousness materially more depraved than that of any person guilty of murder. . . . If the culpability of the average murderer is insufficient to justify the most extreme sanction available to the State, the lesser culpability of the mentally retarded offender surely does not merit that form of retribution. Thus, pursuant to our narrowing jurisprudence, which seeks to ensure that only the most deserving of execution are put to death, an exclusion for the mentally retarded is appropriate.

With respect to deterrence, the interest in preventing capital crimes by prospective offenders, it seems likely that capital punishment can serve as a deterrent only when murder is the result of premeditation and deliberation. . . . Exempting the mentally retarded from that punishment will not affect the cold calculus that precedes the decision of other potential murderers. . . . Indeed, that sort of calculus is at the opposite end of the spectrum from behavior of mentally retarded offenders. The theory of deterrence in capital sentencing is predicated upon the notion that the increased severity of the punishment will inhibit criminal actors from carrying out murderous conduct. Yet it is the same cognitive and behavioral impairments that make these defendants less morally culpable—for example, the diminished ability to understand and process information, to learn from experience, to engage in logical reasoning, or to control impulses—that also make it less likely that they can process the information of the possibility of execution as a penalty and, as a result, control their conduct based upon that information. Nor will exempting the mentally retarded from execution lessen the deterrent effect of the death penalty with respect to offenders who are not mentally retarded. Such individuals are unprotected by the exemption and will continue to face the threat of execution. Thus, executing the mentally retarded will not measurably further the goal of deterrence.

The reduced capacity of mentally retarded offenders provides a second justification for a categorical rule making such offenders ineligible for the death penalty. The risk that the death penalty will be imposed in spite of factors which may call for a less severe penalty . . . is enhanced, not only by the possibility of false confessions . . . but also by the lesser ability of mentally retarded defendants to make a persuasive showing of mitigation in the face of prosecutorial evidence of one or more aggravating factors. Mentally retarded defendants may be less able to give meaningful assistance to their counsel and are typically poor witnesses, and their demeanor may create an unwarranted impression of lack of remorse for their crimes. . . . Mentally retarded defendants in the aggregate face a special risk of wrongful execution.

. . . We are not persuaded that the execution of mentally retarded criminals will measurably advance the deterrent or the retributive purpose of the death penalty. Construing and applying the Eighth Amendment in the light of our evolving standards of decency, we therefore conclude that such punishment is excessive and that the Constitution places a substantive restriction on the State's power to take the life of a mentally retarded offender. . . .

The judgment of the Virginia Supreme Court is reversed and the case is remanded for further proceedings not inconsistent with this opinion.

CASE QUESTIONS

1. What factors does the Court suggest appellate courts consider when deciding whether a challenged sentence is disproportionate?

2. Chief Justice Rehnquist and Associate Justices Scalia and Thomas dissented. Rehnquist pointed out that there really was no national "consensus" for prohibiting executions of the mentally retarded because only 18 of the 50 states had enacted legislation forbidding such executions. All three dissenters also argued that the Court had no business making this decision at all. It should be decided by states through their legislatures and juries—if there is a national consensus, they ask, won't jurors refuse to impose the death penalty on mentally retarded offenders? What do you think of these arguments and concerns?

AUTHOR'S COMMENTARY

The Court's *Penry* decision triggered one of the most important features of federalism, the right of each state to decide for itself whether to accept or reject the U.S. Supreme Court's conclusion. Following *Penry* many states chose the same course of action followed by Michigan with respect to the *Harmelin* decision; they decided to prohibit the execution of mentally retarded persons as a matter of state law.

Internet Tip

An edited version of Chief Justice Rehnquist's dissent in *Atkins v. Commonwealth of Virginia* can be found included in the Chapter 2 portion of the textbook's website.

Chapter Summary

Chapter 2 discusses the explicit and implicit constitutional limitations that limit the way federal and state legislative bodies exercise their lawmaking power.

The prohibitions on bills of attainder and *ex post facto* laws are examples of explicit constitutional prohibitions. Legislative bodies are forbidden to declare someone guilty of a crime—that function is exclusively reserved to the judiciary. Similarly, legislators cannot enact an *ex post facto* law—a statute that either retroactively declares conduct to be criminal that was lawful when it was committed, or imposes a more severe penalty on a convicted offender than was legally permissible at the time the crime was committed.

Due Process Limitations

Other constitutional limitations such as those based on the Due Process Clauses of the Fifth and Fourteenth Amendments are not so clear-cut. Due process has ancient roots going back to the Magna Carta and has been interpreted in many contexts and inconsistently applied. What due process requires varies with the context. As a broad concept, constitutional due process requires that government treat individuals fairly. But the judiciary cannot use this tool casually to remedy unfairness. To do so would undermine the legislative function, which includes determining what fairness requires in a given context.

Due process has both procedural and substantive applications. Each will be discussed in turn.

Substantive Due Process

Laws that establish and define legal rights and duties are classified as substantive law. Thus statutes that perform this function in the criminal law context have to be fundamentally fair to satisfy due process requirements.

Precision

Criminal laws can be so imprecise as to be constitutionally inadequate. There are two types of imprecision—vagueness and overbreadth.

Vagueness is a problem when a statute doesn't make clear to the police (the primary problem) and the public what conduct is prohibited. The legislature is responsible for reasonably defining who it is that should be arrested. This is not a task that can be left to individual police officers to determine—that leads to the rule of police and not the "rule of law."

Overbreadth is a different problem. Some laws that are not unclear are insufficiently focused. An overly broad statute is "insufficiently tailored." By its terms it could legitimately apply not only to a criminal offender but also to someone engaging in constitutionally protected conduct. For example, if the scope of an ordinance that has been enacted to require public protesters to obtain a parade permit can be used to arrest a collection of people parading to church.

The Constitutional Right to Privacy

The federal Constitution does not contain any explicit right to individual privacy rights. The U.S. Supreme Court has interpreted substantive due process as including a limited privacy right (often classified as a "due process liberty interest") which protects individuals from legislative intrusion. The case of *Griswold v. Connecticut*, in which the criminal defendants were accused of providing birth control information to married couples, was the first case to recognize an implicit general right to privacy based on the guarantees in the Due Process Clauses, and elements contained in the First, Ninth, and Fourteenth Amendments. The Supreme Court has also designated other rights to be "fundamental" and deserving of due process protection. The Supreme Court has been careful to restrict the fundamental rights category to the protection of the most important individual rights. The list currently protects the right to enter into interracial marriages, make decisions about procreation, child rearing and education, personal intimacy, and family relationships. The Court's preferences are reflected in both of the cases chosen to illustrate the right to privacy, *Griswold v. Connecticut* and *Lawrence v. Texas*.

Procedural Due Process Limitations

Not all procedural rights included in the Bill of Rights are binding on the states. Only procedural rights that the U.S. Supreme Court has ruled are "incorporated" in the Fourteenth Amendment are essential to due process and are binding on the states. The most basic procedural requirement is that government provide an accused with *notice* of the charges and a *fair hearing*, a principle illustrated in *Jason C. Smith v. State of Idaho*. The U.S. Supreme Court has also made it clear that the procedures that are constitutionally required (besides notice and fair hearing) will vary depending on the circumstances of the case. Criminal defendants, for example, have the most procedural due process protections because their life and/or liberty are at risk. However, only basic due process rights are required in school suspension cases. Because readers should remember that federal procedural due process requirements only establish a procedural floor and not a ceiling, states and local governments can choose to require more extensive procedural protections.

The Equal Protection Clause Limitations

Readers learned that the U.S. Supreme Court has refused to interpret the Equal Protection Clause as guaranteeing equal outcomes. The U.S. Supreme Court uses the Equal Protection Clause to strike down laws which are applied unequally and are intended to single out one group of people for unfavorable treatment. It is most concerned with state classification schemes that discriminate based on race and/or national origin and alienage. Laws that discriminate based on those classifications are "suspect classes" and are subject to "strict scrutiny" by the judiciary. The government can only satisfy "strict scrutiny" review if it can prove that it has a "compelling need" to discriminate and there is no other less discriminatory way to achieve the necessary outcome.

Limitations on Cruel and Unusual Punishments

The federal constitution forbids the federal and state legislatures from using torture and other barbaric methods as punishments. The Supreme Court has determined that the imposition of capital punishment is permissible under the Eighth and Fourteenth Amendments, and states are therefore entitled to determine whether or not to impose capital punishment. At present, 35 states authorize capital punishment. The Supreme Court has been unable to establish a clear policy on the extent to which proportionality is required in non-capital cases. It has ruled on disproportionality grounds that a rapist court not be executed, *Coker v. Georgia*, 433 U.S. 584 (1977), and in *Atkins v. Commonwealth of Virginia*, 536 U.S. 304 (2002), reversed a previous decision (*Penry v. Lynaugh*, 492 U.S. 302 (1989)), which concluded the execution of a mentally retarded offender was not constitutionally prohibited.

 **Discussion Questions**

1. Two Amish families refused to permit their children to attend public schools after completing the eighth grade, in violation of Wisconsin's compulsory-attendance statute. The fathers of the children, Jonas Yoder and Ardin Yutzy, were found guilty of this offense and appealed their convictions to the Wisconsin Supreme Court. They contended that the First Amendment's Free Exercise Clause gave them the right to determine the religious upbringing of their children. This right, they maintained, is incorporated (made applicable to the states) by the Due Process Clause of the Fourteenth Amendment. After the state supreme court ruled in favor of the parents, the State of Wisconsin appealed that decision to the U.S. Supreme Court. Should Wisconsin have the right to

convict these parents for refusing to send their children to school after the eighth grade?

Wisconsin v. Yoder, 406 U.S. 205 (1972)

2. Eddie Lawson was stopped or arrested by members of the San Diego Police Department on some 15 occasions within a two-year period. Although the details of each of these incidents are sketchy, on one occasion he was stopped while walking on a vacant street late at night, and on another occasion while walking late at night in a business area that had been plagued by burglaries. When police officers stopped Lawson they would ask him to produce identification and Lawson would refuse. He was arrested or stopped by police on many occasions, but was twice prosecuted for, and once convicted of, violating California Penal Code Section 647 (e), which requires everyone who loiters or wanders from place to place without apparent reason or business and who refuses to identify himself, to account for his presence when requested by any peace officer to do so, if the surrounding circumstances are such as to indicate to a reasonable man that the public safety demands such identification.

   The statute was interpreted by lower appellate courts to require that persons stopped produce "credible and reliable" identification when asked to do so by a police officer who reasonably suspects that criminal activity may be afoot. Lawson maintained that this statute, as applied to him, was unconstitutionally overly broad. Do you agree? Why or why not?

Kolender v. Lawson, 461 U.S. 352 (1983)

3. Mrs. Inez Moore lived in East Cleveland, Ohio, along with her son, Dale, and her two grandsons, Dale, Jr., and his cousin, John, Jr. Mrs. Moore received a notice from the city that her living arrangements were in violation of a housing ordinance that intended to prevent more than one family to occupy a single dwelling unit. The purposes of this ordinance, according to the city, included preventing overcrowding in the public schools and reducing traffic congestion. Under the terms of the ordinance it was unlawful for Grandmother Moore, cousins John, Jr., and Dale, Jr., and John, Jr.'s uncle, Dale, Sr., to live together as a family in a single-family home. Mrs. Moore was criminally charged with violating the terms of the ordinance when she refused to comply with its terms. She was subsequently tried, convicted, and sentenced to a fine and five days in jail. Mrs. Moore contended that the city was not within its rights under the police power in enacting this ordinance and

claimed federal protection under the Fourteenth Amendment's Due Process Clause. Do you agree? Why or why not?

Moore v. City of East Cleveland, 431 U.S. 494 (1977)

4. A Cincinnati city ordinance made it a crime for "three or more persons to assemble . . . on any of the sidewalks . . . and there conduct themselves in a manner annoying to persons passing by. . . ." Do you see any substantive due process issues with this law?

Coates v. Cincinnati, 402 U.S. 611 (1971)

5. The City of Houston enacted an ordinance making it a crime to "in any manner oppose, molest, abuse or interrupt any policeman in the execution of his duty." Raymond Hill was arrested for verbally challenging Officer Kelley, who was walking toward Charles Hill (a friend of Raymond's), who had been stopping traffic on a busy street so that other vehicles could merge onto the major thoroughfare. The officer took offense when Raymond hollered to Officer Kelley, "Why don't you pick on somebody your own size?" Hill was arrested and charged with "willfully, or intentionally interrupting an officer by verbal challenge during an investigation." Does the ordinance infringe on constitutionally protected speech?

City of Houston v. Hill, 482 U.S. 451 (1987)

NOTES

1. *Goss v. Lopez*, 419 U.S. 565 (1975).
2. See Justice O'Connor's opinion in *Kolender v. Lawson*, 461 U.S. 352 (1983).
3. Ibid.
4. *Grayned v. City of Rockford*, 408 U.S. 104 (1972).
5. Ibid.
6. The state can nevertheless prevail if it can show that its limitation is narrowly drawn and that a compelling reason exists for the state to prevail over the privacy claim. See *Roe v. Wade*, 410 U.S. 113 (1973).
7. *Goss v. Lopez*, 419 U.S. 565 (1975).
8. There are two exceptions. The Fifth Amendment's requirement that the federal government use grand juries in felony prosecutions has not been imposed on the states (see *Hurtado v. California*, 110 U.S. 516, (1984)), nor has the Eighth Amendment's restrictions on excessive bail (see *Stack v. Boyle*, 342 U.S. 1 (1952)). There are also some implementation differences. A criminal jury in state court can constitutionally consist of fewer than the 12 jurors normally required in federal jury trials (see *Williams v. Florida*, 399 U.S. 78, (1970)) but cannot be fewer than six jurors (*Ballew v. Georgia*, 435 U.S. 223, 1978). Similarly, while a federal jury must reach a unanimous verdict, states are permitted to reach non-unanimous verdicts, such as 10-2 or 9-3 (see *Johnson v. Louisiana*, 406 U.S. 223 (1972), and *Apodaca v. Oregon*, 406 U.S. 404 (1972)).

9. *Hurtado v. California*, 110 U.S. 516 (1984).

10. The source of this definition is *Calder v. Bull*, 3 U.S. 386, 390 (1798).

11. *Robinson v. California*, 370 U.S. 660 (1962).

12. *Coker v. Georgia*, 433 U.S. 584 (1977).

13. *Gregg v. Georgia*, 428 U.S. 153 (1976).

14. *Solem v. Helm*, 463 U.S. 277 (1983).

15. Such a result might seem to be impermissible because Michigan's Supreme Court was refusing to follow a rule established in *Harmelin* by the U.S. Supreme Court. But, in fact, the U.S. Supreme Court in *Harmelin* only ruled that as far as the federal Constitution was concerned, a mandatory life sentence for possession of 650 grams or more of cocaine was not a violation of the Eighth and Fourteenth Amendments. The Michigan Supreme Court, however, is the ultimate determiner of the meaning of that state's constitution. In the *Bullock* case, the Michigan Supreme Court decided that Michigan law prohibited the imposition of a life sentence under these circumstances, because such a sentence was disproportionate to the crime.

General Principles of Criminal Liability

93

This chapter introduces the underlying general principles of criminal liability. These principles establish a basic foundation that subsequent chapters will build on as we focus on the elements of particular crimes. We will begin with a discussion of the criminal act and then address criminal intent, concurrence, and causation.

The Criminal Act/*Actus Reus*

One of the most often repeated and traditionally accepted criminal law principles is that persons charged with a criminal offense must be proven to have committed what is traditionally called the **actus reus** for that crime. The *actus reus* consists of proof of one or more voluntary physical acts or omissions (where the law imposes a duty to act). Evil thoughts without willed, bodily acts are usually insufficient to constitute criminal liability.[1] The requirement that the prosecution prove the *actus reus* compels the government to produce tangible evidence of wrongdoing, a more reliable indicator that a person deserves to be punished as a criminal, than evidence that the accused had engaged in "evil thinking." The late Justice Thurgood Marshall expressed it this way: "criminal penalties may be inflicted only if the accused has committed some act, has engaged in some behavior, which society has an interest in preventing, or . . . in historical common law terms, has committed some *actus reus*."[2]

Criminal Act or Status?

Occasionally laws have authorized the criminal prosecution of people who cannot be proven to have engaged in any prohibited criminal acts but who can be linked to a legally prohibited condition. Our next case, *Robinson v. California*, is a good example. The statute that Robinson was charged with violating permitted convictions on the basis of the condition in which he was found by police—in this instance his *status* as a heroin addict. Being addicted to narcotics was a legally prohibited condition under California law.

In the 1960s, many communities enacted vagrancy ordinances similar to the Jacksonville, Florida, ordinance (presented in Figure 3.1). Such ordinances were very broad in their scope and in effect permitted police officers, at their discretion, to arrest "undesirables" and remove them from the streets. The police at that time tended to enforce the vagrancy statutes against persons in particular statuses. Often, the people prosecuted for vagrancy were poor, unemployed ("habitually living without visible means of support"), alcoholic ("common drunkard"), or lazy ("habitually loafing"). Status offenses such as these required no proof of any illegal act—all the prosecutor had to prove was that the arrested person was found in a prohibited condition. Jacksonville's Vagrancy Ordinance was declared unconstitutionally

Figure 3.1. Jacksonville Ordinance Code 26-57 (as of 1965)

> Rogues and vagabonds, or dissolute persons who go about begging, common gamblers, persons who use juggling or unlawful games or plays, common drunkards, common night walkers, thieves, pilferers or pickpockets, traders in stolen property, lewd, wanton and lascivious persons, keepers of gambling places, common railers and brawlers, persons wandering or strolling around from place to place without any lawful purpose or object, habitual loafers, disorderly persons, persons neglecting all lawful business and habitually spending their time by frequenting houses of ill fame, gaming houses, or places where alcoholic beverages are sold or served, persons able to work but habitually living upon the earnings of their wives or minor children shall be deemed vagrants and, upon conviction in the Municipal Court shall be punished as provided for Class D offenses.

vague by the U.S. Supreme Court in 1972.[3] Vagrancy offenses often face constitutional challenge on *vagueness* grounds because they fail to limit the exercise of police discretion and because they fail to provide sufficient notice as to what conduct is prohibited.

ROBINSON v. CALIFORNIA
370 U.S. 660
U.S. Supreme Court
June 25, 1962

AUTHOR'S INTRODUCTION

In *Robinson*, the defendant was found, while addicted to narcotics, within the city of Los Angeles. The government did not offer proof at trial that Robinson had possessed, used, sold, or manufactured narcotics within California. In other words, although the prosecution could prove that he had used narcotics in the past (from the track marks police found on his arms), they could not prove that he had committed any particular drug-related act within California.

The trial judge, over the objection of the defendant, charged the jury that "All that the People must show is either that the defendant did use a narcotic in Los Angeles County, or that while in the city of Los Angeles he was addicted to the use of narcotics." The jury returned a guilty verdict and the trial court entered a judgment of conviction that was affirmed on appeal. The U.S. Supreme Court agreed to review this conviction in order to determine whether a state legislature can, in the proper exercise of its police power, make it a crime for a person to be addicted to narcotics.

Justice Stewart wrote the majority opinion and was careful to pay homage to each state's right in exercise of the police power to "regulate the administration, sale, prescription and use of dangerous and habit-forming drugs." States could, he pointed out, choose to criminalize the unlicensed manufacture, sale, possession, or purchase of narcotics. They could establish a statewide emphasis on public education about the hazards of narcotics, seek to improve underlying social conditions, or even involuntarily confine people as part of a compulsory treatment program. Stewart wrote:

> In short, the range of valid choices which a State might make in this area is undoubtedly a wide one, and the wisdom of any particular choice within the allowable spectrum is not for us to decide. Upon that premise we turn to the California law in issue here.

EXCERPT FROM THE CASE

Mr. Justice STEWART delivered the opinion of the Court.

A California statute makes it a criminal offense for a person to "be addicted to the use of narcotics." This appeal draws into question the constitutionality of that provision of the state law. . . .

This statute . . . is not one which punishes a person for the use of narcotics, for their purchase, sale or possession, or for antisocial or disorderly behavior resulting from their administration. It is not a law which even purports to provide or require medical treatment. Rather, we deal with a statute which makes the "status" of narcotic addiction a criminal offense, for which the offender may be prosecuted "at any time before he reforms." California has said that a person can be continuously guilty of this offense, whether or not he has ever used or possessed any narcotics within the State, and whether or not he has been guilty of any antisocial behavior there.

It is unlikely that any State at this moment in history would attempt to make it a criminal offense for a person to be mentally ill, or a leper, or to be afflicted with a venereal disease. A State might determine that the general health and welfare require that the victims of these and other human afflictions be dealt with by compulsory treatment, involving quarantine, confinement, or sequestration. But, in the light of contemporary human knowledge, a law which made a criminal offense of such a disease would doubtless be universally thought to be an infliction of cruel and unusual punishment in violation of the Eighth and Fourteenth Amendments. . . .

We cannot but consider the statute before us as of the same category. . . . We hold that a state law which imprisons a person thus afflicted as a criminal, even though he has never touched any narcotic drug within the State or been guilty of any irregular behavior there, inflicts a cruel and unusual punishment in violation of the Fourteenth Amendment. To be sure, imprisonment for ninety days is not, in the abstract, a punishment which is either cruel or unusual. But the question cannot be considered in the abstract. Even one day in prison would be a cruel and unusual punishment for the "crime" of having a common cold.

We are not unmindful that the vicious evils of the narcotics traffic have occasioned the grave concern of government. There are, as we have said, countless fronts on which those evils may be legitimately attacked. We deal in this case only with an individual provision of a particularized local law as it has so far been interpreted by the California courts.

Reversed.

CASE QUESTIONS

1. What does the Court find objectionable about Robinson's prosecution?

2. What actions could the State of California have taken that would have passed constitutional review?

AUTHOR'S COMMENTARY

In 1968, the U.S. Supreme Court refused, in the case of *Powell v. Texas*, to extend the principle announced in *Robinson* to persons who were afflicted with chronic alcoholism.[4] The Court, by a 5-4 vote, distinguished the two cases, concluding that while Robinson was prosecuted for being addicted to narcotics, Leroy Powell was convicted for committing a criminal act—being in a public place when drunk. Four of the five justices voting to sustain the conviction emphasized the lack of a consensus among medical experts in 1968 to support the conclusion that chronic alcoholics were incapable of preventing themselves from going out in public when intoxicated.

Although the Court ruled against treating chronic alcoholism the same way as narcotics addiction, reformers turned their focus from the judiciary to the state legislatures. They were often successful in arguing that states should enact **protective custody laws** so that public drunks could be treated as sick persons and not as criminals (see Figure 3.2 for an example of a protective custody law). Protective custody statutes authorize police officers to take intoxicated persons found in public places into custody for their own protection and transport them to treatment facilities or hold them at the police station until they sober up.

Figure 3.2. Excerpts from the Massachusetts Protective Custody Law

---

Title XVI. Chapter III B: Section 8. Incapacitated persons; Assistance to facility or protective custody

Any person who is incapacitated may be assisted by a police officer with or without his consent to his residence, to a facility or to a police station. To determine for purposes of this chapter only, whether or not such person is intoxicated, the police officer may request the person to submit to reasonable tests of coordination, coherency of speech, and breath. . . .

Any person presumed intoxicated and to be held in protective custody at a police station shall, immediately after such presumption, have the right and be informed of said right to make one phone call at his own expense and on his own behalf. Any person assisted by a police officer to a facility under this section shall have the right to make one phone call at his own expense on his own behalf and shall be informed forthwith upon arriving at the facility of said right. The parent or guardian of any person, under the age of eighteen, to be held in protective custody at a police station shall be notified forthwith upon his arrival at said station or as soon as possible thereafter.

If any incapacitated person is assisted to a police station, the officer in charge or his designee shall notify forthwith the nearest facility that the person is being held in protective custody. If suitable treatment services are available at a facility, the department shall thereupon arrange for the transportation of the person to the facility in accordance with the provisions of section seven.

No person assisted to a police station pursuant to this section shall be held in protective custody against his will; provided, however, that if suitable treatment at a facility is not available, an incapacitated person may be held in protective custody at a police station until he is no longer incapacitated or for a period of not longer than twelve hours, whichever is shorter.

A police officer acting in accordance with the provisions of this section may use such force as is reasonably necessary to carry out his authorized responsibilities. If the police officer reasonably believes that his safety or the safety of other persons present so requires, he may search such person and his immediate surroundings, but only to the extent necessary to discover and seize any dangerous weapons which may on that occasion be used against the officer or other person present; provided, however, that if such person is held in protective custody at a police station all valuables and all articles which may pose a danger to such person or to others may be taken from him for safekeeping and if so taken shall be inventoried.

A person assisted to a facility or held in protective custody by the police pursuant to the provisions of this section, shall not be considered to have been arrested or to have been charged with any crime. . . .

Internet Tip

Interested readers can find on the textbook's website with the Chapter 3 materials each of the three opinions in *Powell v. Texas* written by the justices who upheld Powell's conviction, as well as a dissenting opinion.

While it is still constitutional for public drunks to be convicted of a crime, the protective custody laws provide police officers with a valuable alternative to the criminal justice system for addressing public alcoholism. And because the reforms were the product of the normal political processes within each state, and not the result of an unfunded judicial mandate, they were more palatable at the local and state levels of government.

Voluntariness

The prosecution must not only prove that the accused has engaged in criminal conduct, it must also prove that the accused's actions were willed bodily movements, or in legalese, **voluntary acts.** It is difficult, however, to clearly define this term, because involuntariness can logically assume many forms.

Think about each of the scenarios in Figure 3.3. Has the accused committed a voluntary act? The answers to these hypothetical questions can be found in endnote 5.[5]

Figure 3.3. Was the Act Voluntary?

---

1. The accused is sometimes unable to control the movement of his or her limbs because of an illness, disease, or physical trauma (such as a concussion).

2. The accused is at the front of a crowd of people intending to exit a subway car, train, or bus and is suddenly, violently, and unexpectedly shoved from behind and knocked into someone else in front of him who subsequently falls and is seriously injured.

3. The accused falls asleep in a double bed after nursing her two-month-old baby and accidently smothers the child.

4. The accused, a bank teller, hands over her employer's money in response to a robber's demand made at gunpoint.

5. The accused is allergic to bee stings and while hiking in the Adirondack Mountains breaks into a nearby cabin to avoid attack by an enormous swarm of bees.

Figure 3.4. Model Penal Code Voluntary Acts

Section 2.01. Requirement of Voluntary Act; Omission as Basis of Liability; Possession as an Act

(1) A person is not guilty of an offense unless his liability is based on conduct which includes a voluntary act or the omission to perform an act of which he is physically capable.

(2) The following are not voluntary acts within the meaning of this Section:

(a) a reflex or convulsion;

(b) a bodily movement during unconsciousness or sleep;

(c) conduct during hypnosis or resulting from hypnotic suggestion;

(d) a bodily movement that otherwise is not a product of the effort or determination of the actor, either conscious or habitual.

Figure 3.4 presents a portion of the official draft of the American Law Institute's **Model Penal Code** (MPC). Model codes are sets of proposed laws in a given subject area that are prepared as a resource for lawmakers and law reformers. They are not law unless and until they become enacted into law by a lawmaking body such as a state legislature. Many jurisdictions have been influenced by the MPC, and from time to time you will find portions of its contents reprinted in this text. The section of the Model Penal Code in Figure 3.4 is part of a proposed statute that predicates criminal liability on proof of a voluntary act. Other portions of the MPC can be found in Figures 3.5 and 3.7.

STATE OF ARIZONA v. MIGUEL ANGEL LARA

880 P.2d 1124
Court of Appeals of Arizona
April 5, 1994

AUTHOR'S INTRODUCTION

The appellant in the following case argued on appeal that he had introduced evidence as part of his case in chief that entitled him under Arizona law to the voluntary act instruction. The trial court's refusal to give the instruction, appellant maintained, constituted reversible error.

EXCERPT FROM THE CASE

Chief Judge DRUKE:

FACTS AND PROCEDURAL BACKGROUND

On April 9, 1990, appellant was staying with a man named Fernando Bartlett. Around noon, the police received a call from Bartlett complaining of an unwanted person at his house. Tucson police officer Kucsmas responded to the call and was told by Bartlett that he had asked appellant to leave several times without success.

Kucsmas entered the house and walked down a hall to the living room where loud music was playing. As he entered the room, Kucsmas saw appellant sitting on the couch with his feet propped up and a cowboy hat over his face. After Kucsmas asked him to stand up, appellant pushed his hat back on his head and abruptly stood up holding a knife.

Appellant moved toward Kucsmas, making horizontal slashing motions with the knife. As Kucsmas began to back up, he took his radio from his belt and called for assistance. As appellant continued to approach, Kucsmas backed out of the residence and eventually drew his gun. Kucsmas yelled several times, "stop or I'll shoot" and "alto," which is Spanish for "stop." Appellant did not respond. After driving Kucsmas back to a fence at the front of the house, appellant raised the knife above his head and lunged. Kucsmas then shot appellant in the chest severely wounding him.

Appellant was . . . acquitted of attempted first-degree murder, but was found guilty of aggravated assault and was sentenced to a presumptive prison term of 7.5 years.

"VOLUNTARY ACT" INSTRUCTION

Appellant contends that the trial court erred in refusing his requested instruction that the state had to prove that his act of attacking Officer Kucsmas was voluntary. Specifically, appellant argues that Dr. Geffen's trial testimony raised questions about whether appellant acted reflexively rather than voluntarily, thus entitling him to the requested instruction. We agree.

A defendant is entitled to a jury instruction on any theory reasonably supported by the evidence. . . . In the event the trial court fails to instruct the jury on a matter vital to the defendant's rights, such omission constitutes fundamental error. . . .

In this case, Dr. Geffen testified at trial that appellant suffered from "some kind of organic brain impairment that affected the part of his brain which governs the higher mental functions of a human being and plays a role in controlling some of the more primitive tendencies or behavior[s] that are almost automatic, that are instinctive." Dr. Geffen further stated that he would expect a person with such an impairment to "feel threatened and respond to that threat with anger and with rage . . . with almost a preprogrammed kind of massive defense response." When asked about the ability to inhibit that response, Dr. Geffen stated that "with this impairment, a person who begins a certain action impulsively, in reaction to a perceived threat, might continue that action without the ability to inhibit himself; . . . that ability would be reduced very drastically." When crossed by the state as to whether the "reflexive kind of conduct" described by the doctor is "kind of an immediate response," he answered: "Kind of automatic, yes."

Based on this testimony, appellant's defense was that he acted reflexively in response to a perceived threat and was inhibited by his mental impairment from discontinuing his response. Appellant thus requested a "voluntary act" instruction based on A.R.S. § 13-201.

Section 13-201 provides in relevant part that "[t]he minimum requirement for criminal liability is the performance by a person of conduct which includes a voluntary act." Section 13-105(34) defines a "voluntary" act as "a bodily movement performed consciously and as a result of effort and determination." This definition excludes a reflex bodily movement. "The definition of voluntary act in A.R.S. § 13-105 excludes . . . such bodily movements as reflexes or convulsions and movements during unconsciousness, sleep, or hypnosis." . . . Because the evidence in this case reasonably supported appellant's defense that his actions were reflexive rather than voluntary, he was entitled to his requested instruction. . . .

The state nevertheless contends . . . that it was not error to refuse appellant's requested voluntariness instruction because the court's other instructions adequately covered the same subject, specifically, its instructions on premeditation and intent. We find that neither instruction adequately covered the issue of whether appellant's attack was voluntary. The premeditation instruction . . . told the jury that premeditation is one of the elements of first-degree murder and means that "a person either intends or knows that his conduct will result in death to another person." The instruction on intent covered a subject different from appellant's requested instruction on voluntary act. . . . The distinctly punitive nature of criminal law requires that sanctions be reserved for conduct which can be morally condemned. In most instances, the penal law does not condemn conduct alone but rather a state of mind which exhibits an intent to harm, an awareness of harm, an indifference to harm, or a gross deviation from reasonable care. . . .

Criminal liability does not even arise . . . unless the defendant's act is voluntary; it is a "minimum requirement for criminal liability." . . . "If voluntariness is raised, such an act or omission must be established if penal liability is to apply." . . . Simply stated, "a crime consists of both a physical part and a mental part; that is, both an act or omission . . . and a state of mind." . . . Appellant's requested instruction covered the former and the intent instruction the latter, two different subjects.

Accordingly, we hold that the evidence—in this case reasonably supported appellant's requested "voluntary act" instruction—and that the refusal to give it was reversible error because its subject was not adequately covered by the instructions on intent and premeditation. . . .

Reversed and remanded.

CASE QUESTIONS

1. What was the defendant's reason for requesting the voluntary act instruction?

2. Should this case have to be retried merely because the trial court failed to instruct the jury regarding the voluntariness of the act?

AUTHOR'S COMMENTARY

It is important to remember that it is possible for a person to voluntarily commit an *actus reus* and yet still be innocent of a crime. Think about how easy it is, given the similarity of luggage, for an arriving passenger at an airport to mistakenly pick up someone else's luggage. If the arriving passenger checked luggage prior to departure that was of a similar manufacture, color, size, and type as the luggage incorrectly claimed upon arrival, criminal liability will hinge on the existence of criminal intent. If there is no criminal intent, the fact that the arriving passenger has someone else's luggage in her possession will be considered a mistake. If, however, the prosecution can prove that the arriving passenger was fully aware that she had not claimed her own bag, she would have criminal intent and would be subject to prosecution.

Criminal Liability in the Absence of an Act (Omissions)

Although many crimes prohibit specified criminal acts or results, criminal liability also exists where an accused does nothing under circumstances where the law requires conduct. There can be no criminal liability for nonconduct in the absence of a recognized legal duty. Most jurisdictions follow an approach similar to that of the Model Penal Code as excerpted in Figure 3.5.

There are typically four situations in which jurisdictions impose an affirmative duty of action and where inaction is prosecutable:

1. **Statutory duty.** Parents have an affirmative duty to provide food, shelter, and medical care for their children or they are subject to prosecution for child neglect. Drivers have a duty not to leave the scene of a vehicular accident in which a person has been injured or property has been damaged (hit and run). Teachers, doctors, and social workers often have a duty to report apparent child abuse, males have a duty to register with selective service, and taxpayers have a duty to file tax returns.

Figure 3.5. Model Penal Code Ommission as Basis of Liability

Section 2.01. Requirement of Voluntary Act; Omission as Basis of Liability; Possession as an Act

(3) Liability for the commission of an offense may not be based on an omission unaccompanied by action unless:

(a) the omission is expressly made sufficient by the law defining the offense; or

(b) a duty to perform the omitted act is otherwise imposed by law.

---

2. **Contractual duty.** This category includes home health-care workers, daycare providers, and care providers for elders who have contractually obligated themselves to provide for such persons.

3. **Status duty.** This category includes police officers with respect to arrested persons who are apparently injured, lifeguards at a public pool or beach, and public school teachers with their students. Notice that in each of these examples the care provider, although employed by someone else, has no direct contractual relationship with the individuals they are obligated to protect. Parents also have a status duty vis-à-vis their own children.

   Consider the dilemma of David Kaczynski, the brother of Ted Kaczynski, also known as the Unabomber. Ted Kaczynski was a Harvard graduate, received his PhD from Michigan, and had been on the faculty at the University of California, Berkeley. He became a recluse living in Montana in 1971. From 1978-1995, Kaczynski was responsible for killing three people and injuring 28 others with bombs enclosed in packages that he mailed to his victims. After reading excerpts from the Unabomber's "manifesto," David became convinced that his brother, Ted, was the author. His decision to acknowledge the existence of a moral obligation to prevent further loss of life and to contact law enforcement authorities ultimately led to Ted's apprehension. David acted knowing that the government might well seek Ted's execution. Ted Kaczynski pleaded guilty in federal court on January 23, 1998, to the charges against him, and he was sentenced to life imprisonment without possibility of parole.

4. **Assumed duty.** This category applies to someone who has voluntarily assumed a noncontractual duty of providing care for another person who cannot care for himself or herself. Assume, for example, that Bob is a college student living next door to an elderly widow, Mrs. Perez, who doesn't drive and has difficulty getting to the store. Assume further that Bob offers to help this elder by purchasing her groceries for her when he does his weekly shopping. At the end of the school

year, before returning to his home in another state for the summer, Bob will be legally obligated either to find someone else to help Mrs. Perez or to tell relatives, inform municipal/county officials, or recruit a volunteer to replace him. When Bob assumed this duty, other potential care providers would have reasonably concluded that Mrs. Perez's needs for assistance were being met. If that situation were to change, it would be incumbent on Bob to notify relevant authorities and caregivers that he was no longer able to provide this service. He cannot just abandon Mrs. Perez after she has come to rely on him for helping her obtain her food.

COMMONWEALTH OF PENNSYLVANIA v. JOHN BARRY KELLAM

719 A.2d 792
Superior Court of Pennsylvania
October 23, 1998

AUTHOR'S INTRODUCTION

Amy Sullivan was the mother of an infant named Jessica Piper, and John Kellam, the appellant in this case, was her live-in boyfriend. Kellam appealed his convictions for third-degree murder and endangering the welfare of a child on the grounds that he owed the infant victim no legal duty of care. The question to be decided by the appellate court in *Commonwealth v. Kellam* was whether the appellant, John Kellam, although neither the biological or adoptive parent, owed a legal duty of care to his girlfriend's infant daughter.

EXCERPT FROM THE CASE

Judge TAMILIA:

. . . On Sunday, June 30, 1996, at approximately 9:00 P.M., paramedics responded to a 911 call directing them to an emergency at Rear 31, Shady Lane, Uniontown, Fayette County, Pennsylvania. Upon arriving at the house, paramedics found a group of people clustered around the body of a dead infant, who was lying on her back in the middle of the downstairs living room floor. . . .

At the time, appellant . . . resided in the house with appellant's girlfriend and her children, including the infant. However, social workers found no baby formula and little or no baby food in the house. Upon investigation, police established that the infant was kept in an upstairs bedroom, which was extremely hot and smelled of urine and defecation. On the floor of the room, police found dirty diapers, and in the corner, they discovered a baby crib, which contained stuffed animals and a bottle that was dirty and had milk caked along the bottom.

On July 1, 1996, an autopsy revealed that the infant, Jessica M. Piper, had died from a combination of dehydration, malnutrition and hyperthermia. . . . In . . . [the pathologist's] opinion, the child had gone without anything to eat or drink for at least 24 to 48 hours. . . .

During the summer of 1996, . . . [Amy Sullivan, the appellant's girlfriend and the infant's mother] drank heavily and used crack cocaine. On the Friday and Saturday prior to her baby's death, Sullivan stayed out all night drinking, while appellant remained in the house with the children. . . . On Sunday morning, Sullivan returned home and asked appellant about the baby. Appellant replied that he had fed the baby, and she was fine . . . Sullivan then took a nap and did not wake up until 5:00 P.M. . . . At approximately 9:00 P.M., Sullivan checked on the baby and found that she was dead. . . .

. . . [A]ppellant . . . [was subsequently] found . . . guilty of third degree murder and endangering the welfare of a child [and] sentenced to 90 to 240 months incarceration. . . .

Initially, we note that criminal liability may be based on either an affirmative act or a failure to perform a duty imposed by law. . . . Furthermore, the failure to act may constitute the breach of a legal duty (1) where expressly provided by statute, (2) where one stands in a certain status relationship to another, (3) where one has assumed a contractual duty to care for another, or (4) where one has voluntarily assumed the care of another and so secluded the helpless person as to prevent others from rendering aid. . . . In the case of a parent and child, this Court repeatedly has stated that "[a] parent has the legal duty to protect her child, and the discharge of this duty requires affirmative performance." . . .

Appellant claims the duty to act is limited to natural and adoptive parents. We disagree. In this age where children reside in increasingly complex family situations, we fail to understand why criminal liability should be strictly limited to biological, or adoptive parents. In the instant case, appellant resided with the victim and her mother, exercised a great deal of control over the mother, and voluntarily assumed parental responsibilities with regard to the child. We therefore hold that whenever a person is placed in control and supervision of a child, that person has assumed such a status relationship to the child so as to impose a duty to act. . . .

Appellant argues he could not be considered to have had custody "and control over the child because the child's mother was in the house and taking a nap at the time of the infant's death." However, the fact that the infant's mother was physically present at the moment of death is irrelevant. The pathologist who performed the autopsy stated that the child had not had any food or fluids for between 24 and 48 hours. During the vast majority of this time, appellant was the only adult who could care for the dying infant, and as previously stated, he had a duty to do so. Moreover, appellant did more than merely neglect the baby. When Sullivan arrived home on the morning prior to the child's death, appellant actively deceived her about feeding the baby and about the baby's condition at the time.

Judgment of sentence affirmed.

CASE QUESTIONS

1. Under what four circumstances will a legal duty exist such that a person can be found criminally liable for having failed to act? Which theory or theories apply given the facts in this case?

2. Why does the court find that Kellam owed a duty to the infant despite the fact that he was neither a biological nor an adoptive parent?

3. Do you agree with the court's decision?

AUTHOR'S COMMENTARY

There has been an ongoing debate in this country about the wisdom of making it a crime of omission for a person who has observed the commission of a felony not to notify authorities. Assume, for example, that a person is present at a tavern and observes a sexual assault taking place. Assume further that the observer does nothing in particular to encourage or assist the assailant but takes no steps to stop the assaultive conduct or to call the police. Although the person may have a moral duty to either assist the victim or call authorities, should the law impose a legal duty to act in such a situation? Massachusetts enacted the following law in 1983 (See Figure 3.6) in the aftermath of a brutal rape that occurred on March 6, 1983, in Big Dan's Tavern in New Bedford.[6]

Figure 3.6. Massachusetts General Law Chapter 268, Section 40 Reports of Crimes to Law Enforcement Officials

Whoever knows that another person is a victim of aggravated rape, rape, murder, manslaughter or armed robbery and is at the scene of said crime shall, to the extent that said person can do so without danger or peril to himself or others, report said crime to an appropriate law enforcement official as soon as reasonably practicable. Any person who violates this section shall be punished by a fine of not less than five hundred nor more than two thousand and five hundred dollars.

This case gained national attention and Wisconsin, Washington, Florida, and Rhode Island adopted legislation similar to the Massachusetts law.[7]

Readers will notice that the Massachusetts "report or help" statute allows a reporting person to remain anonymous. This is also true of the Wisconsin (940.34 Wis. Stats.), Washington (RCW 9.69.100), Florida (Title XLVI 794.027), and Rhode Island (11-56-1) versions of this law. Why do you suppose all four of these state legislatures felt it necessary to permit anonymous reports? The answer to this question can be found on Loislaw by reading the following Wisconsin case, *State v. LaPlante*, 521 N.W.2d 448 (1994).

Is Possession an Act?

Although criminal law normally requires proof of a criminal act or a failure to act under circumstances where the law requires specified action, the majority rule among the states is that possession of contraband is sufficient to constitute the *actus reus* of a crime. **Actual possession** exists where the object possessed is physically touching the possessor. **Constructive possession** can be found where the possessed object is not actually touching the possessor, but the object is either under the possessor's "dominion and control" or the possessor has "authority" over property. To use other words, constructive possession of property exists where reasonable inferences derived from the proof of the circumstances of the case logically permit the conclusion that the accused was, in fact, controlling property. Constructive possession, for example, was found by a state intermediate appellate court where controlled substances, along with a scale and court documents containing the accused's name and address, were discovered in a locked safe within a house where the accused resided and received his mail.[8]

Most states have adopted a requirement similar to the provision of the Model Penal Code in Figure 3.7.

Figure 3.7. Model Penal Code Possession as an Act

Section 2.01. Requirement of Voluntary Act; Omission as Basis of Liability; Possession as an Act

(4) Possession is an act, within the meaning of this Section, if the possessor knowingly procured or received the thing possessed or was aware of his control thereof for a sufficient period to have been able to terminate his possession.

Model Penal Code, copyright ©1985 by The American Law Institute. All rights reserved. Reprinted with permission.

BYRD v. TEXAS

835 S.W.2d 223
Court of Appeals of Texas
July 22, 1992

AUTHOR'S INTRODUCTION

Byrd was stopped for speeding, and a search of his vehicle disclosed a plastic bag containing a small amount of cocaine residue. He was subsequently charged with, and convicted of, possession of a controlled substance. Byrd argued on appeal that the prosecution had failed to prove that he had engaged in any forbidden conduct. The government's proof that he was in possession of the bag containing cocaine residue was not, he contended, proof of forbidden conduct and therefore could not sustain any criminal prosecution.

EXCERPT FROM THE CASE

Justice VANCE:

. . . Byrd argues that, because "possession" is not an "act or omission," it cannot be used as the basis of a criminal prosecution. Therefore, he says, the indictment fails to allege a forbidden conduct—an essential element of the offense—and thus fails to state an offense against the laws of the State of Texas.

Byrd's argument, however, overlooks section 6.01(a) of the Penal Code, which states: "A person commits an offense only if he voluntarily engages in *conduct*, including an act, an omission, or *possession*." . . . Possession is not an act or omission, but it is conduct. . . . Thus "possession" can form the basis for an offense under the Penal Code. . . . The court did not err in overruling Byrd's motion to quash. . . .

. . . Byrd [also] asserts that, the evidence was insufficient to find him guilty of possession of a controlled substance. . . .

A defendant must exercise care, custody, control, and management over illicit drugs, knowing them to be drugs, before he is guilty of their possession. . . . If the defendant is not in sole possession of the place where drugs are found, the state must prove an affirmative link between the contraband and the defendant to establish his possession. . . . An affirmative link is established by facts and circumstances from which one may reasonably infer that the defendant knew the contraband existed and that he exercised care, custody, control, and management over it. . . . These elements may be established by circumstantial evidence. . . . Possession, however, need not be exclusive. . . .

. . . [T]he evidence shows that Byrd was the driver of the vehicle; he admitted that the "stuff" in the trunk of the vehicle was his; one bag contained a large amount of cash while the other, in close proximity, contained items commonly used to manufacture "rock" cocaine; the second bag contained eight milligrams of cocaine; a drug dog "alerted" on both bags; and half-inch by half-inch plastic bags commonly used for rock cocaine were found in the glove compartment. Thus, we conclude that the trial judge, as a rational trier of the facts, could have found the essential elements of the crime beyond a reasonable doubt. . . .

We affirm the judgment.

CASE QUESTIONS

1. Why did Byrd argue that his indictment for cocaine possession should have been quashed and the evidence suppressed?

2. Did the Court agree with Byrd? Explain.

AUTHOR'S COMMENTARY

The Texas statute provided that Byrd could not be convicted of the crime with which he was charged unless he could be proven to have engaged in criminal "conduct." You will notice that Texas (and some other states) has developed new phraseology to explain what was traditionally called the *actus reus* requirement. These states require proof of "conduct" which has been defined as including proof of a criminal act, a failure to act where action is required, or possession (either actual or constructive). Other jurisdictions maintain the traditional *actus reus* approach. They consider a failure to act to be equivalent to the commission of an act and have defined possession to be an act.

The Texas Court of Appeals emphasized that for Byrd to be guilty of possession, the prosecution had to prove more than that he had exercised dominion and control over a plastic bag containing cocaine residue that was found in his vehicle's trunk. It also had to prove that Byrd knew that the contents of that plastic bag consisted of illegal drugs.

The Model Penal Code provides that criminal liability attaches in a possession case only where the alleged possessor is "knowingly" exercising control over the possessed object. This requirement protects inadvertent possessors from criminal liability. How often do you, when riding as a passenger in a friend's car, look under the seat to make sure that you are not unwittingly exercising dominion and control over stolen goods or drugs? We will discuss the topic of criminal intent later in this chapter.

Internet Tip

The appellant in *State v. Lewis*, 886 A.2d 643 (2005), was convicted of possession of cocaine with intent to distribute while within a park zone. Although appellant was arrested within a park zone, the drugs he was alleged to have possessed were not located within the boundaries of a park. Lewis argued to the New Jersey Supreme Court that the state had a statutory duty to prove that he had actual possession of the drugs and that the drugs possessed were physically located within the park zone. Interested readers can see how the New Jersey Supreme Court decided this case by going to the textbook's website. An edited version of *State v. Lewis* is included in the Chapter 3 materials found in the textbook's website.

Presumptions and *Actus Reus*

Proving the existence of an *actus reus* cannot always be limited to proven facts. Although defendants are logically a good source of factual evidence in criminal prosecutions, they often exercise their constitutional right not to testify at trial (a right protected by the Fifth Amendment's privilege against self-incrimination). To counterbalance the benefit provided the defendant in the Fifth Amendment, the law often specifically permits certain specified facts essential to proving the *actus reus* to be inferred from the proof of other facts. Certain inferential relationships involving **proved facts** and **inferred facts** are given special status and are called *presumptions*. This complex subject is only partially discussed in this chapter. It is important to understand something about this evidentiary device because it affects the proof of the *actus reus* (and also the **mens rea**, which we discuss later).

Presumptions are based on constitutional and legislative provisions and on case law (judicial opinions). They are substitutes for evidence, not evidence itself. The **presumption of innocence** (based in the Due Process Clauses of the Fifth and Fourteenth Amendments) is an example of a presumption that greatly benefits defendants. Because this presumption takes the place of evidence, criminal defendants don't have to prove themselves innocent of the charges against them and the prosecution has the burden of proving guilt.

Some presumptions tend to benefit the prosecution. For example, a defendant's sanity is presumed and statutes are presumed to be constitutional. These presumptions relieve the state from having to prove in every criminal case that the defendant was sane when the alleged crime was committed, and from having to establish a law's constitutionality as part of the government's case in chief.

Figure 3.8. Excerpt from New York Penal Law 265.15 (3) (as of 1967)

<u>The presence in an automobile</u>, other than a stolen one or a public omnibus, of <u>any firearm</u>, defaced firearm, firearm silencer, bomb, bombshell, gravity knife, switchblade knife, dagger, dirk, stiletto, billy, blackjack, metal knuckles, sandbag, sandclub or slingshot <u>is presumptive evidence of its possession by all persons occupying such automobile at the time such weapon, instrument, or appliance is found</u>, except under the following circumstances:

(a) if such weapon, instrument or appliance is found upon the person of one of the occupants therein.

Note: Emphasis added; various other exceptions have been omitted in the interest of saving space.

Many presumptions are essentially neutral. For example, the presumption that witnesses tell the truth eliminates the need for any party calling a witness to establish that witness's veracity (truthfulness) prior to giving testimony and places the burden of proof, regarding untruthfulness, on the opposing party.

The defendants in the next case challenged the prosecution's reliance on a New York statutory presumption excerpted in Figure 3.8.

ULSTER COUNTY COURT v. ALLEN
442 U. S. 140
U.S. Supreme Court
June 4, 1979

AUTHOR'S INTRODUCTION

The four defendants in the next case were occupants in an automobile stopped for speeding by police officers. The defendants were arrested and charged with unlawfully possessing firearms, which had been seized by police from inside the car's passenger compartment and trunk. The prosecution in this case sought to meet its burden of production at trial by directly proving the "basic facts" (that the defendants were found occupying the car from which weapons were seized). The government sought to prove possession (the "elemental fact" in this case), based on reasonable inferences logically derived from proof of the basic facts, because they had no direct proof connecting each of the defendants with the guns in question. The use of inferential proof in this manner was specifically authorized by statute.

EXCERPT FROM THE CASE

Justice STEVENS delivered the opinion of the Court.

A New York statute provides that, with certain exceptions, the presence of a firearm in an automobile is presumptive evidence of its illegal possession by all persons then occupying the vehicle. . . . The United States Court of Appeals for the Second Circuit held that . . . "the statute is unconstitutional on its face." . . . We granted *certiorari* to . . . consider whether the statute is constitutional in its application to respondents. . . .

Four persons, three adult males (respondents) and a 16-year-old girl (Jane Doe, who is not a respondent here), were jointly tried on charges that they possessed two loaded handguns . . . found in a Chevrolet in which they were riding when it was stopped for speeding on the New York Thruway shortly after noon on March 28, 1973. The two large-caliber handguns, which together with their ammunition weighed approximately six pounds, were seen through the window of the car by the investigating police officer. They were positioned crosswise in an open handbag on either the front floor or the front seat of the car on the passenger side where Jane Doe was sitting. Jane Doe admitted that the handbag was hers. . . . The jury convicted all four of possession of the handguns. . . .

Counsel for all four defendants objected to the introduction into evidence of the two handguns, . . . arguing that the State had not adequately demonstrated a connection between their clients and the contraband. The trial court overruled the objection, relying on the presumption of possession created by the New York statute. . . .

Defendants filed a post-trial motion in which they challenged the constitutionality of the New York statute as applied in this case. The challenge was made in support of their argument that the evidence, apart from the presumption, was insufficient to sustain the convictions. The motion was denied, . . . and the convictions were affirmed by the Appellate Division without opinion. . . .

The New York Court of Appeals also affirmed. . . .

Respondents filed a petition for a writ of *habeas corpus* in the United States District Court for the Southern District of New York contending that they were denied due process of law by the application of the statutory presumption of possession. The District Court issued the writ, holding that . . . the mere presence of two guns in a woman's handbag in a car could not reasonably give rise to the inference that they were in the possession of three other persons in the car. . . .

The Court of Appeals for the Second Circuit affirmed. . . .

I

Inferences and presumptions are a staple of our adversary system of fact-finding. It is often necessary for the trier of fact to determine the existence of an element of the crime—that is, . . . "elemental" fact—from the existence of one or more "evidentiary" or "basic" facts. . . . The value of these evidentiary devices, and their validity under the Due Process Clause, vary from case to case, however, depending on the strength of the connection between the particular basic and elemental facts involved and on the degree to which the device curtails the factfinder's freedom to assess the evidence independently. Nonetheless, in criminal cases, the ultimate test of any device's constitutional validity in a given case remains constant: the device must not undermine the factfinder's responsibility at trial, based on evidence adduced by the State, to find the ultimate facts beyond a reasonable doubt. . . .

The most common evidentiary device is the entirely permissive inference or presumption, which allows—but does not require—the trier of fact to infer the elemental fact from proof by the prosecutor of the basic one and which places no burden of any kind on the defendant. . . . In that situation the basic fact may constitute *prima facie* evidence of the elemental fact. . . .

When reviewing this type of device, the Court has required the party challenging it to demonstrate its invalidity as applied to him. . . . Because this permissive presumption leaves the trier of fact free to credit or reject the inference and does not shift the burden of proof, it affects the application of the "beyond a reasonable doubt" standard only if, under the facts of the case, there is no rational way the trier could make the connection permitted by the inference. For only in that situation is there any risk that an explanation of the permissible inference to a jury, or its use by a jury, has caused the presumptively rational factfinder to make an erroneous factual determination.

A mandatory presumption is a far more troublesome evidentiary device. For it . . . tells the trier that he or they must find the elemental fact upon proof of the basic fact, at least unless the defendant has come forward with some evidence to rebut the presumed connection between the two facts. . . .

The trial judge's instructions make it clear that the presumption was merely a part of the prosecution's case, . . . that it gave rise to a permissive inference available only in certain circumstances, rather than a mandatory conclusion of possession, and that it could be ignored by the jury even if there was no affirmative proof offered by defendants in rebuttal. . . . The judge explained that possession could be actual or constructive, but that constructive possession could not exist without the intent and ability to exercise control or dominion over the weapons. . . . He also carefully instructed the jury that there is a mandatory presumption of innocence in favor of the defendants that controls unless it, as the exclusive trier of fact, is satisfied beyond a reasonable doubt that the defendants possessed the handguns in the manner described by the judge. . . . In short, the instructions plainly directed the jury to consider all the circumstances tending to support or contradict the inference that all four occupants of the car had possession of the two loaded handguns and to decide the matter for itself without regard to how much evidence the defendants introduced. . . .

Our cases considering the validity of permissive statutory presumptions such as the one involved here have rested on an evaluation of the presumption as applied to the record before the Court. . . .

III

As applied to the facts of this case, the presumption of possession is entirely rational. . . .

[R]espondents were not "hitchhikers or other casual passengers," and the guns were neither "a few inches in length" nor "out of [respondents'] sight." . . . The argument against possession by any of the respondents was predicated solely on the fact that the guns were in Jane Doe's pocketbook. But several circumstances—which, not surprisingly, her counsel repeatedly emphasized in his questions and his argument, . . . made it highly improbable that she was the sole custodian of those weapons. . . .

The two guns were too large to be concealed in her handbag. . . . The bag was consequently open, and part of one of the guns was in plain view, within easy access of the driver of the car and even, perhaps, of the other two respondents who were riding in the rear seat. . . .

As a 16-year-old girl in the company of three adult men she was the least likely of the four to be carrying one, let alone two, heavy handguns. It is far more probable that she relied on the pocketknife found in her brassiere for any necessary self-protection. Under these circumstances, it was not unreasonable for her counsel to argue and for the jury to infer that when the car was halted for speeding, the other passengers in the car anticipated the risk of a search and attempted to conceal their weapons in a pocketbook in the front seat. The inference is surely more likely than the notion that these weapons were the sole property of the 16-year-old girl.

Under these circumstances, the jury would have been entirely reasonable in rejecting the suggestion which, incidentally, defense counsel did not even advance in their closing arguments to the jury—that the handguns were in the sole possession of Jane Doe. . . .

The permissive presumption, as used in this case, satisfied the . . . [constitutional] test. And, as already noted, the New York Court of Appeals has concluded that the record as a whole was sufficient to establish guilt beyond a reasonable doubt.

The judgment is reversed. So ordered.

CASE QUESTIONS

1. Why was the presumption in this case so important procedurally to the government?

2. Assume that state troopers stop and board a van traveling on the New York Thruway that is occupied by eight passengers sitting two abreast in each of four rows. Assume further that officers discover a purse containing exactly the same number and type of weapons next to a passenger sitting to the driver's right in the front row of the vehicle. Assume further that the district attorney wants to use the same presumption used in *Ulster County v. Allen* to prosecute a passenger in the fourth row for illegal possession of the firearms. Could the presumption be challenged again on constitutional grounds, or is that issue foreclosed by the decision in *Ulster County v. Allen?*

AUTHOR'S COMMENTARY

Although the use of presumptions in criminal cases has been widely accepted in American courtrooms, due process challenges have periodically arisen that have reached the U.S. Supreme Court. In a series of decisions going back to the 1940s, the Court has established constitutional controls over the creation and use of presumptions in criminal trials.

One line of cases has focused on the logical integrity of presumptions—that is, on the strength of the connection between the facts that are proven (called the *basic* or *proved facts*) and the conclusion that is inferred from those facts (called the *presumed* or *elemental fact*). The Court determined that the use of a statutory presumption in a criminal case "must be regarded as . . . unconstitutional, unless it can be said with substantial assurance that the presumed fact is more likely than not to flow from the proved fact[s] on which it is made to depend."[9]

A second line of cases focuses on preserving juror autonomy. It was this issue that Justice Stevens wrote about in the *Allen* case. Stephens explained that it is constitutionally necessary that a judge's instructions to the jury on the use of presumptions preserve juror autonomy in determining whether any elemental fact that is to be presumed has been proven beyond a reasonable doubt. The instructions must make clear that the presumption is *permissive* and that jurors are permitted, but not required, to find the elemental fact. The instructions must additionally make clear that jurors are to find that a presumed fact has been proven *only* if they are satisfied with the proof beyond a reasonable doubt. The Court in *Allen* ruled that the jury instruction in the *Allen* case was permissive and thus there was no due process problem with respect to the jury autonomy issue.

If, however, a jury instruction is ambiguous on juror autonomy or clearly requires jurors to accept proof of an elemental fact, the presumption is classified as *conclusive*, and two due process problems arise. The first problem is the denial of the defendant's Sixth Amendment right to a jury trial. A criminal defendant has a constitutional right in to have a jury decide every factual issue necessary for conviction.[10] If the judge tells the jury that they must find an elemental fact based on the proof of other facts, it is the judge and not the jury who is actually making the decision—a denial of due process. A second problem arises when a judge instructs the jury to find that a particular fact is proven because it is "presumed." In such a situation, a juror who was not convinced that this fact had actually been proven beyond a reasonable doubt might nevertheless follow the judge's instructions and "presume" it.

Let's look at the following hypothetical problem. Assume, for example, that you are a juror in a criminal case in which the prosecution is required to prove facts W, X, Y, and Z beyond a reasonable doubt in order to convict the defendant of the crime charged. Assume further that the trial judge instructs that if jurors find facts W, X, and Y to have been proven beyond a reasonable doubt, that "Z is legally presumed."

Do you see how a juror who is not convinced beyond a reasonable doubt by the government's proof of Z might disregard that doubt and find that Z was proven because of the judge's instructions?

Double Jeopardy Considerations

Before we discuss an interesting aspect of **double jeopardy** law that relates to our discussion of the criminal act, it is necessary to briefly discuss the concepts of **dual sovereignty** and **jeopardy**.

You may recall from Chapter 1 that our federal form of government results in **dual sovereignty** inasmuch as both the federal and state governments are sovereigns. Each of these sovereigns is a complete government with legislative, executive, and judicial branches. Each sovereign's legislature is entitled to enact a statute making it a crime to commit bank robbery. Congress, for example, can make it a federal crime to rob a federally insured bank because doing so harms interstate commerce. California has a legitimate interest in prohibiting all forms of robbery pursuant to its police power. Thus if a person robs a federally insured bank in California, this one criminal act can result in separate prosecutions by both California and the federal government. In such a situation, even though there are two prosecutions, there is, constitutionally speaking, no double jeopardy because each sovereign is legitimately enforcing its own laws, and each is trying the case once.[11]

To understand the concept of double jeopardy we must first understand more about the procedural point in criminal proceedings when jeopardy is said to exist (or as we say in legalese, when jeopardy *attaches*). **Jeopardy**, in the procedural sense, attaches in a bench trial when the first witness is sworn in and in a jury trial when the jury is sworn. If a defendant is convicted of a crime and successfully argues to an appellate court that she or he is entitled to a new trial, she or he cannot claim double

Figure 3.9. Amendment V: Double Jeopardy Clause

> "... nor shall any person be subject for the same offense to be twice put in jeopardy of life or limb ..."

jeopardy when the state reprosecutes the case, because no final judgment was entered by the trial court on the merits of the charges. *Double jeopardy* would occur, however, if a final judgment of conviction or acquittal was awarded in the first trial, and either or both sovereigns brought a second prosecution against the same defendant for the same offense that had been previously adjudicated.

The next case explores another dimension of double jeopardy—the extent to which a prosecutor should be entitled to convert one physical act or episode into multiple criminal convictions and punishments. (See Figure 3.9).

BROWN v. OHIO
432 U.S. 161
U.S. Supreme Court
June 16, 1977

AUTHOR'S INTRODUCTION

In *Brown v. Ohio*, the defendant, Nathan Brown, stole a car from a parking lot in East Cleveland, Ohio, and wasn't arrested until nine days later in Wickliffe, Ohio. The Wickliffe police charged Brown with joyriding on December 8, the day on which he was apprehended. Brown was convicted and sentenced to 30 days in jail and a $100 fine. When he finished serving his sentence on January 8, he was taken into custody by East Cleveland police and was subsequently indicted in that jurisdiction for having engaged in joyriding and auto theft on November 29, the date on which he first stole the car.

Brown appealed, claiming the second prosecution placed him in jeopardy a second time for the same offense, in violation of the double jeopardy clause. This constitutional provision protects criminal defendants, to varying degrees, from multiple trials, convictions, and punishments for the "same offense." Double jeopardy applies in federal cases because it is enumerated in the text of the Fifth Amendment. It also applies in state prosecutions because it has been incorporated into (included within) the Due Process Clause of the Fourteenth Amendment.

The U.S. Supreme Court had to decide whether double jeopardy protections prohibited Ohio from prosecuting Brown in separate trials for alleged offenses committed on the first and last days of a nine-day period in which he was in possession of a car that he had stolen from an East Cleveland parking lot.

Justice POWELL delivered the opinion of the Court.

The question in this case is whether the Double Jeopardy Clause of the Fifth Amendment bars prosecution and punishment for the crime of stealing an automobile following prosecution and punishment for the lesser included offense of operating the same vehicle without the owner's consent. . . .

II

The Double Jeopardy Clause of the Fifth Amendment, applicable to the States through the Fourteenth, provides that no person shall "be subject for the same offense to be twice put in jeopardy of life or limb." It has long been understood that separate statutory crimes need not be identical—either in constituent elements or in actual proof—in order to be the same within the meaning of the constitutional prohibition. . . . The principal question in this case is whether auto theft and joyriding, a greater and lesser included offense under Ohio law, constitute the "same offense" under the Double Jeopardy Clause. . . .

. . . [T]he Fifth Amendment double jeopardy guarantee serves principally as a restraint on courts and prosecutors. The legislature remains free under the Double Jeopardy Clause to define crimes and fix punishments; but once the legislature has acted courts may not . . . attempt to secure that punishment in more than one trial. . . . Where successive prosecutions are at stake, the guarantee serves "a constitutional policy of finality for the defendant's benefit." . . . That policy protects the accused from attempts to relitigate the facts underlying a prior acquittal . . . and from attempts to secure additional punishment after a prior conviction and sentence. . . .

The established test for determining whether two offenses are sufficiently distinguishable to permit the imposition of cumulative punishment was stated in *Blockburger v. United States* . . . :

> The applicable rule is that where the same act or transaction constitutes a violation of two distinct statutory provisions, the test to be applied to determine whether there are two offenses or only one is whether each provision requires proof of a fact which the other does not. . . .

This test emphasizes the elements of the two crimes. "If each requires proof of a fact that the other does not, the **Blockburger** test is satisfied, notwithstanding a substantial overlap in the proof offered to establish the crimes." . . .

We are mindful that the Ohio courts "have the final authority to interpret . . . that State's legislation." . . . Here the Ohio Court of Appeals has authoritatively defined the elements of the two Ohio crimes: Joyriding consists of taking or operating a vehicle without the owner's consent, and auto theft consists of joyriding with the intent permanently to deprive the owner of possession. . . . Joyriding is the lesser included offense. The prosecutor who has established joyriding need only prove the requisite intent in order to establish auto theft; the prosecutor who has established auto theft necessarily has established joyriding as well.

Applying the *Blockburger* test, we agree with the Ohio Court of Appeals that joyriding and auto theft, as defined by that court, constitute "the same statutory offense" within the meaning of the Double Jeopardy Clause. . . . For it is clearly not the case that "each [statute] requires proof of a fact which the other does not." . . . As is invariably true of a greater and lesser included offense, the lesser offense—joyriding—requires no proof beyond that which is required for conviction of the greater—auto theft. The greater offense is therefore by definition the "same" for purposes of double jeopardy as any lesser offense included in it. . . .

III

. . . The Double Jeopardy Clause is not such a fragile guarantee that prosecutors can avoid its limitations by the simple expedient of dividing a single crime into a series of temporal or spatial units. . . . The applicable Ohio statutes, as written and as construed in this case, make the theft and operation of a single car a single offense. Although the Wickliffe and East Cleveland authorities may have had different perspectives on Brown's offense, it was still only one offense under Ohio law. . . . Accordingly, the specification of different dates in the two charges on which Brown was convicted cannot alter the fact that he was placed twice in jeopardy for the same offense in violation of the Fifth and Fourteenth Amendments.

Reversed.

CASE QUESTIONS

1. How should a court go about determining whether successive prosecutions of a defendant are compatible with the requirement of the double jeopardy clause?

2. What is the practical significance of a failure to satisfy the *Blockburger* requirements?

3. What powers, according to the Court, is the double jeopardy clause primarily intended to check?

AUTHOR'S COMMENTARY

Although Brown could not be convicted in separate trials of both joyriding and auto theft, a criminal offender who is charged with breaking into someone else's house and stealing a DVD machine could be prosecuted for each offense in separate trials.

Burglary and theft are not the "same offense" under the *Blockburger* test, because each of these offenses requires proof of at least one fact that is not required for conviction of the other offense. Proof of a theft is not required for conviction of burglary, and proof that a defendant has unlawfully entered or remained in a legally protected structure is not required for conviction of theft.

In *Brown*, Ohio prosecutors sought to try and convict the defendant in *two separate trials* for criminal offenses that were constitutionally the "same offense" under the *Blockburger* test.

 Internet Tip

The Chapter 3 materials included on this textbook's website include a discussion of the double jeopardy clause as it relates to cumulative punishment as well as the U.S. Supreme Court case of *Missouri v. Hunter*. Following the case there is an accompanying author's commentary.

Criminal Intent/*Mens Rea*

With the exception of **strict liability** offenses (which are discussed later in this chapter), criminal offenses require that the prosecutor prove beyond a reasonable doubt that the criminal offender possessed a legally specified degree of **criminal intent/*mens rea*** at the time that the criminal act was committed. The late Justice Robert Jackson explained the rationale for an intent requirement in the following excerpt from *Morissette v. United States* (342 U.S. 46, 1952).

> The contention that an injury can amount to a crime only when inflicted by intention is no provincial or transient notion. It is as universal and persistent in mature systems of law as belief in freedom of the human will and a consequent ability and duty of the normal individual to choose between good and evil. A relation between some mental element and punishment for a harmful act is almost as instinctive as the child's familiar exculpatory "But I didn't mean to" . . . Unqualified acceptance of this doctrine by English common law in the Eighteenth Century was indicated by Blackstone's sweeping statement that to constitute any crime there must first be a "vicious will."

Common-law commentators of the early Nineteenth Century pronounced the same principle. . . .

Crime, as a compound concept, generally constituted only from concurrence of an evil-meaning mind with an evil-doing hand . . . took deep and early root in American soil. As the states codified the common law of crimes, even if their enactments were silent on the subject, their courts assumed that the omission did not signify disapproval of the principle but merely recognized that intent was so inherent in the idea of the offense that it required no statutory affirmation. Courts, with little hesitation or division, found an implication of the requirement as to offenses that were taken over from the common law. The unanimity with which they have adhered to the central thought that wrongdoing must be conscious to be criminal is emphasized by the variety, disparity and confusion of their definitions of the requisite but elusive mental element. However, courts of various jurisdictions, and for the purposes of different offenses, have devised working formulae, if not scientific ones, for the instruction of juries around such terms as "felonious intent," "criminal intent," "malice aforethought," "guilty knowledge," "fraudulent intent," "willfulness," "scienter," to denote guilty knowledge, or *mens rea*, to signify an evil purpose or mental culpability. By use or combination of these various tokens, they have sought to protect those who were not blameworthy in mind from conviction of infamous common-law crimes.

Mens rea offenses can be divided into criminal offenses that are inherently bad (**mala in se**) and that primarily focus on protecting individuals from harm, and offenses that were created by legislative bodies because workable rules were required in order to protect the general welfare of the public (classified as **mala prohibita**). **Mala in se** offenses include murder, rape, robbery, and arson. **Mala prohibita** offenses include exceeding motor vehicle speed limits, driving on the wrong side of the road, and selling cigarettes or alcoholic beverages to underage persons.

Mala in Se Offenses

In the United States, *mala in se* offenses require proof of criminal intent. In part this is because the antecedents of these offenses were often adopted from the English common law crimes, which traditionally required proof of criminal intent for conviction. A second explanation for requiring proof of *mens rea* is that convictions for *mala in se* offenses often result in broad-based social contempt directed at the offender. The procedural significance of requiring proof of criminal intent is that defendants charged with such crimes are legally entitled to present evidence that demonstrates the absence of *mens rea* (a topic we will discuss in Chapter 5, which focuses on defenses). Evidence of the existence of or lack of *mens rea* is inadmissible if the defendant is charged with an offense not requiring proof of criminal intent.

Mala Prohibita Offenses

Some acts that are not intrinsically evil are defined as being criminal by legislative bodies in order to promote the public health, welfare, safety, or morals. Crimes of this type are classified as *mala prohibita* offenses. For example, states commonly make it illegal to sell alcoholic beverages or cigarettes to someone who has not reached a specified minimum age for the lawful consumption of such products. Similarly, under federal law banks can be criminally prosecuted if they fail to provide the government with notice of all cash transactions above a specified dollar amount. This failure, although not inherently evil, is statutorily required because of the government's desire to combat money laundering and the funding of terrorist organizations. A third example is the requirement that automobile drivers stop and yield to pedestrians who are within a crosswalk not controlled by a traffic light. This law protects pedestrians from uncaring motorists who would otherwise deny walkers the opportunity to cross public streets. Legislatures frequently include a *mens rea* requirement for *mala prohibita* offenses. When the legislature declares that conduct is criminal irrespective of the offender's intent it has enacted a **strict liability offense**.

Defining Criminal Intent

Two basic approaches to *mens rea* are prevalent today. One is traditional and based on common law notions of criminal intent; the other is relatively new and based on the Model Penal Code.

The Traditional Common Law Approach

Under the traditional common law approach, *mens rea* consists of **general intent** and **specific intent**.

To prove the existence of **general intent**, the prosecution has to prove that the accused, without any lawful justification or excuse, intended to commit the *actus reus* specified for that crime. The criminal actor would demonstrate a general intent in an arson case by setting fire to a structure that subsequently burns or in a trespass-to-land case by going upon another's land without consent. A person can have general intent without knowing that particular conduct is defined as being criminal and without intending to violate any law.

A **specific intent** crime requires proof of the criminal actor's general intent plus an additional specified type of intent. Specific intent is used to distinguish offenses that have somewhat similar criminal acts. In both common law burglary (a specific intent crime) and trespass (a general intent crime), for example, offenders make unlawful entries. But the burglar has an additional intent at the moment of entry that is not in the mind of the trespasser—the burglar is making an entry in order to commit some other offense. A person who is simply in possession of a controlled substance (a general intent crime) may have engaged in conduct that is very similar to a drug dealer (a specific intent offense). What distinguishes the two drug offenders is that the dealer has not only an intent to possess controlled substances but also an intent to distribute controlled substances to others. The additional intent can assume different forms, including knowledge of certain facts (that property being stored for a friend is stolen, that a person being sheltered is a fugitive from justice, that someone is an illegal alien, or that a particular individual is a police officer). It may also include an intent to commit a felony, or knowledge that one is exercising dominion and control over unlawfully possessed explosives.

It is not unusual for a criminal defendant to challenge the government's proof of intent at trial. In *mens rea* offenses, proof of wrongful intent is an element of the criminal offense and must be proven beyond a reasonable doubt.

STATE v. GORDON
321 A.2d 352
Supreme Judicial Court of Maine
June 17, 1974

AUTHOR'S INTRODUCTION

The defendant in the following case was tried by a jury and convicted of armed robbery, a specific intent crime. Maine's statute required the prosecution to prove beyond a reasonable doubt that the defendant, Gordon, committed the *actus reus* for armed robbery, and additionally that he possessed at that time a specified type of wrongful intent—namely, the intent "to deprive permanently the owner of his property."

Gordon and an accomplice named Stroud were police custody escapees from Vermont who were traveling through Maine in a station wagon that began to have engine problems. As Gordon and Stroud were passing Franklin Prout's house, they noticed Prout's Chevelle. They also noticed that the key was in the Chevelle's ignition. Gordon and Stroud subsequently stole the Chevelle from Prout at gunpoint, but prior to departing with the car, Stroud told Prout that Stroud and Gordon would "take care of [the Chevelle] and see [that Prout] got it back as soon as possible."

Gordon was subsequently convicted of robbery. He argued on appeal that his conviction should be overturned because there was evidence in the trial record that showed that, at the time he and Stroud took the Chevelle, they had not intended to deprive Prout permanently of possession of the vehicle.

EXCERPT FROM THE CASE

Justice WERNICK:

[D]efendant maintains that the evidence clearly established that . . . defendant intended only a temporary use of Prout's Chevelle. Defendant argues that the evidence thus fails to warrant a conclusion beyond a reasonable doubt that defendant had the specific intent requisite for "robbery." (Hereinafter, reference to the "specific intent" necessary for "robbery" signifies the specific intent incorporated into robbery as embracing "larceny.")

Although defendant is correct that robbery is a crime requiring a particular specific intent, . . . defendant wrongly apprehends its substantive content.

. . . The law evaluates the . . . [intention to steal] of "robbery" in terms of the detriment projected to the legally protected interests of the owner rather than the benefits intended to accrue to the wrongdoer from his invasion of the rights of the owner. . . .

[T]he specific intent requisite for "robbery" is defined solely in terms of the injury projected to the interests of the property owner—specific intent "to deprive permanently the owner of his property." . . .

The instant question thus becomes: on the hypothesis . . . that defendant here actually intended to use the Prout automobile "only temporarily" (as he would need it to achieve a successful flight from the authorities), is defendant correct in his fundamental contention that this, *in itself*, negates . . . specific intent of defendant to deprive permanently the owner of his property? We answer that defendant's claim is erroneous.

Concretely illustrative of the point that a wrongdoer may intend to use wrongfully taken property "only temporarily" and yet, without contradiction, intend that the owner be deprived of his property permanently is the case of a defendant who proposes to use the property only for a short time and then to destroy it. At the opposite pole, and excluding . . . specific intent to deprive permanently the owner of his property, is the case of a defendant who intends to make a temporary use of the property and then by his own act to return the property to its owner. Between these two extremes can lie various situations in which the legal characterization of the wrongdoer's intention, as assessed by the criterion of whether it is a specific intent to deprive permanently the owner of his property, will be more or less clear and raise legal problems of varying difficulty.

In these intermediate situations a general guiding principle may be developed through recognition that a "taking" of property is *by definition* "temporary" only if the possession, or control, effected by the taking is relinquished. Hence, measured by the correct criterion of the impact upon the interests of the owner, the wrongdoer's . . . [intention to steal] is fully explored for its true legal significance only if the investigation of the wrongdoer's state of mind extends beyond his anticipated *retention* of possession and includes an inquiry into his contemplated manner of *relinquishing* possession, or control, of the property wrongfully taken.

On this approach, it has been held that when a defendant takes the tools of another person with intent to use them temporarily and then to leave them wherever it may be that he finishes with his work, the fact-finder is justified in the conclusion that defendant had specific intent to deprive the owner permanently of his property. . . .

Similarly, it has been decided that a defendant who wrongfully takes the property of another intending to use it for a short time and then to relinquish possession, or control, in a manner leaving to chance whether the owner recovers his property is correctly held specifically to intend that the owner be deprived permanently of his property.

The rationale underlying these decisions is that to negate, as a matter of law, the existence of specific intent to deprive permanently the owner of his property, a wrongful taker of the property of another must have in mind not only that his retention of possession, or control, will be "temporary" but also that when he will relinquish the possession, or control, he will do it in some manner (whatever, particularly, it will be) he regards as having affirmative tendency toward getting the property returned to its owner. In the absence of such thinking by the defendant, his state of mind is fairly characterized as *indifference* should the owner *never* recover his property; and such indifference by a wrongdoer who is the moving force separating an owner from his property is appropriately regarded as his "willingness" that the owner *never* regain his property. In this sense, the wrongdoer may appropriately be held to entertain specific intent that the deprivation to the owner be permanent. . . .

On this basis, the evidence in the present case clearly presented a jury question as to defendant's specific intent. Although defendant may have stated to the owner, Prout, that defendant

> "would take care of . . . [the automobile] and see [that] . . . [Prout] got it back as soon as possible," defendant himself testified that "[i]n my mind it was just to get out of the area. . . . Just get out of the area and leave the car and get under cover somewhere."

This idea to "leave the car" and "get under cover somewhere" existed in defendant's mind as part of an uncertainty about where it would happen. Because defendant was sort of desperate during the whole day, he had not "really formulated any plans about destination."

Such testimony of defendant, together with other evidence that defendant had already utterly abandoned another vehicle (the station wagon) in desperation, plainly warranted a jury conclusion that defendant's facilely uttered statements to Prout were empty words, and it was defendant's true state of mind to use Prout's

Chevelle and abandon it in whatever manner might happen to meet the circumstantial exigencies of defendant's predicament—without defendant's having any thought that the relinquishment of the possession was to be in a manner having some affirmative tendency to help in the owner's recovery of his property. On this finding the jury was warranted in a conclusion that defendant was indifferent should the owner, Prout, *never* have back his automobile and, therefore, had specific intent that the owner be deprived permanently of his property.

Appeal denied.

CASE QUESTION

What could Gordon have done when he abandoned the Chevelle to avoid legal responsibility for having specific intent to deprive Prout permanently of his vehicle?

AUTHOR'S COMMENTARY

Proving the existence of criminal intent might not, initially, seem to be a difficult hurdle for the prosecution to overcome. But few alleged criminal actors verbalize why they do what they do. Furthermore, because defendants are constitutionally entitled to the privilege against self-incrimination, they are entitled to withhold their knowledge of the facts from the jury or judge at trial. To somewhat offset this benefit to defendants, the law permits the prosecution to inferentially prove a defendant's intent from proof of his or her deeds. Prosecutors often rely on the permissive presumption that a person intends the natural and probable consequences of her/his deliberate acts when establishing the government's case in chief and when arguing to the jury at the end of the trial. We will soon learn more about the constitutional limitations on this presumption in the upcoming case of *Sandstrom v. Montana*.

The Doctrine of Transferred Intent

The common law concept of *mens rea* includes more than general and specific intent, the two categories of criminal intent that we have studied to this point. *Mens rea* also exists where the facts show that the accused actually harmed someone other than the person he intended to injure. Under these circumstances the law *imputes* (treats the accused as having) criminal intent to the defendant. The prosecution's proof that the defendant had *mens rea* to injure the intended victim will transfer and merge with the defendant's *actus reus* against the unintended victim and establish culpability.

The defendants in the following case were convicted of murder based on the doctrine of **transferred intent**.

PEOPLE v. SCOTT

927 P.2d 288
Supreme Court of California
December 19, 1996

AUTHOR'S INTRODUCTION

The defendants in the Scott case, Damien Scott and Derrick Brown, fired an automatic weapon into a public park at an intended target. Their shots missed their mark and instead struck an unintended victim who was merely a bystander in the park.

EXCERPT FROM THE CASE

Justice BROWN:

A jury convicted defendants Damien Scott and Derrick Brown of various crimes for their part in a drive-by shooting which resulted in the death of one person and injury to several others. We must decide in this case whether the doctrine of transferred intent may be used to assign criminal liability to a defendant who kills an unintended victim when the defendant is also prosecuted for the attempted murder of an intended victim.

Under the classic formulation of California's common law doctrine of transferred intent, a defendant who shoots with the intent to kill a certain person and hits a bystander instead is subject to the same criminal liability that would have been imposed had "the fatal blow reached the person for whom intended." . . . In such a factual setting, the defendant is deemed as culpable as if he had accomplished what he set out to do.

Here, it was established at trial that defendants fired an automatic weapon into a public park in an attempt to kill a certain individual, and fatally shot a bystander instead. The case presents the type of factual setting in which courts have uniformly approved reliance on the transferred intent doctrine as the basis of determining a defendant's criminal liability for the death of an unintended victim. Consistent with a line of decisions beginning . . . nearly a century ago, we conclude that the jury in this case was properly instructed on a transferred intent theory of liability for first degree murder.

Moreover, defendants' exposure to a murder conviction based on a transferred intent theory of liability was proper regardless of the fact they were also charged with attempted murder of the intended victim. Contrary to what its name implies, the transferred intent doctrine does not refer to any actual intent that is "used up" once it has been employed to convict a defendant of a specific intent crime against an intended victim. Rather, the doctrine of transferred intent connotes a policy. As applied here, the transferred intent doctrine is but another way of saying that a defendant who shoots with an intent to kill but misses and hits a bystander instead should be punished for a crime of the same seriousness as the one he tried to commit against his intended victim.

In this case, defendants shot at an intended victim, missed him, and killed another person instead. In doing so, defendant committed crimes against two persons. Defendants' criminal liability for causing the death of the unintended victim may be determined on a theory of transferred intent in accordance with the classic formulation of the doctrine under California common law. Their criminal liability for shooting at the intended victim with an intent to kill is that which the law assigns.

The Court of Appeal correctly concluded that the trial court's instruction to the jury on transferred intent as it related to the charge of murder was proper. We affirm the judgment of the Court of Appeal. . . .

I. BACKGROUND

In May 1991, Calvin Hughes became the target of a family vendetta. While Hughes and Elaine Scott were romantically involved, Hughes and his sister, Eugenia Griffin, shared Scott's apartment. After the bloom faded from the romance, relations between Hughes and Scott became increasingly acrimonious and one night Hughes and Scott got into a physical altercation. Defendant Damien Scott and codefendant Derrick Brown, Scott's adult sons, came to her aid and forced Hughes and Griffin out of the apartment.

A few days later, Hughes borrowed Griffin's car and, accompanied by his friend Gary Tripp, returned to Scott's place to retrieve his personal belongings. When Scott attempted to bar his entry, Hughes forced his way into the apartment and gathered his things. On his way out, he heard Scott threaten to page her sons.

Hughes and Tripp drove to Jesse Owens Park in South Los Angeles to meet Griffin. Nathan Kelley and his teenage son, Jack Gibson, had parked nearby. As Hughes stood beside Kelley's car, talking to him through the open window, three cars entered the park. Gunfire erupted. Defendant Scott and codefendant Brown, riding in the first car, sprayed the area with bullets. Hughes took cover behind the front bumper of Kelley's car. When there was a lull in the shooting, Hughes sprinted toward the park gym. A renewed hail of gunfire followed him. A bullet hit the heel of his shoe. The shooting stopped when Hughes took cover behind the gym. The gunmen left the park.

In the aftermath, the victims discovered both Kelley's and Griffin's vehicles had been riddled with bullets; Gary Tripp had been shot in the leg and buttocks; and Jack Gibson had been killed when a bullet struck him in the head. In an amended multicount information, defendant Scott and codefendant Brown were jointly charged with the murder of Jack Gibson (Pen. Code, § 187, subd. (a); all further statutory references are to this code); attempted murder of Calvin Hughes and Gary Tripp (§§ 664, 187, subd. (a)); . . . and assault with a firearm on Calvin Hughes, Nathan Kelley, Gary Tripp, and Eugenia Griffin. (§ 245, subd. (a)(2).) As to each count, the information Page 548 alleged defendants personally used a firearm within the meaning of section 12022.5, subdivision (a)(1). It was further alleged, as to the murder and attempted murder counts, that defendants were armed with a firearm within the meaning of section 12022, subdivision (a)(1).

At a second trial following mistrial due to a deadlocked jury, the prosecutor sought to establish that Jack Gibson was the unintended victim of defendants' premeditated and deliberate intent to kill Calvin Hughes. At the prosecution's request, the trial court instructed the jury on transferred intent using a modified version of CALJIC No. 8.65. The court stated as follows: "As it relates to the charge of murder, where one attempts to kill a certain person, but by mistake or inadvertence kills a different person, the crime, if any, so committed is the same as though the person originally intended to be killed, had been killed." The jury was also instructed on second degree express malice and implied malice murder.

The jury convicted both defendants of second degree murder, two counts of attempted murder, and two counts of assault with a firearm. It found true all of the firearm allegations. The jury acquitted defendants of two counts of assault with a firearm that had been charged in the alternative to the counts of attempted murder.

Defendants appealed their convictions and, in a published decision, the Court of Appeal modified and affirmed the judgments of conviction. In relevant part, the Court of Appeal rejected defendants' argument that a transferred intent instruction only applies when the prosecution elects to charge the defendant with first degree murder of the unintended victim, and not also with attempted murder of the intended victim.

We granted defendant Scott's petition for review.

The jury convicted defendants of second degree murder for fatally shooting the unintended victim. It cannot be determined from the verdicts, however, whether the jury relied on the transferred intent instruction to convict defendants of second degree murder on an express malice theory, or whether it reached that verdict through a finding of implied malice. Consequently, it is necessary to decide whether a transferred intent instruction was properly given in this case.

II. DISCUSSION

The common law doctrine of transferred intent was applied in England as early as the 16th century. (See *The Queen* v. *Saunders & Archer* (1576) 75 Page 549 Eng. Rep. 706, 708 ["And when death followed from his act, although it happened in another person than her whose death he directly meditated, yet it shall be murder in him. . . ."].) The doctrine became part of the common law in many American jurisdictions, including that of California, and is typically invoked in the criminal law context when assigning criminal liability to a defendant who attempts to kill one person but accidentally kills another instead. . . . Under such circumstances, the accused is deemed as culpable, and society is harmed as much, as if the defendant had accomplished what he had initially intended, and justice is achieved by punishing the defendant for a crime of the same seriousness as the one he tried to commit against his intended victim. . . .

Under the classic formulation of the common law doctrine of transferred intent, the defendant's guilt is thus "exactly what it would have been had the blow fallen upon the intended victim instead of the bystander." . . . [indictment should be drawn as though decedent was person at whom shot was fired]; see also 4 Blackstone, Commentaries 201.) . . .

Here, the evidence adduced at trial indicates that defendants shot at an intended victim, missed him, and killed another person instead. . . . [W]e conclude that in light of this evidence, the trial court properly instructed the jury . . . that "[w]hen one attempts to kill a certain person, but by mistake or inadvertence kills a different person, the crime, if any, so committed is the same as though the person originally intended to be killed, had been killed."

Nor is application of the transferred intent doctrine under these circumstances foreclosed by the prosecutor having charged defendants with attempted murder of the intended victim. Contrary to what its name implies, the transferred intent doctrine does not refer to any actual intent that is capable of being "used up" once it is employed to convict a defendant of a specific intent crime against the intended victim. . . .

The legal fiction of transferring a defendant's intent helps illustrate why, as a theoretical matter, a defendant can be convicted of murder when she did not intend to kill the person actually killed. The transferred intent doctrine does not, however, denote an actual "transfer" of "intent" from the intended victim to the unintended victim. . . . Rather, as applied here, it connotes a policy—that a defendant who shoots at an intended victim with intent to kill but misses and hits a bystander instead should be subject to the same criminal liability that would have been imposed had he hit his intended mark. . . . It is the policy underlying the doctrine, rather than its literal meaning, that compels the conclusion that a transferred intent instruction was properly given in this case.

Conversely, reliance on a transferred intent theory of liability for the first degree murder of the unintended victim did not prevent the prosecutor from also charging defendants with attempted murder of the intended victim. As previously recounted, defendants shot at an intended victim, missed him, and killed another individual instead. In their attempt to kill the intended victim, defendants committed crimes against two persons. They may be held accountable for the death of the unintended victim on a theory of transferred intent. Their criminal liability for attempting to kill the intended victim is that which the law assigns, here, in accordance with the attempted murder statute. . . .

III. DISPOSITION

The judgment of the Court of Appeal affirming the judgments of conviction is affirmed. . . .

CASE QUESTIONS

1. What is the judicial policy underlying the doctrine of transferred intent?

2. Why did the Court rule that the defendants could also be charged with attempting to murder the intended victim in this case?

AUTHOR'S COMMENTARY

The doctrine of transferred intent does not apply unless the intended and unintended outcomes are similar. Assume, for example, a criminal actor fires a rifle at person A, purposely trying to kill A. Assume further that the shot misses A and hits and knocks a flower pot off a balcony which strikes person B in the head, causing B's death. The outcomes in the two cases are too dissimilar for application of the doctrine of transferred intent. The *Scott* defendants, however, meant to shoot one individual and ended up shooting a bystander. The intended and unintended outcomes were the same and the transferred intent doctrine properly applied.

The Court in *Scott* made reference to the sixteenth-century English case which first invoked the concept of transferred intent, *Queen v. Saunders & Archer*, but chose not to summarize the facts of that early case. This void was filled by an Arizona court in *State v. Johnson.*, 205 Ariz. 413 (App. 2003):

> BROWN, J.
>
> ¶ 12 Transferred Intent . . .
>
> The origin of the doctrine of transferred intent has been traced to the medieval criminal law of England. . . . *The Queen v. Saunders & Archer*, 2 Plowd. 473, 474, 75 Eng. Rptr. 706, 707 (1576), defendant John Saunders intended to poison his wife so he could marry another woman. He placed poison in an apple and gave it to her. Sadly, she gave part of it to their young daughter who ate it and died. . . . Saunders did not intend to kill his daughter, but he was nonetheless guilty of her murder. . . . The court "transferred" his intent to kill his wife to the death of his daughter. . . . The doctrine of transferred intent became part of the common law in many American jurisdictions and now exists in various forms in both criminal and tort law. . . .

The Model Penal Code Approach

In the earlier excerpt from the *Morissette* case, Supreme Court Justice Robert Jackson pointed out some of the various terms that judges and legislatures have resorted to as they sought to clarify the concept of *mens rea* and define discrete categories of mental culpability. The general frustration with the common law's "inconsistencies, ambiguities, and backward-looking tendencies" spurred interest in an alternative approach. The Model Penal Code's alternative approach to criminal intent is included in this text because it has been widely accepted throughout the nation.

The Model Penal Code's rational and structured approach was designed to cure one of the more troublesome characteristics of the common law—its reliance on general and specific intent. The MPC replaces the common law's archaic terminology, ancient and often ambiguous historical roots, and inconsistent applications with four mental states: **purposely**, **knowingly**, **recklessly**, and **negligently** (see Figure 3.10).

A person who has a conscious desire to produce a prohibited result or harm can be said to have acted *purposely*. For example, a person acts purposely when he or she strikes another in order to injure the other person.

A person who is aware that a prohibited result or harm is very likely to occur but does not consciously intend the specific outcome that occurs can be said to have acted *knowingly*. For example, if a person sets fire to a house, the person may hope that the people inside escape injury and that only the building will be destroyed yet also be aware that it is likely the people inside will be seriously injured or killed.

A person who *consciously disregards the welfare of others* and creates a significant and unjustifiable risk of harm can be said to have acted *recklessly*. The risk in such cases has to be one that would not have been consciously undertaken or created by a law-abiding person. Assume, for example, that a driver consciously takes her eyes off the road to look after her crying baby and is aware in a general sense that this conduct would potentially jeopardize the safety of other drivers and pedestrians who might, or might not, be approaching her vehicle. This driver, by choosing to care for her child, would be demonstrating her willingness to put others at risk of death or serious injury and can be said to have acted recklessly. Had she been aware that a particular pedestrian or driver was likely to be hit by her vehicle if she were to tend to the baby, she would have acted knowingly.

A driver who is unaware that his conduct poses a substantial and unjustifiable risk to another person's welfare can be said to have acted *negligently*—if the risk taken is *objectively* unreasonable under the circumstances. This means that reasonableness will be determined from the perspective of what *a hypothetical reasonable person* would have done under the circumstances. Assume, for example, that a driver takes her eyes off the road to look after her crying baby under circumstances where a reasonable person would have safely stopped the vehicle before attending to the child. Such a driver would be acting negligently if she were unaware that her conduct had created a substantial and unjustifiable risk of harm to others.

Figure 3.10. Model Penal Code: Kinds of Culpability

Section 2.02 General Requirements of Culpability

* * *

(2) *Kinds of Culpability Defined.*

(a) *Purposely.*

A person acts purposely with respect to a material element of an offense when:

(I) if the element involves the nature of his conduct or a result thereof, it is his conscious object to engage in conduct of that nature or to cause such a result; and

(II) if the element involves the attendant circumstances, he is aware of the existence of such circumstances or he believes or hopes that they exist.

(b) *Knowingly.*

A person acts knowingly with respect to a material element of an offense when:

(I) if the element involves the nature of his conduct or the attendant circumstances, he is aware that his conduct is of that nature or that such circumstances exist; and

(II) if the element involves a result of his conduct, he is aware that it is practically certain that his conduct will cause such a result.

(c) *Recklessly.*

A person acts recklessly with respect to a material element of an offense when he consciously disregards a substantial and unjustifiable risk that the material element exists or will result from his conduct. The risk must be of such a nature and degree that, considering the nature and purpose of the actor's conduct and the circumstances known to him, its disregard involves a gross deviation from the standard of conduct that a law-abiding person would observe in the actor's situation.

(d) *Negligently.*

A person acts negligently with respect to a material element of an offense when he should be aware of a substantial and unjustifiable risk that the material element exists or will result from his conduct. The risk must be of such a nature and degree that the actor's failure to perceive it, considering the nature and purpose of his conduct and the circumstances known to him, involves a gross deviation from the standard of care that a reasonable person would observe in the actor's situation.

FURR v. STATE

822 S.W.2d 380
Supreme Court of Arkansas
March 6, 1992

AUTHOR'S INTRODUCTION

Arkansas has statutorily adopted the Model Penal Code's approach to criminal intent in its definition of the intent element of murder in the first degree. The Arkansas Supreme Court, in the following case, had to determine whether the evidence introduced at the appellant's trial was legally sufficient to sustain a trial jury's conclusion that the appellant had acted "purposely."

The appellant in *Furr v. State*, Jesse Furr, was charged with the murder of his stepmother. Furr maintained at trial that the killing was accidental and asked the trial court to enter a directed verdict of acquittal for that reason. He was convicted of first-degree murder, however, and sentenced to life imprisonment. He appealed on the ground that the evidence introduced at trial did not rise to the level required to support a finding of purposeful conduct, required *mens rea* for the crime.

EXCERPT FROM THE CASE

Justice NEWBERN:

... Murder in the first degree is purposely causing the death of another person. ... "A person acts purposely with respect to his conduct or a result thereof when it is his conscious object to engage in conduct of that nature or to cause such a result." Ark. Code. Ann. § 5-2-202(1) (1987). ...

Intent is seldom capable of proof by direct evidence and must usually be inferred from the circumstances surrounding the killing. ... The intent necessary for first degree murder may be inferred from the type of weapon used, the manner of its use, and the nature, extent, and location of the wounds.

The evidence with respect to Furr's purposeful mental state at the time of the crime, viewed in the light most favorable to the State, was substantial. From Dr. Malak's expert testimony that the gun used in the shooting was fired at close, or point blank, range the inference could easily be drawn that it was the purpose of the person firing to kill the victim. ... The jury was free to determine the weight to be given the expert testimony, and they could reject or accept all or any part of it they believed to be true. ...

The State also presented evidence that Furr stole some money, a truck, and two guns from his stepmother after the shooting and then fled the scene.

Furr testified he had no intent to return the money or the guns. A jury could reasonably conclude from this evidence that Furr purposely killed his stepmother for financial reasons.

Furr claimed his finger accidentally hit the trigger and the gun went off, but the trier of fact is not required to believe the testimony of any witness. This is especially true when the witness is the accused.

We find the evidence supporting the conviction to have been substantial. The record of trial has been examined for error . . . and we have found no errors prejudicial to Furr.

Affirmed.

CASE QUESTIONS

1. What was the *mens rea* required for conviction of first-degree murder in Arkansas?

2. Why did the Court conclude that the defendant's claim that the shooting was accidental should be rejected and the trial court's judgment of conviction be affirmed?

AUTHOR'S COMMENTARY

The reason that the Arkansas Supreme Court "viewed Furr's purposeful mental state at the time of the crime in the light most favorable to the State" in this case was because the defendant/appellant was convicted at his jury trial. When a convicted defendant/appellant appeals and alleges that the evidence presented at trial was legally insufficient, the court views disputed facts in favor of the prevailing party at trial. Thus the court would accept as proof Dr. Malak's testimony, the evidence of Furr's conduct after the shooting, and inferences drawn from this evidence.

Presumptions and Criminal Intent

As we saw in the earlier *actus reus* discussion, a presumption is an evidentiary device permitting a factfinder to infer proof of an element of a criminal offense (In *Ulster County Court v. Allen* the elemental fact was possession of a firearm) from proof of certain basic facts (presence in an automobile and seizure of firearms from that same vehicle). The U.S. Supreme Court's ruling in the following case changed the then prevailing practice with respect to the use of presumptions to inferentially prove criminal intent.

SANDSTROM v. MONTANA

442 U.S. 510
U.S. Supreme Court
June 18, 1979

AUTHOR'S INTRODUCTION

The defendant in the case of *Sandstrom v. Montana* admitted to doing the acts alleged by the state. His defense was that although he did commit the act which took the life of the victim (the *actus reus*), he did not act purposely or knowingly. He therefore lacked the necessary *mens rea* required for conviction of deliberate homicide. The prosecutor, relying on the commonly used presumption in criminal cases at that time, asked the judge to instruct the members of the jury that "the law presumes that a person intends the ordinary consequences of his voluntary acts." The defendant objected to such an instruction on the grounds that it would violate the Due Process Clause.

EXCERPT FROM THE CASE

Justice BRENNAN delivered the opinion of the Court.

The question presented is whether, in a case in which intent is an element of the crime charged, the jury instruction, "the law presumes that a person intends the ordinary consequences of his voluntary acts," violates the Fourteenth Amendment's requirement that the State prove every element of a criminal offense beyond a reasonable doubt. . . .

II

The threshold inquiry in ascertaining the constitutional analysis applicable to this kind of jury instruction is to determine the nature of the presumption it describes. . . . That determination requires careful attention to the words actually spoken to the jury, . . . for whether a defendant has been accorded his constitutional rights depends upon the way in which a reasonable juror could have interpreted the instruction.

[Montana] . . . argues, first, that the instruction merely described a permissive inference—that is, it allowed but did not require the jury to draw conclusions about defendant's intent from his actions—and that such inferences are constitutional. . . . These arguments need not detain us long, for even . . . [Montana] admits that "it's possible" that the jury believed they were required to apply the presumption. . . . Sandstrom's jurors were told that "[t]he law presumes that a person intends the ordinary consequences of his voluntary acts." They were not told that they had a choice, or that they might infer that conclusion; they were told only that the law presumed it. It is clear that a reasonable juror could easily have viewed such an instruction as mandatory. . . .

We do not reject the possibility that some jurors may have interpreted the challenged instruction as permissive, or, if mandatory, as requiring only that the defendant come forward with "some" evidence in rebuttal. However, . . . unless these kinds of presumptions are constitutional, the instruction cannot be adjudged valid. . . . It is the line of cases urged by petitioner, and exemplified by *In re Winship*, . . . that provides the appropriate mode of constitutional analysis for these kinds of presumptions.

In *Winship*, this Court stated:

> Lest there remain any doubt about the constitutional stature of the reasonable-doubt standard, we explicitly hold that the Due Process Clause protects the accused against conviction except upon proof beyond a reasonable doubt of every fact necessary to constitute the crime with which he is charged. . . .

. . . The petitioner here was charged with and convicted of deliberate homicide, committed purposely or knowingly. . . . It is clear that under Montana law, whether the crime was committed purposely or knowingly is a fact necessary to constitute the crime of deliberate homicide. Indeed, it was the lone element of the offense at issue in Sandstrom's trial, as he confessed to causing the death of the victim, told the jury that knowledge and purpose were the only questions he was controverting, and introduced evidence solely on those points. . . . Moreover, it is conceded that proof of defendant's "intent" would be sufficient to establish this element. Thus, the question before this Court is whether the challenged jury instruction had the effect of relieving the State of the burden of proof enunciated in *Winship* on the critical question of petitioner's state of mind. . . .

We consider first the validity of a conclusive presumption. This Court has considered such a presumption on at least two prior occasions. In *Morissette v. United States*, . . . [the Court] held:

> It follows that the trial court may not withdraw or prejudge the issue by instruction that the law raises a presumption of intent from an act. It often is tempting to cast in terms of a "presumption" a conclusion which a court thinks probable from given facts. . . . [But] [w]e think presumptive intent has no place in this case. A conclusive presumption which testimony could not overthrow would effectively eliminate intent as an ingredient of the offense. A presumption which would permit but not require the jury to assume intent from an isolated fact would prejudge a conclusion which the jury should reach of its own volition. A presumption which

would permit the jury to make an assumption which all the evidence considered together does not logically establish would give to a proven fact an artificial and fictional effect. In either case, this presumption would conflict with the overriding presumption of innocence with which the law endows the accused and which extends to every element of the crime." . . .

As in *Morissette* . . . a conclusive presumption in this case would "conflict with the overriding presumption of innocence with which the law endows the accused and which extends to every element of the crime," and would "invade [the] fact-finding function" which in a criminal case the law assigns solely to the jury. The instruction announced to David Sandstrom's jury may well have had exactly these consequences. Upon finding proof of one element of the crime (causing death), and of facts insufficient to establish the second (the voluntariness and "ordinary consequences" of defendant's action), Sandstrom's jurors could reasonably have concluded that they were directed to find against defendant on the element of intent. The State was thus not forced to prove "beyond a reasonable doubt . . . every fact necessary to constitute the crime . . . charged," . . . and defendant was deprived of his constitutional rights as explicated in *Winship*.

A presumption which, although not conclusive, had the effect of shifting the burden of persuasion to the defendant, would have suffered from similar infirmities. If Sandstrom's jury interpreted the presumption in that manner, it could have concluded that upon proof by the State of the slaying, and of additional facts not themselves establishing the element of intent, the burden was shifted to the defendant to prove that he lacked the requisite mental state.

Because David Sandstrom's jury may have interpreted the judge's instruction as constituting either a burden-shifting presumption like that in *Mullaney*, [*Mullaney v. Wilbur*, 421 U.S. 684 (1975)] or a conclusive presumption like those in *Morissette* and *United States Gypsum Co.*, [*U.S. v. U.S. Gypsum Co.*, 438 U.S. 422 (1978)] and because either interpretation would have deprived defendant of his right to the due process of law, we hold the instruction given in this case unconstitutional. . . .

IV

Accordingly, the judgment of the Supreme Court of Montana is reversed, and the case is remanded for further proceedings not inconsistent with this opinion.

It is so ordered.

CASE QUESTIONS

1. What is the fundamental difference between a "permissive" presumption and a "conclusive" presumption?

2. Why is it constitutionally impermissible in this case for a trial court to instruct the jury to conclusively presume intent?

3. What is constitutionally wrong with a burden-shifting presumption?

AUTHOR'S COMMENTARY

On remand from the U.S. Supreme Court, the case was retried, this time without the flawed instruction. David Sandstrom was convicted and sentenced to life imprisonment.

The *Sandstrom* case is much more than a precedent-setting U.S. Supreme Court decision. It is the story of a courageous and determined lawyer overcoming incredible odds. Public defender Byron Boggs, a Harvard Law School graduate, was responsible for representing indigent defendants from three scarcely populated counties in rural southwest Montana. This is why he was assigned in 1976 to represent David Sandstrom. Boggs, three years out of law school and inexperienced in criminal defense to begin with had no experience whatsoever in murder cases. Yet it was he who was assigned to defend a person accused of the most serious type of crime—capital murder. Attorney Boggs had kept current with relevant federal and state appellate court decisions. He was familiar with the U.S. Supreme Court's decisions in *In re Winship* (1970) and *Mullaney v. Wilbur* (1975). He was also aware that objections to conclusive presumptions relating to proof of *mens rea* had been raised in other jurisdictions. Boggs anticipated that such a presumption was likely to be used at trial since this presumption had been commonplace in Montana criminal trials since 1889. The fact that he had fully briefed the presumption issue prior to trial assisted him greatly in making a solid record that would be essential in the event of an appeal. Boggs objected in particular to the trial judge's fifth jury instruction, which contained the constitutionally impermissible conclusive presumption of *mens rea*. Judge Robert Boyd's response to Bogg's objection was to dismissively tell Attorney Boggs: "You can give those to the Supreme Court. The objection is overruled." Boggs took the trial court's suggestion to heart and actually took his objection to both the Montana and United States Supreme Courts. Undaunted by the Montana Supreme Court's adverse ruling in his initial appeal, Boggs pressed on. Amazingly, the U.S. Supreme Court granted his petition for certiorari, and Boggs then personally argued the case before the U.S. Supreme Court. Unquestionably, it was highly improbable that this young, inexperienced public defender from rural Montana trying his first murder case would win a new trial for his client in the U.S. Supreme Court. But because of Attorney Boggs' effort, competence, and perseverance, new constitutional ground was broken, and the prevailing practice in criminal trials throughout the country was changed for the better.[12]

Internet Tip

The Maryland Supreme Court, in the case of *Thornton v. State*, 919 A.2d 678 (2005), showed that *Sandstrom* can apply to bench trials as well as jury trials.

Maryland is a state which continues to follow the common law approach to criminal intent (i.e., defines *mens rea* into specific and general intent). The Court explained:

> Similar to the facts in *Sandstrom*, . . . [when] the trial judge in the present case stated that "we are called upon to be responsible for our actions," and that, if "you do something like that, the consequences are yours[;]" he, shifted the burden of proof to the defendant, by presuming that he intended the consequences of his actions. . . .

Maryland's highest court continued:

> In summary, the trial judge's mistaken conclusions of law, which modified the specific intent requirement and unconstitutionally shifted the burden of proof to Thornton, warrants our reversal of Thornton's conviction for murder in the second degree and a remand of the case for a new trial.

Interested readers will find an edited excerpt from the *Thornton* case in the Chapter 3 materials included on this textbook's website.

Concurrence

Generally speaking, for a crime to occur the *actus reus* and *mens rea* must merge. This is called concurrence. One who has engaged in prohibited conduct without criminal intent or has criminal intent but has not committed a criminal act cannot be convicted of a crime. Assume that a man is pushing through a crowd on a big city sidewalk hoping to catch a bus that is about to depart from the curb. Assume that the man bumps into a senior citizen and knocks her to the ground. If the man intended to bump the woman, then concurrence would exist. If he bumped her accidentally, although the man might be civilly liable, there would be no merger of *mens rea* and *actus reus*, and therefore no criminal act.

Strict Liability

Strict liability offenses (also called **public welfare** offenses) represent a major exception to the normal requirement that criminal liability be predicated on the existence of both a criminal act and criminal intent. In strict liability offenses the law provides for convictions of offenders without regard to the existence of, or lack of, a culpable mind. Examples of strict liability offenses include violation of laws against vehicular speeding, pure food and drug regulations, and regulations making vendors strictly liable for selling alcoholic beverages and cigarettes to minors.

The late Justice Robert Jackson explained the rationale for strict liability crimes in the following excerpt from *Morissette v. United States*:

> [Strict liability] . . . crimes . . . depend on no mental element but consist only of forbidden acts or omissions. This . . . is made clear from examination of a century-old but accelerating tendency, discernible both here and in England, to call into existence new duties and crimes which disregard any ingredient of intent. The industrial revolution multiplied the number of workmen exposed to injury from increasingly powerful and complex mechanisms, driven by freshly discovered sources of energy, requiring higher precautions by employers. Traffic of velocities, volumes and varieties unheard of came to subject the wayfarer to intolerable casualty risks if owners and drivers were not to observe new cares and uniformities of conduct. Congestion of cities and crowding of quarters called for health and welfare regulations undreamed of in simpler times. Wide distribution of goods became an instrument of wide distribution of harm when those who dispersed food, drink, drugs, and even securities, did not comply with reasonable standards of quality, integrity, disclosure and care. Such dangers have engendered increasingly numerous and detailed regulations which heighten the duties of those in control of particular industries, trades, properties or activities that affect public health, safety or welfare.
>
> While many of these duties are sanctioned by a more strict civil liability, lawmakers, whether wisely or not, have sought to make such regulations more effective by invoking criminal sanctions to be applied by the familiar technique of criminal prosecutions and convictions. This has confronted the courts with a multitude of prosecutions, based on statutes or administrative regulations, for what have been aptly called "public welfare offenses." These cases do not fit neatly into any of such accepted classifications of common-law offenses, such as those against the state, the person, property, or public morals. Many of these offenses are not in the nature of positive aggressions or invasions, with which the common law so often dealt, but are in the nature of neglect where the law requires care, or inaction where it imposes a duty. Many violations of such regulations result in no direct or immediate injury to person or

property but merely create the danger or probability of it which the law seeks to minimize. While such offenses do not threaten the security of the state in the manner of treason, they may be regarded as offenses against its authority, for their occurrence impairs the efficiency of controls deemed essential to the social order as presently constituted. In this respect, whatever the intent of the violator, the injury is the same, and the consequences are injurious or not according to fortuity. Hence, legislation applicable to such offenses, as a matter of policy, does not specify intent as a necessary element. The accused, if he does not will the violation, usually is in a position to prevent it with no more care than society might reasonably expect and no more exertion than it might reasonably exact from one who assumed his responsibilities. Also, penalties commonly are relatively small, and conviction does no grave damage to an offender's reputation. Under such considerations, courts have turned to construing statutes and regulations which make no mention of intent as dispensing with it and holding that the guilty act alone makes out the crime.

PEOPLE v. JUAN J. CORIA
985 P.2d 970
Supreme Court of California
October 28, 1999

AUTHOR'S INTRODUCTION

Juan Coria was convicted under a statute that made it an offense to manufacture methamphetamine. The case was appealed to the state supreme court because the parties disputed whether the offense required proof of *mens rea* or was a strict liability offense.

EXCERPT FROM THE CASE

Judge CHIN:

... Defendant Juan Josuel Coria was arrested after he left a clandestine laboratory which was set up for the extraction of pseudoephedrine from cold tablets, a step in the process of manufacturing methamphetamine. Defendant admitted he received $500 for helping others "wash ephedrine pills," but claimed he agreed to do so without knowing this was an illegal act. According to defendant, he initially thought he was helping to salvage "discarded or dirty" pills so they could be resold. When, during the course of the "washing," he learned from the others that it was being done to make methamphetamine, defendant became scared and left.

A jury found him not guilty of conspiring to manufacture methamphetamine . . . and not guilty of possessing pseudoephedrine with the intent to manufacture methamphetamine, but convicted him of manufacturing methamphetamine. . . .

On appeal, defendant contends the trial court erred in instructing the jury that, to be guilty of manufacturing methamphetamine . . . it was not necessary for defendant to have been aware it was methamphetamine that was being manufactured via the extraction process.

This instruction was derived from *People v. Telfer* . . . which held that manufacturing of methamphetamine is a strict liability offense, i.e., knowledge of the physical character of the substance being manufactured is not an element of the offense and, "[s]o long as the product of the defendant's activity was methamphetamine . . . the defendant is guilty, even if he did not know that methamphetamine would be that product." . . .

DISCUSSION

Section 11379.6, . . . makes it unlawful to engage in the chemical synthesis of a substance as one part of the process of manufacturing a controlled substance. . . .

At the prosecution's request and over defense counsel's objection, the trial court modified . . . [the jury instruction] to inform the jurors that "[a]wareness of the physical character of the substance being manufactured, i.e., that the product of the chemical synthesis is methamphetamine is not necessary." . . .

Defendant contends the trial court erred in giving this portion of the instruction, thereby incorrectly converting section 11379.6 into a strict liability crime. . . .

Telfer declined to extend this knowledge requirement to the crime of manufacturing a controlled substance. . . .

Telfer . . . stands for the proposition that knowledge of the character of the substance being manufactured is not an element of section 11379.6, and that lack of such knowledge is not a defense. Because a person may be guilty of manufacturing methamphetamine without achieving the end product . . . the holding of *Telfer*, applied to this case via the challenged instruction, means that defendant was guilty of violating section 11379.6 if he engaged in any step of the manufacturing process, without knowledge that he was engaging in the process of manufacturing methamphetamine, and without actually producing methamphetamine.

For reasons which follow, we reject the *Telfer* holding. . . .

Generally, [t]he existence of a *mens rea* is the rule of, rather than the exception to, the principles of Anglo-American criminal jurisprudence. . . . In other words, there must be a union of act and wrongful intent, or criminal negligence. . . . "So basic is this requirement that it is an invariable element of every crime unless excluded expressly or by necessary implication." . . . In addition, Penal Code section 26 provides that a person is incapable of committing a crime where an act is performed in ignorance or mistake of fact negating criminal intent; a crime cannot be committed by mere misfortune or accident. . . .

There is an exception to the *mens rea* requirement for certain so-called public welfare crimes. Such offenses generally are based upon the violation of statutes which are purely regulatory in nature and involve widespread injury to the public. . . . "Under many statutes enacted for the protection of the public health and safety, e.g., traffic and food and drug regulations, criminal sanctions are relied upon even if there is no wrongful intent. These offenses usually involve light penalties and no moral obloquy or damage to reputation. Although criminal sanctions are relied upon, the primary purpose of the statutes is regulation rather than punishment or correction. The offenses are not crimes in the orthodox sense, and wrongful intent is not required in the interest of enforcement." . . .

It is this public welfare exception upon which *Telfer* relied in concluding that section 11379.6 is a strict liability offense. . . .

The analogy is inapt. Section 11379.6 is more than a mere regulatory statute which imposes light penalties with no damage to reputation. . . . Manufacturing methamphetamine is a felony, which is "as bad a word as you can give to man or thing." . . .

The United States Supreme Court has emphasized that felony offenses which bear harsh punishment are not the type of "public welfare" offenses for which courts will readily dispense with the *mens rea* requirement when construing a statute. . . .

Although section 11379.6, like any other law relating to narcotics or controlled substances, undoubtedly has public health and safety features, its provisions forbid the manufacture of controlled substances for mere personal use or consumption, as well as for sale or distribution to the public. Moreover, from the standpoint of public health and safety, manufacturing controlled substances appears akin to selling those substances. Yet as previously noted, our case law holds that if the defendant is prosecuted for *possession or sale* of a controlled substance, his knowledge of the character of the substance possessed is an essential element of the offense. . . . Logically, a defendant prosecuted for manufacturing those substances should be similarly treated.

Moreover, there is a " 'prevailing trend' away from the imposition of criminal sanctions in the absence of culpability where the governing statute, by implication or otherwise, expresses no legislative intent or policy to be served by imposing strict liability." . . . For crimes which impose severe punishment, the usual presumption that a defendant must know the facts that make his conduct illegal should apply. . . .

. . . The legislative history contains no suggestion whatever that the Legislature intended to treat manufacturing of controlled substances differently than sales or possession, with respect to the requisite criminal knowledge or intent. . . .

. . . Not all acts of chemical synthesis are illegal; only the manufacture of specific controlled substances is prohibited. (§ 11379.6.) If this were not so, chemistry classes could not be taught at educational institutions. Moreover, the mere possession of pseudoephedrine is not prohibited and punishable by imprisonment absent an intent to manufacture methamphetamine. . . . In other words, because chemical synthesis ordinarily is "traditionally lawful conduct," we may infer the Legislature did not intend to eliminate a *mens rea* requirement in section 11379.6 that the accused know of the character of the substance being manufactured.

Simply stated, there is no reason in law or logic to construe section 11379.6 as a strict liability offense and thus permit the conviction of a person for manufacturing methamphetamine, a felony, for extracting pseudoephedrine from pills if the person does not know the extraction was performed for the purpose of, or as part of the process of, manufacturing methamphetamine. Merely engaging in chemical synthesis is not enough; the defendant must have knowledge of the facts which make the chemical synthesis unlawful, i.e., that methamphetamine is being manufactured. . . .

By telling the jury it did not matter if defendant lacked knowledge that methamphetamine was being manufactured, the instruction . . . both removed an element of the charged offense from the jury's consideration . . . and . . . negated his defense that he did not know what actually was going on at the residence, and that he ceased participating in the chemical synthesis and asked to leave when he learned of the true facts.

. . . That the jurors convicted defendant on count III, but found him not guilty on counts I and II, suggests the jury believed his defense but felt constrained to convict him on the charge of manufacturing methamphetamine.

Hence, the instructional error was not harmless, and defendant is entitled to a new trial on count III. . . .

We affirm the judgment of the Court of Appeal.

CASE QUESTIONS

1. What are the characteristics of what the court referred to as "public welfare crimes"?

2. Why does the court conclude that the statute in this case should be interpreted as requiring proof that the defendant knew that his conduct was contributing to the manufacture of methamphetamine?

AUTHOR'S COMMENTARY

As was seen in this case, courts are generally reluctant to dispense with the *mens rea* requirement and treat an offense as strict liability. This is especially true where an offense was classified as *mala in se* under the common law and traditionally contained a *mens rea* requirement. It is also important to note that defendants charged with strict liability offenses are barred from raising intent based defenses—this will be further addressed in Chapter 5.

Internet Tip

Interested readers will find an edited excerpt of *People v. Sean King*, 133 P.3d 636 (2006), included in the materials associated with Chapter 3 on the textbook's website. In this case, the California Supreme Court rejects the state attorney general's argument that a criminal possession of weapons statute should be classified as a strict liability offense. The court explains the theory of strict liability, and by applying the theory to the facts of the case, illustrates why this particular statute required proof of *mens rea*.

Causation

Crimes can be classified in terms of whether they target specified conduct (such as perjury, indecent exposure, forgery, armed criminal action, or reckless operation of a motor vehicle) or criminalize specified consequences of acts (outcomes) rather than the acts themselves (such as child abuse, murder, and criminal damage to property). When a crime criminalizes an outcome, the prosecution must prove beyond a reasonable doubt not only that the accused committed the *actus reus* with the specified culpable mind but also that the defendant's criminal act caused the prohibited outcome.

In a homicide case, for example, the prosecution must prove that the defendant's conduct caused death. To be convicted of a threatened battery assault, the defendant's actions must have caused the victim reasonably to have feared an impending battery. In a battery, the defendant's conduct must have caused a harmful or offensive touching. Proving **causation** generally involves establishing that the defendant was both the factual cause and the proximate cause of the harmful outcome.

Factual Causation

Criminal liability attaches only to conduct that is determined to be the factual cause of the harmful outcome. **Factual causation** is often called *but for* causation or in Latin, *sine qua non* causation—"but for the act of the defendant, the victim would not have been harmed as and when he was." If the defendant sets in motion a chain of events that eventually results in harm, the defendant may be found to be the "but for" cause of the harm. A criminal actor is generally responsible for the natural and probable consequences of his acts. A key to establishing causation is the legal concept of "proximate cause." Proof of factual causation is necessary to criminal liability, but not sufficient by itself. For criminal liability to exist, *proximate causation* (legal causation) must be proven beyond a reasonable doubt.

Proximate Causation

Proximate cause is a flexible concept. It permits factfinders to sort through various factual causes and determine which cause should be found to be the *legal cause* for the harmful consequences. For example, an accused is responsible only for the reasonably foreseeable consequences that follow from his or her acts. If the causation chain is stretched too far, the harm caused may be so remote that it would be unfair to attribute legal responsibility to the alleged criminal actor.

COMMONWEALTH v. BERGGREN
496 N.E.2d 660
Supreme Judicial Court of Massachusetts
August 26, 1986

AUTHOR'S INTRODUCTION

The appellant in *Berggren* was operating a motorcycle that was being pursued by a police officer in a marked cruiser. Berggren admitted at trial that he knew an officer was in pursuit, but he was afraid he would lose his license if apprehended so he decided not to stop. During the pursuit, Officer Michael Aselton hit his brakes prior to entering an intersection, and when the cruiser's brakes locked, it struck a tree. Aselton died as a result of this collision. The state charged Berggren with vehicular homicide by negligence. The state supreme court agreed to determine if the agreed-upon facts were legally sufficient to charge Berggren with Aselton's death.

EXCERPT FROM THE CASE

Justice LYNCH:

[T]he question [is] whether the stipulated facts would be sufficient to support a conviction of motor vehicle homicide by negligent operation. . . .

The defendant essentially contends that since he was one hundred yards ahead of the patrolman's cruiser and was unaware of the accident, his conduct cannot be viewed as directly traceable to the resulting death of the patrolman. The defendant, however, was speeding on a motorcycle at night on roads which his attorney at oral argument before this court characterized as "winding" and "narrow." He knew the patrolman was following him, but intentionally did not stop and continued on at high speed for six miles. From the fact that the defendant was "in fear of his license," it may reasonably be inferred that he was aware that he had committed at least one motor vehicle violation. Under these circumstances, the defendant's acts were hardly a remote link in the chain of events leading to the patrolman's death. . . . The officer's pursuit was certainly foreseeable, as was, tragically, the likelihood of serious injury or death to the defendant himself, to the patrolman, or to some third party. The patrolman's death resulted from the "natural and continuous sequence" of events caused by the defendant's actions. . . .

We conclude that the proper standard of causation for this offense is the standard of proximate cause. . . . We further conclude that, should the jury find the facts as stipulated in the instant case, and should the only contested element of the offense of motor vehicle homicide by negligent operation be that of causation, these facts would support a conviction. . . .

CASE QUESTIONS

1. Explain the difference between factual and legal causation based on the facts of this case.

2. Berggren claimed to have been unaware of the collision involving the officer's cruiser and the tree, and he insisted that he never intended that the officer die. Why should this defendant be criminally responsible for causing the death of the officer?

Independent, Intervening Cause

The law provides that an accused is not responsible for consequences that follow the intervention of an **independent, intervening cause**. An intervening cause is a causal force that is the product of external forces and is unrelated to the actions of the accused. An intervening cause is one that a reasonable person would not have reasonably foreseen and that changes the outcome attributable to the defendant's conduct. Where an intervening cause exists, it severs the causal chain leading back to the accused, and the accused cannot be the proximate cause of the harm.

PEOPLE v. SAAVEDRA-RODRIGUEZ
971 P.2d 223
Supreme Court of Colorado
February 11, 1999

EXCERPT FROM THE CASE

Justice MARTINEZ delivered the Opinion of the Court.

We granted *certiorari* to review the court of appeals' ruling that a defendant on trial for homicide should have been allowed to present evidence of inadequate medical treatment as the intervening cause of the victim's death. . . . The trial court determined that the defendant had not offered sufficient evidence to submit the defense to the jury. The court of appeals ordered a new trial. We hold that grossly negligent medical treatment is an intervening cause of death only if the initial wound would probably not have been fatal without the treatment. We also hold that a defendant need only offer some evidence that the medical treatment was the intervening cause of death to be entitled to submit the defense to a jury. We reverse the decision of the court of appeals because the defendant's offer of proof did not meet this standard.

I

On September 9, 1994 the defendant, Patricio Saavedra-Rodriguez, stabbed Pedro Avila in the chest. The victim was found by his roommates and brought to the hospital by ambulance. Upon arrival at North Colorado Medical Center, the victim was treated by an emergency room doctor, Dr. Claman; a surgeon, Dr. Wikholm; and several nurses. Despite treatment, the victim's condition deteriorated and he did not survive. According to the autopsy, the victim died of a stab wound that penetrated approximately four and one-half inches into the victim's chest cavity, punctured his lung, and cut a one-inch hole in his heart.

During treatment of the victim, Drs. Claman and Wikholm disagreed about the severity of the wound, the appropriate course of treatment, and whether to continue resuscitative measures. Dr. Claman subsequently filed an "incident report" with the hospital criticizing Dr. Wikholm's treatment. The hospital's internal peer review concluded that Dr. Wikholm failed to provide "aggressive trauma management."

The defendant was charged with second degree murder. Based upon the victim's medical records and interviews with hospital personnel, who were involved in the victim's care, the defendant sought to raise an intervening cause defense. The prosecution moved to prevent the defense based on its argument that, although Dr. Wikholm's care may have been substandard, it did not rise to the level of an intervening cause.

At the pretrial hearing on the prosecution's motion to prevent the defendant from presenting an intervening cause defense, the parties disputed the standard of proof required for an intervening cause defense. The prosecution argued that the defendant had the burden of proving within a reasonable degree of medical certainty that Dr. Wikholm's gross negligence caused the death. The defense argued that, in order to raise the defense, there need be only a scintilla of evidence to support an intervening cause theory.

The defense made an offer of proof as to the testimony of a number of medical practitioners. This testimony would have been that Dr. Wikholm made several errors in his diagnosis and treatment of the victim. Additional testimony would have been that Dr. Wikholm unnecessarily delayed treatment and that given proper timely treatment the patient may have had a better chance of survival. Finally, the defense would have offered testimony that the patient survivability rate after a heart wound is higher than 50 percent and in certain circumstances increases to 80 percent if afforded proper treatment.

Although the defendant offered to present testimony of doctors and nurses who were critical of Dr. Wikholm's care, he did not offer testimony that Dr. Wikholm's allegedly substandard care was the cause of the victim's death. In fact, all of the doctors would have testified that the cause of the victim's death was the stab wound inflicted by the defendant.

In a written order issued on October 19, 1995, the trial court disallowed the defendant's intervening cause defense. The court found that . . . a defendant is entitled to an intervening cause instruction only if the improper medical care is a cause "but for which death would not have occurred." According to the trial court's reasoning, the victim would have died from the stab wound had no care been rendered. Therefore, "no acts or omissions by [Dr. Wikholm] changed the course of natural effects that flowed from the stabbing of the victim." Furthermore, the trial court concluded that, despite evidence that given proper medical care the defendant would have had a better chance of survival, the treatment received by the victim did not contribute to his death, it merely failed to prevent it. Therefore, the physician's treatment did not constitute an intervening cause.

The defendant was found guilty of manslaughter . . . and the trial court entered a judgment of conviction. The court of appeals reversed the conviction and ordered a new trial. . . . The court of appeals held that . . . "once a physician undertakes a duty to treat a victim, grossly negligent delay in diagnosing and providing medical treatment can amount to an intervening cause of death if adequate timely medical treatment would have saved the victim's life." . . . The court of appeals found that the question of whether Dr. Wikholm's care amounted to gross negligence constituting an intervening cause should have gone to the jury. . . .

We agree with the trial court. We hold that improper medical treatment does not relieve the defendant of liability for the death of the victim unless the treatment is grossly negligent and death probably would not have otherwise occurred. . . .

II

... A conviction for criminal homicide requires proof beyond a reasonable doubt that death was a natural and probable consequence of the defendant's unlawful act. ... The prosecution therefore must prove that the defendant's conduct was the actual cause of death, in the sense that it began a chain of events the natural and probable consequence of which was the victim's death. However, under certain circumstances, the defendant may be relieved of liability for the death of the victim if there has been an independent intervening act. ... An independent intervening cause is an act of an independent person or entity that destroys the causal connection between the defendant's act and the victim's injury and, thereby becomes the cause of the victim's injury.

In [*People v.*] *Calvares* we adopted Wharton's rule on intervening cause:

> To warrant a conviction for homicide, the death must be the natural and probable consequence of the unlawful act, and not the result of an independent intervening cause in which the accused does not participate, and which he could not foresee. If it appears that the act of the accused was not the proximate cause of the death for which he is being prosecuted, but that another cause intervened, with which he was in no way connected, and but for which death would not have occurred, such supervening cause is a defense to the charge of homicide. ...

We explained that an intervening cause is a defense to the charge of homicide if it is unforeseeable, and a cause without which death would not have occurred. We discuss these components in turn.

For an independent intervening cause to relieve a defendant of liability it must not be reasonably foreseeable. Simple negligent medical treatment, although hopefully unusual, is sufficiently ordinary that we consider it foreseeable. "[N]egligence, unfortunately, is entirely too frequent a human conduct to be considered 'abnormal.' " ... For this reason, we have previously stated that mere negligence on the part of an attending physician does not constitute a defense. ... Therefore, one who has inflicted a wound or injury upon another is criminally responsible for the victim's death even where different or more skillful medical treatment might have saved the victim's life, or where death was immediately caused by a surgical operation rendered necessary by the wound or injury. ...

In *Calvares* we recognized that unlike simple negligence, gross negligence is sufficiently extraordinary, to be classified as unforeseeable. ... Where medical treatment is so deficient as to constitute gross negligence or intentional malpractice, such medical treatment is abnormal and not reasonably foreseeable. ...

We have established that gross negligence is unforeseeable. However, in order for the gross negligence to discharge the defendant of liability for homicide, the maltreatment must also be the cause but for which death would not have occurred. ... Grossly negligent medical treatment is the cause but for which death would not have occurred when it disrupts the natural and probable sequence of events following the defendant's act and intervenes to cause the victim's death.

We are concerned that this component, the cause but for which death would not have occurred, could be misunderstood as merely requiring an event in a sequence of events which produced death. Indeed, this appears to be the misunderstanding of the court of appeals, which stated that grossly negligent delay in diagnosing and treating could amount to an intervening cause if proper treatment would have saved the victim's life. Rather, in order for grossly negligent medical treatment to relieve the defendant of liability, it must interrupt the natural and, probable sequence of events to cause death. This interruption only occurs when death would not have been the probable and natural result without the grossly negligent medical treatment.

To determine whether grossly negligent medical treatment was the cause of death, we look to the initial trauma to the victim as well as to the nature of the improper treatment. We consider the defendant's act, the nature of the wound inflicted by the defendant, the location of the wound on the victim, the natural and probable result of the injury, and the actual result of the medical treatment. The inquiry should focus on whether the wound inflicted by the defendant is the type of wound that would generally endanger or destroy life and from which the victim would likely die if little or no treatment is provided. Accordingly, a defendant is not relieved of liability, even in the face of grossly negligent medical treatment, if the original wound would likely have been fatal without the treatment.

Conversely, if the wound inflicted upon the victim would probably not have been fatal, but the victim dies as a result of the physician's grossly negligent treatment, the physician's gross negligence is an intervening act that relieves the defendant of criminal liability for the death. . . .

We find it persuasive that other courts have also drawn distinctions based upon the seriousness of the original wound. . . . By drawing this distinction, we hold a defendant criminally liable for death that results from the original injury but relieve a defendant of criminal liability for death that results from grossly negligent medical treatment. . . .

In sum, in order to discharge a defendant of liability for homicide, an intervening act must be an unforeseeable act but for which the victim would not have died. Grossly negligent medical treatment is not foreseeable. Thus, if the treatment is grossly negligent and the wound inflicted by the defendant would not have been likely to cause death absent the medical treatment, the medical treatment constitutes an independent intervening act relieving the defendant of liability for the victim's death. . . .

Having explained the essential components of the intervening cause defense, we now consider the quantum of evidence necessary to raise this defense and determine that the defendant's offer of proof did not meet this standard. . . .

The quantum of evidence that must be offered by the defendant in order to be entitled to an instruction on a theory of defense is "a scintilla of evidence." ... Therefore, a defendant must present a scintilla of evidence, or some evidence, that grossly negligent medical treatment is the cause of death, which would not have otherwise occurred, in order to be entitled to submit the issue to the jury. The court, not the jury, must make threshold determinations of whether an affirmative defense can be supported by the evidence. ...

Here the defendant did not meet the foundational requirements necessary to present an affirmative defense. The defendant offered proof of improper medical care. He failed to offer any evidence that would show that the victim's wound was unlikely to result in death had little or no treatment been provided. Therefore, he has not offered evidence that Dr. Wikholm's medical care may have caused the victim's death. Thus, the, defendant has not offered a scintilla of evidence that the medical care constituted gross negligence absent which death would not have occurred. In order to present an intervening cause defense to the jury the defendant must present evidence that the natural chain of causation flowing from the defendant's act was broken, as where the defendant did not inflict a fatal wound and the victim died only from the effects of the subsequent act. ...

Here, the defendant offered testimony that the victim might have survived the injury had he been given immediate and proper treatment. However, he did not offer any evidence to show that the physician's treatment was the sole cause of death. Nor did he meet the lesser standard that the victim would have been likely to survive absent the medical care that was provided. Accordingly, the trial court correctly excluded evidence of deficient medical care because there was no evidence that the medical care was the cause of death.

III

In sum, improper medical treatment is an intervening cause of death only if it is grossly negligent and the initial wound would not likely have been fatal without the treatment. A defendant need only offer some evidence that the medical treatment was the intervening cause of death to be entitled to submit the defense to a jury. Accordingly, we reverse the court of appeals and remand with directions to consider any unresolved issues.

CASE QUESTIONS

1. Why did the state supreme court conclude that the physician's treatment of the defendant did not amount to an intervening cause?

2. Why, according to the state supreme court, is proof of simple medical negligence insufficient to amount to an intervening cause?

AUTHOR'S COMMENTARY

This case was really about what evidence the defendant had to introduce at trial to be entitled to have the judge instruct the jury on what is called an affirmative defense. Defendants, when raising an *affirmative defense*, are essentially saying "yes, I did the act with which I am charged, but I am not legally responsible for the crime with which I am charged because of a legally recognized justification or excuse." We study affirmative defenses at the beginning of Chapter 6.

Saavedra-Rodriguez was accused of stabbing Pedro Avila to death and was charged with second degree murder. Saavedra-Rodriguez wanted to defend against second-degree murder by raising an affirmative defense called *independent, intervening cause.* He offered to produce hospital documents and testimony from hospital staff members that would show that one of the emergency room doctors had negligently treated the victim, Pedro Avila, and he argued that this evidence would show that the causal chain that began with his admitted stabbing of Avila was severed by the doctor's inadequate treatment, and that it was the doctor who was the legal cause of Avila's death. The trial court found Saavedra-Rodriguez's offer of proof legally inadequate and refused to permit the defense. The trial court explained that the defense's proof demonstrated that the emergency room doctors had not prevented Avila's death, but did not establish that the doctor's conduct had caused the death. The appeals court reversed, believing that the defendant's evidence had met the legal threshold for raising the affirmative defense, but the Colorado Supreme Court disagreed. To raise the independent, intervening cause affirmative defense, said the supreme court, a defendant has to offer some proof that the lack of medical care caused the death. In other words, Saavedra-Rodriguez had to produce both some evidence of grossly negligent medical treatment and some evidence that the stab wound "would not have been fatal without the treatment." The trial court, said the state supreme court, correctly refused to instruct the jury on the independent, intervening cause affirmative defense.

 Chapter Summary

In Chapter 3, readers learn about the architecture of crimes. The basic principles learned apply generally to all federal and state crimes. The elements discussed in this chapter include proof of a criminal act or legal equivalent (*actus reus*), criminal intent (*mens rea*), **concurrence**, and causation. Each topic is summarized in the order addressed in the textbook.

The Criminal Act Requirement

This requirement forces government to have tangible evidence that someone should be criminally prosecuted. One cannot be punished solely for having criminal thoughts. Thoughts without more action pose no threats to other individuals or the society. And involuntary actions will not constitute a criminal act. Thus if a person with epilepsy strikes someone as a result of a convulsion, the act is involuntary and there has been no criminal act. But sometimes the law makes it a crime to have failed to act where the law provides there is a duty to act. For example, parents are required to provide their children with food, clothing, and shelter. It can be a crime to not fulfill this legal duty.

Some crimes require proof that the defendant was in possession of specified items, such as controlled substances or stolen property. In most instances the prosecution will be able to prove that the defendant had actual possession of the forbidden items. But sometimes the prosecution cannot prove actual possession but can prove "constructive possession." Possession, whether actual or constructive, can be legally defined as a criminal act.

Sometimes the law provides that if the government has proof of one or more specified facts that an unproven fact can be inferred. In this scenario the prosecution is relying on a permissive "statutory presumption." The presumption will serve as a legally permissible substitute for evidence and will help it "prove" the commission of a criminal act. Criminal defendants benefit greatly from the most widely know presumption—the presumption of innocence. Because of this presumption, the defendant does not have to present any evidence of innocence to win the case, and the prosecution has the burden of proving guilt beyond a reasonable doubt. The discussion of the criminal act concluded with a discussion of double jeopardy. Readers were reminded that it is not double jeopardy for a criminal defendant to be prosecuted by both the federal and state governments for a single criminal act. The reason goes back to the discussion of sovereignty in Chapter 1. If a single act violates both federal and state statutes, each can insist on trying the defendant. There is no constitutional double jeopardy problem because each sovereign is prosecuting the defendant once.

The Criminal Intent Requirement

Proof of a criminal act or the legal equivalent of a criminal act is not the only essential element in a criminal case. Proof of criminal intent is equally important in most but not all prosecutions (the exception is for strict liability offenses). For most crimes a criminal offender must have possessed a culpable level of criminal intent at the time the criminal act was committed. Historically, crimes in common law countries have been classified as either *mala in se* (offenses which were inherently bad) and *mala prohibita* (offenses which have been declared to be crimes by legislatures exercising the police power but which are not inherently evil). *Mala in se* offenses have traditionally required proof of criminal intent. Legislatures often require proof of criminal intent for most *mala prohibita* but sometimes require no proof of criminal intent at all (strict liability offenses).

Today there are two basic approaches to criminal law—the traditional common law approach and the increasingly popular Model Penal Code approach.

The Common Law Approach

Under the common law, criminal law crimes either required proof of "general intent" or "specific intent." General intent crimes only require proof of an intent to commit the *actus reus* specified for each offense and no additional criminal intent. Specific intent crimes require the accused to have intended to commit the *actus reus* plus an additional intent or knowledge. If the facts show that defendant A, although intending to hit B, misses and accidently hits C, the Doctrine of Transferred Intent will apply and the defendant's intent to hit B will transfer to C.

The Model Penal Code Approach

The Model Penal Code completely rejects the common law approach. It establishes four levels of culpable criminal intent ranging in order from the most culpable to the least culpable level; purposeful, knowing, reckless, and negligent. Each level is distinctly different from the other three. These distinctions between levels help legislators, lawyers, judges, and jurors better understand exactly what intent must be proven to convict an accused.

Concurrence

The prosecution must prove that a defendant possessed the level of *mens rea* called for in the statute at the time of the commission of the criminal act.

Strict Liability Offense Exception

Some *mala prohibita* offenses require no proof of *mens rea*. For these offenses, proof of the criminal act is sufficient for conviction. If a court after researching the matter is in doubt as to whether an offense requires proof of intent, it will usually determine whether the offense in question was classified as *mala in se* under the common law.

If the answer is yes, the ambiguous statute will usually be interpreted as requiring proof of intent.

Causation

Some crimes require more than proof of a criminal act—they require proof of an outcome. Sometimes it must be proved that the defendant committed a criminal act, possessed criminal intent, and caused the prohibited outcome. Prosecutors generally prove causation by establishing that the defendant was both the *factual cause* and the *proximate cause* of the harmful outcome. The prosecutor may also have to overcome a defense claim that an *independent, intervening cause* severed the causation chain linking the defendant to the outcome.

 Discussion Questions

1. Dennis and Lorie Nixon's 16-year-old daughter, Shannon, was afflicted with a medical condition known as diabetes acidosis. All three members of the Nixon family were members of the Faith Tabernacle Church, whose members rely on spiritual healing rather than medical treatment. When Shannon became ill, her parents followed their church's religious practices and relied on prayer to help their daughter. Shannon weakened, became comatose, and died. Dennis and Lorie Nixon were charged with involuntary manslaughter and endangering the welfare of a child. The Nixons responded to the charges by raising two defenses. One, the "mature minor" defense, would permit mature minors to make their own decisions about seeking medical care and thereby relieve parents of that duty. Second, the parents argued that Shannon had a fundamental privacy right under the federal and state constitutions to refuse medical care. Pennsylvania recognizes, by statute, that persons who are 18 or older, or who have graduated from high school, become pregnant, or married, are legally entitled to make their own decisions about medical treatment. Should the parents' failure to take Shannon to the hospital subject them to criminal liability if they acted in conformity with their daughter's wishes under these circumstances?

Pennsylvania v. Nixon, J-44-2000, Supreme Court of Pennsylvania (11/27/2000)

2. Feola was prosecuted and convicted of assaulting two federal officers. His defense was that he did not know that the men who were assaulted were under-cover officers. The federal statute prohibiting assaults on federal agents was silent as to whether knowledge was required for conviction. Should the statute

be interpreted so as to require that the government prove that the accused was aware that the persons he was assaulting were federal officers?

United States v. Feola, 420 U.S. 671 (1975)

3. Shaughnessy, while a passenger in an automobile, was driven onto private property, where she was stopped and charged with violating an ordinance prohibiting entry onto private property without the owner's permission. Should she be convicted on this evidence?

People v. Shaughnessy, 319 N.Y.S.2d 626 (1971)

4. A truck driver stopped his vehicle, rolled down the window, and asked a 13-year-old girl for directions. When the girl was unable to tell him the location of the street, he instructed her to get in his truck. The truck driver was convicted of attempted kidnapping. The conviction was appealed. Based on this evidence, who should win?

Commonwealth of Massachusetts v. Banfill, 597 N.E.2d 47 (1992)

5. After receiving a gunshot wound to his head, a shooting victim decided to go on a liquids-only diet and removed his feeding tube. After the man's death, the shooter was prosecuted for causing this death. The defense argued that the removal of the feeding tube constituted an independent, intervening cause. Do you agree with the defense?

People v. Velez, 602 N.Y.S.2d 758 (1993)

6. Should siblings and parents be legally obligated, either by statute or by status, to turn in other family members who they believe have committed crimes, as did David Kaczynski? Or are such decisions better left to individuals and their consciences? What are the pluses and minuses of each position from your point of view? Which position do you believe would make for better public policy?

NOTES

1. We see in later chapters that in some contexts words can become what are called verbal acts, *In re Winship*, 397 U.S. 358 (1970), which makes them part of the *actus reus*—this is especially true for the crimes of solicitation and conspiracy.
2. *Powell v. Texas*, 392 U.S. 514 (1968).
3. *Papachristou v. City of Jacksonville*, 405 U.S. 156 (1972).
4. *Powell v. Texas*, 392 U.S. 514 (1968).

5. Answers to voluntary act questions:
   (1) A person's bodily movements while experiencing an epileptic seizure, for example, are not considered voluntary for purposes of a criminal prosecution.
   (2) Again, the person who was knocked into the third individual was acting involuntarily.
   (3) A sleeping parent who rolls over and inadvertently smothers the baby is not engaging in a voluntary act.
   (4) There is no voluntary act because the teller was acting under duress. Duress is a recognized defense in which the accused admits to having engaged in the conduct alleged by the government, but claims that there were mitigating circumstances-in this scenario, the present threat of death or serious bodily injury at the hands of the armed robber.
   (5) There would be no voluntary act here because the biker could claim the defense of "necessity"—he broke into the cabin only because it was necessary under these circumstances for him to avoid being stung—it could have cost him his life.
6. Six men were charged with aggravated rape. Four defendants were convicted and two were acquitted. Three of the convicted defendants received prison sentences of 9-12 years and the fourth was sentenced to a prison term of 6-8 years. The convictions and sentences were affirmed by the Massachusetts Supreme Judicial Court, see *Commonwealth v. Vieira*, 519 N.E.2d 1320 (1988). The victim, age 25, died in a car crash in 1986. She was survived by her husband and two daughters.
7. Many of the most disturbing facts from the New Bedford case were included in Hollywood's 1988 movie, *The Accused*, in which Jodie Foster played the victim and for which Foster won an Academy Award. Statutes of this type are sometimes called "Good Samaritan Statutes." Wisconsin adopted its "Good Samaritan Statute" in 1984 in the aftermath of Big Dan's Tavern case and Washington did the same in 1987.
8. *People v. Profit*, Docket No. 228726, Michigan Court of Appeals (2002), unpublished.
9. *Leary v. United States*, 385 U.S. 6 (1969).
10. *In re Winship*, 397 U.S. 358 (1970).
11. It should be noted, however, that many states prohibit prosecutions where dual sovereignty exists and the accused has been successfully prosecuted in federal court.
12. The basic facts in this commentary relating to the *Sandstrom* case were obtained in a telephone conversation with Byron Boggs on March 16, 2009.

Complicity and Vicarious Liability

 ## Complicity

Crimes are committed by individuals acting entirely alone, as well as by people who receive assistance from others. Assistance can be provided at the preparatory stages, in the actual commission of the substantive crime, and in the aftermath of the event. After police officers have apprehended bank robbers, for example, they may discover that several people other than the actual robbers have helped the perpetrators commit the offense. These other individuals may have helped plan the robbery, procure necessary equipment, or recruit other participants with specialized skills (such as car thieves, safe crackers, forgers, and chemists). Subsequent investigation may disclose that the robbers also received assistance from colleagues who were outside the bank performing as lookouts and getaway drivers, and that still other individuals provided transportation, food, clothing, and shelter in the aftermath of the robbery.

The law provides that persons who knowingly contribute to the commission of a crime are subject to prosecution as accomplices.

Complicity Under the Common Law

Criminal liability normally attaches to persons who directly perpetrate a crime and to those who encourage and assist others to commit crimes. Under the common law, a person who personally commits the *actus reus* is classified as a **principal in the first degree**. A person who is not a perpetrator but who aids or abets the commission of a crime and is present when criminal conduct occurs is classified as a **principal in the second degree**. A person who aids or abets prior to the commission of a crime but is not present when the crime is perpetrated is classified as an **accessory before the fact**. And lastly, a person who provides assistance to a perpetrator after the commission of a crime (such as hiding the offender from authorities) is classified as an **accessory after the fact**.

PEOPLE v. NORRIS
600 N.W.2d 658
Michigan Court of Appeals
October 8, 1999

AUTHOR'S INTRODUCTION

James Norris, the appellant in this case, was alleged to have aided and abetted the commission of a mall jewelry store robbery. He was convicted of armed robbery as an accomplice (in Michigan a person who aids or abets is called "a party to the crime") because he helped to plan the crime and drove the getaway car.

EXCERPT FROM THE CASE

Judge BANDSTRA:

This case arises from a jewelry store robbery in which store employees were sprayed with a device containing military tear gas and oleoresin capsicum. The chemical spray caused the employees to suffer extreme eye pain and irritation, burning sensations on the skin and in the nose, mouth, and lungs, breathing diffi-culties, and a cornea defect in both eyes of one of the victims that was consistent with having been chemically sprayed. Several perpetrators were involved in the rob-bery in which twenty Rolex watches, valued at approximately $100,000, were taken. Numerous witnesses observed the robbery, and the perpetrators were immediately apprehended following the robbery. The prosecutor alleged that although defendant was not present during the robbery, he participated in the planning and acted as the getaway driver.

Following a jury trial, defendant was convicted of armed robbery. . . . He now appeals. . . .

Defendant argues that there was insufficient evidence to support his armed robbery conviction because the prosecutor failed to prove that the chemical device containing tear gas and oleoresin capsicum that an accomplice used to spray store employees constituted a "dangerous weapon" within the meaning of the armed robbery statute. . . .

The armed robbery statute does not define the term "dangerous weapon." . . . However, "[w]hether an object is a dangerous weapon depends upon the object itself and how it is use[d]." . . . Further, a dangerous weapon has been described as either (1) a weapon designed to be dangerous and capable of causing death or serious injury (e.g., a loaded gun); or (2) any other object capable of causing death or serious injury that the defendant used as a weapon (e.g., a screwdriver used as a knife). . . . Whether an object is a dangerous weapon under the circum-stances of the case is a question for the factfinder. . . .

In the present case, the victims testified that they experienced extreme eye pain and burning sensations that required two of them to seek medical treatment. William Henry testified that he experienced severe pain on his face and in his left eye and had to be taken to the hospital to have his eyes flushed. He further testified that as a result of being sprayed, he needs glasses to read and has blurred vision in his left eye. Further, Henry's ophthalmologist testified that, although not permanent, Henry had a cornea defect in both eyes that was consistent with having been chemically sprayed. Dorothy Fox, who was also taken to the hospital to have her eyes flushed, testified that the spray permeated her clothing and caused a severe burning sensation on her skin and in her eyes, nose, and mouth that lasted, "several hours, not even until the morning hours until it started going away. . . ." The spray also penetrated and burned her lungs, making it difficult to breathe. Kathleen Sharbo testified that, although she did not go to the hospital after the incident, she was unable to wear her contacts for a month because the spray irritated her eyes. Under the facts of this case, we conclude that the evidence . . . was sufficient to permit a reasonable jury to conclude that the tear gas mixture was a dangerous weapon within the meaning of the armed robbery statute. . . .

Defendant also argues that the evidence was insufficient to support his armed robbery conviction because the facts failed to prove that he was an active participant. We disagree. One who procures, counsels, aids, or abets in the commission of an offense may be convicted and punished as if he committed the offense directly. . . . To establish that a defendant aided and abetted a crime, the prosecutor must prove that (1) the crime charged was committed by the defendant or some other person, (2) the defendant performed acts or gave encouragement that assisted the principal in committing the crime, and (3) the defendant intended the commission of the crime or knew the principal intended its commission at the time he gave aid or encouragement. . . . Mere presence, even with knowledge that an offense is about to be committed or is being committed, is insufficient to establish that a defendant aided or assisted in the commission of the crime. . . .

Here, a store employee testified that, about an hour before the robbery occurred, defendant entered the store with a group of other men and then left, but that she did not see him a second time when the store was robbed. One witness testified that the three black males she saw rob the store subsequently ran toward a white car parked just outside the mall, where a fourth black male was waiting inside. Other witnesses testified that they saw the three men enter the white car already occupied by a fourth black male and drive away. Officers Daly and Turner testified that they followed the white car from the mall parking lot to a lot across the street where the four occupants jumped out of the car and ran. They pursued the two suspects who had exited the driver's side of the vehicle. Turner testified that when the two suspects ran in different directions, he chased and eventually apprehended the suspect whom he identified as defendant. . . . In addition, following the robbery, traces of an ultraviolet dye like that contained in the chemical spray used at the robbery were found on defendant's shirt.

Jermaine Johnson, who testified for the prosecution pursuant to a plea agreement, stated that he and five others, including defendant, came from Ohio to rob the jewelry store. He testified that when they arrived, they went to the jewelry store they were going to rob and then went to a restaurant where they, including defendant, discussed their plans before returning to commit the robbery. After the robbery, he and three others drove away in a white car that one of them had stolen to use as a getaway car. . . .

[W]e conclude that there was sufficient evidence to permit the jury to infer that defendant actively participated in planning the robbery and that he drove the getaway vehicle . . . (factors to consider in determining aider and abettor's state of mind include close association between the defendant and the principal, the defendant's participation in planning or executing the crime, and evidence of flight after the crime); . . . (the defendant's conviction as an aider and abettor of an armed robbery was supported by eyewitness testimony identifying the defendant as the driver of the getaway car). . . . There was sufficient evidence to conclude that defendant committed armed robbery beyond a reasonable doubt.

We affirm.

CASE QUESTIONS

1. What was the defendant's argument to the Michigan Court of Appeals regarding his conviction for armed robbery?

2. What, according to the court, must the prosecution prove to establish the *actus reus* for the crime of aiding and abetting?

3. What did the court conclude and why?

AUTHOR'S COMMENTARY

One of the more difficult questions in aiding and abetting cases is determining when an individual has crossed the line separating criminal from noncriminal conduct. Is a patron who sits at a bar and quietly watches other patrons participate in a gang rape in another part of the bar an accessory before the fact? Is the patron, although not personally assaulting the victim, aiding and abetting the rapists if he claps, whistles, and chants "Go, go, go"?

It can be argued that an otherwise passive observer who does nothing to affirmatively indicate encouragement or support for the attackers is not an accessory. The converse, however, can also be argued. If a "mere" observer remains at the scene and does nothing to disassociate himself/herself from what is transpiring, isn't the observer's passive presence and unwillingness to assist the victim or call police a source of encouragement to the rapists? If the observer had even loudly slammed the door on the way out of the bar the attackers might have assumed that the police were being called and abandoned their attacks. But if aiding and abetting is defined to include observing patrons who clap, whistle, and chant, but who do not personally assault the victim, such patrons may in some jurisdictions be subject to prosecution to the same extent as those who actually attacked the victim.

Proving Complicity

The prosecution establishes a defendant's liability as an accomplice by first proving the elements of the underlying offense and then proving that the defendant assisted the perpetrator(s). In such cases, the acts of the perpetrators are imputed to (made the legal responsibility of) the accomplices as long as the accomplice intended the commission of the crime, or knew that the perpetrator(s) intended its commission at the time the aid or encouragement was given.

States possess broad powers to determine what conduct will be deemed criminal. Such decisions can involve difficult policy choices. For example, should

Figure 4.1. New Mexico Harboring Statute

> **30-22-4. Harboring or aiding a felon.**
>
> Harboring or aiding a felon consists of any person, not standing in the relation of husband or wife, parent or grandparent, child or grandchild, brother or sister by consanguinity or affinity, who knowingly conceals any offender or gives such offender any other aid, knowing that he has committed a felony, with the intent that he escape or avoid arrest, trial, conviction or punishment.
>
> In a prosecution under this section it shall not be necessary to aver, nor on the trial to prove, that the principal felon has been either arrested, prosecuted or tried.
>
> Whoever commits harboring or aiding a felon is guilty of a fourth degree felony.

uninvolved family members be subject to arrest if they fail to notify the police that a "wanted" family member is hiding in the family home to avoid arrest? The legislature can decide to make it a crime to withhold such information from authorities or to answer untruthfully when asked by authorities if the wanted person is present in the home. An alternative approach would be for the state to leave this moral question to the family members involved and their consciences.

In Figure 4.1 you see New Mexico's answer to the question.

STATE v. MOBBLEY
650 P.2d 841
Court of Appeals of New Mexico
August 3, 1982

AUTHOR'S INTRODUCTION

In the following case, New Mexico's harboring statute is applied to some very challenging facts. The case also illustrates how a policy that seems to be relatively unambiguous at first reading can become much less clear when applied to particular facts.

EXCERPT FROM THE MAJORITY OPINION

Judge Wood:

The criminal information charged that defendant did "knowingly aid Andrew Needham knowing that he had committed a felony with the intent that he escape arrest, trial, conviction and punishment . . . ." The issue is whether the agreed upon facts are such that defendant may not be prosecuted for the offense of aiding a felon.

Defendant is married to Ricky Mobbley. Police officers went to a house and contacted defendant; they advised defendant that felony warrants had been issued for Ricky Mobbley and Andrew Needham. The officers asked defendant if "both were there." Defendant denied that the men were there, although she knew that both men were in the house. Hearing noises, the officers entered the house and discovered both men. Defendant could not have revealed Needham without also revealing her husband. The criminal charge was based on the failure to reveal Needham. . . .

The power to define crimes is a legislative function. . . . Section 30-22-4, . . . applies to "any person, not standing in the relation of husband or wife, parent or grandparent, child or grandchild, brother or sister by consanguinity or affinity." There is no claim that any of the exempted relationships applies as between defendant and Needham. As enacted by the Legislature, Section 30-22-4, . . . applies to the agreed facts.

Defendant contends that such a result is contrary to legislative intent because statutes must be interpreted in accord with common sense and reason, and must be interpreted so as not to render the statute's application absurd or unreasonable. . . . We give two answers to this contention.

First, where the meaning of the statutory language is plain, and where the words used by the Legislature are free from ambiguity, there is no basis for interpreting the statute. . . . Section 30-22-4, *supra*, applies to "any person" not within the relationship exempted by the statute. Defendant is such a person.

Second, if we assume that the statute should be interpreted, our holding that Section 30-22-4, *supra*, applies to the agreed facts accords with legislative intent. Statutes proscribing harboring or aiding a felon grew out of the common law of accessories after the fact. . . .

. . . At common law, only one class was excused from liability for being accessories after the fact. Wives did not become accessories by aiding their husbands. No other relationship, including that, of husband to wife, would suffice. Today, close to half of the states have broadened the exemption to cover other close relatives. . . . This broadening of the excemption [*sic*] may be justified on the ground that it is unrealistic to expect persons to be deterred from giving aid to their close *relations*. . . .

In 1875 New Mexico adopted the common law. . . . The present statute . . . was a part of the Criminal Code enacted in 1963. . . .

Limiting the exemptions . . . to relatives named in that statute accords with the legislative intent as shown by legislative history. In light of the limited exemption at common law, and legislation limited to relatives, it is not absurd and not unreasonable to hold that if defendant aided Needham, Section 30-22-4, *supra*, applies to that aid.

Except for one fact, there would have been no dispute as to the applicability of Section 30-22-4, *supra*. That one fact is that defendant could not have revealed

Needham without also revealing her husband. The statute does not exempt a defendant from prosecution when this fact situation arises; to judicially declare such an additional exemption would be to improperly add words to the statute. . . . Also, such a judicial declaration would be contrary to the rationale for this type of statute; it is unrealistic to expect persons to be deterred from giving aid to their close relations. . . .

We recognize that defendant was placed in a dilemma; if she answered truthfully she revealed the presence of her husband; if she lied she took the chance of being prosecuted. . . .

Defendant contends we should follow two Arkansas decisions which support her position. . . . We decline to do so. Our duty is to apply the New Mexico statute, not the Arkansas law of accomplices.

The order of the trial court, which dismissed the information, is reversed. The cause is remanded with instructions to reinstate the case on the trial court's docket.

It is so ordered.

EXCERPT FROM THE DISSENTING OPINION

Judge LOPEZ:

I respectfully dissent. The majority holds that the defendant can be charged with the offense of harboring or aiding Andrew Needham . . . because she does not qualify under any of the exemptions listed in the statute with respect to Needham. It arrives at this holding in spite of the fact that the defendant could not have revealed the presence of Needham in the house without also revealing the presence of her husband. This holding negates the legislative intent of the statute to exempt a wife from being forced to turn in her husband. Under the majority ruling, the defendant would have had to turn in Needham to escape being charged . . . which would have been tantamount to turning in her husband.

Whether the rationale underlying the legislative exemption is a recognition "that it is unrealistic to expect persons to be deterred from giving aid to their close relations, . . . or an acknowledgment of human frailty, . . . that rationale is ignored by requiring a wife to turn in her husband if he is with another suspect." Such a result requires a proverbial splitting of analytic hairs by attributing the defendant's action, in denying that Needham was at the house, to an intent to aid Needham rather than her husband. . . .

The practical effect of the majority opinion, which requires a wife to turn in her husband if he is with a co-suspect, is to deny the wife's exemption in Section 30-22-4. The reasons for refusing to force a wife to inform on her husband are the same whether or not he is alone. The statute should not be construed so narrowly as to frustrate the legislative intent to exempt a wife from turning in her husband. . . . Although the court should not add to the provisions of a statute, it may do so to prevent an unreasonable result. . . .

Given the wife's exemption from turning in her husband contained in Section 30-22-4, it would be unreasonable to require her to do just that by revealing Needham.

For the foregoing reasons, I cannot agree that the defendant in this case can be charged under Section 30-22-4 for refusing to tell the police that Needham was in the house. I would affirm the action of the trial court in dismissing the information against the defendant.

CASE QUESTIONS

1. Had you been one of the judges deciding this case, how would you have ruled and how did you logically arrive at your conclusion?

2. Do you agree or disagree with the legislative premise underlying statues such as the New Mexico statute at issue in this case? In your opinion, is the list of statutorily exempted statuses too broad, too narrow, or just about right?

 Internet Tip

State of Utah v. Ashlee M. Briggs is an accomplice liability case recently decided by the Utah Supreme Court. The court's opinion includes interesting facts and a nice explanation of the elements of accomplice liability. This case is included in the supplemental materials for this chapter that can be found online at the textbook's website. You can also find this case online via Loislaw. Search for *State of Utah v. Ashlee M. Briggs*, 197 P.3d 628 (2008).

AUTHOR'S COMMENTARY

Modern statutes have legislatively consolidated the common law categories of principles in the first and second degree and accessories before the fact into one statute so that all aiders and abettors prior to the commission of a crime can be punished as principals.

Today, accomplices after the fact are often treated more leniently than was the case under the common law. They are often prosecuted for **obstructing justice** or for hindering arrest and not convicted of the offense committed by the perpetrator. Oregon's statute (see Figure 4.2) reflects this policy.

Figure 4.2. Oregon Hindering Arrest Statute (Oregon Revised Statutes 162.325)

> ORS 162.325 provides, in part:
>   (1) A person commits the crime of hindering prosecution if, with intent to hinder the apprehension, prosecution, conviction or punishment of a person who has committed a crime punishable as a felony, . . . the person: . . .
>   (c) Provides or aids in providing such person with money, transportation, weapon, disguise or other means of avoiding discovery or apprehension; . . .
>   (2) Hindering prosecution is a Class C felony.

OREGON v. ALLRED
CA A103666
Court of Appeals of Oregon
January 26, 2000

AUTHOR'S INTRODUCTION

The defendant in the following case was charged with violating Oregon's hindering arrest statute. This statute carries a maximum sentence of five years incarceration upon conviction (the penalty for a Class C felony conviction in Oregon). Under the common law approach, however, an accessory after the fact in a murder case could have been convicted and sentenced as a murderer.

EXCERPT FROM THE CASE

Judge LINDER:

Defendant appeals his sentence for hindering prosecution. The sole issue on appeal is whether the trial court erred in imposing . . . sentence. We conclude that the trial court erroneously interpreted . . . the particular sentencing guideline. . . . [C]onsequently, we vacate the sentence for hindering prosecution and remand for resentencing.

Defendant pleaded guilty in connection with hindering the prosecution of Jesse Fanus, an individual who was suspected of murder. Defendant is a long-time friend of Fanus's father and has known Fanus since he was an infant. Fanus was a fugitive from the police and a suspect in the murder of retired Marine Corps General Marion Carl and in the shooting of Carl's wife in the course of a home invasion robbery. On June 29, 1998, defendant was driving through Roseburg and by chance saw Fanus on the street at a time that Fanus was in the vicinity of police officers, but apparently was not noticed by them. Defendant stopped his car, told Fanus he should get in, and drove him to Medford. Defendant did not know if Fanus had committed the crime. He suspected Fanus might have done so, however, because he knew that Fanus and Fanus's brother had acquired a shotgun and he was concerned that they would get themselves into trouble with it. En route to Medford, Fanus told defendant that he had shot Carl with a shotgun and that he had disposed of the weapon. Defendant suggested that Fanus go to Los Angeles because it is a big city where "a person could get lost." Once in Medford, defendant provided Fanus with some clothing and put him on a bus to California. One week later, California police arrested Fanus in suburban Los Angeles. While Fanus was on the run, defendant did not disclose Fanus's whereabouts to anyone. When the police questioned defendant after apprehending Fanus, defendant initially denied any knowledge of the matter. He admitted his involvement only after learning that Fanus had told police that defendant had driven him to Medford.

Defendant was charged with and convicted of hindering prosecution. . . .

Hindering prosecution is a descendant of the common-law crime of accessory after the fact. . . . At common law, accessorial liability "rested on the notion that one who helps an offender avoid justice becomes in some sense an accomplice in the original crime." . . . One guilty of accessory after the fact was, in effect, derivatively liable for the underlying crime. Consistent with the notion of derivative liability, the accessory had to have knowledge that the principal committed the crime, the principal had to be tried first or jointly with the accessory, the principal's conviction was a prerequisite to punishment of the accessory, and the accessory was subject to the same sentence as the principal. . . .

The Model Penal Code (MPC) broke "decisively" from the common-law view of the offense by rejecting its tradition of accessorial liability and adopting instead "the alternative theory of prosecution for obstruction of justice." . . . The MPC therefore reformulated the crime as that of hindering apprehension or prosecution. It aimed the prohibition at the "purposeful efforts to aid another to evade justice" and did so "without regard to whether the person assisted in fact committed a crime and with penalties not invariably tied to those prescribed for the underlying offense." . . .

In revising the Oregon Criminal Code in 1971, the legislature substantially adopted the MPC's approach. . . . The legislature repealed the former accessory statute . . . and replaced it with hindering prosecution, codified as ORS 162.325. Although borrowing in part from the MPC, Oregon did not abandon accessorial liability altogether. Rather, it retained the requirement that the person aided be one "who has committed a crime punishable as a felony." . . . Significantly, however, Oregon shifted the emphasis to the public's interest in preventing the obstruction of justice. The legislature changed the mental state required for hindering prosecution by deleting the requirement that a defendant know that the person he or she aided in fact had committed a felony. Instead, the mental state required is the intent to hinder apprehension or prosecution, thus aiding the offender in "escaping justice." . . .

As that history reflects, hindering prosecution in Oregon is still based in part on accessorial liability for the crime committed by the aided felon, but the penal goal of the offense is to prevent the obstruction of justice. Consistent with that objective, hindering prosecution does not require that an offender know that he or she is aiding someone who in fact committed a crime; it does not require that the person aided have recidivist tendencies; it does not require actual success in avoiding prosecution. . . .

Conviction affirmed; sentence vacated; remanded for resentencing.

CASE QUESTIONS

1. How did the Oregon legislature depart from the common law crime of accessory after the fact?

2. Could a defendant be convicted of hindering prosecution in Oregon if the perpetrator of the crime has committed a misdemeanor rather than a felony?

AUTHOR'S COMMENTARY

As discussed elsewhere in this text, the Model Penal Code has functioned as a catalyst in encouraging state legislatures to reexamine their criminal laws. Oregon, as a sovereign state, has full authority to determine the nature and scope of its criminal law, limited only by the Oregon and federal constitutions. One of the advantages of federalism is its flexibility and its ability to produce innovation. Oregon considered the Model Penal Code proposals regarding accessory law as part of its revision process and accepted many of its suggestions. It agreed with the drafters of the MPC that accessory laws should focus on preventing the obstruction of justice, and to change the intent requirement from proof that an accused obstructor knew that the person aided had committed a felony to proof that the alleged obstructor intended that the aided person avoid apprehension or prosecution. As states go through this process across the country, a national redefinition of criminal law takes place, but with variation, experimentation, and much thought and deliberation.

Vicarious Liability

We learned in Chapter 3 that criminal liability generally requires proof that a defendant has personally either committed a criminal act or failed to act under circumstances where the law requires action. There is a limited exception to this

Figure 4.3. Iowa Vicarious Liability Statute

> **Iowa Code 703.4 Responsibility of employers.**
>
> An employer or an employer's agent, officer, director, or employee who supervises or directs the work of other employees, is guilty of the same public offense committed by an employee acting under the employer's control, supervision, or direction in any of the following cases:
>
> 1. The person has directed the employee to commit a public offense.
>
> 2. The person knowingly permits an employee to commit a public offense, under circumstances in which the employer expects to benefit from the illegal activity of the employee.
>
> 3. The person assigns the employee some duty or duties which the person knows cannot be accomplished, or are not likely to be accomplished, unless the employee commits a public offense, provided that the offense committed by the employee is one which the employer can reasonably anticipate will follow from this assignment.

general rule that allows for the imposition of what is called vicarious criminal liability. Where a criminal prosecution is based on **vicarious liability**, the defendant, who has not personally committed an *actus reus*, is nevertheless held responsible for criminal acts that were actually committed by others. Legislatures often enact statutes expressly making employers vicariously liable for criminal acts committed by their employees. The Iowa statute in Figure 4.3 is an example.

UNITED STATES v. PARK
421 U.S. 658
U.S. Supreme Court
June 9, 1975

AUTHOR'S INTRODUCTION

In *United States v. Park*, the president of a retail food chain was convicted by a jury of allowing food to be stored in a warehouse contaminated by rodents, contrary to federal food and drug laws. The question of whether a corporate chief executive can be held vicariously responsible for criminal acts committed by other corporate employees was before the U.S. Supreme Court for decision.

EXCERPT FROM THE CASE

Chief Justice BURGER:

Acme Markets, Inc., is a national retail food chain with approximately 36,000 employees, 874 retail outlets, 12 general warehouses, and four special warehouses. Its headquarters, including the office of the president, respondent Park, who is chief executive officer of the corporation, are located in Philadelphia, PA. In a five-count information filed in the United States District Court for the District of Maryland, the Government charged Acme and respondent with violations of the Federal Food, Drug, and Cosmetic Act. Each count of the information alleged that the defendants had received food that had been shipped in interstate commerce and that, while the food was being held for sale in Acme's Baltimore warehouse following shipment in interstate commerce, they caused it to be held in a building accessible to rodents and to be exposed to contamination by rodents. These acts were alleged to have resulted in the food's being adulterated. . . .

Acme pleaded guilty to each count of the information. Respondent pleaded not guilty. The evidence at trial . . . demonstrated that in April 1970 the Food and Drug Administration (FDA) advised respondent by letter of unsanitary conditions in Acme's Philadelphia warehouse. In 1971 the FDA found that similar conditions existed in the firm's Baltimore warehouse. An FDA consumer safety officer testified concerning evidence of rodent infestation and other insanitary conditions discovered during a 12-day inspection of the Baltimore warehouse in November and December 1971. The witness testified with respect to the inspection of the basement of the "old building" in the warehouse complex: "We found extensive evidence of rodent infestation in the form of rat and mouse pellets throughout the entire perimeter area and along the wall." "We also found that the doors leading to the basement area from the rail siding had openings at the bottom or openings beneath part of the door that came down at the bottom large enough to admit rodent entry. There were also roden[t] pellets found on a number of different packages of boxes of various items stored in the basement, and looking at this document, I see there were also broken windows along the rail siding." . . . On the first floor of the "old building," the inspectors found: "Thirty mouse pellets on the floor along walls and on the ledge in the hanging meat room. There were at least twenty mouse pellets beside bales of lime Jello and one of the bales had a chewed rodent hole in the product. . . ."

The Government also presented testimony by the Chief of Compliance of the FDA's Baltimore office, who informed respondent by letter of the conditions at the Baltimore warehouse after the first inspection. The letter, dated January 27, 1972, included the following: "We note with much concern that the old and new warehouse areas used for food storage were actively and extensively inhabited by live rodents. Of even more concern was the observation that such reprehensible conditions obviously existed for a prolonged period of time without any detection, or were completely ignored . . . ." "We trust this letter will serve to direct your attention to the seriousness of the problem and formally advise you of the urgent need to initiate whatever measures are necessary to prevent recurrence and ensure compliance with the law." . . . Acme's Baltimore division vice president, . . . [testified] on behalf of Acme and respondent and described the steps taken to remedy the insanitary conditions discovered by both inspections. The Government's final witness, Acme's vice president for legal affairs and assistant secretary, identified respondent as the president and chief executive officer of the company and read a bylaw prescribing the duties of the chief executive officer. . . . He testified that respondent functioned by delegating "normal operating duties," including sanitation, but that he retained "certain things, which are the big, broad, principles of the operation of the company," and had "the responsibility of seeing that they all work together." . . .

At the close of the Government's case in chief, respondent moved for a judgment of acquittal on the ground that "the evidence in chief has shown that Mr. Park is not personally concerned in this Food and Drug violation." The trial judge denied the motion, stating that *United States v. Dotterweich* . . . (1943), was controlling.

Respondent was the only defense witness. He testified that, although all of Acme's employees were in a sense under his general direction, the company had an "organizational structure for responsibilities for certain function" according to which different phases of its operation were "assigned to individuals who, in turn, have staff and departments under them." He identified those individuals responsible for sanitation, and related that upon receipt of the January 1972 FDA letter, he had conferred with the vice president for legal affairs, who informed him that the Baltimore division vice president "was investigating the situation immediately and would be taking corrective action and would be preparing a summary of the corrective action to reply to the letter." Respondent stated that he did not "believe there was anything [he] could have done more constructively than what [he] found was being done." . . .

On cross-examination, respondent conceded that providing sanitary conditions for food offered for sale to the public was something that he was "responsible for in the entire operation of the company," and he stated that it was one of many phases of the company that he assigned to "dependable subordinates." Respondent was asked about and, over the objections of his counsel, admitted receiving, the April 1970 letter addressed to him from the FDA regarding insanitary conditions at Acme's Philadelphia warehouse. . . . He acknowledged that, with the exception of the division vice president, the same individuals had responsibility for sanitation in both Baltimore and Philadelphia. Finally, in response to questions concerning the Philadelphia and Baltimore incidents, respondent admitted that the Baltimore problem indicated the system for handling sanitation "wasn't working perfectly" and that as Acme's chief executive officer he was responsible for "any result which occurs in our company." . . .

At the close of the evidence, respondent's renewed motion for a judgment of acquittal was denied. . . . Respondent's counsel objected to the instructions on the ground that they failed fairly to reflect our decision in *United States v. Dotterweich*. . . . The trial judge over-ruled the objection. The jury found respondent guilty on all counts of the information, and he was subsequently sentenced to pay a fine of $50 on each count.

The Court of Appeals reversed the conviction and remanded for a new trial. . . . The Court of Appeals concluded that the trial judge's instructions "might well have left the jury with the erroneous impression that Park could be found guilty in the absence of 'wrongful action' on his part," . . . and that proof of this element was required by due process. It held, with one dissent, that the instructions did not "correctly state the law of the case," . . . and directed that on retrial the jury be instructed as to "wrongful action," which might be "gross negligence and inattention in discharging . . . corporate duties and obligations or any of a host of other acts of commission or omission which would 'cause' the contamination of food." . . .

We granted *certiorari* because of an apparent conflict among the Courts of Appeals with respect to the standard of liability of corporate officers under the Federal Food, Drug, and Cosmetic Act as construed in *United States v. Dotterweich*, . . . and because of the importance of the question to the Government's enforcement program. We reverse.

I

The question presented by the Government's petition for *certiorari* . . . and the focus of this Court's opinion, was whether "the manager of a corporation, as well as the corporation itself, may be prosecuted under the Federal Food, Drug, and Cosmetic Act of 1938 for the introduction of misbranded and adulterated articles into interstate commerce." . . . In *Dotterweich*, a jury had disagreed as to the corporation, a jobber purchasing drugs from manufacturers and shipping them in interstate commerce under its own label, but had convicted Dotterweich, the corporation's president and general manager. The Court of Appeals reversed the conviction on the ground that only the drug dealer, whether corporation or individual, was subject to the criminal provisions of the Act, and that where the dealer was a corporation, an individual connected therewith might be held personally only if he was operating the corporation "as his 'alter ego.'" . . .

In reversing the judgment of the Court of Appeals and reinstating Dotterweich's conviction, this Court looked to the purposes of the Act and noted that they "touch phases of the lives and health of people which, in the circumstances of modern industrialism, are largely beyond self-protection." . . . It observed that the Act is of "a now familiar type" which "dispenses with the conventional requirement for criminal conduct—awareness of some wrongdoing. In the interest of the larger good it puts the burden of acting at hazard upon a person otherwise innocent but standing in responsible relation to a public danger." . . .

Central to the Court's conclusion that individuals other than proprietors are subject to the criminal provisions of the Act was the reality that "the only way in which a corporation can act is through the individuals who act on its behalf." . . . The Court also noted that corporate officers had been subject to criminal liability under the Federal Food and Drugs Act of 1906, ... and it observed that a contrary result ... would be incompatible with the expressed intent of Congress to "enlarge and stiffen the penal net and to discourage a view of the Act's criminal penalties as a 'license fee for the conduct of an illegitimate business.'" ...

At the same time, however, the Court was aware ... that literal enforcement "might operate too harshly by sweeping within its condemnation any person however remotely entangled in the proscribed shipment." ... A limiting principle, in the form of "settled doctrines of criminal law" defining those who "are responsible for the commission of a misdemeanor," was available. In this context, the Court concluded, those doctrines dictated that the offense was committed "by all who ... have ... a responsible share in the furtherance of the transaction which the statute outlaws." ...

The Court recognized that, because the Act dispenses with the need to prove "consciousness of wrongdoing," it may result in hardship even as applied to those who share "responsibility in the business process resulting in" a violation. It regarded as "too treacherous" an attempt "to define or even to indicate by way of illustration the class of employees which stands in such a responsible relation." The question of responsibility, the Court said, depends "on the evidence produced at the trial and its submission—assuming the evidence warrants it—to the jury under appropriate guidance." The Court added: "In such matters the good sense of prosecutors, the wise guidance of trial judges, and the ultimate judgment of juries must be trusted." ...

II

The rule that corporate employees who have "a responsible share in the furtherance of the transaction which the statute outlaws" are subject to the criminal provisions of the Act was not formulated in a vacuum. ... Cases under the Federal Food and Drugs Act of 1906 reflected the view both that knowledge or intent were not required to be proved in prosecutions under its criminal provisions, and that responsible corporate agents could be subjected to the liability thereby imposed. ... Moreover, the principle had been recognized that a corporate agent, through whose act, default, or omission the corporation committed a crime, was himself guilty individually of that crime. The principle had been applied whether or not the crime required "consciousness of wrongdoing," and it had been applied not only to those corporate agents who themselves committed the criminal act, but also to those who by virtue of their managerial positions or other similar relation to the actor could be deemed responsible for its commission.

In the latter class of cases, the liability of managerial officers did not depend on their knowledge of, or personal participation in, the act made criminal by the statute. ... Rather, where the statute under which they were prosecuted dispensed with "consciousness of wrongdoing," an omission or failure to act was deemed a sufficient basis for a responsible corporate agent's liability. It was enough in such cases that, by virtue of the relationship he bore to the corporation, the agent had the power to prevent the act complained of. . . .

The rationale of the interpretation given the Act in *Dotterweich*, as holding criminally accountable the persons whose failure to exercise the authority and supervisory responsibility reposed in them by the business organization resulted in the violation complained of, has been confirmed in our subsequent cases. Thus, the Court has reaffirmed the proposition that "the public interest in the purity of its food is so great as to warrant the imposition of the highest standard of care on distributors." . . . In order to make "distributors of food the strictest censors of their merchandise," . . . the Act punishes "neglect where the law requires care, or inaction where it imposes a duty." . . . "The accused, if he does not will the violation, usually is in a position to prevent it with no more care than society might reasonably expect and no more exertion than it might reasonably exact from one who assumed his responsibilities." . . . Courts of Appeals have recognized that those corporate agents vested with the responsibility, and power commensurate with that responsibility, to devise whatever measures are necessary to ensure compliance with the Act bear a "responsible relationship" to, or have a "responsible share" in, violations. . . . Thus *Dotterweich* and the cases which have followed reveal that . . . the Act imposes not only a positive duty to seek out and remedy violations when they occur but also, and primarily, a duty to implement measures that will insure that violations will not occur. The requirements of foresight and vigilance imposed on responsible corporate agents are beyond question demanding, . . . but they are no more stringent than the public has a right to expect of those who voluntarily assume positions of authority in business enterprises whose services and products affect the health and well-being of the public that supports them. . . .

The Act does not, . . . make criminal liability turn on "awareness of some wrong-doing" or "conscious fraud." The duty imposed by Congress on responsible corporate agents is, we emphasize, one that requires the highest standard of foresight and vigilance, but the Act, in its criminal aspect, does not require that which is objectively impossible. The theory upon which responsible corporate agents are held criminally accountable for "causing" violations of the Act permits a claim that a defendant was "powerless" to prevent or correct the violation to "be raised defensively at a trial on the merits." If such a claim is made, the defendant has the burden of coming forward with evidence, but this does not alter the Government's ultimate burden of proving beyond a reasonable doubt the defendant's guilt, including his power, in light of the duty imposed by the Act, to prevent or correct the prohibited condition. Congress has seen fit to enforce the accountability of responsible corporate agents dealing with products which may affect the health of consumers by penal sanctions cast in rigorous terms, and the obligation of the courts is to give them effect so long as they do not violate the Constitution.

III

... Turning to the jury charge in this case, it is of course arguable that isolated parts can be read as intimating that a finding of guilt could be predicated solely on respondent's corporate position. But this is not the way we review jury instructions, because "a single instruction to a jury may not be judged in artificial isolation, but must be viewed in the context of the overall charge." ...

Reading the entire charge satisfies us that the jury's attention was adequately focused on the issue of respondent's authority with respect to the conditions that formed the basis of the alleged violations. Viewed as a whole, the charge did not permit the jury to find guilt solely on the basis of respondent's position in the corporation; rather, it fairly advised the jury that to find guilt it must find respondent "had a responsible relation to the situation," and "by virtue of his position . . . had . . . authority and responsibility" to deal with the situation. The situation referred to could only be "food . . . held in unsanitary conditions in a warehouse with the result that it consisted, in part, of filth or . . . may have been contaminated with filth." ...

We conclude that, viewed as a whole and in the context of the trial, the charge was not misleading and contained an adequate statement of the law to guide the jury's determination. ...

Reversed.

CASE QUESTIONS

1. What was the defendant/respondent's legal argument on appeal as to why his conviction should be reversed?

2. According to the U.S. Supreme Court majority, why was Mr. Park's conviction justified?

AUTHOR'S COMMENTARY

Complicity has a different theoretical basis than criminal liability based on vicarious liability. Although accomplices actually assist a perpetrator in the commission of an offense, a defendant who is vicariously liable is prosecuted for acts that were committed, independently, by someone else. The perpetrators-in-fact in these cases are often lower-level employees of a corporation. In the case you have just read, *U.S. v. Park*, the company's president was criminally charged and convicted because he was responsible for the operation of the Acme Markets, Inc. His culpability lay in his *failure to foresee* the possibility of warehouse contamination and his *lack of vigilance* in establishing and maintaining procedures and systems at Acme Markets that would have prevented or disclosed the existence of unsanitary conditions.

Parental Liability for Failure to Supervise a Child

Some jurisdictions have enacted laws that make parents and guardians criminally liable if they are ineffective parents.

A 1995 Salt Lake City ordinance imposed vicarious criminal liability on parents who have "neglected their parenting duties." The City's stated rationale for this policy is stated in Salt Lake City Ordinance 11.60.010:

> The increasing number of criminal episodes committed by children is a negative reflection on our society's attention to family stability, and demonstrates the breakdown of meaningful parental supervision of children. Those who bring children into the world or assume a parenting role, but fail to effectively train, guide, teach, and control them, should be accountable at law. Those who need assistance and training should be aided. Those who neglect their parenting duties should be encouraged to be more diligent through criminal sanctions, if necessary. This chapter should be construed to achieve these remedial objectives.

The substantive requirements for conviction of this offense are contained in 11.60.020, which is set forth in its entirety in Figure 4.4.

According to one law review author, Salt Lake City made a serious commitment to enforce its newly adopted ordinance for a few years. The police chief, however, had concluded by 1998 that this attempt had not been effective, had cost too much, and advocated that the ordinance be repealed.[1]

Internet Tip

The drafters of the Salt Lake City ordinance were careful to recognize that there were some situations in which parents should not be held criminally responsible. They recognized these as "affirmative defenses" in 11.60.030 of the ordinances. Readers can find a complete version of Salt Lake City's "failure to supervise" ordinance included in the Chapter 4 materials posted online at the textbook's website. Affirmative defenses will be extensively discussed in Chapter 5.

As sovereign states under our federal system, New Hampshire and Utah have the right to make their own determinations as to whether parents should be subject to vicarious criminal liability. We will see in the next case that New Hampshire and Salt Lake City, a governmental entity created under the Constitution and laws of the State of Utah, have followed different paths.

Figure 4.4. Excerpts from Salt Lake City Ordinances of 1995

11.60.020 Failure to supervise a child

A person commits the offense of failing to supervise a child or tending to cause the delinquency of a child, if the person

A. Is the parent, lawful guardian, or other person over the age of eighteen years who is lawfully charged with the care or custody of a child, which adult person resides within the corporate limits of the city; and

B. Fails to provide appropriate and reasonable supervision of the child; or who aids, contributes or becomes responsible for the neglect, abuse or delinquency of the child. For purposes of this section, a person is responsible for the delinquency of a child or has failed to provide appropriate and reason able supervision when

1. The child has committed three or more delinquent acts within a two-calendar-year period, which events have been referred to the juvenile court, or

2. The person fails to undertake counseling requirements ordered by a juvenile court having jurisdiction over the child, or

3. The person fails to take meaningful or reasonable disciplinary or remedial action in response to prior delinquent acts of the child, or

4. The act or failure to act by the person demonstrates a willful lack of commitment to prevent future delinquent acts by the child;

C. Solicits, requests, commands, encourages, or intentionally aids or acts with the child in violation of any federal, state, or local law; or

D. Aids, contributes to, or becomes legally responsible for the neglect, abuse, or delinquency of the child; or

E. Willfully abuses, neglects, or abandons the child in any manner likely to cause the child unnecessary suffering or serious injury to his/her health or morals; or

F. Provides, encourages, or permits the child to possess or consume an alcoholic beverage or a controlled substance.

11.60.060 Penalty/counseling

Violation of this chapter is a Class B misdemeanor. To fulfill the primary objective and purpose of this chapter, it is the legislative intent that:

A. Upon a first conviction under this chapter, the court sentence the defendant to complete a program of appropriate counseling;

B. Upon a second conviction under this chapter, the court sentence the defendant to perform not less than one hundred hours of community service, and to complete a program of appropriate counseling.

[A person convicted of a Class B Misdemeanor in Utah is subject to a jail sentence not exceeding six months.]

STATE v. AKERS

400 A.2d 38
Supreme Court of New Hampshire
March 23, 1979

AUTHOR'S INTRODUCTION

Melvin Akers and Marshal Fox were each criminally prosecuted for conduct engaged in by their minor sons. The sons were alleged to have illegally operated snowmobiles at unreasonable speeds on a "public way." The state maintained that the state's Off Highway Recreational Vehicle statute, 269-C:24 IV, should be interpreted so as to make the parents of minor children criminally, as well as civilly, liable for the illegal actions of their minor children. Both fathers appealed their convictions to the New Hampshire Supreme Court, maintaining that the legislature never intended to impose vicarious liability on parents and that the state constitution's due process clause prohibits the state from imposing criminal sanctions on defendants solely because of their status as parents.

EXCERPT FROM THE MAJORITY OPINION

GRIMES, J.

The case before us presents an issue of first impression. We are called upon to determine whether, under New Hampshire's Constitution and Criminal Code, parents of minors can be held criminally responsible for their children's offenses solely on the basis of their parental status. We hold that parents cannot be held criminally responsible vicariously for the offenses of the child. . . .

RSA 269-C:24 IV, which pertains to the operation and licensing of Off Highway Recreational Vehicles (OHRV), provides that "[t]he parents or guardians or persons assuming responsibility will be responsible for any damage incurred or for any violations of this chapter by any person under the age of 18." . . . The defendants argue that . . . the statute under which they were convicted, was not intended by the legislature to impose criminal responsibility, and . . . if in fact the legislative intention was to impose criminal responsibility, then the statute would violate N.H. Const. pt. I, art. 15 and U.S. Const. amend. XIV, 1.

We first address the defendants' claim that the legislature's intention in enacting RSA 269-C:24 IV did not encompass the imposition of criminal sanctions on parents whose minor children have committed violations under chapter 269-C. In considering this claim, we are guided by the legislature's own mandate that in interpreting its enactments, we must construe "[w]ords and phrases . . . according to the common and approved usage of the language." . . .

The language of RSA 269-C:24 IV, "parents . . . will be responsible . . . for any violations of this chapter by any person under the age of 18," clearly indicates the legislature's intention to hold the parents criminally responsible for the OHRV violations of their minor children.

It is a general principle of this State's Criminal Code that "[a] person is not guilty of an offense unless his criminal liability is based on conduct that includes a voluntary act or the voluntary omission to perform an act of which he is physically capable." . . . See generally *United States v. Park*, 421 U.S. 658 (1975). RSA 269-C:24 IV seeks to impose criminal liability on parents for the acts of their children without basing liability on any voluntary act or omission on the part of the parents. Because the statute makes no reference at all to parental conduct or acts, it seeks to impose criminal responsibility solely because of their parental status contrary to the provisions of RSA 626:1 I.

The legislature has not specified any voluntary acts or omissions for which parents are sought to be made criminally responsible and it is not a judicial function to supply them. It is fundamental to the rule of law and due process that acts or omissions which are to be the basis of criminal liability must be specified in advance and not ex post facto. . . .

It is argued that liability may be imposed on parents under the provisions of RSA 626:8 II(b), which authorizes imposing criminal liability for conduct of another when "he is made accountable for the conduct of such other person by the law defining the offense." This provision comes from the Model Penal Code 2.04(2)(b). The illustrations of this type of liability in the comments to the Code all relate to situations involving employees and agents, and no suggestion is made that it was intended to authorize imposing vicarious criminal liability on one merely because of his status as a parent. . . .

Without passing upon the validity of statutes that might seek to impose vicarious criminal liability on the part of an employer for acts of his employees, . . . we have no hesitancy in holding that any attempt to impose such liability on parents simply because they occupy the status of parents, without more offends the due process clause of our State constitution. N.H. CONST. pt. I, art. 15.

Parenthood lies at the very foundation of our civilization. The continuance of the human race is entirely dependent upon it. It was firmly entrenched in the Judaeo-Christian ethic when "in the beginning" man was commanded to "be fruitful and multiply." Genesis I. Considering the nature of parenthood, we are convinced that the status of parenthood cannot be made a crime. This, however, is the effect of RSA 269-C:24 IV. Even if the parent has been as careful as anyone could be, even if the parent has forbidden the conduct, and even if the parent is justifiably unaware of the activities of the child, criminal liability is still imposed under the wording of the present statute. There is no other basis for criminal responsibility other than the fact that a person is the parent of one who violates the law.

. . . Because the net effect of the statute is to punish parenthood, the result is forbidden by substantive due process requirements of N.H. Const. pt. I, art. 15.

Exceptions sustained.

CASE QUESTION

Do you think that legal rules applying to persons in the status of president of Acme Markets, Inc., (i.e., the Park case) should also be applicable to people in the status of parent?

AUTHOR'S COMMENTARY

Two judges dissented in the *Akers* case. The author of the dissenting opinion, Justice Bois, argued that *U.S. v. Park* supports the proposition that "imposing criminal liability based on status for certain violations of a mala prohibitum nature does not offend constitutional requirements." The dissenters reasoned that given the "demonstrable public interest to assure the safe operations of off highway recreational vehicles, and the minor penalties imposed" on violators, there was no violation of fundamental fairness.

Internet Tip

The dissent in *Akers* is included in the Chapter 4 materials posted online at the textbook's website.

Can a Corporation Be Convicted of a Crime?

The traditional notion that corporations could not be criminally prosecuted has deep historical roots. According to U.S. Supreme Court Justice William R. Day (1903–1922), the rule is traced back to 1701 and is credited to Justice Hold, at that time the Chief Justice of England.[2] Hold ruled that criminal prosecutions could be brought against corporate employees but not against the corporations, themselves. The U.S. Supreme Court changed Hold's rule in federal courts in the 1909 case of *New York Central Railroad Company v. United States*, 212 U.S. 481. Justice Day, writing for the Court, declared "It is true that there are some crimes which, in their nature, cannot be committed by corporations. But there is a large class of offenses . . . wherein the crime consists in purposely doing the things prohibited by statute. In that class of crimes, we see no good reason why corporations may not be held responsible for and charged with the knowledge and purposes of their agents, acting within the authority conferred upon them. . . . If it were not so, many offenses might go unpunished and acts be committed in violation of law where, as in the present case, the statute requires all persons, corporate or private, to refrain from certain practices, forbidden in the interest of public policy."[3] Hold's rule continued to prevail at the state level. Oregon, for example, continued to support the traditional rule in 1961 in the case of *State of Oregon v. Pacific Powder Company.* However, in the 1970s, states began to change course, and today corporations are prosecuted for many crimes—even homicides as we will see in the next case.

VAUGHAN AND SONS, INC. v. STATE
Court of Criminal Appeals of Texas
737 S.W.2d 805
September 16, 1987

AUTHOR'S INTRODUCTION

During the 1980s, state legislatures began to enact statutes that authorized prosecutions of corporations for criminally negligent homicides. In Kentucky, a company's conviction for manslaughter was upheld in the 1980 case of *Commonwealth v. Fortner LP Gas Co., Inc.* Texas was also one of the leaders. The *Vaughan* case you are about to read, from Texas, was included in this textbook because the court explains why it is necessary to switch from the traditional rule to a more modern approach.

EXCERPT FROM THE CASE

Onion, Presiding Judge.

Appellant, Vaughan and Sons, Inc., a Texas corporation, was convicted by a jury of criminally negligent homicide. . . . The information alleged that appellant, acting through two of its agents, caused the death of two individuals in a motor vehicle collision. . . . Punishment was assessed by the trial court at a fine of $5,000.00. . . .

On appeal the appellant contended . . . that the "penal code provisions for prosecution of corporations and other artificial legal entities do not extend to any type of criminal homicide, therefore the trial court erred in failing to grant appellant's motion to set aside the information."

The Court of Appeals agreed and reversed the conviction. . . . The Court of Appeals wrote in part: "A superficial reading of the negligent homicide statute construed with the Penal Code definition of 'person' . . . indicates that a corporation could indeed be found guilty of the crime charged. But the actual question before this court is whether a legislative intent plainly appears which includes corporations within the criminal field of negligent homicide by use of the term 'person.' "

After reviewing other statutes, etc., the Court of Appeals concluded: "Therefore, without a stronger, clearer indication from the legislature that the policy for holding corporations criminally responsible for homicide has changed, we decline to so hold. We should make haste slowly when it is in the direction of holding either an individual or a corporation criminally liable for a crime, especially one so serious as homicide, when it is committed by someone other than the person charged."

Thus, the Court of Appeals ruled that even though the statutes so state, the Legislature could not have intended to include corporations within the class of culpable parties because corporations are unable to formulate "intent" in their "artificial and soulless" form. . . .

We granted the State's petition for discretionary review to determine the correctness of the holding of the Court of Appeals. . . .

At common law a corporation could not commit a crime. . . . W. LaFave & A. Scott, Criminal Law, Sec. 33 (1972). . . . "This position was predicated on the rationale that a corporation had no mind and hence could not entertain the appropriate criminal intent required for all common law crimes. Also, the absence of physical body precluded imprisonment, the primary punishment available at common law. Illegal acts of a corporate agent were not imputed to the corporate entity because they were considered ultra vires and therefore without the authority of the corporation." . . .

The rule that a corporation could not be tried for any criminal offense was once widely accepted, not just in Texas, but throughout the nation. Today, however, the general rule is that a corporation may be held liable for criminal acts performed by its agents acting on its behalf. . . .

Prior to the 1974 Penal Code and the conforming amendments thereto corporate criminal responsibility was recognized only to a very limited extent in Texas. . . . Texas was then apparently the only state that did not provide for general criminal liability. See . . . Keeton & Searcy, *A New Penal Code for Texas*, 33 Tex. B. Journal 980, 985 (1970). "While there were a few statutes that imposed criminal liability in limited situations, mainly for pollution or willful violations of economic regulatory legislation, . . . even these were virtually negated by the absence of a procedure under which Texas corporations could be prosecuted." . . . Three earlier criminal cases left considerable doubt whether a corporation could be successfully prosecuted as a possible defendant. . . . *Thompson v. Stauffer Chemical Co.* . . . involved an appeal from a district court judgment holding void a judgment of a Justice of the Peace Court, and enjoining the Justice of the Peace from issuing execution thereon. . . . The Court of Civil Appeals . . . rested its decision on the following basis: "It is our view that the matters of which appellant complains are matters which the Legislature will have to afford relief for, if any relief be afforded. *There is no procedure in the Code of Criminal Procedure whereby a corporation as such, can be prosecuted for misdemeanor in Texas, and we cannot give our approval to the method employed.* The Corporation was never arrested; nor entered an appearance; was tried and convicted 'in absentia;' and we think that such Justice of Peace Court judgment of conviction was void." (Emphasis supplied.)

The Texas Supreme Court refused the writ of error, "no reversible error." Thus there was no practical procedure for bringing a corporation into court for criminal prosecution.

Former Penal Code Article 22 did define "person," but it was held that the word used therein extended only to a corporation as the "person" or "party" who, or whose property was affected by the crime. . . . Further, most of the Penal Code statutes, in defining offenses, used the term "whoever" or "person" without any indication that corporations were to be included therein.

It is not difficult to see why it could be said that prior to the 1974 Penal Code "a corporation or a partnership could not be indicted or tried under the criminal laws of Texas." . . .

The Legislature, recognizing that for years Texas was the only jurisdiction in which corporations bore no general criminal responsibility, and aware of the previous roadblocks in case law to the prosecution of corporations for criminal offenses, enacted statutes to remedy the situation. . . . [T]he legislature defined "person" in both the Penal Code . . . and the Code of Criminal Procedure . . . so as to expressly embrace corporations. To leave no doubt the Legislature also similarly defined "person" in the Code Construction Act. . . . In the accusatory and definitional part of most offenses found in the Penal Code the term "person" (as defined elsewhere) is used without qualification. Observe that this was done in . . . Penal Code, Sec. 19.01, defining criminal homicide, and in the statute in question in this case, V.T.C.A., Penal Code, Sec. 19.07 (Criminal Negligent Homicide). . . . And the Legislature was not content to rest upon the definitions of "person" to impose corporate criminal responsibility. It also enacted Sec. 7.22 of the Penal Code as general statute to indicate its intention that corporations were to be rendered criminally responsible for the conduct of its agents acting within the scope of its employment in committing offenses. For fear there would be no procedure for summoning corporations into court Chapter 17A was added to the Code of Criminal Procedure. And to overcome the fact that corporations cannot be placed in jail or imprisoned, the Legislature provided a schedule of fines in V.T.C.A., Penal Code, Sec. 12.51 in lieu of imprisonment where corporations were convicted.

The intention of the Legislature could hardly be made clearer given the history, the reform intended and the literal meaning of the statutes involved. Taken collectively, the foregoing statutes furnish the basis for overcoming the obstacles which in the past have prevented the criminal prosecution of corporations.

It is the State's contention that a corporation is a "person" under general definitional statute of the Penal Code . . . and since the crime of criminally negligent homicide can be committed by a "person" . . . it follows that the crime can be committed by a corporation. We agree. . . .

The Court of Appeals stated that those jurisdictions which have addressed the issue of corporate criminal liability ". . . are divided as to criminal responsibility for personal crimes such as homicide or rape, though the majority still agrees that a corporation cannot commit a crime requiring specific intent." No authority is cited. In 18B Amer. Jur. 2d, Sec. 2137, pp. 959-960, it is stated: "It is now *generally accepted* that a corporation may be indicted for a crime to which a specific intent is essential, and that the intent is essential, and that the intent of its employees or agents may be imputed to the corporations." (Emphasis supplied.) . . .

In 19 C.J.S., Corporations, Sec. 1363, pp. 1075-1076, it was pointed out that: "A corporation may be criminally liable for crimes which involve a specific element of intent as well for those which do not, and, although some crimes require such a personal, malicious intent that a corporation is considered incapable of committing them, nevertheless under the proper circumstances the criminal intent of its agent may be imputed to it so as to render it liable, the requisites of such imputation being essentially the same as those required to impute malice to corporations in civil actions." . . .

An examination of decisional law from other states indicates that where there are corporate criminal responsibility statutes similar to our own Texas statutes, it appears to have been consistently held that a corporation is liable for specific intent crimes and offenses of criminal negligence. . . .

Given the history of corporate criminal liability in Texas prior to the 1974 Penal Code, the various provisions of the 1974 Penal Code and other statutes enacted to bring about a change, the clear statutory language, and the analogous case authority, we reject the reasoning of the Court of Appeals and conclude that a corporation may be criminally prosecuted for the misdemeanor code offense of criminally negligent homicide under V.T.C.A., Penal Code, Sec. 19.07, for corporations have been made subject thereto. . . .

The Court of Appeals judgment is reversed and the cause remanded to that court for consideration of appellant's points of error.

CASE QUESTIONS

1. According to the Texas Court of Criminal Appeals, why did the common law prohibit the criminal prosecution of corporations?

2. What steps did the Texas legislature take in 1974 to enable the criminal prosecution of corporations?

Internet Tip

Edited excerpts of the *State of Oregon v. Pacific Powder Company*, 360 P.2d 530 (1961), and *Commonwealth v. Fortner LP Gas Co., Inc.*, 610 S.W.2d 941 (1980), cases can be found in the Chapter 4 materials posted online at the textbook's website.

AUTHOR'S COMMENTARY

Corporations, although not persons in the human sense, are legally classified as persons and share many attributes with human persons. They can both own tangible and intangible property, earn income, incur debt, file lawsuits and be sued, pay taxes, make charitable contributions, and so on.

Corporations can also, like human persons, commit crimes. Obviously, convicted corporations, unlike human persons, cannot be put in jail. They can, however, be seriously punished. Upon conviction, corporations can be heavily fined, the company's reputation can be damaged, the value of its goods can diminish, the value of its stock can depreciate (vicariously punishing the stockholders, too), and many professional reputations may be ruined.

Criminal charges are generally brought against corporations where prosecutors believe that it is necessary to make an example of a corporation itself for reasons of

Figure 4.5. Excerpt from Iowa Statute on Corporate Criminality

> **Iowa Code 703.5 Liability of corporations, partnerships, and voluntary associations**
>
> A public or private corporation, partnership, or other voluntary association shall have the same level of culpability as an individual committing the crime when any of the following is true:
>
> 1. The conduct constituting the offense consists of an omission to discharge a specific duty or an affirmative performance imposed on the accused by law.
>
> 2. The conduct or act constituting the offense is committed by an agent, officer, director, or employee of the accused while acting within the scope of the authority of the agent, officer, director or employee and in behalf of the accused and when said act or conduct is authorized, requested, or tolerated by the board of directors or by a high managerial agent.
>
> "High managerial agent" means an officer of the corporation, partner, or other agent in a position of comparable authority with respect to the formulation of policy or the supervision in a managerial capacity of subordinate employees.

deterrence. Sometimes the public interest is not adequately protected by prosecutions against the humans who actually were the perpetrators and accomplices. We have seen several recent examples of companies whose cultures have become so corrupted that sanctions against the company, as well as its culpable employees, are necessary to protect the public interest. The consequences of a criminal prosecution can be devastating to a corporation—especially if it is convicted of the charges. The consequences that may result from corporate prosecutions include official condemnation, financial penalties, the heaping of disgrace on its public image (which will presumably devalue the company's stock), and even bankruptcy.

Thus a company is itself prosecuted for criminal conduct based on a theory of vicarious liability. It is made criminally responsible for the acts of its agents and employees (see Figure 4.5).

UNITED STATES v. IONIA MANAGEMENT

Docket Nos. 07-5801-cr, 08-1387-cr
U.S. Court of Appeals for the Second Circuit
January 20, 2009

AUTHOR'S INTRODUCTION

Ionia Management, the appellant in this case, was a Liberian corporation with headquarters in Greece. This company managed a Bahamian-flagged oil tanker named the M/T Kriton. The Kriton was inspected by the U.S. Coast Guard because the Kriton was in the process of delivering oil and petroleum products to various ports up and down the eastern seaboard of the United States. One of the reasons the Coast Guard wanted to inspect the Kriton was to determine if the Kriton's crew was complying with a federal law known as the Act to Prevent Pollution on Ships ("APPS"). The APPS was enacted by Congress to fulfill obligations our country assumed when the United States became a party to two international treaties. The Coast Guard's inspection was to determine if the Kriton was properly recording how it was disposing of its oily waste water. The law required that the crew detail its procedures in a legally required "oil record book" (the ORB). The Coast Guard inspectors discovered that crew members were not complying with the law. Instead of processing the water containing quantities of oil waste through the ship's apparatus known as the Oil Water Separator, crew members had been directed to bypass the separator and illegally pump the waste directly into the sea through what they called the "magic hose." The Coast Guard further determined that the Kriton ORB contained false entries, that the magic hose had been hidden, and that members of the Kriton Crew had otherwise sought to obstruct the investigation and conceal wrongdoing.

The government subsequently sought and obtained grand jury indictments charging Ionia with conspiracy, falsifying records, and obstruction of justice. The case was tried to a jury in the District of Connecticut, and Ionia was convicted of all the charges. Ionia appealed the case to the U.S. Court of Appeals for the Second Circuit.

EXCERPT FROM THE PER CURIAM OPINION

PER CURIAM: . . .

Ionia now appeals . . . arguing: (1) that the District Court erred in instructing the jury that Ionia could be found liable for violating the APPS, [Act to Prevent Pollution on Ships] 33 U.S.C. § 1908(a), for failing to "maintain" an ORB [Oil Record Book] when the *Kriton*'s crew only *possessed* the falsified ORB and did not *make* any false entries when it was in U.S. waters; (2) that the jury instruction on vicarious corporate liability was erroneous and constructively amended the indictment, and that the evidence was insufficient to establish . . . [corporate] criminal liability; (3) [and] that the District Court constructively amended the indictment when it failed to instruct the jury that it had to find "material" falsification to convict under 18 U.S.C. § 1519. . . .

Ionia's argument about the APPS concerns an issue that this Court has not yet addressed. We therefore interpret for the first time the regulation that requires subject ships to "maintain" an ORB. . . . In doing so, we join the Fifth Circuit in holding that this provision imposes a duty on ships, upon entering the ports or navigable waters of the United States, to ensure that its ORB is accurate (or at least not knowingly inaccurate). We find that this requirement complies with international law as required by . . . [federal statute], which provides that "[a]ny action taken under [the APPS] shall be taken in accordance with international law." In addition, it is supported by the regulation's plain text and is necessary to advance the aims of the international treaties governing pollution on the high seas. Accordingly, we conclude that the District Court did not err in its jury instruction.

With respect to the remaining issues on appeal, we address them summarily as Ionia has failed to demonstrate that there were any errors based on the established precedents of our Circuit. . . .

II. REMAINING CLAIMS

Ionia's remaining claims do not require the Court to interpret new areas of law and, hence, can be addressed summarily. We assume the parties' familiarity with the additional facts, procedural history, and scope of the issues pertinent to these remaining claims.

A. CORPORATE CRIMINAL LIABILITY (RESPONDEAT SUPERIOR)

We find that Ionia's claim that there was not sufficient evidence to convict it on a *respondeat superior* theory to be meritless. The Court reviews challenges to the sufficiency of the evidence *de novo* . . . affirming if "after viewing the evidence in the light most favorable to the prosecution, *any* rational trier of fact could have found the essential elements of the crime beyond a reasonable doubt," . . . . The record reflects that there was ample evidence for a jury to have reasonably found that the *Kriton*'s crew acted within the scope of their employment. The crew members acted within their authority to maintain the engine room, discharge waste, and record relevant information, when they used the "magic hose." They testified that they acted at the direction of their supervisors not just (a) in the discharging of the oil, and (b) in the making and maintaining of the false ORB entries, but also (c) in lying to the Coast Guard. The jury could, moreover, infer from the expert testimony about the maintenance and expense involved in using the Oil Water Separator that the crew used the bypass hose to benefit Ionia and subsequently lied to protect the company.

Ionia's appeal that the jury charge on *respondeat superior* was erroneous and constructively amended the indictment also fails. . . . Ionia contends that the District Court erred because . . . it failed to instruct the jury that corporate criminal liability can only stem from the actions of so-called "managerial" employees. That contention seems at odds with our precedents in *United States v. Twentieth Century Fox Film Corp.*, 882 F.2d 656, . . . and *United States v. George F. Fish, Inc.*, 154 F.2d 798. . . . But regardless of these, there was overwhelming evidence that the *Kriton*'s Chief Engineers specifically directed crew members to use the "magic hose," and so Ionia's argument is without merit in any event.

Furthermore, we refuse to adopt the suggestion that the prosecution, in order to establish vicarious liability, should have to prove as a separate element in its case-in-chief that the corporation lacked effective policies and procedures to deter and detect criminal actions by its employees. . . . Adding such an element is contrary to the precedent of our Circuit on this issue. *See Twentieth Century Fox Film Corp.*, 882 F.2d at 660 (holding that a compliance program, "however extensive, does not immunize the corporation from liability when its employees, acting within the scope of their authority, fail to comply with the law"). And this remains so regardless of asserted new Supreme Court cases in other areas of the law. As the District Court instructed the jury here, a corporate compliance program may be relevant to whether an employee was acting in the scope of his employment, but it is not a separate element.

B. FALSIFICATION UNDER 18 U.S.C. § 1519

Ionia next asserts that the District Court's jury charge as to falsification under 18 U.S.C. § 1519 constructively amended the indictment by failing to instruct the jury that the falsification had to be "material." . . . Here, Ionia was on notice of the "core criminality" to be proven at trial. Moreover, the evidence shows that the falsification in this case was indisputably material, and thus Ionia's rights were not substantially affected. . . .

III. CONCLUSION

We have carefully considered all of Ionia's claims, and we find them to be without merit.

Accordingly, the judgment of the District Court and the jury verdict are AFFIRMED.

CASE QUESTION

Why did the Second Circuit agree with the district court that Ionia Management Corporation was vicariously responsible for criminal violations of the Act to Prevent Pollution on Ships (APPS)?

AUTHOR'S COMMENTARY

Thirty-five years ago, when the author was an assistant district attorney, prosecutors and police officers would occasionally give first-time misdemeanor offenders "a break" so that they could avoid the consequences of having a criminal record. The prosecutor in such cases would essentially dictate the conditions of what was essentially an "informal probation." The offender's choice was either to agree to the terms or face prosecution. The conditions often provided that the miscreant apologize and make restitution to the victim, required the accused to get counseling/get a job/get education, and "stay out of trouble" for a specified period of time. If the miscreant breached the agreement and the statute of limitations hadn't expired, the prosecutor could file the criminal charges.

Since 2000, a number of U.S. Attorneys have been following similar practices in cases of **corporate criminality**. There are two types of documents which set forth the terms to which the miscreant corporation must agree to avoid the full force of a criminal prosecution. One is called a non-prosecution agreement. The second type is called a deferred prosecution agreement.

A prosecutor who is willing to negotiate a non-prosecution agreement will enter into negotiations with the allegedly offending company after the investigative process has concluded but prior to taking the evidence to the grand jury. The prosecutor will offer to agree not to seek an indictment if the company agrees to various terms which often include acknowledging wrongful conduct, paying financial penalties, making restitution, cooperating with the government, and undertaking specified reforms. The primary benefit to the corporation is that it avoids the possibility of being branded a criminal corporation, which could lead to the corporation's demise. Thousands of Arthur Andersen employees lost their jobs after the legendary accounting firm was convicted by a jury in the aftermath of the Enron debacle.

The primary difference between a non-prosecution agreement and deferred prosecution agreement is that the negotiations in the former occur prior to the filing of criminal charges. In a deferred prosecution agreement, the prosecutor initiates a formal prosecution and then indicates a willingness to dismiss these charges if the corporate defendant agrees to the prosecution's terms. The corporation has to balance the cost of complying with the government's terms as set forth in the deferred prosecution agreement against the consequences of being indicted and tried for the alleged criminal offenses.

Today, federal prosecutors and corporate criminal defendants are doing an end-run around the traditional adversarial criminal trial in which judges determine guilt and innocence and impose sanctions. Increasingly, litigation is being replaced with leveraged negotiations. This alternative dispute resolution approach to corporate criminal conduct features prosecutors who "propose" settlement terms and "negotiate" with corporations. The prosecution has the upper hand in these negotiations, because only by reaching agreement with the government can the company guarantee its own survival.

The negotiation in lieu of prosecution approach has proven quite controversial. Four members of the U.S. House of Representatives have introduced proposed legislation to regulate the use of deferred and non-prosecution agreements. The 2009 version of the bill is called the "Accountability in Deferred Prosecution Act of 2009". It proposes that the Attorney General issue guidelines for both types of agreements, that the full text of such agreements be posted on the Department of Justice website, and that every negotiated agreement be submitted to a district court judge for approval.[4]

Chapter Summary

Prior to Chapter 4, the discussion has focused on crimes committed by the principle actor, the individual who, without the assistance of others, has personally and directly committed a criminal offense. In many instances, however, many individuals may have contributed to the commission of a crime. This chapter explained how the criminal law treats accomplices and explains when an individual can be found vicariously liable for a crime committed by someone else.

Complicity

Whenever a criminal offense has been committed, and it is determined that more than one person contributed to its commission, it is likely that there will be accomplices. Today, the common law distinctions are generally not recognized, and all individuals who aided or abetted the commission of the crime, whether as a principle or an accessory before the fact, will be prosecuted as "parties to the crime." A person convicted as a party to the crime is punishable exactly like a principal. Thus, the lookout who encouraged the principal to commit the crime and facilitated the commission of the crime is prosecuted and convicted of bank robbery just like the individual who entered the bank and pointed the weapon at the teller. The *actus reus* committed by the principal will be imputed to the accomplices (this means that the law will consider the accomplices as also having committed the *actus reus*). The prosecution will first prove the identity of the principal and then prove the commission of the criminal act and the *mens rea* required for conviction of armed robbery. They will then focus on proving that the accomplice, while possessing the same level of criminal intent as the principal, encouraged and facilitated the commission of the crime.

Accomplice liability also exists for those who obstruct justice by harboring or otherwise assisting an offender in the aftermath of a crime to avoid capture and prosecution. Also known as an "accessory after the fact," this form of complicity requires proof that the accomplice had knowledge that the fugitive had committed a crime at the time that the assistance was rendered. The sentence for this form of accomplice liability is usually less than that given to persons who are convicted as principals or aiders and abettors of the initial substantive offense.

Vicarious Liability

Sometimes, laws impose vicarious liability on individuals for criminal acts committed by others. This type of liability is premised on the existence of a relationship between the person being prosecuted and the person who commits the *actus reus*. The employer-employee and parent-child relationships and the relationship between a corporation and its agents and employees are three examples of relationships in which vicarious liability was imposed that were discussed in this chapter.

Discussion Questions

1. Even though the rebate period had elapsed, salesmen at a Pontiac dealership told potential customers that they would try to get the customers cash rebates from GM. The salesmen forged the customers' signatures on the rebate applications and fraudulently backdated the transaction dates so that they would appear to have occurred within the authorized rebate time period. The dealership, a corporation, was prosecuted for theft and forgery, both of which

required proof of specific intent. Can a corporation be convicted of a specific intent crime?

State v. Christy Pontiac-GMC, Inc., 354 N.W.2d 17 (1984)

2. The following factual summary was found by the court:

> ... the Green Bay police received a report that in the late evening hours of May 24 and early morning hours of May 25, 2002, twenty-one cars had been broken into and personal property had been stolen. One of the items stolen was a faceplate from a car's Pioneer radio. On May 25, the police stopped a vehicle that had been identified by its license plate approximately twelve hours earlier as the car used by four young Asians in an unsuccessful attempt to steal property from one of these cars. They found Ying sitting in the back seat and observed next to him a Pioneer faceplate stolen from one of the cars the night before. In addition, property stolen from other vehicles the night before, such as CDs and stereo equipment, was found in the car. Ying also matched the general description of the young Asians who had been observed breaking into a car twelve hours earlier.

Do these facts support a probable cause finding that the defendant, Ying, participated in the commission of a theft either as a principal or as an aider and abettor?

State v. Ying, N.V. No. 02-2626 (2002)

3. Iverson was the founder, president, and chairman of the board of a chemical company named CH2O, Inc. The company asked its customers to return the drums in which the company's products were shipped so that they could be reused. However, the returned drums had to be cleaned by the company before they could be reused, and the water used in the drum-cleaning operation was too polluted with metals to be disposed of through public sewers. Between 1985 and 1988, Iverson and his employees disposed of the contaminated wastewater down sewer drains on property that he owned. From 1988 to 1992, Iverson's chemical company employed professionals to handle the wastewater, but at enormous cost. In 1992, Iverson purchased a warehouse that was connected to the Olympia sewer and discharged its wastewater down that drain until 1995. Although Iverson had officially announced his retirement prior to purchase of the warehouse, he continued to be compensated by the chemical company and he continued to be listed as president of the company on official documents. He was also supervising other employees in the wastewater disposal operation. He was prosecuted and convicted of violating the Clean Water Act, the Washington Administrative Code, and the Olympia Code and was sentenced to one year in jail, three years supervised release, and a $75,000 fine. Should the trial

court have permitted the jury to find Iverson, as a "responsible corporate officer," criminally liable for violating the Clean Water Act?

United States v. Iverson,, 162 F.3d 1015, U.S. Court of Appeals (9th Cir. 1998)

4. Standefer, who was in charge of Gulf Oil Company's tax department, was indicted for aiding and abetting an IRS agent to violate federal law by accepting illegal gifts. The indictment alleged that Standefer's complicity consisted of approving the expenditure of Gulf Oil funds to pay for five vacations taken by the IRS agent, who happened to be the government officer responsible for auditing Gulf Oil's tax returns. Prior to Standefer's indictment, the agent had been found not guilty on four of ten counts for which he stood trial. Should an aider and abettor be subject to criminal prosecution for offenses that the principal was acquitted of committing?

Standefer v. United States, 447 U.S. 10 (1980)

NOTES

1. L.J. Harris, "An Empirical Study of Parental Responsibility Laws: Sending Messages, but What Kind and To Whom?" 18 *Utah Law Review* 5, 17 (2006).
2. See Justice Day's opinion in *New York Central Railroad Company v. United States*, 212 U.S. 481 (1909), in which he cites Chief Justice Holt's comment included in an anonymous case reported in 88 Eng. Rep. 1518 (K.B. 1701).
3. *New York Central Railroad Company v. United States*, 212 U.S. 481.
4. See H.R. 1947, the Accountability In Deferred Prosecution Act of 2009.

Criminal Defenses

As criminal law evolved from its common law roots to the present, it had to recognize the legitimacy of defendants' claims that they should not be held criminally responsible because of special considerations that justified, excused, or mitigated their conduct. Today, there are essentially three strategies available to a criminally accused person who intends to go to trial. One option is to create reasonable doubt exclusively through the use of the government's own witnesses. Because criminal defendants are presumed innocent of the charges placed against them and because the prosecution has the constitutional responsibility of proving a defendant's guilt beyond a reasonable doubt, an accused can defeat the government by poking holes in the prosecution's case. This can be achieved by challenging both the nature and the quality of its proof, and by impeaching the credibility of its witnesses and physical evidence. Where the evidence is legally insufficient, the defendant can win if the judge is convinced that the prosecution has failed its **burden of production**. A second option is for the defendant to convince the fact-finder (the judge in a bench trial or the jury) that the government has failed to establish guilt beyond a reasonable doubt and has therefore failed to satisfy its **burden of persuasion**. The third option is for the defendant to introduce evidence that proves a defense. The defendant could prove an **alibi** or **good character defense**, or present evidence of an **affirmative defense**. We begin this chapter by exploring the affirmative defenses.

 ## Affirmative Defenses

When a defendant seeks to establish an affirmative defense, he or she is essentially saying, "I did it but . . ." and then presents evidence of extenuating circumstances. The defendant thus admits to having committed the act that was the basis for the prosecution but claims that other factors should be taken into consideration that mitigate against criminal responsibility.

Affirmative defenses are different from other defensive strategies in that they do not challenge the adequacy of the government's case in chief. In an affirmative defense, the defendant raises new issues that bear on whether the accused should be found criminally responsible for actions that the defendant acknowledges committing. The U.S. Supreme Court has ruled that states are not constitutionally required to recognize affirmative defenses and can dispense with any or all of them if they wish. The Court has also made clear that states can determine whether the prosecution or defense should ultimately bear the burden of persuasion with respect to the proof of affirmative defenses. Prosecutors do not, said the justices, have any Fourteenth Amendment due process obligation to disprove the existence of affirmative defenses beyond a reasonable doubt. Therefore, said the justices, states have the right to determine that defendants wishing to raise affirmative defenses bear both the burden of production and the burden of persuasion with regard to such defenses.[1]

Justification Defenses

When a defendant raises a *justification defense*, the accused claims that even though an *actus reus* was committed, he or she acted rightly under the circumstances. Examples of this form of affirmative defense include **self-defense**, **defense of others**, **defense of property**, and **necessity (choice of evils)**.

Self-Defense and Defense of Others

One of the primary reasons society establishes police forces, public prosecutors, and judicial systems is so that the rule of law replaces mob rule in the determination of guilt and imposition of sentences. It is an alternative to allowing the victims of crime and their families to take the law into their own hands in order to obtain "justice." The law provides victims with both civil and criminal remedies, both of which ultimately provide for the resolution of the dispute in a court of law. In many instances this approach works reasonably well.

Self-defense is one of the oldest defenses. Its use is justified when a defender threatens to use, or uses, reasonable force to protect himself or herself from an attacker's unlawful use, or threatened use, of force directed against the defender. The defender must reasonably be in fear of imminent danger of death or serious bodily harm, and the amount of force used in self-defense must not be greater than what is reasonably necessary to thwart the attacker. If the defendant in a homicide case believed that taking the life of an alleged attacker was reasonable and necessary under the circumstances, and the factfinder agrees that a hypothetically reasonable person would have acted as the defendant did, a *perfect self-defense* has been established. If, however, the defendant in a murder case, while believing that the taking of life under the given circumstances was reasonable and necessary, is found to have used excessive force, an *imperfect self-defense* is established. An imperfect self-defense will reduce a murder to the less serious crime of manslaughter.

Using force in defense of others is justifiable if the defender reasonably believes the attacker is unlawfully threatening or using force against a third person (the target of the attack). A defender is permitted to defend another person from attack only if that other person would have been legally entitled to use force in self-defense. The "defender," however, cannot claim to have acted reasonably if he or she was the initial aggressor, or goaded or taunted the attacker into launching an attack.

COLORADO v. STEVEN SILVA

987 P.2d 909
Colorado Court of Appeals
April 15, 1999

AUTHOR'S INTRODUCTION

Steven Silva, the defendant/appellant in the next case, was convicted of attempted manslaughter. He appealed his convictions claiming that the trial judge had improperly given the jury a provocation instruction when there was no evidence in the record that he had engaged in provocative conduct prior to his use of force in defense of one of his friends.

EXCERPT FROM THE CASE

Judge DAVIDSON:

Defendant, Steven Silva, appeals from the judgment of conviction entered upon jury verdicts finding him guilty of attempted reckless manslaughter, first degree assault, and second degree assault. We reverse and remand for a new trial.

According to the evidence presented at trial, the two victims and their three friends went to a bar. However, two of the friends were denied admittance because of their age and decided to wait in the truck in which they were riding while the others went inside briefly. Also in the bar were defendant and his two friends. They left at about the same time as the victims.

Prior to the affray giving rise to the charges against defendant, there was no meeting or altercation between the two groups. However, as one of the victims' friends was about to get into the truck, he instead approached defendant and one of his friends. Words were exchanged and the other of defendant's friends came around from the far side of the truck and hit the victims' friend. The victims then came over and began hitting the person who had struck the first blow. Defendant and his friends and the victims and their friends entered into the affray.

As one of defendant's friends was fighting with the first victim, defendant jumped on his back, took out his knife, and began stabbing the first victim in the arm. The second victim, not knowing that defendant had a knife, knocked defendant off of the first victim. Defendant then turned around and swung at the second victim, stabbing him in the chest and arm. The victims and their friends fled.

Defendant and his friends remained at the bar where defendant subsequently was arrested. . . .

At trial, defendant asserted the affirmative defense of self-defense and defense of others. In support of his claim, he presented evidence that he had used justifiable force when the victims and their friend returned the first blow, made by defendant's friend, with excessive force. Therefore, he asserted, he had acted reasonably in coming to his friends' defense with his knife. Defendant was convicted of the charges from which he now appeals.

I

Defendant first contends that the trial court erred in instructing the jury concerning self-defense. . . . [H]e argues that the instruction was not supported by the evidence and was misleading to the jury. We agree. The trial court has the duty to instruct the jury properly on all matters of law. . . . An instruction on self-defense is warranted if there is some evidence to support it. However, the court should not instruct on an abstract principle of law unrelated to issues in controversy. . . .

A

Defendant argues that the trial court violated his right to present a defense by instructing the jury on the issue of provoking the victim as an exception to self-defense. We agree. . . .

[W]e consider defendant's contention as properly raised and preserved. If the record contains any evidence tending to establish the affirmative defense of self-defense, then a defendant is entitled to have the jury properly instructed as to such defense. . . .

Here, the trial court, over defendant's objection, instructed the jurors . . . that:

> 3. A person is not justified in using physical force if:
>   a. with intent to cause bodily injury or death to another person, he provokes the use of unlawful physical force by that person.

Under the common law, a defendant could not avail himself of the defense of self-defense if the necessity for such defense was brought on by a deliberate act of the defendant, such as being the initial aggressor or acting with the purpose of provoking the victim into attacking. . . .

According to the plain language of the statute, a defendant's assertion of self-defense is lost if he or she acted with intent to provoke the victim into attacking first in order to provide the defendant with the excuse to injure or kill the victim. . . .

In order to warrant the giving of this instruction, the prosecution has the burden of establishing that the defendant intended to harm the victim and that he or she intended the provocation to goad the victim into attacking him or her as a pretext for injuring or killing the victim. . . .

In contrast to the initial aggressor limitation, the provocation limitation applies in situations where the defendant was not the initial aggressor.

An instruction on provoking the victim, therefore, should be given if: (1) self-defense is an issue in the case; (2) the victim makes an initial attack on the defendant; and (3) the defendant did some act intended to cause the victim to make such attack and provide a pretext for injuring the victim. . . .

Here, although there was no . . . confrontation between defendant and his friends and the victim and his friends either in the bar or in the parking lot as the two groups walked to their vehicles, there was conflicting evidence as to the cause of the fight. Evidence was presented that an argument started between defendant and one of his friends and one member of the other group after both groups had begun to get into their trucks; however, no witness could recall the content of the discussion or who had spoken first.

Even if the defendant had started the argument, mere words generally are not sufficient to be considered provoking . . . (one who has injected himself into a mild situation is not deprived of right of self-defense if the situation, beginning with only argument, develops to a point where physical force would be justified to protect himself); . . . (insulting language is not a provoking incident). Further, the victims who were stabbed were not present when words first were exchanged. Indeed, the victims did not enter the fight until after defendant's friend had thrown the first punch.

. . . [W]e conclude there simply was no evidence presented that defendant intended to provoke a fight with the victims or their friend so that he could inflict injury upon them under the guise of such provocation. In the absence of such evidence, it was error for the trial court to give the jury an instruction on provoking the victim. . . .

B

Reversible error occurs if the instructions create a reasonable possibility that the jury could have been misled or improperly contribute to a defendant's conviction. Jury instructions must be considered as a whole in determining whether a particular instruction was so misleading as to constitute reversible error. . . .

If, as here, an affirmative defense is available under the statutory scheme, the trial court has the duty to determine if sufficient evidence has been presented to raise a factual issue as to the existence of the defense. . . .

Similarly, whether the evidence presented warrants giving a further instruction as to exceptions to the asserted affirmative defense also lies within the court's province.

Here, the court gave the provocation of the victim instruction over defendant's objection because it found the evidence to be in "total disarray." Although it is appropriate for the jury to resolve questions of fact, the court has the duty to determine first which issues have been raised by the evidence presented.

. . . Here, because the trial court did not ensure that the jury received a proper instruction setting forth the rule of law relied upon by defendant in support of his theory of the case, we conclude that the judgment of conviction cannot stand and the case must be remanded for a new trial.

II

Because certain issues may arise again on retrial, we address them here. . . .

A

Defendant argues that the trial court erred in instructing the jurors concerning the initial aggressor exception to self-defense and defense of others. Specifically, defendant argues that, because he was not the initial aggressor, the evidence was insufficient to support the giving of this instruction. The People contend that the instruction was proper because defendant's friend, as the initial aggressor, could not assert self-defense and, therefore, likewise, defendant could not assert defense of others. Assuming that the same or similar evidence is introduced on retrial, we conclude that the evidence creates questions of fact for the jury to determine whether the friend was the initial aggressor and, if so, whether defendant was justified in using physical force to come to his friend's aid. We further conclude that the instructions given by the trial court, with some modification, will properly inform the jury of these fact questions and the law necessary to make its determination.

1.

A reasonable belief that one is defending against the use of unlawful force is the touchstone of self-defense and, thus, of defense of others. . . .

In determining whether an initial aggressor instruction is appropriate under the circumstances of a case in which hostilities begin and escalate among a group of people, the conduct of the defendant in the context of the situation must be the focus of any analysis of the defendant's right to self-defense. . . .

It is undisputed that defendant did not strike the first blow and, therefore, was not himself the initial aggressor. That he may have uttered some insult or engaged in an argument also would not justify identifying defendant as the initial aggressor. However, there was conflicting testimony as to how the fight actually began. Defendant's friend testified that he threw the first punch when he saw one of the other persons take an aggressive stance and draw his arm back as if to hit defendant's other friend. The victims testified, to the contrary, that defendant's friend threw the first punch without any provocation. This evidence created questions of fact for the jury as to who, other than defendant, was the initial aggressor, and whether defendant responded reasonably under the circumstances once the fight began . . . (person may respond with physical force to reasonably perceived threat of physical force without being the initial aggressor). . . .

As a general rule, a person coming to the aid of a third party with a reasonable belief that his or her intervention is necessary to prevent injury to the third party is entitled to assert defense of others to absolve or mitigate a charge of assault or homicide. The affirmative defense of defense of others is not absolutely barred by the wrongful actions of the third party. . . .

The majority of jurisdictions today, for public policy reasons, allow a defendant to assert some form of defense of others based on a reasonable belief by a defendant that intervention was necessary to protect the person he or she perceived as being under attack. . . . Model Penal Code § 3.09, comment 2 (person should not be convicted of crime requiring intent if person was acting under a mistake that, had the facts been as he or she supposed, would have left that person free from guilt).

Similarly, under the Colorado statute defining self-defense, . . . a person coming to the aid of a third party must have a reasonable belief that the third party is in imminent danger of becoming the victim of unlawful force. The statute does not require that such person have actual knowledge of the circumstances surrounding the use of force by another, but requires only a reasonable belief of the necessity to intervene. . . .

Thus, on retrial, regardless whether defendant's friend, and not defendant, was the initial aggressor, if the same or similar evidence is presented, questions of fact concerning defendant's action under the circumstances of the fight are raised for the jury's determination and the jury must be instructed accordingly.

2.

. . . Here, although no evidence was presented that defendant, himself, was the initial aggressor, as discussed, the evidence was sufficient to raise a question of fact concerning defendant's right to come to the defense of another person who might have been the initial aggressor. Thus, on remand, if the same or similar evidence is presented, it would be proper for the trial court to instruct the jury concerning the limitation on an initial aggressor's right to assert self-defense, and the right of the defendant to act upon his reasonable belief under the circumstances. However, to clarify the applicable law under the circumstances of this case, the court should also instruct the jury that defendant, in coming to the aid of another who is the initial aggressor, may defend the other only from that which he reasonably believes to be the use of excessive force. . . .

The judgment is reversed and the cause is remanded for further proceedings consistent with the views expressed in this opinion.

CASE QUESTIONS

1. When is a defendant entitled to an instruction on the defense-of-others affirmative defense?

2. The court identified two circumstances under which the defense-of-others affirmative defense would be unavailable. What were they?

3. The appellate court concluded that the trial judge had incorrectly instructed the jury regarding self-defense and the defense of others. What exactly was the error?

AUTHOR'S COMMENTARY

Not all states agree with Colorado's approach in defense of third-person cases where the intervening person (and the defendant in a pending prosecution) mistakenly assumed that the attacker was the victim. In some jurisdictions, the right of the intervenor to claim self-defense is dependent on whether the person aided was entitled to use self-defense. The reasonableness of the intervenor's actions is decided by the trier of fact and involves a determination of whether a hypothetically reasonable person would have acted similarly under those circumstances.

Defense of Property and Habitation

As a general rule, it is unreasonable for a person who is not in physical danger to defend his or her property with force intended to, or likely to, cause death or great bodily harm to another. The public policy underlying this rule is the greater importance placed on preserving life as opposed to protecting property rights. But the use of reasonable levels of force less than that intended to, or likely to, cause death or great bodily harm to others is often permitted in defending one's property from "interference" by another.

Many states also recognize a homeowner's right to use deadly force against an intruder who has unlawfully entered the owner's home to cause bodily injury to an occupant or to commit a felony. This right has historically been recognized for over 200 years in Anglo-American jurisprudence as the "castle doctrine." Colorado, by statute, has greatly expanded the protections afforded home occupants who use force against intruders in a statute known as the "make my day" law (see Figure 5.1).

Figure 5.1. Excerpt from Colorado Section 18-1-704.5 Use of Deadly Physical Force Against an Intruder

(1) The general assembly hereby recognizes that the citizens of Colorado have a right to expect absolute safety within their own homes.

(2) Notwithstanding the provisions of section 18-1-704 [the self-defense statute], any occupant of a dwelling is justified in using any degree of physical force, including deadly physical force, against another person when that person has made an unlawful entry into the dwelling, and when the occupant has a reasonable belief that such other person has committed a crime in the dwelling in addition to the uninvited entry, or is committing or intends to commit a crime against a person or property in addition to the uninvited entry, and when the occupant reasonably believes that such other person might use any physical force, no matter how slight, against any occupant. . . .

COLORADO v. MARK JANES
982 P.2d 300
Colorado Supreme Court
June 1, 1999

AUTHOR'S INTRODUCTION

The Colorado Supreme Court in the next case had to decide whether that state's defense of habitation statute provides both an immunity from prosecution and an affirmative defense.

EXCERPT FROM THE CASE

Chief Justice MULLARKEY:

We granted *certiorari* ... to determine whether the jury was properly instructed as to certain affirmative defenses raised at trial by the defendant, Mark Kelso Janes (Janes). ...

On June 15, 1995, Janes was arrested and charged with heat-of-passion manslaughter for the shooting death of Linford Tillman, a former lover and roommate who had moved out of their rented condominium approximately one month before the shooting.

The record indicates that on the day of the shooting Tillman had been drinking and at approximately 2:00 A.M. had used his own key to enter the condominium to attempt a reconciliation with Janes. During their conversation, Tillman discovered that Janes had been in bed with another man. Tillman became agitated, pulled the man from the bed, and assaulted him. Janes asked Tillman to stop, threatened to call the police, and retrieved a gun. Tillman continued the assault and moved towards Janes, who then shot Tillman in the chest.

Janes was arrested and charged with manslaughter. Claiming immunity under section 18-1-704.5, 6 C.R.S. (1998), which justifies under certain circumstances the use of deadly physical force against an intruder (the "make-my-day" statute), Janes filed a pretrial motion to dismiss the charges filed against him. That motion was denied.

At trial, Janes raised the "make-my-day" statute as an affirmative defense. ... Janes also raised self-defense as an affirmative defense.

The trial court rejected Janes's tendered instructions on self-defense. Janes objected to the instructions given to the jury as to the affirmative defenses. He was convicted and sentenced to six years of probation. Contending, among other things, that the trial court erred in instructing the jury, Janes appealed the judgment of conviction entered against him.

... [T]he court of appeals reversed the judgment of the trial court and ordered a new trial based upon its conclusion that the tendered jury instructions failed to indicate that the "make-my-day" defense is an affirmative defense and that, as such, the prosecution has the burden to disprove the existence of the defense. . . .

The court of appeals also held that there was sufficient evidence in the record to support Janes's theory of self-defense. . . . We granted the People's petition for *certiorari* review.

II. "MAKE-MY-DAY" DEFENSE

The People contend that the court of appeals erred when it concluded that the jury instructions did not properly allocate the burden of proof as to the "make-my-day" defense. . . .

Pursuant to this statute, a district court is authorized to dismiss a pending criminal charge prior to trial when the defendant establishes the statutory conditions for immunity by a preponderance of the evidence. . . . One such condition requires a defendant to prove by a preponderance of the evidence that the victim knowingly made an unlawful entry. . . . If the pretrial motion to dismiss on grounds of statutory immunity is denied, the defendant may raise the "make-my-day" statute at trial as an affirmative defense to criminal charges arising out of the defendant's use of physical force against an intruder into his home. The burden of proof generally applicable to affirmative defenses applies to such a defense. . . . Under that standard, if a defendant presents some credible evidence supporting the applicability of an affirmative defense, the prosecution then bears the burden of proving beyond a reasonable doubt the guilt of the defendant as to the issue raised by the affirmative defense as well as all other elements of the offense charged. . . .

Here, Janes asserted and the jury was instructed as to the affirmative defenses of self-defense and "make-my-day." . . . Instruction No. 12 provided as follows:

> To find the defendant not guilty based upon the lawful use of deadly physical force against an intruder, you must find that the victim made a knowingly unlawful entry into the defendant's apartment. An entry that is uninvited is not necessarily unlawful. This defense is not available if the victim entered the apartment in the good faith belief he was making a lawful entry. . . .

Because the "make-my-day" statute creates an immunity defense when raised before trial as well as an affirmative defense when raised at trial, it poses special problems when instructing a jury. Although the elements of the "make-my-day" defense remain the same, the burden of proof is very different.

When the "make-my-day" statute is asserted as an affirmative defense at trial, the defendant no longer has the burden to prove all elements of the statute by a preponderance of the evidence. Rather, the burden of proof is, as it always is, on the prosecution to prove beyond a reasonable doubt that the defendant is guilty of the crime charged. . . . Effectively, this requires the People to disprove the affirmative defense beyond a reasonable doubt. However, the language of Instruction

No. 12 eliminated that burden by telling the jury that the "make-my-day" statute does not apply unless the defendant proves that the intruder's entry was knowingly unlawful. . . .

Logically, the jury could have concluded that the burden was on the defendant to prove the conditions set forth in Instruction No. 12. . . .

Clearly it is not the defendant's burden at trial to prove that the victim did not enter in good faith.

. . . [W]e conclude that the jury instructions, when read as a whole, confused or misled the jury as to the burden of proof applicable to the affirmative defense of "make-my-day." Thus, we affirm the judgment of the court of appeals as to this issue.

CASE QUESTIONS

1. Assume that a homeowner in Colorado shoots an intruder who has unlawfully entered the shooter's home in the nighttime. What additional protection does the "make-my-day" law provide an accused beyond that already provided by the regular self-defense statute?

2. What consequences do you anticipate may result from the court's ruling that the state has to disprove a defendant's "make-my-day" affirmative defense beyond a reasonable doubt?

AUTHOR'S COMMENTARY

As we saw in the Chapter 1 with *Katko v. Briney*, there are cases in which individuals have resorted to the use of mechanical devices called *spring guns* that have been deployed to defend vineyards, homes, and unoccupied structures from trespassers. Often, the person setting the trap rigs a wire from a weapon to the inside of a door in an interior room. When the door is opened, the firearm discharges. The use of such dangerous devices to defend property is prohibited by statute in several states and is widely prohibited by case law in others. It is against public policy to use lethal force to defend mere property against trespassers.[2]

Necessity (Choice of Evils)

Under the common law, people accused of crime could defend by establishing that while their actions constituted technical violations of the criminal law, they had acted out of *necessity*. The defense of necessity (also known as choice of evils) was traditionally available in cases where the accused was confronted with having to select from two or more options, all of which would produce harm, and where committing a criminal act would produce a less serious harm than choosing other options.

To succeed with this defense, the accused must have had no reasonable alternative to violating the law. As Chief Justice Rehnquist explained, "Under any definition of these defenses one principle remains constant: if there was a reasonable, legal alternative to violating the law, 'a chance both to refuse to do the criminal act and also to avoid the threatened harm,' the defenses will fail."[3]

STEVEN MCCULLOUGH v. STATE OF INDIANA
888 N.E.2d 1272
Court of Appeals of Indiana
June 30, 2008

AUTHOR'S INTRODUCTION

Steven McCullough was convicted after a bench trial of felony criminal confinement (two counts), misdemeanor battery, and of being a habitual offender.

He appealed these convictions to an intermediate court of appeals, claiming that the evidence at trial was legally insufficient and that he had acted out of necessity. McCullough argued that his efforts to prevent McGuire from jumping out of a moving vehicle, which the state claimed constituted criminal confinement and battery, were actually necessary under the circumstances to prevent McGuire from suffering serious injury. McCullough maintained that because his conduct was undertaken for McGuire's benefit, he had established a valid necessity defense. He was sentenced to prison for two years with another four years to be served in a "community corrections facility."

EXCERPT FROM THE CASE

Crone, Judge.

... On June 3, 2007, three days after he was released to parole, McCullough insisted that his friend, Carol McGuire, leave her home and drive with him to his mother's house. The two left in McGuire's car, with McCullough driving. Instead of going to his mother's house, McCullough showed McGuire a garage from which he was considering starting a car detailing business. During the drive, the two began arguing. McCullough was screaming and angry, and McGuire was scared. Even though the car was moving, McGuire unbuckled her seat-belt and tried to get out of the car six or seven times. Each time, McCullough grabbed her left arm to prevent her from jumping out of the car. When they stopped at a stop sign or a stoplight, McCullough put his arm across McGuire's chest. McGuire asked McCullough to let her out of the car, but he continued to drive in the center lane. McGuire asked McCullough to drop her off at two different friends' houses, but McCullough refused. McCullough told McGuire that if she told anyone about what he had done, he would go back to jail, and she would "have to deal with" him and his family. . . . Finally, McCullough drove McGuire home and left. Two days later, McGuire, who had a bruise on her left wrist, reported the incident to police.

. . . . In sentencing McCullough, the trial court stated,

> The Court in its sentence found most significant that you had recently violated the conditions of your parole, that you have a history of criminal and delinquent activity. That's undeniable and that the Court finds that you are in need of correctional and rehabilitative treatment that could be best provided by commitment to a penal facility and that imposition of any reduced or sentence or suspension, more than the Court suspended would depreciate the seriousness of the crime to the victim in this matter. The Court does take into consideration the effect that this offense had on the victim. Additionally, by looking at your past and considering the amount of time that past [sic] between your release from the Department of Correction and the commission of this offense, the risk that you would commit another crime, the nature and the circumstances of the crime committed. The mitigator that the Court does find and does note was that this crime resulted from circumstances that are unlikely to reoccur. . . . It's with great seriousness that I impose this sentence today. The change that your family has seen, I hope will continue and you will not have bitterness in your heart about the sentence. I heard the facts of this case. I found that the State met their burden of proof beyond a reasonable doubt. I have the certainty that I need as a human being and as a Judge to render my sentence in this matter I heard the facts of the case and I made my decision accordingly. I don't make it recklessly. I heard the facts of the case and from hearing both sides, this is my sentence. . . .

DISCUSSION AND DECISION . . .

McCullough contends that there is insufficient evidence to support his convictions for confinement and battery. . . . A person who knowingly or intentionally confines another person without the other person's consent by using a vehicle commits class C felony confinement. Ind. Code §§ 35-42-3-3(b)(1)(B).

A person who knowingly or intentionally touches another person in a rude, insolent, or angry manner that results in bodily injury to another person commits class A misdemeanor battery. Ind. Code §§ 35-42-2-1(a)(1). " 'Bodily injury' means any impairment of physical condition, including physical pain." Ind. Code §§ 35-41-1-4.

Here, the State presented evidence that McCullough would not let McGuire out of the car despite her repeated requests and repeated attempts to exit the car. This is sufficient evidence to prove that he confined her. Further, McGuire testified that during their argument, McCullough was angry and screaming and that when he grabbed her arm to pull her back into the car, he was "hurting" her arm. . . . McGuire's arm was bruised as a result of McCullough's actions. This is sufficient evidence to prove that McCullough committed battery.

McCullough acknowledges that his conduct "[t]echnically . . . meets the statutory definition of confinement." . . . He argues, however, that he was acting out of necessity and claims, "It is reasonable, and even commendable, that McCullough did not allow McGuire to jump out of the moving car." . . . Generally, necessity may be an appropriate defense when, "under the force of extreme circumstances, conduct that would otherwise constitute a crime is justifiable and not criminal because of the greater harm which the illegal act seeks to prevent." *Toops v. State*, (Ind. Ct. App. 1994). The traditional elements of a necessity defense include:

(1) the act charged as criminal must have been done to prevent a significant evil;

(2) there must have been no adequate alternative to the commission of the act;

(3) the harm caused by the act must not be disproportionate to the harm avoided;

(4) the accused must entertain a good-faith belief that his act was necessary to prevent greater harm;

(5) such belief must be objectively reasonable under all the circumstances; and

(6) the accused must not have substantially contributed to the creation of the emergency . . .

[T]o negate a claim of necessity, the State must disprove at least one element of the defense beyond a reasonable doubt. The State may refute a claim of the defense of necessity by direct rebuttal, or by relying upon the sufficiency of the evidence in its case-in-chief. The decision whether a claim of necessity has been disproved is entrusted to the fact-finder. Where a defendant is convicted despite his claim of necessity, this court will reverse the conviction only if no reasonable person could say that the defense was negated by the State beyond a reasonable doubt. . . .

Here, the State established that McCullough's commission of the confinement and battery were unnecessary. Simply put, McCullough could have stopped the car and let McGuire get out as she requested, or McCullough himself could have gotten out of the car. McCullough did neither. Consequently, McCullough's claim of necessity fails. There is sufficient evidence to support the convictions. . . .

CASE QUESTIONS

1. The court recited the traditional elements of the necessity defense. Do you see any problems with these elements?

2. Apply the traditional elements of the necessity defense to the facts of this case. What do you conclude?

In the famous 1843 case of *Regina v. Dudley*,[4] four sailors—Dudley, Stevens, Brooke, and Parker (a 17-year-old boy)—had to abandon a yacht because of a storm some 1,600 miles from land. They took refuge in an open lifeboat and set out for safety. After 12 days they had consumed what food they had and on the 18th day they were still some 1,000 miles from land. At that time, Stevens and Dudley, over Brooke's objection, decided that Parker should be killed for food so that the rest might live. Dudley actually stabbed Parker to death. Stevens and Dudley's plan was successful, and four days later all three survivors were rescued by another ship. Stevens and Dudley were prosecuted for murder and were convicted after unsuccessfully arguing the defense of necessity. The Court of Queen's Bench concluded that killing an innocent person to save other lives should not be recognized as legally "necessary." Their death sentences were commuted to six months in prison by Queen Victoria.

Excuse Defenses

When a defendant raises an **excuse defense**, the accused claims that even though an *actus reus* was committed, he or she should be excused from criminal responsibility because of the circumstances. Examples of this form of affirmative defense include **duress**, **child's minority**, **intoxication**, **insanity**, mistake, and entrapment.

Duress

Duress is a complete defense where the accused honestly and reasonably believed that he or she would suffer imminent death or serious bodily harm unless he or she committed a criminal act. Threats to damage a person's reputation or property are not enough to raise this defense. This defense is traditionally not available to an accused charged with a homicide, and some jurisdictions also exclude aggravated assault and other offenses involving serious bodily harm.[5] It is also clear, however, that a threat of future harm is insufficient to excuse a criminal act.

Internet Tip

In 2007, the case of *State of Connecticut v. Gabriel P. Heinemann* was decided by the Supreme Court of Connecticut. Heinemann, a 16 year-old male, appealed his burglary, robbery, larceny, conspiracy, and theft of a firearm convictions,

(continued)

claiming that the trial court had incorrectly instructed the jury on duress. The trial judge had given the standard duress instruction, which included language permitting the jury to consider the relative age differences between this defendant and the individuals who had allegedly threatened him. But the defendant asked the court to go further. Heinemann wanted the court to permit the jury to "recognize the differences between a juvenile and an adult in maturity, sense of responsibility, vulnerability and personality traits, which make it more difficult for adolescents to resist pressures because of their limited decision-making capacity and their susceptibility to outside influences." The defendant contended that the law often distinguishes between mature adults and minors recognizing that teen-aged juveniles are less able than mature adults to make decisions and "evaluate risks." Therefore, he maintained, these factors should have been considered by the jurors who had to determine whether or not he had made an objectively reasonable effort to resist those who were coercing him, an essential requirement of the duress defense.

Interested readers can learn about the court's decision in this case by going to Loislaw and searching for *State of Connecticut v. Gabriel P. Heinemann*, 920 A.2d 278 (2007).

Child's Minority

A person lacks capacity to commit a crime when he or she is not fully competent because of age. All states have established a minimum age below which a child cannot be held criminally responsible, even for a homicide. Age also is a factor in determining whether a person is prosecuted in a juvenile court or as an adult (see Figure 5.2), and all states have a procedure for transferring some cases involving juvenile offenders from the jurisdiction of the juvenile court to the adult court.

Intoxication

The traditional common law rule was that persons who voluntarily became intoxicated were fully responsible for their criminal conduct. Some states continue to follow this rule. Many states, however, permit a voluntarily intoxicated defendant to prove that the use of drugs or alcohol prevented the formation of specific intent.

Figure 5.2. Revised Code of Washington 9A. 04.050

Children under the age of eight years are incapable of committing crime. Children of eight and under twelve years are presumed to be incapable of committing crime, but this presumption may be removed by proof that they have sufficient capacity to understand the act or neglect, and to know that it was wrong.

Voluntary intoxication is never recognized as a defense to general intent or strict liability offenses.

Involuntary intoxication or an involuntary drugged condition is generally recognized as a defense to all *mens rea* offenses. Few defendants can avail themselves of its use. It typically arises where the alleged criminal actor was tricked or coerced into ingesting the drugs or alcohol. It is common for states to require that an involuntarily intoxicated defendant prove that the extent of intoxication was so severe that he or she was unable to distinguish right from wrong.

STATE OF HAWAII v. TONY SOUZA
813 P.2d 1384
Supreme Court of Hawaii
July 24, 1991

AUTHOR'S INTRODUCTION

Tony Souza was charged with the attempted murder of Ryan Agbayani. Souza, who maintained at trial that he had acted while under the influence of "ice," requested an instruction on self-induced intoxication.

The requested instruction would have permitted evidence of self-induced intoxication to be used by the defendant at trial to negate the *mens rea* element required for conviction. The trial court rejected the request and instead instructed the jury that while such evidence was admissible to prove *mens rea*, it was inadmissible to disprove intent. Souza was subsequently convicted of attempted second-degree murder and appealed.

EXCERPT FROM THE CASE

Chief Justice Lum:

II

Appellant primarily contends that Hawaii Revised Statutes Section 702-230 and thus the court's self-induced intoxication instruction which recites a portion of the statute are unconstitutional. According to appellant, the instruction deprived him of his right to present a complete defense by preventing the jury from considering relevant evidence relating to his mental state at the time of the offense. We disagree.

The legislature ... clearly indicated that the purpose of the statute ... is to prevent defendants who willingly become intoxicated and then commit crimes from using self-inflicted intoxication as a defense. . . . The statute, in pertinent part, specifically provides that

> [e]vidence of the nonself-induced or pathological intoxication of the defendant shall be admissible to prove or negative the conduct alleged or the state of mind sufficient to establish an element of the offense. Evidence of self-induced intoxication of the defendant is not admissible to negative the state of mind sufficient to establish an element of the offense. . . .

Contrary to appellant's assertion, the operation of [the statute] does not deprive a defendant of the opportunity to present evidence to rebut the *mens rea* element of the crime. The statute merely prohibits the jury from considering self-induced intoxication to negate the defendant's state of mind. Appellant could still have attempted to convince the jury that he did not act "intentionally or knowingly" as required for murder in the second degree. Moreover, the statute does not relieve the State of the burden of establishing that a defendant had the requisite *mens rea*.

Furthermore, we find that voluntary intoxication is a "gratuitous" defense and not a constitutionally protected defense to criminal conduct. . . . Voluntary intoxication does not result from a disease or defect of the mind, but rather from a state that is voluntarily self-induced. Therefore, the legislature's decision to prohibit the use of self-induced intoxication as a defense does not implicate any recognizable constitutional right.

The legislature was entitled to redefine the *mens rea* element of crimes and to exclude evidence of voluntary intoxication to negate state of mind.

Redefinition of the kind and quality of mental activity that constitutes the *mens rea* element of crimes is a permissible part of the legislature's role in the "constantly shifting adjustment between the evolving aims of the criminal law and the changing religious, moral, philosophical and medical views of the nature of man." . . .

We conclude that our legislature is entitled to determine that the goals of Hawaii's penal code would be better achieved by prohibiting voluntary intoxication from negating a defendant's state of mind. Accordingly, we find section 702-230 constitutional. . . .

Affirmed.

CASE QUESTIONS

1. Why does the court conclude that the legislature has the right to refuse to recognize self-induced intoxication as a defense?

2. What factors is the legislature entitled to consider in determining the goals of the state's penal code?

AUTHOR'S COMMENTARY

Approximately one-third of the states have prohibited the use of voluntary intoxication as a defense in any criminal prosecution. The U.S. Supreme Court, by a vote of 5–4 decided in the case of *Montana v. Egelhoff*, 518 U.S. 37 (1996), that states were not constitutionally required to recognize the voluntary intoxication defense. In the aftermath of that decision, approximately one-third of the states changed their laws to prohibit its use in the guilt determination phase of the trial. Voluntary intoxication testimony is permitted in many courts for mitigation purposes in conjunction with sentencing hearings.

Internet Tip

The U.S. Supreme Court's opinion in *Montana v. Egelhoff* can be found with the Internet materials associated with Chapter 5 on this textbook's website.

Insanity

Before we examine the substance of the insanity defense, it is important to make sure that readers do not confuse the question of the defendant's sanity with the question of the defendant's competency to stand trial. The U.S. Supreme Court reemphasized in its 1996 ruling in the case of *Cooper v. Oklahoma*, 515 U.S. 348 (1996), its continued support for the proposition that constitutional due process forbids any criminal proceeding against a criminal defense unless the accused "has sufficient present ability to consult with his lawyer with a reasonable degree of rational understanding . . . [and] a rational as well as factual understanding of the proceedings against him." The rationale for this rule is that it is fundamentally unfair to put a person on trial who cannot reasonably understand the nature of the proceedings against him or her and who cannot meaningfully communicate with the defense attorney in defending against the government's charges. Whenever there is a question of the defendant's present competency to stand trial, a hearing must be held to resolve this question. The hearing will often consist of a duel between qualified mental heath experts who testify about their conclusions and rationales. A defendant who is found to be incompetent will often be indefinitely hospitalized until such time as competency is restored. Some jurisdictions limit the amount of time that incompetents can remain in this legal limbo and require the government either to start to initiate a civil commitment proceeding or release the person.

A criminal defendant can claim insanity if he or she lacks the legal capacity to be criminally responsible for what would otherwise constitute criminal conduct. Some jurisdictions refuse to recognize insanity as an affirmative defense,[6] and the U.S. Supreme Court has ruled that states are constitutionally entitled to choose such a policy.[7] Since jurisdictions differ on what it means to lack legal capacity in such circumstances, there is no simple, uniform definition of insanity.

Internet Tip

Justice David Souter provided a brief but excellent overview (with footnotes) of this country's approach to insanity in criminal cases in his majority opinion in *Clark v. Arizona*, 548 U.S. 735 (2006). Interested readers can access this case on Loislaw.

Criminal law students often wrongfully assume that insanity is a medical rather than a legal term. *Insanity* is actually a legal term whose precise meaning varies with the contexts in which it is used. In the civil law context, a person determined to be insane will be ruled incompetent to enter into contracts or to make a will. In extreme cases, insane people can be civilly committed.

The first insanity test was developed by the English House of Lords in the aftermath of Daniel M'Naghten's unsuccessful attempt to murder Prime Minister Robert Peel (M'Naghten missed Peel but killed Edward Drummond, Peel's private secretary).[8] In *M'Naghten*, the Law Judges ruled that a criminal defendant could be excused from criminal responsibility only if (1) he was not, because of mental illness, aware of the nature and quality of his actions, or (2) he did know what he was doing; he was unable, when he acted, to distinguish right from wrong.

For approximately 100 years, the **M'Naghten rule** was the test followed in all American jurisdictions. Many states, such as Colorado, continue to follow the "right-wrong" dichotomy that is characteristic of the *M'Naghten* approach (see Figure 5.3).

Figure 5.3. Colorado Insanity Statute 16-8-101.5. Insanity defined—offenses committed on and after July 1, 1995

> (1) The applicable test of insanity shall be:
> (a) A person who is so diseased or defective in mind at the time of the commission of the act as to be incapable of distinguishing right from wrong

with respect to that act is not accountable; except that care should be taken not to confuse such mental disease or defect with moral obliquity, mental depravity, or passion growing out of anger, revenge, hatred, or other motives and kindred evil conditions, for, when the act is induced by any of these causes, the person is accountable to the law; or

(b) A person who suffered from a condition of mind caused by mental disease or defect that prevented the person from forming a culpable mental state that is an essential element of a crime charged, but care should be taken not to confuse such mental disease or defect with moral obliquity, mental depravity, or passion growing out of anger, revenge, hatred, or other motives and kindred evil conditions because, when the act is induced by any of these causes, the person is accountable to the law.

(2) As used in subsection (I) of this section:

(a) "Diseased or defective in mind" does not refer to an abnormality manifested only by repeated criminal or otherwise antisocial conduct.

(b) "Mental disease or defect" includes only those severely abnormal mental conditions that grossly and demonstrably impair a person's perception or understanding of reality and that are not attributable to the voluntary ingestion of alcohol or any other psychoactive substance but does not include an abnormality manifested only by repeated criminal or otherwise antisocial conduct.

(3) This section shall apply to offenses committed on or after July 1, 1995.

STATE OF COLORADO v. ROBIN V. TALLY

7 P.3d 172
Colorado Court of Appeals
April 29, 1999

AUTHOR'S INTRODUCTION

In the following Colorado case, Robin Tally claimed that he had been insane at the time he killed the victim and had acted while under a "delusion." This delusion, he said, was the product of a mental disease or defect. His request for a supplemental insanity instruction was denied by the trial court.

Robin Tally was charged with murder in the first degree for killing a co-worker. Tally claimed that he had been insane and that he believed, at the time of the incident, that God intended that Tally kill the victim. The jury found Tally to be sane and guilty as charged, and judgment was entered on the verdict. Tally appealed his conviction, contending that the trial judge committed prejudicial error in rejecting two requested instructions regarding the affirmative defense of insanity.

EXCERPT FROM THE CASE

Judge CRISWELL:

Defendant . . . argues that the instruction given by the court with respect to "deific delusions" was inadequate and that it should have been supplemented by one tendered by him. We disagree.

Section 16-8-101, C.R.S. . . . , requires that, to be legally insane, a defendant must be incapable of distinguishing right from wrong at the time of the commission of the act. The term "wrong" for this purpose is moral wrong, as distinguished from legal wrong. Further, "moral wrong" refers to an act measured by societal standards of morality rather than by a purely personal and subjective moral standard. . . .

In this sense, the fact that the individual acts under the delusion that God is compelling the act, the so-called deific-decree delusion . . . is an integral factor in assessing a person's cognitive ability to distinguish right from wrong. . . .

Here, the court told the jurors, among other things, that, with reference to the defense of insanity: *Incapable of distinguishing right from wrong* refers to cognitive inability, due to a mental disease or defect, to distinguish right from wrong as measured by a societal standard of morality, even though the person may be aware that the conduct in question is criminal. . . .

Defendant sought an instruction that, among other things, would have told the jurors that:

If Mr. Tally committed the act under a delusion, caused by mental disease or defect, that God had given him permission to commit the act, he must be judged insane.

While the tendered instruction might properly have been given, we conclude that the instruction given by the court was proper and adequately informed the jurors of the issue to be decided by them. . . .

The judgment is affirmed.

CASE QUESTION

When the "right-wrong" test is used to determine if an accused should be legally responsible for a criminal act, the definition of the meaning of "wrong" is of great importance. How did the court define the term *wrong* in this case?

AUTHOR'S COMMENTARY

The insanity standard historically followed in this country has been the traditional *M'Naghten* rule. During the last 30 years, however, many jurisdictions have abandoned *M'Naghten* in favor of the approach in the Model Penal Code, because they view the traditional rule's scope as too narrow. The Model Penal Code defines legal incapacity more broadly and includes a volitional dimension in addition to the traditional focus on cognition. The MPC rule provides that there is no criminal responsibility where an accused is unable to confine his conduct to legally established limits because of mental disease or defect. The *M'Naghten* rule is also criticized because it places too much emphasis on the opinions of expert witnesses. Critics say that the ultimate conclusions about an accused's cognitive capacity should be clearly reserved for the fact-finding judge or jury.

Approximately half of the states follow the MPC approach with respect to the insanity defense. The next case is from Rhode Island, a jurisdiction that replaced *M'Naghten* with a modified version of the Model Penal Code standard.

STATE v. DAVID BARRETT

768 A.2d 929
Supreme Court of Rhode Island
April 6, 2001

AUTHOR'S INTRODUCTION

David Barrett shot and killed Joseph Silvia in a service station parking lot in East Providence, Rhode Island. The two had been involved in an altercation in which each had threatened to kill the other. Prior to the arrival of the police, Barrett took a bag of marijuana out of his pocket and instructed a friend to get rid of it before officers arrived on the scene. After police arrived, Barrett was taken into custody, transported to the police station, and advised of his Miranda rights. After waiving his Miranda rights, Barrett subsequently admitted to having shot Silvia.

EXCERPT FROM THE CASE

Justice BOURCIER:

On July 18, 1995, David Barrett shot and killed Joseph Silvia. He was later indicted, tried by a Superior Court jury, and convicted of second-degree murder, and of carrying firearms without a license. In this appeal, he challenges his conviction for second-degree murder, contending that at the time that he shot Silvia he was of such diminished mental capacity as to be incapable of having formed the required intent and premeditation necessary for conviction. . . . We take up Barrett's appellate contentions in the order of their presentation. . . .

DIMINISHED CAPACITY

At his Superior Court trial, it was generally conceded that Barrett had a long history of bipolar disorder. Whether at the time he shot and killed Silvia that mental defect had prevented Barrett from being able to appreciate the wrongfulness of shooting Silvia, or from conforming his conduct to the requirements of the law, was both questioned and disputed.

Bipolar disorder, also called manic depression, is a mental illness characterized by episodes of both depression and a highly elevated mood. Other symptoms of the disease may include paranoia, intense agitation and energy, and aggressiveness. The severity of the disease differs individually but generally falls along a spectrum, ranging from highly symptomatic and highly impaired (manic) to less impaired and less symptomatic (hypomanic).

In *State v. Johnson*, . . . 399 A.2d 469 (1979), we adopted the Model Penal Code standard for determining a person's ability to form the intent necessary for criminal culpability. We said in that case that:

> A person is not responsible for criminal conduct if at the time of such conduct, as a result of mental disease or defect, his capacity either to appreciate the wrongfulness of his conduct or to conform his conduct to the requirements of law is so substantially impaired that he cannot justly be held responsible. The terms 'mental disease or defect' do not include an abnormality manifested only by repeated criminal or otherwise antisocial conduct. . . .

We found great merit in the Model Penal Code test because it recognized that in the determination of a defendant's alleged insanity or diminished capacity, that issue was delegated to a fact-finder or trial jury and is essentially a legal rather than a medical question, which permits a trial jury or fact-finder to consider volitional as well as cognitive impairments in determining a defendant's responsibility. . . . The Court in *Johnson* was particularly influenced by the Model Penal Code's recognition that in lieu of our then prevailing M'Naghten Rule, the Model Code permitted "a reasonable three-way dialogue between the law-trained judges and lawyers, the medical trained experts and the jury." . . . In Barrett's trial in the Superior Court, that three-way dialogue was played out.

At Barrett's trial, the severity of his bipolar disorder was vigorously contested. Both the state's prosecutor and defense counsel proffered and relied upon the medical opinion testimony of well-qualified experts, who offered opposing opinions concerning the extent and severity of Barrett's diminished capacity at the time of the shooting.

Two of those expert witnesses, Dr. Thomas Paolino and Dr. Thomas Gutheil, testified as defense witnesses for Barrett. Doctor Paolino, a board certified psychiatrist, who interviewed Barrett on nine separate occasions before Barrett's trial, testified that at the time of the shooting Barrett suffered from bipolar disorder in the manic phase, with psychotic and paranoid characteristics. When questioned on direct examination concerning whether or not as a result of this mental disease the defendant Barrett was able to appreciate the wrongfulness of his conduct at the time of the shooting, Dr. Paolino testified:

> My opinion is that David Barrett was convinced that Joseph Silvia was going to kill or severely injure him or his friends. It's my opinion that he didn't think it was wrong to shoot him, because he didn't know of any alternatives because . . . of his psychosis. In essence, the psychosis which includes the paranoid delusions, mania, and grandiosity denied him any alternatives. In the psychotic mind he was—either shoot or his friends and then he would be either killed or severely injured. If he were not psychotic or paranoid he wouldn't even be carrying a gun in the first place. Basically paranoia, mania, and the delusions, grandiosity essentially left him no options or alternatives then to [sic] what he did.

Doctor Paolino ruled out that Barrett's anger played any role in the shooting, and concluded that Barrett, at the time of the shooting, was not capable of conforming his conduct to the requirements of the law. . . .

On cross-examination, however, Dr. Paolino conceded that moments after the shooting Barrett was aware of what he had done, knew right from wrong, and was then able to conform his conduct to the law as evidenced by Barrett's decision to discard and conceal from the police the marijuana that he had in his vehicle. Doctor Paolino disputed, however, that this meant that Barrett was legally sane or of full mental capacity when moments earlier he had shot Silvia. In essence, Dr. Paolino testified that Barrett could have had a "manic" attack as a result of his altercation with Silvia that led to the shooting, and then Barrett could have become non-manic moments after the altercation ended.

Doctor Gutheil, also a board certified psychiatrist, testified for Barrett. Although he interviewed Barrett on only one occasion, he relied mostly for his diagnosis on the extensive reports of Dr. Paolino. He opined, as did Dr. Paolino, that Barrett was suffering from bipolar disorder at the time of the shooting. He testified that Barrett's ability to conform his behavior at that time to the requirements of the law and to appreciate the wrongfulness of actions was "substantially impaired" when he shot and killed Silvia. He concluded that Barrett was "very frightened, convinced he was going to die, and feeling endangered throughout that entire block of time as events escalated."

Doctor Gutheil, unlike Dr. Paolino, however, questioned whether Barrett's decision, following the shooting, to discard and conceal . . . marijuana to avoid its detection, and his culpability, indicated that Barrett was then able to conform his conduct to the law. . . . Under cross-examination, Dr. Gutheil, however, unlike Dr. Paolino, conceded that on the day of the shooting, Barrett exhibited only symptoms of hypomania, a milder form of bipolar disorder. Whereas Dr. Paolino had testified that on the day of the shooting, Barrett could not be hypomanic by definition, Dr. Guthiel testified that Barrett, on that day, was hypomanic. He also conceded that he could not rule out that anger—not just paranoia—played a role in Barrett's decision to track down, shoot and kill Silvia.

Following his arrest and questioning at the . . . police station, Barrett was . . . interviewed by Dr. Martin Bauermeister, a psychiatrist in charge of psychiatric services for the Department of Corrections. He testified that when he attempted to speak with Barrett, Barrett told him that he had been advised by his lawyer not to talk to the doctor. Doctor Bauermeister noted in his medical record that Barrett seemed rational, made rational statements and that he "noticed no evidence of psychotic misinterpretation of reality." When asked by defense counsel if it was "possible for someone who is psychotic to be calm a period of time," the doctor replied, "Yes. Not all crazy people are crazy all the time."

Doctor Robert Cserr (Dr. Cserr), a practicing board certified psychiatrist, was called as a prosecution witness. Doctor Cserr, based on one interview he had with Barrett and based on his review of Barrett's extensive medical record, acknowledged that Barrett had a long history of mental illness. Doctor Cserr opined, from his review of Barrett's medical history, that Barrett had become "increasingly grandiose" in the weeks before the shooting, and that his bipolar disorder was in a manic to "hypomanic/manic" stage on the morning of the killing. He also acknowledged that Barrett's mental illness played some role in the shooting. "I think without the mental illness he probably wouldn't have gone to the station, or remained there, or when confronted [by Silvia] might have left. So, there is some degree of impairing his judgment. . . ."

However, Dr. Cserr said that Barrett was not legally insane at the time when he shot and killed Silvia, and that Barrett at that time was able to understand the wrongfulness of his actions and, as well, his need to conform his behavior to the requirements of the law. . . .

Doctor Cserr rejected the suggestion that Barrett believed that he could not drive away from the Mobil station as a result of mental illness. He also interpreted Barrett's tracking down and threatening Silvia, before he shot Silvia . . . as indicative of "some degree of composure." . . . Doctor Cserr also found that Barrett's discarding of marijuana to conceal it from the police was evidence not only of his sanity, but also of his then presence of mind and ability to think on how to avoid detection, positing that "it's hard to say that you don't know about something major [the shooting] and yet you're totally tuned into something relatively minor that can get you into trouble." He challenged defense counsel's suggestion that it would be possible for Barrett to be psychotic at the time of the killing and not be psychotic just moments later at the time of his deciding to dispose of the marijuana. Doctor Cserr steadfastly maintained that, despite some mental impairment, Barrett was not of such diminished capacity at the time of the shooting as to preclude his ability to appreciate the wrongfulness of what he was doing or to conform his conduct to that required of him by the law. . . .

In short, Dr. Cserr appears to have agreed with the observation made by Dr. Bauermeister that "not all crazy people are crazy all the time." Thus, the trial jury had before it for its consideration, the various expert opinions from the medical witnesses. The mere fact that two of those opinions supported Barrett's diminished capacity defense as opposed to only one supporting the state's position that Barrett was capable of forming the requisite mental intent necessary for conviction of murder is not in itself dispositive of the issue of Barrett's mental condition at the time of the shooting. Trial jurors are uniformly reminded that in their evaluation of expert witness opinion trial testimony they should not decide disputed issues of fact solely upon the number of the witnesses testifying for or against a particular fact issue, but instead, upon the quality of the evidence concerning that fact issue. In this case it is perfectly obvious that the trial jurors opted to accept the opinion testimony offered by Dr. Cserr and to reject in great part the opinion testimony proffered by Drs. Paolino and Guthiel. That was the trial jury's choice to make.

We, of course, recognize from the trial record that there was evidence of Barrett's sometimes bizarre behavior and nonconformist actions indicative of his long-standing psychological infirmity. That evidence alone, however, did not, as Barrett now contends, require a conclusion by the trial jury that Barrett lacked the required mental capacity to have been able at the time . . . to conform his conduct to the requirements of the law. . . . We discern in the trial record more than sufficient evidence to support the jury's finding that, beyond a reasonable doubt, Barrett had the substantial and necessary mental capacity to conform his conduct to the requirements of the law at the time he went to the Mobil station on July 18, 1995, and when he tracked down, shot and killed Silvia. . . .

Implicit in the jury's verdict in this case is its finding that Barrett, at the time he shot Silvia, was not of such diminished mental capacity as to be unable to appreciate the wrongfulness of his conduct, or to conform his conduct to the requirements of the law. Barrett's guilt for that murder in the second degree finds ample support in the trial record. Barrett's contention that the trial jury misconceived the trial evidence and erred in not accepting the medical opinions proffered by his witnesses is without merit. . . .

THE NEW TRIAL MOTION

Barrett's final appellate contention of trial error is that he believes that the trial justice erred in denying his motion for a new trial. He argues that the trial justice overlooked or misconceived material trial evidence concerning the nature and extent of his insanity and diminished capacity.

He points out that the trial justice recognized only that he suffered from "some mental health problem" and passed over what he contends was other voluminous evidence that established far beyond a fair preponderance of all of the trial evidence that he was legally insane at the time that he shot and killed Silvia. In doing so, Barrett chooses to conveniently ignore the undeniable fact that twelve jurors and later, a learned and experienced trial justice, all had reviewed, considered and rejected that same evidentiary contention.

We have carefully reviewed the trial justice's decision in which he denied Barrett's new trial motion. We discern therein sufficient reference to the material trial evidence and sufficient explanation for the reasons given by him for denying the motion. We thus are able to conclude that he adequately reviewed the trial jury's findings, and the trial evidence that the jury relied on to make its findings. We are also satisfied that he properly exercised his own independent judgment upon the weight and credibility of the trial evidence in determining whether that evidence was sufficient to satisfy the state's burden to have proven beyond a reasonable doubt that at the time Barrett shot and killed Silvia, he both appreciated the wrongfulness of what he was doing, realized that he could be held responsible for what he was doing, and that he could have, but did not then conform his conduct to the requirements of the law. . . .

Under the rule we adopted in *Johnson*, the state in this case was required to prove beyond a reasonable doubt that Barrett was capable of forming the malicious intent, however brief, to unlawfully kill Silvia during his somewhat deliberate but yet unfortunate confrontation with Silvia at the Mobil station in East Providence. In addition, the state, and to that same degree of proof, was required to prove that the shooting of Silvia by Barrett was done with malice, arising from either Barrett's express intent to kill Silvia or to inflict great bodily harm on him from wanton recklessness.

. . . Barrett by alleging his diminished capacity "conceded his responsibility for the act but claims that, in light of his abnormal mental condition, he is less culpable." . . .

While Barrett had no burden of proof to meet and carry, he did, because of his assertion of an insanity or diminished capacity defense, assume the burden of presenting sufficient evidence of his diminished capacity, and to persuade the trial jury that it was of sufficient degree to have prevented him from forming the required intent and malice essential for conviction on the murder charge. . . . This, of course, did not relieve the state of its initial and continuing trial burden to prove beyond a reasonable doubt Barrett's ability to form the necessary intent required for conviction of the crime of murder.

In *Johnson*, . . . we [ruled] that the determination of whether a particular defendant was insane, or of such diminished capacity to commit the particular criminal act, must be left to the jury. "Without question the essential dilemma in formulating any standard of criminal responsibility is encouraging a maximum informational input from the expert witnesses while preserving to the jury its role as trier of fact and ultimate decision maker." . . . We concluded in *Johnson* that "because impairment is a matter of degree, the precise degree demanded is necessarily governed by the community sense of justice as represented by the trier of fact." . . .

We are satisfied from our review of the trial record and trial exhibits that the trial justice in this case diligently exercised his independent judgment on the totality of the trial evidence and on the jury's findings and verdict. He concluded there-from that the trial evidence:

> supports the conclusion that the defendant shot Mr. Silvia out of anger and not because he was suffering from an abnormal mental condition which rendered him incapable of forming the specific intent to kill Mr. Silvia. The record is replete with instances of the defendant reacting in an untoward fashion when he is angered. . . .

The mere fact that Barrett now disagrees with the jury's verdicts and with the trial justice's acceptance and approval of those verdicts, does not serve to transform what he wishes into reality. . . .

CONCLUSION

For the reasons herein above set out, the defendant's appeal is denied and his convictions are affirmed. The papers in this case are remanded to the Superior Court. . . .

CASE QUESTION

What are the principal differences between the Rhode Island insanity rule and the *M'Naghten* rule?

AUTHOR'S COMMENTARY

Some jurisdictions have chosen to somewhat broaden the *M'Naghten* rule by following Alabama's lead and adopting the **irresistible impulse test**.[9] According to this test, a person who knew the nature and quality of his actions, and who knew that what he was doing was wrong, would still not be criminally responsible if he was unable to exercise self-control because of mental disease or defect and was overcome by an irresistible impulse. Although this test is more expansive than *M'Naghten*, it is not as broadly conceived as the MPC's approach, which exempts those who substantially lack the capacity to conform their conduct to legal standards because of a mental disease or defect.

Mistake of Fact

Sometimes a person, although committing an *actus reus*, honestly and reasonably misunderstands the true facts and lacks the state of mind required for conviction of a crime. To illustrate this defense, let's consider a hypothetical set of facts readers encountered in Chapter 3 involving a passenger retrieving her suitcase from an airport's baggage carousel. Under the facts of that example, the passenger picked up a suitcase that looks, in all respects, like the one that she checked with the airline prior to taking a flight. Readers were asked to assume that this passenger failed to carefully examine the baggage tags and then mistakenly took another passenger's suitcase. She had in fact taken someone else's bag, put it in her car's trunk, and exited the airport, believing at all times that the bag in her trunk was her own. Despite the fact that she has committed an *actus reus*, and had taken and carried away another's bag, she did not have the requisite criminal intent. Her testimony, if believed and if found to be reasonable after a comparison of the suitcase she brought to the airport with the one that she mistakenly claimed at the carousel, would establish a valid **mistake of fact** defense. Note that she did not claim to have made a mistake about the lawfulness or constitutionality of her actions. The mistake was purely one of fact.

JOSEPH W. MARQUARDT JR. v. STATE OF MARYLAND
882 A.2d 900
Court of Special Appeals of Maryland
September 8, 2005

AUTHOR'S INTRODUCTION

This case focuses on events that occurred between March 12-14, 2003. Joseph Marquardt and his wife, Catherine Burns, were experiencing marital difficulties. Both had a history of alcohol and drug abuse. On March 12, Joseph was living at their residence, and Catherine was at that time staying with friends. Although Joseph had completed a rehabilitation program and claimed to have overcome his addictions, he believed Catherine was away from home "smoking crack." She had done this previously and would be gone for "days at a time."

Joseph received a phone call from Catherine saying that she was at the hospital, subsequently went to the hospital, and learned that Catherine was three months pregnant. The parents agreed to reconcile and the celebrate the coming birth of their child on March 14th.

Joseph could not find Catherine when he came home after work on March 14th and spent the next two days looking for her and contacting his addiction counselor and both his and his wife's probation officers to see if they could provide help to Catherine. Nothing came from these efforts. Even prior to the events of March 12-14, Joseph had contacted several public and private agencies and his wife's parents to see if they would help Catherine deal with her addiction. After learning that his wife was pregnant, Joseph was adamant that Catherine's and his child not become a "crack baby."

Joseph was also searching for Catherine on his own, disregarding police advice that he step aside and "let the law handle it" if he discovered where Catherine was staying. Instead, Joseph offered to pay a $100 reward for information about where his wife was staying. He received a tip that Catherine was currently in an apartment in a building located at 17 Bay Street. He went to that address, broke the glass on the front door, and soon learned that he was at the wrong address. Joseph apologized to the resident, who's dwelling he had unlawfully entered, offered to make restitution, and left for a second apartment building located at 13 Bay Street.

At the second apartment building, Joseph broke into the building and used a baseball bat to break into apartment one, within which he found Catherine and her friend, Robert Lambert. When Lambert ran toward Joseph, Joseph hit Lambert on the head with the bat. Joseph then grabbed Catherine, and against her will, forced her to accompany him out of apartment one and the apartment building and into his truck.

While Joseph was driving the truck, Catherine managed to call 911 on her cell phone. She left it on so that police could listen to what was happening and so that she could be rescued. Catherine subsequently escaped from the truck, was found by police, and taken to a hospital. The police 911 recording consisted of Joseph and Catherine arguing while in the truck. Catherine was heard saying that Joseph was hitting her and threatening to kill her. Joseph was also heard on this recording making several threats to kill his wife if she didn't stop smoking "crack."

PROCEDURAL FACTS

Marquardt was charged, convicted, and sentenced for assaulting two people, burglarizing two dwellings, maliciously destroying property (3 counts), and one count of false imprisonment. Marquardt raised four issues on appeal, one of which is relevant to our current discussion and is included in this excerpt from the case report.

The relevant issue as stated by the court was:

"2. Did the circuit court err in refusing to instruct the jury on the defenses of necessity . . . and mistake of fact?"

EXCERPT FROM THE CASE

KENNEY, Judge.

II. JURY INSTRUCTIONS

A. NECESSITY

Appellant requested that the circuit court instruct the jury on the defense of necessity. . . .

Appellant argues that the defense was applicable because he faced a choice between acting to prevent his wife from abusing drugs or doing nothing, "thereby risking that his wife's placenta would break loose and she would bleed to death and/or that their child would die or be born with serious disabilities." The State counters that the defense was not applicable because "the crimes were disproportionate to the threat," and "the threatened harm is future, rather than immediate, personal injury." Furthermore, the State asserts that the defendant had other alternatives than resorting to violence, such as continuing to convince Burns to seek treatment.

We begin with a discussion of the defense of necessity . . .

In *Frasher v. State*, this Court stated that "[i]t is essential to a crime that the [appellant] committed a voluntary act," therefore, "it is a defense as to all crimes except taking the life of an innocent person that the [appellant] acted under a compelling force of coercion or duress." . . .

This "compulsion may be by necessity, that is duress arising from circumstances, or by the application of duress on the defendant by another person." . . . Quoting "R. Perkins, *Criminal Law*, 847 (1957)," the *Frasher* Court stated: " 'If a choice exists but only between two evils, one of which is the commission of a wrongful act, and the emergency was not created by the wrongful act of another person it is spoken of as an act done in a case of necessity.' " . . .

The rationale of the necessity defense is not that a person, when faced with the pressure of circumstances of nature, lacks the mental element which the crime in question requires. Rather, it is this reason of public policy: the law ought to promote the achievement of higher values at the expense of lesser values, and sometimes the greater good for society will be accomplished by violating the literal language of the criminal law." (quoting W. LaFave & A. Scott, Jr., *Criminal Law* § 50 (1972)).

The Court noted five elements necessary to consider before applying the defense of necessity:

"**1**—The harm avoided—this need not be physical harm but also may be harm to property as, for instance, where a firefighter destroys some property to prevent the spread of fire which threatens to consume other property of greater value.

2—The harm done—this is not limited to any particular type of harm but includes intentional homicide as well as intentional battery or property damage. An illustration is supplied:

[A]s where A, driving a car, suddenly finds himself in a predicament where he must either run down B or hit C's house and he reasonably chooses the latter, unfortunately killing two people in the house who by bad luck happened to be just at that place inside the house where A's car struck—it is the harm-reasonably-expected, rather than the harm-actually-caused, which governs.

3—Intention to avoid harm—to have the defense of necessity, the defendant must have acted with the intention of avoiding the greater harm. Actual necessity, without the intention, is not enough. However, an honest and reasonable belief in the necessity of his action is all that is required.

4—The relative value of the harm avoided and the harm done. The defendant's belief as to the relative harmfulness of the harm avoided and the harm done does not control. It is for the court, not the defendant, to weigh the relative harmfulness of the two alternatives. To allow the defense the court must conclude that the harm done by the defendant in choosing the one alternative was less than the harm which would have been done if he had chosen the other.

5—Optional courses of action; imminence of disaster. The defense of necessity applies when the defendant is faced with this choice of two evils: he may either do something which violates the literal terms of the criminal law and thus produce some harm, or not do it and so produce a greater harm. If, however, there is open to him a third alternative, which will cause less harm than will be caused by violating the law, he is not justified in violating the law. For example, "[a] prisoner subjected to inhuman treatment by his jailors is not justified in breaking prison if he can bring about an improvement in conditions by other means." . . .

The . . . cases makes clear that, in order for the defense of necessity to have been warranted in this case, appellant must have presented "some evidence" that there was a choice between two evils, that no legal alternatives existed, that the harm appellant caused was not disproportionate to the harm avoided, and that the emergency was imminent. . . . Appellant runs afoul of the last requirement, or namely, that the emergency he was seeking to prevent was imminent.

Appellant testified, without corroboration, that he called a hospital the night of the incident and was told if Burns continued to use cocaine she might suffer internal bleeding from a ruptured placenta later during pregnancy, but there was no evidence of an immediate or imminent danger that would warrant appellant acting in the manner that he did. Rather than helping, his actions could have caused more serious harm to Burns and perhaps a miscarriage terminating her pregnancy. . . . In addition, Lambert could have been more seriously injured or even killed. A tenuous relationship between present actions and a possible future harm is not enough to support a necessity instruction. . . .

Appellant did not establish a *prima facie* case of necessity. Accordingly, the circuit court did not err in refusing to give a defense of necessity instruction.

B. MISTAKE OF FACT

Appellant contends that, "[a]ssuming that the lower court erred by failing to instruct the jury on necessity of circumstances, it further erred in denying [appellant's] request for an instruction on mistake of fact." . . . He asserts that his belief in breaking into 17 Bay Street instead of 13 Bay Street to retrieve Burns was reasonable, "given the information he had regarding her location as well as the general stress and excitement of the moment," and that "had the address been correct, [his] actions would have been justified under the defense of necessity. Therefore, the refusal to provide the instruction on mistake of fact was error."

In other words, he contends that, acting out of necessity, he could reasonably break into 13 Bay Street, and that he mistakenly entered 17 Bay Street, which was reasonable under the circumstances. A necessary element of the mistake of fact defense is that his conduct would not have amounted to a crime had the circumstances been as he believed them to be. Appellant's mistake of fact argument is based on his necessity defense and fails with the failure of that defense. Appellant was not justified in breaking into either 13 or 17 Bay Street.

CASE QUESTION

Since Marquardt's conduct at 17 Bay Street was based on a factual mistake as to where Lambert lived, why isn't this factual mistake legally sufficient for the court to give the mistake-of-fact instruction?

AUTHOR'S COMMENTARY

It is important to emphasize that the mistake of fact defense negates the possibility that the accused possessed criminal intent to commit the charged offense. When successful, it is a complete bar to criminal liability for *mens rea* offenses. The mistake of fact defense, however, is unavailable to someone charged with a strict liability crime.

Mistake of Law

A person who mistakenly believes that his conduct was lawful when he committed it is attempting to maintain a *mistake of law* defense. The traditional general rule is that "ignorance of the law is no excuse." People are presumed to know the law. In our society, citizens, it is argued, have ready access to the law. Any person who has access to a computer can access virtually all the statutes enacted by the federal and state legislatures. Today, many of the recent decisions of state and federal appellate courts interpreting these statutes are also available online.

Imagine how difficult it would be for society to protect itself if the prosecution had to prove that every defendant was personally aware of the existence of the particular laws that made his or her actions criminal!

Yet there are some circumstances in which exceptions to the general rule are recognized. In one famous case a person was prosecuted for not registering with police as required by law. The U.S. Supreme Court ruled that under the particular circumstances of her case, where there was no proof that the defendant had actual notice of any duty to register and little probability that a reasonable person would be aware of such a duty, due process barred her conviction.[10]

KIPP v. STATE OF DELAWARE

704 A.2d 839
Delaware Supreme Court
January 13, 1998

AUTHOR'S INTRODUCTION

In the case of *Kipp v. State of Delaware* we will see that the mistake-of-law defense also applies where a criminal defendant's allegedly criminal acts result from misinformation supplied by a judge.

EXCERPT FROM THE CASE

Justice HOLLAND:

This is an appeal following a bench trial in the Superior Court. The defendant-appellant, Hugh A. Kipp, Jr. ("Kipp"), was convicted of three counts of Possession of a Deadly Weapon by a Person Prohibited. The State has confessed error on appeal and submits that Kipp's judgments of conviction should be reversed.

FACTS

On the morning of September 17, 1995, several police officers went to Kipp's home in Wilmington. They were investigating a "man with a gun" complaint from Kipp's girlfriend, Lisa Zeszut ("Zeszut"). At first Kipp refused to come out of his house, but eventually surrendered to the police. Kipp was taken to Wilmington Hospital for a psychological evaluation.

The police searched the house for other weapons. The police found a handgun and two unloaded shotguns. The police discovered ammunition for those weapons scattered on the bedroom floor. The police also found two hunting bows, with arrows. Upon checking Kipp's criminal record, police ascertained that he was a person prohibited from possessing deadly weapons.

Kipp was originally charged with five counts of Possession of a Deadly Weapon by a Person Prohibited. Based on a complaint by Zeszut, Kipp was also charged with Aggravated Menacing, Possession of a Deadly Weapon During Commission of a Felony, Terroristic Threatening and Offensive Touching. Zeszut, however, did not cooperate with the prosecution. Those charges were dismissed prior to trial.

The only defense offered by Kipp at trial was that he was unaware of his status as a "person prohibited." Kipp was a "person prohibited" as a result of his guilty plea to Assault in the Third Degree in 1990. Kipp testified he was told that he would not be prohibited from possessing weapons as a result of the plea.

The 1990 guilty plea form, which was submitted into evidence, has a space which provides that a guilty plea will result in loss of the right to possess deadly weapons. That portion of the form was marked "N/A". Kipp testified that "N/A" meant the provision did not apply to him. The completed guilty plea form was provided to the judge during the 1990 plea colloquy. Neither the prosecutor nor the judge, however, brought the error on the guilty plea form to Kipp's attention.

After hearing all of the evidence, the Superior Court concluded that the two hunting bows were not deadly weapons. Therefore, it dismissed the two counts of Possession of a Deadly Weapon by a Person Prohibited involving the bows. The Superior Court found Kipp guilty of three counts of Possession of a Deadly Weapon by a Person Prohibited in connection with his possession of the three firearms.

PERSON PROHIBITED STATUTE INCLUDES
VIOLENT MISDEMEANORS

Under II Del. C. § 1448(b), "[a]ny prohibited person . . . who knowingly possesses, purchases, owns or controls a deadly weapon while so prohibited shall be guilty of possession of a deadly weapon by a person prohibited." A person is a "prohibited person" for purposes of § 1448(b) when, *inter alia*, he or she has "been convicted in this State or elsewhere of a felony or a crime of violence involving physical injury to another . . ." II Del. C. § 1448(a)(1). Assault in the Third Degree is a misdemeanor crime of violence involving physical injury to another. II Del. C. § 61 I. A person who has been convicted of a violent misdemeanor is prohibited from possessing a deadly weapon for the five-year period from the date of conviction. II Del. C. § 1448(d).

KIPP'S CONTENTION GUILTY PLEA INVALID

Kipp does not contest the fact that he pled guilty on October 23, 1990 to Assault in the Third Degree, a violent misdemeanor. Nor does he contest the fact that he had three firearms in his possession on September 17, 1995. Kipp does not contest the fact that, within five years of pleading guilty to a violent offense, he possessed three deadly weapons. His sole contention on appeal is that his 1990 guilty plea was not made knowingly. Therefore, Kipp submits that his 1990 conviction for Assault in the Third Degree is invalid. Accordingly, he argues that his conviction for Possession of a Deadly Weapon by a Person Prohibited should be set aside.

DEADLY WEAPON PROHIBITION CONSTITUTES
COLLATERAL CONSEQUENCE

The judge's failure to inform Kipp in 1990 that he would, upon conviction, be prohibited from possessing deadly weapons did not render the 1990 guilty plea involuntary. A defendant's loss of the future right to possess deadly weapons upon entry of certain guilty pleas is merely a collateral consequence of such a plea. . . . "Without a doubt, the defendant must understand the consequences of pleading guilty, but this does not include informing him of collateral civil or criminal consequences of the plea." . . . Therefore, Kipp's 1990 conviction for Assault in the Third Degree is valid.

MISTAKE OF LAW STATE CONFESSES ERROR

Nevertheless, the State has confessed error in Kipp's case on appeal. Under the facts presented, the State concedes that Kipp presented a valid mistake of law defense. This Court has held that, in very narrow circumstances, mistake of law can be a defense to a criminal charge. . . . That defense is cognizable when the defendant: (1) erroneously concludes in good faith that his particular conduct is not subject to the operation of the criminal law; (2) makes a "bona fide, diligent effort, adopting a course and resorting to sources and means at least as appropriate as any afforded or under our legal system, to ascertain and abide by the law"; (3) "act[s] in good faith reliance upon the results of such effort"; and (4) the conduct constituting the offense is "neither immoral nor anti-social." . . .

Kipp presented evidence that he was misled in connection with his plea to Assault in the Third Degree. His 1990 guilty plea form, which was introduced at trial, and his testimony indicated he was told that the prohibition against possession of a deadly weapon which would result from a guilty plea was "not applicable" to the plea which he was entering. Kipp testified that he was told that prohibition was not applicable to him because he was pleading to a misdemeanor.

Kipp's plea agreement and truth-in-sentencing guilty plea form were submitted to the judge in 1990 at the plea colloquy before his guilty plea to Assault in the Third Degree was accepted. Apparently, the prosecutor and the judge who accepted his guilty plea failed to notice the "not applicable" notation on the guilty plea form. The judge referred to the plea agreement in the plea colloquy, but never informed Kipp that the "not applicable" notation was incorrect with respect to the prohibition against future possession of a deadly weapon which would result from the plea.

Under II Del. C. § 1448, a person is guilty of possession of a deadly weapon by a person prohibited when he is: (a) a person prohibited; and (b) knowingly possesses a deadly weapon. Thus, to be guilty of the offense, the defendant need only know that he or she possessed the weapon. Section 1448 does not require the defendant to know that it was criminal to do so. . . .

Ignorance of the law is not a defense to crime. . . . But "[a] defendant is not charged with knowledge of a penal statute if he is misled concerning whether the statute is not being applied." . . . A mistake of law defense is appropriately recognized where the defendant demonstrates that he has been misled by information received from the State. . . .

Under the unique circumstances of this case, the State concedes on appeal that Kipp presented a proper and complete mistake of law defense. . . . In relying on the advice of counsel, memorialized in an official guilty plea document presented to and not corrected by either the prosecutor or the judge, Kipp had "made a bona fide, diligent effort, adopting a course and resorting to sources and means at least as appropriate as any afforded under our legal system, to ascertain and abide by the law. . . ." The State submits that Kipp's three convictions for possession of a deadly weapon by a person prohibited should be reversed. . . .

CONCLUSION

The mistake of law defense is based upon principles of fundamental fairness. . . . A review of the record and the applicable law supports the State's confession of error. The State's confession of error "is in accordance with the highest tradition of the Delaware Bar and the prosecutor's unique role and duty to seek justice within an adversary system." . . .

The judgments of conviction are reversed. This matter is remanded to the Superior Court for further proceedings in accordance with this opinion.

CASE QUESTIONS

1. In Delaware, when is the mistake of law defense appropriately recognized?

2. Why was Kipp's mistake about the lawfulness of his conduct excusable under the circumstances of this case?

3. Why doesn't the state normally have to prove that a defendant is aware of the requirements of the law he or she is accused of violating?

AUTHOR'S COMMENTARY

Exceptions to the general rule that ignorance of the law is no excuse are sometimes recognized where a criminally accused person relies on the holdings of an appellate court, where a defendant has relied on a statute that was subsequently ruled to be unconstitutional (because statutes are presumptively constitutional), and where one of the elements of the crime requires that the accused be proven to have possessed knowledge of the illegality of particular conduct.

A criminal defendant cannot ordinarily defend by proving that he had relied on an attorney's advice as to the legality of contemplated conduct and that the advice had turned out to be incorrect. The problem with recognizing reliance on an attorney's bad advice as a defense is that it would become too easy for an accused to avoid criminal responsibility and because it would have the effect of elevating the advice of attorneys over the actual requirements of the law.[11]

Entrapment

Entrapment is a defense intended to deter police investigators from inducing a customarily law-abiding person into committing a criminal offense. This defense is available in situations where police officers persuade someone to commit a crime who would not otherwise have done so. Assume, for example, that undercover police officers approach an unemployed worker who has not otherwise been involved with controlled substances. Assume further that after three weeks they are able to persuade the worker to become a drug pusher and supply them with drugs and that they subsequently arrest him when he finally gives in and takes their advice. The worker has been entrapped by the police officers. It is they who are the moving force in the commission of the crime. The worker was not predisposed to commit the crime. If, however, the accused is predisposed to sell drugs and police officers merely provide the person with an opportunity to make a sale, there has been no entrapment.

Either a court or the jury, depending on the jurisdiction, determines whether the police conduct has gone too far and whether this defense is proven.

WISCONSIN v. JAMES L. SCHUMAN
595 N.W.2d 86
Wisconsin Court of Appeal
April 15, 1999

AUTHOR'S INTRODUCTION

James L. Schuman, the defendant in the next case, was convicted of solicitation to commit first-degree murder and attempted first-degree murder. His request for a jury instruction on entrapment was refused by the trial court, and he appealed to the intermediate court of appeals.

EXCERPT FROM THE CASE

Judge EICH:

James L. Schuman was convicted, after a jury trial, of attempted first-degree intentional homicide and solicitation to commit first-degree intentional homicide. He was sentenced to thirty-five years in prison. . . .

The charges arose from a police undercover operation in La Crosse in early 1997. The operation began after Herbert Miller—a convicted felon and an acquaintance of Schuman—reported to the La Crosse Police Department that Schuman had approached him on several occasions asking whether he could find someone to kill Schuman's wife, with whom Schuman was involved in a drawn-out, bitter divorce proceeding. As a result of Miller's accusations, a Wisconsin Department of Justice investigator, Eric Szatkowski, posing as a "hit man" (ostensibly located by Miller), telephoned Schuman, and the two men agreed to meet. During their first and subsequent meetings and conversations—all of which were taped by Szatkowski— Schuman said that his wife had ruined his life and put his children in foster homes, and that he wanted her killed. After several discussions of the details of such an endeavor, Schuman agreed to pay Szatkowski $10,000 to kill his wife, and indicated he would pay additional sums for the death of her father if he was "in the way." Miller also told Szatkowski that he wanted the killing to take place during the weekend of February 28, 1997, when he would be out of town with his two children. In subsequent conversations, Schuman reaffirmed his desire to have his wife killed—and her boyfriend, too, if necessary—and the two men continued to discuss the "details," including Szatkowski's payment.

On the morning of February 27, 1997, Schuman was arrested as he was preparing to leave town with his children. Schuman's defense at trial was that he was never really seeking a "hit man," but only wanted to find someone who would play "dirty tricks" on his wife—such as planting drugs on her or scaring her—in an attempt to shorten the divorce proceedings and get his children out of foster care; and he testified that he agreed to meet with Szatkowski "just to talk and see what kind of prank he was gonna pull." He testified that it wasn't until Szatkowski mentioned a gun that he (Schuman) first realized he was "confront[ing] . . . a killer" and that, at this point he became frightened, fearing what might happen if he just "walk[ed] away" from the discussions—even though he had every intention of backing out before the plan could be consummated. Schuman stated that throughout their conversations, he interpreted various statements made by Szatkowski as "direct threats" as to what would happen if Schuman backed out and went to the police; and he feared that his precipitous withdrawal would jeopardize his and his children's safety.

Thus, according to Schuman, even though his taped conversations with Szatkowski included discussions of methods and opportunities for killing Schuman's wife, those conversations should not be taken at face value, but rather must be understood in the context of Schuman's state of mind at the time—that he was only pretending to go along with the plan out of fear.

At the close of evidence, Schuman requested that the jury be instructed on the defense of entrapment. The court denied the request, stating that there was no evidence of "objectionable inducements" on Szatkowski's part which would warrant such an instruction. Schuman renewed the request when the jury, during its deliberations, sent a question to the court asking: "What is the legal definition of entrapment?" to which the court replied: "The court has given you the instructions that you are to consider regarding this case." As indicated, the jury found Schuman guilty of attempted first-degree intentional homicide (of his wife) and solicitation to commit first-degree intentional homicide (of his wife's boyfriend).

There is no question that the government may use undercover agents to enforce the law, and that "[a]rtifice and stratagem may be employed to catch those engaged in criminal enterprises." . . . However, those agents "may not originate a criminal design, implant in an innocent person's mind the disposition to commit a criminal act, and then induce commission of the crime so that the Government may prosecute." . . . And that is the essence of the defense of entrapment: a situation where the "evil intent" and the "criminal design" of the offense originate in the mind of the government agent, and the defendant would not have committed an offense of that character except for the urging of the agent. . . . Establishing the defense is a two-step process:

> To establish the defense of entrapment, the defendant must show by a preponderance of the evidence that [he or] she was induced to commit the crime. If the defendant meets [that] burden of persuasion, then the burden falls on the state to prove beyond a reasonable doubt that the defendant was predisposed to commit the crime. . . .

A trial court is justified in declining to give a requested instruction in a criminal case—including an instruction on the defense of entrapment—if it is not reasonably required by the evidence. . . . And when the appeal is from such a denial, we must view the evidence in the most favorable light it will reasonably admit from the standpoint of the accused. . . . Only "slight evidence" is required to create a factual issue and thus put the defense before the jury. . . .

The evidence may be "weak, insufficient, inconsistent, or of doubtful credibility" . . . but the defendant is entitled to the instruction unless the evidence is rebutted by the prosecution to the extent that "no rational jury could entertain a reasonable doubt as to either element." . . .

Considering the evidence, as we must, in the light most favorable to Schuman, he testified that he never told Miller, Szatkowski, or anyone else, that he wanted his wife killed. He testified that it was Miller who first approached him, after overhearing him talking on the phone with his children about the divorce. According to Schuman, Miller offered to get one of his friends to play a "dirty trick" on Schuman's wife. Schuman also testified that there was nothing in his conversations with either Miller or Szatkowski prior to his first meeting with Szatkowski to indicate that he was being set up with a "hit man." According to Schuman, it was only when Szatkowski mentioned a firearm that he first believed he was dealing with a professional hit man who intended to do much more to his wife than simply play a "dirty trick" on her. At this point, Schuman said, he only discussed details about killing his wife "just to give [Szatkowski] something to satisfy him at the moment so [Schuman] could get out of there." He said his aim in all this was to convince Szatkowski that he "wasn't gonna run to the police."

Schuman explained that his plan was to get some money for Szatkowski's expenses so he could tell him he didn't want things to go any further and then could abort the plan prior to its execution. As indicated, Schuman also testified that he interpreted various statements made by Szatkowski as threats as to what would happen if he went to the police, and that he continued to "play along" because, while he intended to back out at all times, he feared that any sudden withdrawal would place both him and his children in danger. The question is not whether we, or the trial court, believe, or are willing to give credence to Schuman's testimony. The test for evidentiary support for a requested jury instruction is, as we have indicated, whether "a reasonable construction of the evidence will support the defendant's theory, viewed in the most favorable light it will reasonably admit from the standpoint of the accused." ... And in making that determination, neither the trial court nor the reviewing court may weigh the evidence, but instead may only ask whether a reasonable construction of the evidence, viewed favorably to the defendant, supports the alleged defense. If this question is answered affirmatively, then it is for the jury, not the trial court or [the appellate] court, to determine whether to believe defendant's version of the events. . . .

The United States Court of Appeals for the Ninth Circuit made a similar point in Kessee, supra. In that case, the defendant, responding to a police informant's requests to enter into a drug deal, eventually proposed selling drugs to the informant, telling him that he had engaged in more than fifty such deals in the past. Charged with conspiracy and possession of drugs with the intent to distribute, the defendant requested an entrapment instruction based on his testimony that he had never dealt drugs before, but falsely portrayed himself as an experienced dealer in order to impress the informant who, he said, had lured him into the transaction. The trial court denied the request. . . .

The trial judge's skepticism [as to the defendant's story] was certainly well-founded. At least one juror would have to be very impressed by Kessee's testimony on the stand, so impressed as to accept unlikely stories to explain the way Kessee sounded on the telephone, his inconsistencies, and his statements to the police. Nevertheless, the jury, not the trial judge, had the power to decide whether Kessee's account on the witness stand was the truth. . . . Kessee presented "some evidence" for each of the two elements of entrapment, so "[t]he weight and credibility of the conflicting testimony are issues properly reserved [to] the jury. The jury could have believed . . . that he was falsely boasting when he described himself as a major drug dealer." . . . We are in a similar position here. While Schuman's story stretches the imagination, we cannot say that no reasonable juror, having observed him testify at trial, could (a) determine that his participation in the scheme was induced by Szatkowski, or (b) entertain a reasonable doubt that he was predisposed to commit the charged crimes. Because Schuman's testimonial account of that participation, if true, established an issue of fact, it was for the jury, not the trial judge—and not this court—to assess his credibility or the believability of his story, and to resolve any conflicts in the evidence. Our task under the applicable law, as we have pointed out earlier in this opinion, is not to consider or assess these matters, but simply to determine whether, viewing the evidence in the light most favorable to Schuman, his testimony reasonably supports the giving of the requested instruction. And we conclude that it does.

By the Court—Judgment and order reversed and cause remanded with directions.

CASE QUESTIONS

1. How much evidence of entrapment must a defendant present in order to be entitled to an entrapment instruction?

2. What, according to the court, is the "essence of entrapment"?

3. Why was the trial court reversed on appeal?

AUTHOR'S COMMENTARY

Wisconsin, like a majority of the states and the federal courts, has adopted a *subjective test* for determining whether a criminal defendant has been entrapped. The subjective test provides that entrapment has occurred when a nonpredisposed defendant has been induced to commit the crime by the government. It preserves the defense for an accused who would not have committed the crime but for the government's inducement(s) and denies its protections to a defendant who was predisposed to commit the crime prior to being subjected to government inducements.

A significant minority of states have rejected the subjective approach in favor of an *objective test*. States adopting the objective approach view the purpose of the **entrapment defense** as the deterrence of police misconduct. According to this approach, entrapment occurs when the government's conduct would have persuaded or induced an ordinary, law-abiding person to commit the criminal act. This test entirely disregards the question of the defendant's predisposition to commit the crime.

 # Other Defenses

In some situations a defendant can defend against the prosecution's charges by proving the existence of an alibi or present a good character defense. Neither of these defenses is classified as an affirmative defense because the defendant who raises them does not admit to having committed any *actus reus*.

Alibi

It is essential that the government, in every criminal case, establish that the defendant could have been at the scene of the crime. A defendant who claims to have been at some other location such that it would have been impossible for him or her to be present at the time and place where the crime was committed is raising an **alibi defense**.

The alibi defense attacks the *actus reus* element, something that the government has to prove to sustain its burdens of production and persuasion.

Many jurisdictions require that the defendant notify the prosecution at the arraignment or prior to trial that the defendant may present an alibi defense. This notice ensures that the government will have an opportunity to investigate the facts and adequately prepare for trial. Without such notice, the prosecution would be seriously disadvantaged at trial.

ANDERSON BROWN v. STATE OF DELAWARE
958 A.2d 833
Supreme Court of Delaware
October 6, 2008

AUTHOR'S INTRODUCTION

Bakr Dillard and Anderson Brown, the defendants in this case, were convicted by a jury of murder, robbery, and conspiracy and were sentenced to life imprisonment. They appealed their convictions and sentences to the Delaware Supreme Court claiming that the trial court committed reversible error by refusing to give the jurors an instruction on the alibi defense.

EXCERPT FROM THE CASE

HOLLAND, Justice.

...On March 26, 2005, Dion Gibbs ("Gibbs") and Steven Cleveland ("Cleveland") were visiting friends on Spruce Street on the east side of Wilmington until around midnight. While walking back to Cleveland's house, they were accosted by four men on Kirkwood Street. According to Gibbs, one of the assailants held a gun to his head and demanded his valuables. While Gibbs emptied his pockets, Cleveland protested vigorously and was struck in the face with the gun and told to "shut-up." Gibbs was then ordered to remove his clothing and to run in the opposite direction. As Gibbs was running away, he heard several gunshots.

At 12:45 A.M., the police received a "shots fired" complaint and arrived at the scene shortly thereafter. Cleveland, who had been shot several times, was still alive. Before he died, Cleveland told the police that four men tried to rob Gibbs and Cleveland. Two of the men carried handguns. Cleveland did not know their identities. Gibbs also did not know any of the assailants, but told the police that one had a "Sunni" beard.

Neighborhood residents Ruth Ann Clark and Joanne Brown, who shared a house on Kirkwood Street, were the only witnesses who claimed to have seen the robbery and the shootings. Both gave unsworn statements to the police. Although the record does not include a transcript of those videotaped statements, the statements were substantially as follows: Clark stated that she had witnessed the conclusion of the robbery, as well as the shootings. She identified three of the four robbers by their nicknames: "Bam" (Andrew Brown), "AD" (Anderson Brown) and "Breeze" (Dillard), but did not know the fourth. Clark described Dillard as having a "Sunni" type beard.

According to Clark, two of the four assailants carried firearms: Andrew Brown and the fourth man she could not identify. Clark saw one of the victims (Gibbs) strip naked and run in the direction of 9th Street. She then saw Anderson Brown and Dillard tussling with Cleveland. Clark saw one person hit Cleveland with a gun and saw Andrew Brown fire several shots at Cleveland, after which the four men ran up Kirkwood Street in the direction of 10th Street.

Joanne Brown's statement was not as precise. She did not claim to have witnessed the robbery or the shootings, but stated that she saw "Bam," "AD" and "Breeze" on the corner of 10th and Kirkwood Streets shortly before the shooting. Later she saw the "naked boy" flee up the block in the direction of 9th Street, heard gunshots, and then saw the backs of four men fleeing from the scene. She believed that those were the same men she had seen earlier. Joanne Brown stated that Dillard was wearing a "ROCA" coat with green lettering.

Police arrested Andrew Brown, Anderson Brown, and Dillard. Andrew Brown was tried separately and convicted of First Degree Intentional Murder, First Degree Felony Murder, First Degree Robbery (two counts), weapons offenses (four counts) and Conspiracy. . . . Anderson Brown and Dillard were charged with the same offenses and were tried together before a Superior Court jury.

Clark and Joanne Brown testified at both Andrew Brown's trial and at the joint trial of Anderson Brown and Bakr Dillard. On both occasions, Clark disavowed her unsworn statement to the police. At the Anderson Brown/Dillard trial, Clark testified that she was a drug addict and that on the night of the robbery, she had been using cocaine and was high. Clark further testified that Anderson Brown was present but was "really trying to stop it," and that Dillard "was not there." Similarly, Joanne Brown stated that she was "high all the time" and had used drugs on the night of the robbery. As a result, she testified that she did not remember seeing the Brown brothers or Dillard that night or ever seeing a naked person. Because Clark's and Joanne Brown's trial testimony was inconsistent with their previous statements to the police, the State introduced as evidence their above-described out-of-court videotaped statements to the police. Those statements were played for the jury pursuant to Title 11, section 3507 of the Delaware Code. . . .

ALIBI DEFENSES

Dillard denied having participated in the robbery, and raised a defense of alibi. Dillard testified that at the time of the robbery he was in Tiara Flonnory's apartment located off of Maryland Avenue, outside the Wilmington city limits. Flonnory was Dillard's girlfriend and they had a daughter together, whom Dillard was responsible for watching while Flonnory was at work.

Dillard testified that on March 26, 2005, he woke up at Flonnory's apartment around 10:00 A.M. or 11:00 A.M. and spent some time with his daughter until Flonnory returned home from work around 2:30 P.M. or 3:00 P.M. He then left Flonnory's apartment around 3:00 P.M. or 4:00 P.M. and went to the east side of Wilmington, where Kirkwood Street is located. Dillard hung out at his cousin's house on Lombard Street and then "walked around for a little while." At around 8:00 P.M., he left the east side and drove to Nikesha Whye's house in Newark . . .

A little before 10:00 P.M., Dillard left Newark and drove back to Flonnory's apartment in Wilmington. Dillard testified that he remained there overnight because he had to watch his daughter while Flonnory was at work the next day. Dillard further testified that his nickname was "Breeze," that at the time of his arrest he had a "Sunni" beard (which he had shaved off in the meantime), and that he owned a "ROCA" coat (but was not sure if he was wearing it on the night of the robbery).

Both Whye and Flonnory testified at trial in support of Dillard's alibi defense. Whye testified that on March 26, 2005, Dillard came to her apartment a little after 8:00 P.M. and that he was still there when she went to sleep some time after 9:00 P.M. Whye stated that she did not hear anybody leave the apartment after she went to bed, but that when she woke the next morning, Dillard was not there.

Flonnory testified that she was working as a cook at the Mary Campbell Center and that her shift on March 26 and 27, 2005, was from 6:00 A.M. until 2:30 P.M. She stated that when she came back from work on March 26, 2005 (at around 3:00 P.M.), Dillard was in her apartment. He left the house at some point and returned around 10:00 P.M. because Flonnory "had to be [at] work the next morning, and [Dillard] had to watch the baby." Flonnory testified that she went to bed at around 12:00 A.M. or 12:30 A.M. and that when she woke up the next morning at around 4:30 A.M. to go to work, Dillard was in bed with her.

Anderson Brown also denied having participated in the robbery and claimed that he was in Philadelphia with his girlfriend on March 26 and 27, 2005.

Brown's girlfriend, Aigner Gardner, testified at trial that she and Brown were in Philadelphia at her father's house on the night of the shooting. She testified that they spent the evening together watching television, hanging out, eating and sleeping. She also testified that they did not return to Delaware until the following day, March 27, 2005.

ALIBI INSTRUCTION DENIED

Based on the evidence presented, both defendants requested that an alibi instruction be given to the jury. The record on appeal does not disclose the entire content of the proffered alibi instruction. The transcript of the hearing indicates, however, that the requested instruction included language similar to the Superior Court's standard alibi instruction: "If the evidence on [the alibi] raises in your mind a reasonable doubt as to the defendant's guilt, you must give him the benefit of that doubt and return a verdict of not guilty."

The trial judge reviewed the proposed alibi instruction in its entirety but refused to give it to the jury. The trial judge reasoned that an alibi instruction was redundant, because he/she intended to give an instruction on burden of proof. The trial judge stated:

> I find that [the proposed instruction] is an unnecessary commentary on the evidence. If I do that, I probably should list every single bit of evidence in the case and say, if this piece of evidence raises a reasonable doubt, you must find the defendant not guilty. . . . Obviously, counsel, however, can make this argument. It is [a] perfectly valid legal argument.

Instead of the proffered alibi instruction, the trial judge gave a general instruction on burden of proof (with no specific reference to the alibi defense). That general instruction informed the jury that "[t]he burden of proof is upon the State to prove all of the facts necessary to establish each and every element of the crime charged beyond a reasonable doubt." After closing arguments and before the jury deliberated, the judge reiterated that instruction. "Furthermore, because the burden of proof, as described earlier, is upon the State to prove the existence of all elements of the crime beyond a reasonable doubt, a defendant is not required to present any evidence on his own behalf."

The jury returned a verdict finding both Dillard and Brown guilty of Felony Murder in the First Degree, Manslaughter (a lesser-included offense of Intentional Murder in the First Degree), Robbery in the First Degree (two counts) and Conspiracy in the Second Degree. Both defendants then moved for a judgment of acquittal. Anderson Brown also moved for a new trial, challenging, among other things, the trial judge's refusal to give the requested alibi instruction. The trial judge denied those motions. . . .

ALIBI INSTRUCTION REQUIRED

In *Jackson v. State*, this Court held that where there was sufficient evidence to justify a charge on alibi, "[it] was prejudicial error to deny the substance of that request" and reversal was required. . . . Two years later, in *Gardner v. State*, we again held that an alibi instruction should be given if "there is some credible evidence showing that the defendant was elsewhere when the crime occurred . . . [and] if a defendant requests an instruction on alibi. . . ." In *Gardner*, we also held that where the defendant makes no specific request for an alibi instruction, "a duty to . . . instruct the jury upon alibi may arise [in certain circumstances], so that the failure to do so would amount to a manifest defect affecting the defendant's substantial rights and thus constitute plain error." . . .

This Court has defined the alibi defense as " 'a denial of any connection with the crime,' and is based upon evidence that the defendant 'was somewhere other than at the place the crime is alleged to have been committed when it is alleged to have been committed.' " . . . It is well settled that our holding in *Jackson* requires the trial judge to instruct the jury on the alibi if the defendant requests the instruction and presents some credible evidence of the alibi. . . . This Court has defined "some credible evidence" as evidence that is "capable of being believed." . . . Sworn testimony constitutes "some credible evidence" since the jury must assess the credibility and decide whether to believe any sworn testimony presented at trial. . . .

Here, the general instructions given by the Superior Court informed the jury that "[t]he burden of proof is upon the State to prove all of the facts necessary to establish each and every element of the crime charged beyond a reasonable doubt" and that "a defendant is not required to present any evidence on his own behalf." Although the general instructions accurately addressed each party's burden of proof, or lack thereof, a specific instruction on alibi was required under this Court's holding in *Jackson*. . . . The jury should have been instructed that they "must acquit the defendant[s] if they find that the evidence [of each defendant's alibi] raises a reasonable doubt as to [each] defendant's guilt. . . ."

Unlike the defenses contained within the Delaware Code, the alibi defense is not an affirmative defense and is not required to be proven "to the jury's satisfaction." . . . Without an alibi instruction in this case, the jury was erroneously "left free to assume that the defendant b[ore] the burden of proving alibi." . . . An alibi instruction is required so that a jury does not make a determination of guilt based on the "failure of the defense rather than because the evidence introduced by the [state] ha[d] satisfied the jury of the defendant's guilt beyond a reasonable doubt." . . .

Thirty years ago, our holding in *Jackson* established that a trial judge must give the jury an alibi instruction where sufficient credible evidence is presented and a timely request is made. Relying on *Jackson*, Dillard and Brown argue that the trial judge was obligated to give the requested alibi instruction and that the failure to do so was prejudicial error requiring reversal. We agree. The sworn testimony of the alibi witnesses presented by Dillard and Brown, along with the defendants' requests for the alibi instruction, required the trial judge to provide the alibi instruction. . . . We hold that the Superior Court committed reversible error by not providing the jury with an alibi instruction.

CONCLUSION

The judgments of the Superior Court are reversed and these matters are remanded for further proceedings in accordance with this opinion.

CASE QUESTIONS

1. Why isn't alibi classified as an affirmative defense?

2. How is a court supposed to determine whether enough evidence of alibi has been introduced to warrant the alibi instruction?

3. Why should this trial judge have known that he/she had an obligation to instruct the jury in this case on the alibi defense?

AUTHOR'S COMMENTARY

Although the Delaware Supreme Court reversed the convictions of the two defendants in this case, it is likely that the prosecutors would recharge them and they would face trial again on the same charges. In this case the trial judge made a serious mistake in not instructing the jury on alibi. Had this been a minor error without constitutional implications, the error would generally be classified as "harmless" and the convictions upheld.

In a case like this where the appellate courts determine that there was a serious error with the jury instructions, the prosecutors will normally have the right to require these defendants to face a new trial. It is true that these defendants, if recharged, would in fact be facing a second trial for these alleged crimes. However, constitutionally speaking, they would not be placed in "jeopardy" a second time for the same offenses because there was no valid resolution of their guilt or innocence in that "first trial." Thus, a second trial under these circumstances would not create any Double Jeopardy problem.

Good Character Defense

A defendant charged with a crime can introduce reputation or opinion testimony to prove that he or she was well known in the community to have character traits that are inconsistent with the charges brought by the prosecution. If the defendant is charged with any crime of violence, reputation evidence can be offered that shows the accused to be a practitioner of nonviolence and a peaceful, law-abiding person. A defendant in a crime involving fraud, theft, or perjury could similarly defend with reputation or opinion testimony as to the defendant's honesty and integrity. From proof of these character traits, the defense attorney can argue that the charges against the defendant are utterly inconsistent with the client's character and that reasonable doubt exists as to whether the defendant, a person of sterling qualities, could have committed the alleged crime.

Chapter Summary

Legislators cannot anticipate every conceivable factual situation to which a law might apply when drafting a bill. This is especially true with American criminal law, which has common law roots dating back to medieval times. It has long been acknowledged that criminal laws cannot be rigidly applied without exceptions, because to do so produces unacceptable outcomes under some circumstances.

We have learned in previous chapters that government is required to comply with the U.S. Constitution's substantive and procedural requirements in a prosecution. And sometimes, for reasons of public policy, the charges against a factually guilty defendant are dismissed after a judicial determination that essential evidence of guilt has to be suppressed because police officers violated a defendant's constitutional rights. Even the legislature can be at fault if it enacts a law that is ex post facto, too vague, or overly broad. Other procedural requirements may also bar a prosecution, such as where prosecutors fail to file charges prior to the expiration of the statute of limitations.

The focus in this chapter was on some of the most common criminal defenses. These are the defenses that have been legally recognized as essential to a fair determination of whether an accused should be convicted of a crime. We first looked at the affirmative defenses. When a defendant raises an affirmative defense she admits that even though she committed the alleged act she should not be convicted of a crime. She can claim to have acted reasonably given the facts of that case—her conduct was justified under those circumstances, such as where the accused successfully proves "necessity." Or she might claim that there were circumstances that should mitigate against her conviction—such as where she claims that she acted in self-defense. Other recognized defenses "excuse" the accused, such as situations in which the accused acted under a mistaken assumption of the facts. Other defenses discussed included alibi and good character.

Discussion Questions

1. Government agents repeatedly sent Keith Jacobson mail for over two years in an effort to see if he would violate the Child Protection Act of 1984. This act makes it a federal crime for a person to knowingly receive mail containing child pornography. Jacobson, ultimately, did order pornographic photographs of minors engaging in sex and was subsequently arrested and charged with violating the CPA. What would the government have to prove to overcome Jacobson's entrapment defense?

Jacobson v. United States, 503 U.S. 540 (1992)

2. Assume that prisoners A and B share a cell in the local county jail and that A threatens to sexually assault B later on that night after B has gone to sleep. B, afraid to go to sleep, waits until A is asleep and kills him. Would self-defense be available to B if he is charged with murdering A?

State v. Schroeder, 261 N.W.2d 759 (1978)

3. Assume that a citizen is being arrested by a police officer and that the officer is acting without an arrest warrant or probable cause. Should a citizen have the right to use force to resist this unlawful arrest?

Commonwealth v. Moreira, 447 N.E.2d 1224 (1983)

4. Should the necessity defense be available to parents who took their two children to work with them and left them for three hours in an unheated car at a time when the temperature was below freezing? The parents based their necessity on the fact that they could not find a child-care provider and feared becoming homeless again if they were discharged by their employer for not being on the job.

People v. Turner, 619 N.E.2d 781 (1993)

5. Should the necessity defense be available to an intoxicated driver who believed that a friend was having a life-threatening medical emergency?

State v. Brodie, 529 N.W.2d 395 (1995)

NOTES

1. *Patterson v. New York*, 432 U.S. 197 (1977). The Supreme Court's opinions in this case have been included in the Chapter 5 materials on the textbook's website.
2. *Katko v. Briney*, 183 N.W.2d 677 (1971).
3. *United States v. Bailey*, 444 U.S. 394 (1980).
4. L.R. 14 Q.B.D. 273 (1884).
5. However, some states allow necessity to reduce a first-degree murder conviction to second-degree murder.
6. Idaho Code 18-207, Montana Code Ann. 46-14-102, 46-14-311, Utah Code Ann. 76-2-305, and Kansas Stat. Ann. 22-3220.
7. *Montana v. Cowan*, 114 S.Ct 1371 (1994).
8. *Daniel M'Naghten's Case*, House of Lords, 10 CI. & D. 200, 8 Eng. Rep. 718 (1843).
9. *Parsons v. State*, 2 S0. 854 (1886).
10. *Lambert v. California*, 355 U.S. 225 (1957).
11. *Hopkins v. State*, 69 A.2d 465 (1950).

Crimes Against Persons

Fear of being physically harmed by others is a fundamental concern of all people. It is not surprising, therefore, that the crimes we are studying in this chapter—murder, **manslaughter**, rape and sexual assault, battery, assault, kidnapping, and false imprisonment—are as feared today as they were long ago. On the surface, crimes that threaten personal bodily integrity today retain a resemblance to those of the past, but on closer examination we see that contemporary social conditions and attitudes have brought about significant changes. For instance, centuries-old offenses such as the once-distinct crimes of assault and battery have generally merged into a single offense, and the archaic legal approach to rape prior to the late 1970s has been replaced with comprehensive, gender-neutral sexual assault statutes.

Homicide

A **homicide** is committed when one person kills another person. In some circumstances people have a lawful right to take life and are exempt from criminal liability. Examples of noncriminal killings include the taking of life by soldiers in combat, by police officers in apprehending a fleeing felon who has just used deadly force, and by individuals legitimately acting in reasonable self-defense. In addition, many accidental killings do not rise to the level of criminal negligence.

Two types of criminal homicide were recognized under the common law; murder and manslaughter. Both crimes required proof of an intentional and unlawful killing, but a murder conviction also required proof of "**malice aforethought.**" Courts over the centuries have defined malice aforethought unsystematically, so the only practical way to determine its meaning is to research the precedents within each jurisdiction where malice continues to be an element of murder.[1] In general terms, *malice* exists whenever one person kills another without any lawful justification or excuse (i.e., malice does not exist where a police officer properly uses deadly force or where a person takes another's life in reasonable self-defense).

Under the common law, malice was recognized when any of four mental states of mind were proven: the perpetrator had specific intent to kill and did so; the perpetrator killed but only intended to commit serious bodily harm; the perpetrator killed an unintended victim in conjunction with the commission of an arson, kidnapping, rape, robbery, or burglary; and depraved heart murders (in which the perpetrator acted with extreme recklessness). State statutes often contain definitions of malice. For example, Nevada's definition is presented in Figure 6.1.

Figure 6.1. Nevada Definition of Malice

Nevada Revised Statute § 200.020 Malice: Express and implied defined.

1. Express malice is that deliberate intention unlawfully to take away the life of a fellow creature, which is manifested by external circumstances capable of proof.

2. Malice shall be implied when no considerable provocation appears, or when all the circumstances of the killing show an abandoned and malignant heart.

First-Degree Murder

The classification of murder into degrees began in 1794 when Pennsylvania and other states began to question the common law rule that all murderers deserve capital punishment. One problem with the common law approach was that juries at that time thought the death penalty to be inappropriate in some cases and were acquitting the defendants.[2]

The 1794 statute provided that proof of an *intentional killing* and *malice* were required for both first- and second-degree murder, but only **first-degree murder** required proof of *premeditation* (the perpetrator thought before acting) and *deliberation* (the action was not accidental or spontaneous). Many other states followed Pennsylvania's approach and it continues to be followed even today. Jurisdictions that retain the traditional premeditation requirement can differ, however, as to how long premeditation must occur. In Virginia, for example, even a moment's premeditation is sufficient,[3] but a Washington statute (RCW 9A.32.020) provides that "... the premeditation required in order to support a conviction of the crime of murder in the first degree must involve more than a moment in point of time."

TABLE 6.1	ELEMENTS OF PREMEDITATED FIRST DEGREE MURDER
Criminal act	Unlawful killing of another person
Criminal intent	Specific intent preceded by premeditation and deliberation
Causation	Factual and legal causation

To illustrate some of these differences we will examine the first-degree murder statutes of three states: Hawaii, Virginia, and Nebraska.

Figure 6.2. Hawaii Definition of First-Degree Murder

> **Hawaii Revised Statute 707-701 Murder in the first degree.**
>
> (1) A person commits the offense of murder in the first degree if the person intentionally or knowingly causes the death of:
>
> (a) More than one person in the same or separate incident;
>
> (b) A law enforcement officer, judge, or prosecutor arising out of the performance of official duties;
>
> (c) A person known by the defendant to be a witness in a criminal prosecution;
>
> (d) A person by a hired killer, in which event both the person hired and the person responsible for hiring the killer shall be punished under this section; or
>
> (e) A person while the defendant was imprisoned.
>
> (2) Murder in the first degree is a felony for which the defendant shall be sentenced to imprisonment as provided in section 706-656.

Hawaii

Hawaii's homicide laws have been greatly influenced by the Model Penal Code (MPC). Hawaii, following the MPC, no longer requires proof of malice in murder prosecutions. It has also adopted the MPC's approach to *mens rea* and for conviction requires that defendants be proven to have acted intentionally or knowingly. Hawaii initially followed the MPC and enacted a unitary murder statute in 1972 (i.e., refusing to segment murder into degrees). It had second thoughts in 1987, however, and as shown in Figure 6.2, now recognizes two degrees of murder. The strength of the Hawaii/MPC approach is that it simplifies the law conceptually. It avoids many of the ambiguities and the centuries of legal baggage accompanying the common law approach.

Virginia

In Virginia and other capital punishment states, it is common for there to be two categories of first-degree murder. This is deemed necessary in order to delineate which first-degree murder offenders should be subjected to the death penalty. In Virginia, the more serious category is called *capital murder.* Virginia has statutorily defined 13 offenses as constituting capital murder. The 13th and most recent addition to Virginia's list is homicides resulting from the commission or attempted commission of terrorist acts (see Figure 6.3).

Note how Virginia retains common law concepts in its first-degree murder and capital murder statutes. Both require for conviction that an accused act with

Figure 6.3. Virginia Definitions of Murder

Virginia Statute 18.2-31. Capital murder defined; punishment.

The following offenses shall constitute capital murder, punishable as a Class I felony:

1. The willful, deliberate, and premeditated killing of any person in the commission of abduction, . . . when such abduction was committed with the intent to extort money or a pecuniary benefit or with the intent to defile the victim of such abduction;

2. The willful, deliberate, and premeditated killing of any person by another for hire;

3. The willful, deliberate, and premeditated killing of any person by a prisoner confined in a state or local correctional facility . . . or while in the custody of an employee thereof;

4. The willful, deliberate, and premeditated killing of any person in the commission of robbery or attempted robbery;

5. The willful, deliberate, and premeditated killing of any person in the commission of, or subsequent to, rape or attempted rape, forcible sodomy or attempted forcible sodomy or object sexual penetration;

6. The willful, deliberate, and premeditated killing of a law-enforcement officer . . . or any law-enforcement officer of another state or the United States having the power to arrest for a felony under the laws of such state or the United States, when such killing is for the purpose of interfering with the performance of his official duties;

7. The willful, deliberate, and premeditated killing of more than one person as a part of the same act or transaction;

8. The willful, deliberate, and premeditated killing of more than one person within a three-year period;

9. The willful, deliberate, and premeditated killing of any person in the commission of or attempted commission of a violation of §§ 18.2-248 [18.2-248 prohibits the manufacturing, selling, giving, distributing or possessing with intent to manufacture, sell, give or distribute a controlled substance or an imitation controlled substance], involving a Schedule I or II controlled substance, when such killing is for the purpose of furthering the commission or attempted commission of such violation;

10. The willful, deliberate, and premeditated killing of any person by another pursuant to the direction or order of one who is engaged in a continuing criminal enterprise as defined in subsection I of §§ 18.2-248;

11. The willful, deliberate and premeditated killing of a pregnant woman by one who knows that the woman is pregnant and has the intent to cause the involuntary termination of the woman's pregnancy without a live birth;

Figure 6.3. Virginia Definitions of Murder (continued)

> 12. The willful, deliberate and premeditated killing of a person under the age of fourteen by a person age twenty-one or older; and
>
> 13. The willful, deliberate and premeditated killing of any person by another in the commission of or attempted commission of an act of terrorism as defined in §§ 18.2-46.4.
>
> Murder, other than capital murder, by poison, lying in wait, imprisonment, starving, or by any willful, deliberate, and premeditated killing, or in the commission of, or attempt to commit, arson, rape, forcible sodomy, inanimate or animate object sexual penetration, robbery, burglary or abduction, except as provided in §§ 18.2-31, is murder of the first degree, punishable as a Class 2 felony.

purposeful intent, deliberation, and premeditation. Notice also the number and variety of Virginia's enumerated offenses. The decision to permit murder prosecutions where a homicide accompanies the commission of enumerated offenses (**felony murder**) is also an expression of Virginia's right to exercise its sovereign powers in defining crimes and punishments.

Nebraska

Nebraska's statute (shown in Figure 6.4), like Virginia's, incorporates some components of common law murder but includes fewer offenses as enumerated crimes than does Virginia. Note also that Nebraska's statute includes crimes not found on Virginia's list (and vice versa).

Figure 6.4. Nebraska Definition of First-Degree Murder

> A person commits murder in the first degree if he or she kills another person
> (1) purposely and with deliberate and premeditated malice, or
> (2) in the perpetration of or attempt to perpetrate any sexual assault in the first degree, arson, robbery, kidnapping, hijacking of any public or private means of transportation, or burglary, or
> (3) by administering poison or causing the same to be done; or if by willful and corrupt perjury or subornation of the same he or she purposely procures the conviction and execution of any innocent person. The determination of whether murder in the first degree shall be punished as a Class I or Class IA felony shall be made pursuant to sections 29-2519 to 29-2524.

STATE v. ROY J. TOWNSEND
15 P.3d 145
Washington Supreme Court
January 4, 2001

AUTHOR'S INTRODUCTION

Townsend, the appellant in the following case, challenged his conviction on the grounds that his trial attorney had been incompetent. Townsend argued that the attorney's errors contributed to the trial jury's finding that he had committed a premeditated killing. Townsend argued that he did not act with premeditated intent and therefore should have been convicted of **second-degree murder** and not first-degree murder.

EXCERPT FROM THE CASE

Judge MADSEN:

On November, 1, 1996, Roy Townsend, Jack Jellison and the victim, Gerald Harkins, attended a party at Mike Brock's home. Several hours prior to the party, Brock mentioned to Townsend that he was angry at Harkins for spreading rumors about Brock's sister. After hearing the rumors, Townsend replied "either you can deal with it or I can deal with it." . . .

Brock suggested a hunting trip, at which time Brock would confront Harkins about the rumors. Brock later decided to not go hunting. Harkins, however, left the party in his pickup truck with Townsend and Jellison to go hunting. On the way, they stopped at Townsend's house where they picked up a spotlight and Townsend changed clothes. After the stop, Harkins drove while Townsend sat in the passenger seat, using a spotlight to search for deer and occasionally taking shots at road signs with his .45 caliber pistol.

Eventually, Harkins turned the truck onto a road which was blocked by a locked gate that prevented further access to the road. Townsend exited the vehicle and shot the lock several times but was unsuccessful in opening the gate. Townsend then got into the back of the pickup truck and Harkins turned the truck around. Later, Harkins turned onto a side road in another attempt to get up into the mountains. This road, too, was impassable, blocked by a large mound of dirt. As Harkins began backing up to go back down the hill, Jellison, then sitting in the passenger seat, heard a shot from the rear of the truck. Turning around, Jellison saw that Townsend had fallen out of the truck and lay on the ground many feet away from the truck. Townsend then asked "[a]re you guys okay?" . . . Jellison replied that they were fine, but then Harkins slumped over his arm and Jellison realized that Harkins had been shot. Jellison jumped out of the truck and yelled to Townsend "[O]h my God, you shot him. What the hell are you doing?" . . . Townsend said that it was an accident.

Townsend asked if Harkins was still alive. Jellison noticed that Harkins was still breathing and that his eyes were open, staring at him. They argued about taking Harkins to the hospital but Townsend insisted that they could not do so since the police would never believe that the shooting was an accident. Jellison asked why the police would not believe them if it was an accident and Townsend reminded Jellison of their prior criminal histories. Townsend then approached the driver's side of the truck, looked inside, and raised the gun up to "the general area where the head was laying." . . . Townsend said "God forgive me," and pulled the trigger again. . . .

Townsend moved Harkins' body over to the passenger seat and Jellison drove the truck back to the gate where Townsend dumped the body nearby in the dense woods. Jellison and Townsend drove back to Townsend's house and told Townsend's roommate, Mike Drury, that Harkins had been accidentally shot. Later, Townsend moved Harkins' truck and burned it. He took the gun with him to Yakima.

Several days after Harkins' death, Yakima police arrested Townsend for armed robbery and placed him in the Yakima County jail. While in custody, Townsend contacted Harkins' father and told him that he had information regarding his 18-year-old son's death. In exchange for a promise of "help" with his armed robbery charges, Townsend provided substantial information, including the general location of Harkins' body.

The State charged Townsend with first degree murder, second degree murder, second degree arson, and third degree theft. At a pre-trial hearing, and again during *voir dire*, there were references to the death penalty. . . .

Defense counsel did not object to any of the comments.

At the conclusion of trial, the jury found the petitioner guilty of first degree murder, second degree arson, and first degree theft. The trial judge imposed an exceptional sentence of 800 months, approximately one and one-half times the standard range. On appeal, the petitioner principally asserted that his counsel was ineffective when he failed to object to statements about the death penalty. The Court of Appeals . . . found that the statements were not erroneous. . . .

DISCUSSION

. . . The law of Washington holds. . . . "The question of the sentence to be imposed by the court is never a proper issue for the jury's deliberation, except in capital cases." . . . This is not a capital case, and the State provides no authority in Washington that allows the jury to hear about the potential punishment in a noncapital trial.

This strict prohibition against informing the jury of sentencing considerations ensures impartial juries and prevents unfair influence on a jury's deliberations. The only exception that allows juries to know about sentencing consequences is in a death penalty trial, and even then the jury is to consider the penalty only after a determination of guilt.

Considering the long-standing rule that no mention may be made of sentencing in noncapital cases we conclude that counsel's failure to object to the instruction fell below prevailing professional norms. . . .

Counsel's deficient performance is the failure to object to erroneous oral instructions to the jury. Under Washington law, when assessing the impact of an instructional error, reversal is automatic unless the error "is trivial, or formal, or merely academic, and was not prejudicial to the substantial rights of the party assigning it, and in no way affected the final outcome of the case." . . . Petitioner does not suggest that the jury would have acquitted him. . . . Instead, the petitioner contends that the interference in the jury's deliberations led to his conviction of first degree murder rather than second degree murder.

Premeditation is "the deliberate formation of and reflection upon the intent to take a human life" and involves "the mental process of thinking beforehand, deliberation, reflection, weighing or reasoning for a period of time, however short." . . .

There was ample evidence of premeditation. Townsend brought a gun and had spoken with Mike Brock about "taking care of" Harkins. After shooting Harkins the first time, which may have been accidental, Jellison told Townsend that Harkins was still breathing and alive. Jellison recommended that they take Harkins to the hospital. Townsend declined, telling Jellison that no one would believe that the shooting was an accident since they both had criminal records. After that, Townsend went to the window of Harkins' truck, raised the pistol, said "God forgive me," and shot Harkins in the head, killing him. The evidence overwhelmingly supports a finding of premeditation.

Accordingly, counsel's failure to object to the statements informing the jury that this was not a capital case in no way affected the outcome. The petitioner has failed to show that he was prejudiced in any way. . . .

The conviction is affirmed.

CASE QUESTION

How long, according to the Washington Supreme Court, must the accused have planned the killing in order to satisfy the premeditated intent requirement?

AUTHOR'S COMMENTARY

Washington, like Nebraska, requires proof of premeditation for a first-degree murder conviction. In this case, the fact that Townsend declined to take the victim (who was then still alive) to the hospital, reasoning that any claims of an accidental shooting would be unbelievable, was clear evidence of a thinking process that precedes the victim's death. This thinking process was reinforced when Townsend shot the helpless victim a second time in the head while saying "God forgive me." There was no provocation on the part of the victim; this killing was brutal and without justification or excuse, clearly establishing malice. There were also no causation problems with this case. Establishing factual and proximate causation (you may recall the discussion of these topics in Chapter 3) was straightforward, as the defendant was shown to have twice shot the victim and caused his death.

Second-Degree Murder

For a second-degree murder conviction, the prosecution is required to prove three elements: intent to kill, death, and causation.

TABLE 6.2   ELEMENTS OF SECOND-DEGREE MURDER

Criminal act	Unlawful killing of another person not amounting to first degree murder
Criminal intent	Specific intent (without premeditation and deliberation)
Causation	Factual and proximate causation

In many instances prosecutors charge murder in the second degree because the proof of premeditation is lacking, the offense committed is not an enumerated offense under the first-degree murder statute, the law does not recognize the felony murder doctrine, or there are mitigating circumstances that warrant a manslaughter charge (see Figure 6.5). In some states, murder in the second degree is defined in terms of the killing of another person for spite, revenge, or hatred and (in some jurisdictions) for reckless indifference to human life (depraved heart).

In practical terms, since jurors are sometimes unable to agree on a first-degree murder verdict because they are split over whether premeditation has been proven,

Figure 6.5. Second-Degree Murder Definitions

> **Hawaii Revised Statute §§ 707-701.5 Murder in the second degree**
> (1) Except as provided in section 707-701, a person commits the offense of murder in the second degree if the person intentionally or knowingly causes the death of another person. . . .
> **§§ 18.2-32 Virginia's second degree murder statute**
> All murder other than capital murder and murder in the first degree is murder of the second degree and is punishable by confinement in a state correctional facility for not less than five nor more than forty years.
> **Excerpt from Nebraska Statute §§ 28-304. Murder in the second degree**
> (1) A person commits murder in the second degree if he causes the death of a person intentionally, but without premeditation. . . .

they will sometimes return a verdict on the lesser-included offense of murder in the second degree.

STATE OF NEBRASKA v. TYLER J. KEUP
655 N.W.2d 25
Supreme Court of Nebraska
January 10, 2003

AUTHOR'S INTRODUCTION

Tyler Keup was charged with the murder in the first degree of Maricela Martinez. Keup entered a not guilty plea and waived his right to a jury trial. After both parties had rested their cases at trial, the judge granted Keup's motion to dismiss the first-degree murder charge. The court explained that the dismissal was required because the state had not produced any evidence of premeditation. The court also ruled, however, that Keup might still be subject to conviction of lesser-included offenses. Keup was subsequently convicted of second-degree murder, use of a weapon to commit a felony, and being a felon in possession of a firearm and was sentenced to prison for a term of 25 to 60 years. Keup appealed.

EXCERPT FROM THE CASE

Judge GERRARD:

In June or July 2000, Keup told a friend, Michael L., that Keup wanted a handgun. Michael stole a ".25 millimeter semi-automatic handgun" in a burglary, and on August 3, Michael sold the gun to Keup for $72. Keup later showed the gun to two of his friends. Keup told them that Keup intended to scare a person who had "ripped [Keup] off" in a drug-related transaction.

On August 4, 2000, Keup telephoned Martinez and tried to arrange the purchase of drugs. Tanya Lynn Barnett, Martinez' roommate, told Martinez to call Keup back so that they could "rip him off," meaning that they would take Keup's money but not provide drugs. Barnett then left the residence to go shopping. Keup went to Martinez' residence while Barnett was gone.

Keup took the gun with him when he went to Martinez' residence. Keup testified that he had no plan or intent to shoot Martinez and that he took the gun in order to trade or sell it to get drugs. Keup testified at trial that he and Martinez were playing with the gun by pointing it at each other and, in jest, threatening to fire. Keup's testimony at trial was that although he knew the gun was loaded, he thought the safety was on, and was pointing the gun at Martinez' head with his finger on the trigger and the hammer pulled back when the gun just "went off."

Sgt. Mark F. Bohaty, an expert from the Nebraska State Patrol Criminalistics Laboratory, testified that he later tested the weapon and was unable to induce an accidental discharge. Bohaty also testified that he conducted a "trigger-pull test," intended to determine how much force could be applied to the trigger of the gun before the gun would fire. Bohaty testified that between 4 and 5.25 pounds would need to be applied, depending on which part of the trigger was pressed, before the trigger would activate. This was well above the industry standard of 3 pounds.

Keup testified that after the shooting, he grabbed his cigarettes, fled Martinez' residence, and went home, where, because he was scared, he lied to his parents and said that he had seen Martinez commit suicide. Additionally, Barnett testified that after she returned home, she noticed that Keup's telephone number had been erased from the caller identification device at Martinez' residence, although she and Martinez never erased telephone numbers from the device and all of the other calls remained in the device's memory.

When Barnett returned home, she called the 911 emergency dispatch service. Police responded and found Martinez dead, seated on her couch, with an apparent wound to the right temple. A single, small-caliber firearm casing was found on the floor 2 to 3 feet from Martinez' body. Martinez was taken to the hospital and was determined to have suffered a single gunshot wound to the head. It was determined, based on the bullet path and nature of the wound, that the gun was between 1 and 2 inches from Martinez' head when discharged.

Lt. Rick Ryan, of the North Platte Police Department, was at the hospital following Martinez' transport there, when he received a telephone call from Keup's father. Keup's father said that Keup had witnessed a suicide. Ryan met with Keup and Keup's parents at the police station. Keup's father brought a small handgun that had been given to him by Keup. This gun was later identified as the gun sold to Keup by Michael and was also determined to have discharged the shell casing that was found near Martinez' body.

Keup and his parents were read their *Miranda* rights and waived those rights and agreed to speak to Ryan. Keup stated to Ryan that Keup had telephoned Martinez and gone to Martinez' residence to retrieve some personal belongings. Keup told Ryan that Martinez had produced the gun, that Keup had handled it and given it back to Martinez, and that then, while Keup was looking away, the gun went off. Keup claimed to Ryan that because Keup was a convicted felon and Keup's fingerprints were on the gun, Keup took the gun and fled the scene.

Ryan asked Keup to take a polygraph examination, which was administered by Investigator Randy Billingsley of the North Platte Police Department. Based on the examination, Billingsley told Keup that Keup was being untruthful. The results of the polygraph examination were admitted into evidence at trial only as foundation for Keup's ensuing statements to Billingsley. When accused by Billingsley, Keup broke down and admitted that he had shot Martinez. Keup still claimed that the gun was Martinez' and that Keup had unloaded it and was playing with it when it went off. At trial, Keup admitted lying to both Ryan and Billingsley. . . .

The primary issue contested at trial was whether the gun fired accidentally or Keup fired the gun intentionally. After the close of the evidence and closing arguments, the district court concluded that Keup had pulled the trigger and fired the weapon intentionally, and was guilty of second degree murder. . . .

While in a bench trial of a criminal case the court's findings have the effect of a verdict and will not be set aside unless clearly erroneous, an appellate court has an obligation to reach an independent, correct conclusion regarding questions of law. . . .

ELEMENTS OF INTENT

A person commits murder in the second degree if he or she causes the death of a person intentionally, but without premeditation. . . . The intent to kill may be inferred, sufficient to support a murder conviction, from the defendant's deliberate use of a deadly weapon in a manner likely to cause death. . . .

Keup's argument with respect to the element of intent is somewhat perplexing. Keup's argument appears to be directed less at the sufficiency of the evidence to support a finding that Keup acted intentionally than at the district court's purportedly erroneous legal basis for that finding. Nonetheless, we note that to the extent Keup is arguing the evidence of intent was insufficient, that argument is without merit. The district court's factual finding that Keup acted intentionally is supported by competent evidence, described above, which, viewed and construed most favorably to the State, is sufficient to support the conviction. . . .

Keup's primary argument seems to be that in making detailed findings of fact for the record, the district court somehow demonstrated a misunderstanding of the element of intent. A review of the district court's findings, however, reveals no error sufficient to overcome the presumption that the district court was familiar with and applied the proper rules of law. . . .

From circumstances around a defendant's voluntary and willful act, a finder of fact may infer that the defendant intended a reasonably probable result of his or her act. . . . The evidence presented in this case indicates that when the weapon was discharged, Keup was deliberately pointing the weapon at Martinez' head, at a distance of 1 to 2 inches, with his finger on the trigger and the hammer cocked. The State's firearms expert, Bohaty, testified that the trigger on the weapon required between 4 to 5.25 pounds of force before the weapon would discharge and that Bohaty was unable to induce an accidental discharge of the weapon. The evidence adequately supports the inference that Keup's firing of the weapon required a conscious and appreciable effort by Keup; thus, Keup's intent to cause Martinez' death may be inferred from the evidence. . . . [T]he court correctly applied the law to the facts of the instant case with regard to the element of intent. Keup's assignment of error is without merit.

LESSER-INCLUDED OFFENSES

Keup argues that the district court erred when, after dismissing the charge of first degree murder, the district court considered lesser-included homicide offenses. However, Keup waived any error in this regard by failing to present the issue to the district court with a timely objection. An appellate court will not consider an issue on appeal that was not presented to or passed upon by the trial court. . . .

We find no plain error in the district court's consideration of the lesser-included offense of second degree murder. In a bench trial, where the State fails to demonstrate a *prima facie* case on the crime charged, but does so on a lesser-included offense, the trial court may, in its discretion, dismiss the charge and consider all properly submitted evidence relative to a lesser-included offense of the crime charged in the information. . . . We have repeatedly held that second degree murder is a lesser-included offense of first degree murder. . . . Thus, the district court did not commit plain error when it dismissed the first degree murder charge but considered the lesser-included offense of second degree murder. . . .

The evidence is sufficient to sustain the district court's finding that Keup acted intentionally, and the court applied the correct legal standards in reaching that conclusion. Keup did not object to the district court's consideration of lesser-included offenses and has shown no basis for finding the court's consideration of lesser-included offenses to be plain error. Because Keup's assignments of error are without merit, the judgment of the district court is affirmed.

Affirmed.

CASE QUESTIONS

1. Why did the trial court convict Keup of second-degree murder rather than the crime with which he was charged in the information, first-degree murder?

2. Assume for purposes of argument that the Nebraska Supreme Court had found that Keup did not intend to kill Martinez. What difference would such a ruling have made in the outcome of this case?

AUTHOR'S COMMENTARY

This case points out once again the importance of inferential proof in a criminal case. The government's proof of intent in the Keup case rested on inferences drawn from the following proved facts: Keup engaged in a voluntary act when he pointed a deadly weapon that he knew was both loaded and cocked, within one to two inches of the victim's head; a firearms expert testified that the firearm used in the shooting was the weapon that discharged the shell casing that was found next to the victim's body; that same weapon was the firearm that was given to Keup by Michael L.

Finally; and this same firearm did not accidently discharge when properly tested by the firearms expert. It is reasonable for a factfinder to conclude from this evidence that Keup intended the natural and probable consequences of his voluntary acts that resulted in the shooting and subsequent death of Martinez.

Felony Murder

The felony-murder rule originated in England during the sixteenth century and was the law in that country until it was repealed by Parliament in the Homicide Act of 1957. Because the felony-murder rule holds felons vicariously liable for any deaths that occur during the commission of certain statutorily specified crimes, it is controversial. Its supporters argue that the rule serves as a deterrent to the commission of dangerous felonies and creates an incentive for felons to avoid the use of violence when committing crimes. Seven states, exercising their constitutional rights as sovereigns, have abolished the rule by statute or by judicial decision,[4] arguing that it is illogical for the law to permit prosecutors to satisfy the *mens rea* element of first-degree murder by proving that the accused intended to commit a felony. Opponents also argue that the felony-murder rule deviates from the law's traditional focus on personal moral accountability. Is it fair, they ask, to subject an accomplice who did not actually kill anyone to the same punishment as someone who did?

In a felony-murder case, given that the intent to commit a felony is imputed (i.e., is a substitute for) evidence of intent to kill, there is no possibility of mitigating circumstances reducing the offense to manslaughter.

Most state felony-murder statutes provide that persons who commit or attempt to commit certain statutorily specified felonies (which are often referred to as the "predicate crimes") are vicariously responsible for any deaths that are causally connected to the commission of the crime, occurring during the commission of the felony, or any subsequent flight. The *mens rea* requirement in a felony case is that the prosecution prove that the defendant had the intent to commit the predicate felony.

TABLE 6.3	ELEMENTS OF FELONY MURDER
Criminal act	Homicide
Criminal intent	Intent to commit felony
Circumstances	Victim died in conjunction with commission of predicate felony or flight
Causation	Victim's death is causally related to the commission of the felony[5]

PEOPLE v. LISL E. AUMAN
109 P.3d 647
Colorado Supreme Court
September 26, 2002

AUTHOR'S INTRODUCTION

What follows is a highly abbreviated summary of a recent Colorado case. The opinion in this case has been extensively edited in the interests of saving space to focus on the mechanics of the felony-murder rule.

Lisl Auman and three friends (one of whom, Matthaeus Jaehnig, was armed with a shotgun and two assault rifles) traveled in two cars (one of which was a stolen Trans Am) to a rooming house in the mountains outside of Denver known as the Lodge, where Auman's former boyfriend lived. Auman wanted to collect some personal possessions that were still located in her former boyfriend's room. While Jaehnig stayed outside as the "lookout," Auman and her other two friends entered the Lodge and went to the ex-boyfriend's room. The trio used bolt cutters on the padlock that secured the door and broke into the room. They collected Auman's belongings and also stole some items belonging to the ex-boyfriend. After the trio left the Lodge, Jaehnig and Auman started toward Denver, and the second car went in the opposite direction. Residents of the rooming house in the meantime called police because they became suspicious, and they provided officers with the license plate numbers of the two cars. Officers located the Trans Am and when Jaehnig, the driver, refused to pull over, a lengthy high speed pursuit ensued. At one point in this pursuit, Auman briefly steered the Trans Am so that Jaehnig could lean out the window and fire at police. Eventually, the fleeing car stopped at another friend's condominium. Jaehnig exited the car and escaped on foot. Auman remained in the car and surrendered to police. She was handcuffed and placed in a police cruiser. Five minutes later, Jaehnig shot and killed a pursuing police officer and committed suicide with the dead officer's sidearm. Auman was convicted of murder in the first degree (felony murder), second-degree burglary, and other crimes and was sentenced to life in prison without possibility of parole. She appealed on a variety of grounds, two of which are included in the excerpt that follows.

EXCERPT FROM THE CASE

BENDER, Justice.

II. ... PROCEEDINGS BELOW

Auman was convicted of felony murder for her role in an alleged burglary which resulted in the shooting death of a Denver police officer, Bruce VanderJagt, on November 12, 1997. ...

Auman was charged with several criminal offenses, including first degree felony murder, attempted first degree murder, first degree assault, menacing, first degree burglary, and conspiracy to commit first degree burglary. At the request of Auman's counsel, and as lesser included offenses to the charge of first degree burglary, the court instructed the jury on second degree burglary and first degree criminal trespass.

At the preliminary hearing, the trial court found that the burglary, flight, and shooting were connected by a "continuing sequence of events." Relying on our holding in *People v. McCrary*, . . . (1976), and, after viewing the facts in the light most favorable to the prosecution, the court concluded, as a matter of law, that immediate flight had not terminated upon Auman's arrest and that the question of whether she was guilty of felony murder could thus be submitted to the jury. . . .

At trial, . . . [i]n closing, the People argued that Auman committed felony murder because she was guilty of burglary and because Officer VanderJagt's death was caused by Jaehnig in immediate flight from that burglary. The People argued that Auman's arrest did not terminate her liability for felony murder while Jaehnig's immediate flight continued and while she lied to and withheld information from police. The People also argued that Auman did not meet the statutory affirmative defense to felony murder because, among other things, she did not immediately disengage herself from immediate flight upon having reasonable grounds to believe that Jaehnig was armed or dangerous.

In response, Auman's counsel argued that . . . immediate flight had terminated upon Auman's arrest, thereby terminating her liability for felony murder. . . .

The trial court submitted a jury instruction which tracked the language of the felony-murder statute and included the immediate flight element. The court declined to submit supplemental instructions tendered by the People and Auman. . . .

The jury acquitted Auman of first degree burglary . . . but found her guilty of first degree felony murder, second degree burglary, conspiracy to commit first degree burglary and menacing.

Auman appealed her convictions to the court of appeals. She made numerous arguments, asserting that the trial court had committed reversible error in improperly instructing the jury on the required elements of second degree burglary and theft. The court rejected each of these arguments. . . .

Auman now appeals to this court, arguing that arrest, as a matter of law, terminates liability under Colorado's felony-murder statute. She also asserts that the trial court committed reversible error in improperly instructing the jury. . . .

III. WHETHER AUMAN'S ARREST TERMINATED HER LIABILITY FOR FELONY MURDER

A. THE FELONY-MURDER STATUTE: FOUR REQUIREMENTS

On its face, Colorado's felony-murder statute is broad in scope. The words of the statute provide that if a person commits a specifically enumerated felony and an innocent party dies during that felony or during immediate flight from that felony, then that person commits felony murder:

> A person commits the crime of murder in the first degree if: . . . [a]cting either alone or with one or more persons, he [or she] commits or attempts to commit . . . burglary . . . and, in the course of or in furtherance of the crime that he [or she] is committing or attempting to commit, or of immediate flight therefrom, the death of a person, other than one of the participants, is caused by anyone. § 18-3-102(1)(b), 6 C.R.S. (1999).

Pursuant to the terms of this statute, it does not matter that the defendant had no intent to kill or that the defendant did not cause the killing. Liability arises from the defendant's participation in, and intent to commit, one of the specifically named, or predicate, felonies. According to the felony-murder doctrine, the intent to kill is imputed from the participant's intent to commit the predicate felony. . . . Our felony-murder statute provides severe penalties for those who participate in specifically enumerated felonies involving a risk of death when death is caused during a felony or in immediate flight from that felony. . . .

Under this statute, a defendant who commits a predicate felony may be liable when death occurs during either of two events, namely: (1) "in the course of or in furtherance of the crime that [the defendant] is committing or attempting to commit;" or, (2) "in the course of or in furtherance . . . of immediate flight therefrom." . . . Here, we address only whether the death was caused in the course of or in furtherance of immediate flight from the predicate felony, which in this case was burglary.

According to the plain language of the immediate flight provision of the statute, there are four limitations on liability for felony murder when a death occurs during flight from the predicate felony.

First, the flight from the predicate felony must be "immediate," which requires a close temporal connection between the predicate felony, the flight, and the resulting death. *See Webster's New World College Dictionary* 713 (4th ed. 1999) (defining "immediate" as "without delay" or "of the present time").

Second, the word "flight" limits felony-murder liability in such cases to those circumstances in which death is caused while a participant is escaping or running away from the predicate felony. . . .

Third, the death must occur either "in the course of" or "in furtherance of" immediate flight, so that a defendant commits felony murder only if a death is caused during a participant's immediate flight or while a person is acting to promote immediate flight from the predicate felony. . . .

Fourth, the immediate flight must be "therefrom," indicating that the flight must be from the predicate felony, as opposed to being from some other episode or event.

In 1971, the General Assembly added the words "immediate flight therefrom" to the statute. . . . When these words are read together with the initial words of the statute, which provide that one may act "either alone or with one or more persons," immediate flight terminates when a sole participant in the subject felony is subject to complete custody, or, alternatively, when all participants in a predicate felony involving more than one participant are subject to complete custody. . . .

The plain language of our statute supports the legal principle that a co-participant in a predicate felony may be liable for felony murder even after arrest while another participant remains in immediate flight. The statute deems conduct as murder when one participates in the predicate felony and a death is caused in the course of or in furtherance of "immediate flight," which, by its terms, is not limited to the flight of any particular participant. The felony-murder statute regards all participants as liable for felony murder when a person acts "with one or more persons" in the commission of a specifically enumerated felony and death is "caused by anyone" "in the course of or in furtherance . . . of immediate flight" from the predicate felony. . . .

Just as important as what the statute says is what the statute does not say. As it is worded, the statute does not differentiate between liability for participants in the predicate felony who are in immediate flight and those who are not; nor does the statute state that some participants may be liable for a death that occurs in the course of or in furtherance of immediate flight but that others may not. The statute also does not state that if a co-participant's actual flight ends as a result of arrest, and another participant remains in flight, that immediate flight has ended for the co-participant under arrest. Most importantly, the statute does not say that a co-participant may be liable for felony murder for only those deaths caused during that co-participant's immediate flight. We should not construe these omissions by the General Assembly as unintentional. . . .

B. IMMEDIATE FLIGHT BEFORE AND AFTER OUR PRESENT STATUTE

Colorado's former felony-murder statute provided that "[a]ll murder . . . which is committed in the perpetration . . . [of a predicate felony] . . . shall be deemed murder of the first degree. . . ." In *Bizup v. People,* . . . (1962), a pre-code case, we interpreted this statute and held that the perpetration of the predicate felony encompasses the act of flight from that felony. In addition, in *McCrary,* another pre-code case, we upheld the defendant's conviction for felony murder even though the flight of the defendant and his co-participant was purportedly interrupted . . . before the eventual killing. . . . Under *Bizup* and *McCrary,* the concept of flight is broad. Together, these pre-code cases stand for the proposition that, as a matter of law, felony murder does not terminate where death occurs during continuous flight from the predicate felony, nor does it terminate where intervening events interrupt flight.

In interpreting the phrase "immediate flight therefrom," we have relied upon and applied *Bizup, McCrary*, and other pre-code cases construing the meaning of flight under our pre-code statute. . . . We conclude that the General Assembly's 1971 addition of the words "immediate flight therefrom" incorporates into our present statute the concept derived from these pre-code cases that a defendant may be liable for felony murder for a death caused either during the predicate felony or during immediate flight from that felony.

Our pre-code precedent concerning immediate flight is consistent with judicial decisions from New York interpreting that state's felony-murder statute, *N.Y. Penal Law* § 125.25(3) (McKinney 1967) . . . the statute upon which our General Assembly largely modeled section 40-3-102(1)(b).]. . . . Like the Colorado General Assembly, New York's legislature added the words "immediate flight therefrom" to its statute to clarify that felony-murder liability does not terminate upon the completion of the predicate felony. . . .

Further, under New York's statute, arrest does not terminate immediate flight or liability for felony murder as a matter of law. . . .

Our present felony-murder statute requires a jury to decide factual issues relating to the effect of arrest on felony-murder liability, such as whether, in spite of arrest, the temporal connection between the predicate felony, flight, and death is "immediate," and whether a death following a defendant's arrest is still "in the course of or in furtherance of" immediate flight from the predicate felony.

We hold that under our statute and precedent, each felony-murder case involving immediate flight must be decided according to its unique set of circumstances. As a matter of law, arrest, by itself, does not terminate a co-participant's liability for felony murder when a death occurs at the hands of another participant who remains in flight. Hence, whether Auman's arrest terminated her liability for felony murder was properly left to the jury. . . .

IV. THE TRIAL COURTS INSTRUCTION . . . ON THE LACK OF AN INTERVENING CAUSE . . .

B. THE LACK OF AN INTERVENING CAUSE INSTRUCTION

We now turn to Auman's final argument on this issue, in which she contends that the trial court erred by not submitting an intervening cause instruction to the jury. Auman claims that Jaehnig may have been fleeing from police for reasons unforeseeable to her, such as because the Trans Am he was driving was stolen or because he had high levels of methamphetamines in his system, . . . and not because of the alleged burglary. . . .

In *People v. Calvaresi*, we stated that to be liable for a homicide offense under Colorado law, death must be a "natural and probable consequence of the [defendant's] unlawful act." . . . (quoting 1 *Wharton's Crim. Law & Pro.* § 200, at 448 (12th ed. 1957)). . . .

If an act of some other person, or intervening cause, breaks the causal connection between the defendant's unlawful acts and the victim's injury, then the defendant is relieved of liability. . . . As a threshold matter, a defendant is not entitled to an intervening cause instruction unless the following three conditions are met: first, a defendant must introduce competent evidence to show that the ultimate harm would not have occurred in the absence of the claimed intervening cause; second, a claimed intervening cause must be one that the defendant could not foresee; and third, such a cause must be one in which the defendant does not participate. . . .

. . . Auman claimed that Jaehnig's actions—driving a stolen Trans Am and using methamphetamines—were intervening causes, but she failed to introduce any evidence to show that Officer VanderJagt's death would not have occurred absent these alleged intervening causes. Because Auman failed to satisfy one of the threshold requirements warranting an intervening cause instruction, the trial court did not commit reversible error in not submitting an intervening cause instruction to the jury.

Further, the two contributing causes alleged by Auman do not meet the threshold requirements to be deemed intervening causes because they occurred, or existed, prior to Auman's unlawful acts. Accordingly, there was no conduct which "intervened" to break the chain of causation between Auman's unlawful acts and Officer VanderJagt's death. Thus, we hold that the trial court did not commit reversible error in not submitting an intervening cause instruction to the jury.

CASE QUESTIONS

1. Given what you know about this case, are you pro or con making Lisl Auman vicariously liable for the death of Officer VanderJagt?

2. Do you agree with the Colorado Supreme Court that the officer's death was within the realm of reasonable foreseeability?

AUTHOR'S COMMENTARY

Although the Colorado Supreme Court rejected Auman's arguments with respect to the issues discussed in the case excerpt, it ultimately reversed her conviction. We return to this case in Chapter 7 and learn why the Court reversed Auman's conviction and what subsequently happened in this case.

Internet Tip

Michigan has no statute that defines the elements of murder. According to an 1854 decision of the Michigan Supreme Court, "[m]urder is where a person of sound memory and discretion unlawfully kills any reasonable creature in being, in the peace of the state, with malice prepense or aforethought, either express or implied."[6] The Michigan Supreme Court decided in 1980 to define murder so as to preclude the use of the felony-murder doctrine. The Court said:

> We conclude that Michigan has no statutory felony-murder rule which allows the mental element of murder to be satisfied by proof of the intention to commit the underlying felony. Today we exercise our role in the development of the common law by abrogating the common-law felony-murder rule. We hold that in order to convict a defendant of murder, as that term is defined by Michigan case law, it must be shown that he acted with intent to kill or to inflict great bodily harm or with a wanton and willful disregard of the likelihood that the natural tendency of his behavior is to cause death or great bodily harm. We further hold that the issue of malice must always be submitted to the jury.

People v. Aaron, 299 N.W.2d 304 (1980). Justice Fitzgerald's opinion in this case, which was too long to include in this textbook's website, can be found by searching on Loislaw.

Manslaughter

Manslaughter has long been recognized as a mitigated murder. The key difference in these crimes is that the perpetrator of a manslaughter does not premeditate and deliberate before killing the victim. Under the common law, manslaughter existed in two forms, the first voluntary and the second involuntary. Although some states (and the Model Penal Code) only recognize one form of manslaughter, most states and the federal government have retained both traditional forms.

Voluntary Manslaughter

Voluntary manslaughter is an appropriate charge where the perpetrator intentionally killed the victim in response to extreme provocation that caused the perpetrator to lose all self-control. The traditional language that describes this state of mind is that the perpetrator, after being adequately provoked, killed while "in the sudden heat of passion." The crime is murder and not manslaughter if the perpetrator kills after having calmed down and regained self-control. The rationale here is that provoked killings should not be punished as murder. In voluntary manslaughter cases, the killing, although intentional, is neither premeditated nor deliberate and lacks malice because of mitigating circumstances. But the scope of what constitutes a legally sufficient provocation is not unlimited. Courts will not, for example, find that words alone can form the basis of a legally sufficient provocation that would justify the use of a deadly weapon in the commission of a homicide.

TABLE 6.4	ELEMENTS OF VOLUNTARY MANSLAUGHTER
Criminal act	Unlawful killing
Criminal intent	Intent to kill
Extenuation	Reasonable provocation and sudden heat of passion or imperfect self-defense
Causation	Factual and proximate causation

There must also be proof of causation beyond a reasonable doubt to sustain a voluntary manslaughter conviction. This means that the proof must show that the extreme provocation produced the heat of passion, which in turn is causally linked to the victim's death.

The questions as to whether the accused was adequately provoked, and whether he or she killed while in the heat of passion, are decided at trial by the factfinder (the jury or judge in a bench trial). These questions are framed at trial in terms of whether a hypothetical "reasonable person" would have been provoked by the circumstances in the case and if so, whether a reasonable person would have regained self-control at the point in time when the victim was killed.

Voluntary manslaughter is also charged when the accused kills while using unnecessary or excessive force in self-defense (imperfect self-defense), or where the defendant is the aggressor and precipitates a fight that is causally linked to the death of the victim.

Involuntary Manslaughter

The victim in an **involuntary manslaughter** case is unintentionally killed by a person committing a misdemeanor or engaging in reckless or grossly negligent conduct. If the actor is aware that the conduct engaged in exposed the victim to a high risk of death or serious bodily injury, the actor has acted recklessly. If the actor is unaware of the risk, but has not acted as a reasonable person would have acted, the actor has acted in a grossly negligent manner. Parents who, for religious reasons, have refused to take their minor child to the hospital for medical care are often prosecuted for involuntary manslaughter. Similarly, when one of two persons participating in a fistfight unintentionally causes the death of the other by hitting him with his fists, involuntary manslaughter may be charged.

TABLE 6.5	ELEMENTS OF INVOLUNTARY MANSLAUGHTER
Criminal act	Unlawful killing
Circumstances	Occurring as a result of the commission of a misdemeanor or as a result of a culpably negligent act
Criminal intent	Reckless or gross negligence
Causation	Factual and proximate causation

Proof of causation is required for conviction of involuntary manslaughter, as it is in all homicide offenses. This means that the illegal or culpably negligent conduct must have been the factual and proximate cause of the victim's death. Some states have statutorily defined the commission of specified misdemeanor offenses that result in a homicide as constituting involuntary manslaughter.

STATE v. KENNETH W. WOOD
561 S.E.2d 304
North Carolina Court of Appeals
March 19, 2002

AUTHOR'S INTRODUCTION

Kenneth Wood observed a stranger (Roger McDaniel) attempt to lure a six-year-old boy into the stranger's vehicle. Wood and his friend, Pasour, who were friends of the boy's mother, Tina Padgett, went looking for the stranger. When they discovered where he lived, the two broke down the front door to his apartment and entered it while he was absent. When they saw McDaniel coming toward them from behind his apartment building, they moved toward him. The three wrestled near McDaniel's truck, and when McDaniel attempted to retrieve a handgun from underneath his shirt, Wood and Pasour disarmed him. They continued to fight until McDaniel fell to the ground, at which point witnesses observed Wood kick McDaniel in the head and stomach. McDaniel's spinal cord was injured, and he sustained other injuries and died. Wood was charged with first-degree murder, but after a jury trial he was convicted of the lesser-included offense of second-degree murder and of felonious breaking and entering. He appealed because the trial court had denied his requests for instructions on involuntary manslaughter and heat of passion and had overruled his objection to the trial court's intended instruction on self-defense.

EXCERPT FROM THE CASE

Judge SMITH:

Defendant ... alleges the trial court erred in denying defendant's requested instruction on the lesser included offense of involuntary manslaughter. ...

The trial court "has an obligation to fully instruct the jury on all substantial and essential features of the case embraced within the issue and arising on the evidence." ...

The purpose of a charge is to give a clear instruction which applies the law to the evidence in such a manner as to assist the jury in understanding the case and in reaching a correct verdict. ...

Involuntary manslaughter is "the unlawful and unintentional killing of another human being, without malice, which proximately results from an unlawful act not amounting to a felony ... or from an act or omission constituting culpable negligence." ... Culpable negligence is "such reckless or careless behavior that the act imports a thoughtless disregard of the consequences of the act or the act shows a heedless indifference to the rights and safety of others." ...

In this case, the trial court instructed the jury on the elements of first degree murder, second degree murder, and voluntary manslaughter, which is the unlawful killing of a human being without malice, premeditation, or deliberation. ... As mentioned above, several witnesses observed the altercation between defendant, Michael Pasour, and the victim, Roger Dale McDaniel. In fact, Kristy Harbison testified that she watched defendant "stomp" the victim in the face. Chris James testified that he observed the attack and saw defendant kick the victim in the head and stomach. James also testified that after the beating the men pranced around as if they were happy, and "they gave each other a high five." This evidence is wholly inconsistent with involuntary man slaughter, which involves a killing resulting from culpable negligence or from an act not amounting to a felony. Defendant's assignment of error to the contrary is overruled. ...

Defendant next argues the trial court erred in denying defendant's request for an instruction that defendant's actions were brought about by heat of passion. Heat of passion is a killing done without premeditation and under the influence of a "sudden passion." ... Heat of passion has been defined by our Supreme Court as "any of the emotions of the mind known as rage, anger, hatred, furious resentment, or terror, rendering the mind incapable of cool reflection." ... Defendant contends that the deadly assault resulted from the heat of passion aroused by the victim's alleged attempt to abduct the 6-year-old boy.

... [T]he testimony presented at trial indicates that a significant amount of time passed following the attempted abduction. ... This evidence of the time and acts involved does not support a jury instruction on the heat of passion brought about by a sudden provocation which would "naturally and reasonably arouse the passions of an ordinary man beyond his power of control." . . .

. . . [D]efendant testified that following the attempted abduction, he was upset but "not furious." After failing to find McDaniel in his apartment, defendant and Pasour attempted to return to defendant's truck when McDaniel appeared from behind the apartment building and approached the two men. According to defendant, when McDaniel went for a weapon under his clothing, the two men grabbed him and tried to separate him from the handgun. Once the weapon was free, defendant admitted that he kicked the gun "at least six" times to remove it from the immediate vicinity of the altercation. He claimed he purposefully did not pick up the weapon because he had a criminal record and did not want his fingerprints on the gun. Defendant then claims he turned and noticed Pasour hitting and kicking McDaniel, and he persuaded Pasour to stop the attack because he "did not want the man to die." He testified that he rolled McDaniel onto his stomach because he heard him choking and apparently wanted to help him breathe more easily until the authorities arrived. This evidence indicates that defendant was capable of cool reflection during the confrontation which ended in McDaniel's death. The trial court did not err in refusing defendant's requested instruction on heat of passion. . . .

Defendant next argues the trial court erred in overruling defendant's objections to an instruction that defendant would lose the benefit of self-defense if the jury determined that he was the aggressor in bringing on the fight resulting in McDaniel's death. The trial court instructed the jury that defendant would be excused from murder or manslaughter based on self-defense, if he was not the aggressor in bringing on the fight, and did not use excessive force under the circumstances. If the Defendant voluntarily and without provocation entered the fight, he would be considered the aggressor. Self-defense completely excuses a defendant for the killing of another person if four conditions are met:

(1) it appeared to defendant and he believed it to be necessary to kill the deceased in order to save himself from death or great bodily harm; and

(2) defendant's belief was reasonable in that the circumstances as they appeared to him at the time were sufficient to create such a belief in the mind of a person of ordinary firmness; and

(3) defendant was not the aggressor in bringing on the affray, i.e., he did not aggressively and willingly enter into the fight without legal excuse or provocation; and

(4) defendant did not use excessive force, i.e., did not use more force than was necessary or reasonably appeared to him to be necessary under the circumstances to protect himself from death or great bodily harm. . . .

If only the first two elements of self-defense are met, the defendant loses the right to perfect self-defense but may nevertheless be entitled to imperfect self-defense and in that case would be guilty of at least voluntary manslaughter. . . . In the instant case, however, more than sufficient evidence was presented to indicate that defendant could have been the aggressor in the fight resulting in the victim's death. . . . On this evidence, the jury could find that defendant was the aggressor or voluntarily entered the fight resulting in the death of McDaniel. Thus the trial court's jury instruction on the issue of self-defense was not error. . . .

Defendant has offered no argument in support of the remaining assignments of error in the record. Therefore they are deemed abandoned. . . .

No error.

CASE QUESTIONS

1. From your reading of this case, why do you think that the jury refused to convict the defendant of first-degree murder, the crime with which he was charged in the indictment, and convicted him of murder in the second degree?

2. Why did the court of appeals sustain the trial court's instruction on self-defense?

AUTHOR'S COMMENTARY

Kenneth Wood sought to mitigate the crime with which he was charged, first-degree murder, to voluntary manslaughter by arguing that he had acted in the sudden heat of passion after adequate provocation. The trial and appellate courts rejected this claim because too much time had passed between the occurrence of the provocation and McDaniel's death. The appellate court found Wood's conduct during the confrontation with McDaniel to be consistent with "cool reflection," rather than that of a person still under the "heat of passion," and refused to instruct the jury on heat of passion as requested by Wood.

Wood also argued that the trial court should not have instructed the jury to the effect that Wood would "lose the benefit of self-defense if the jury determined that he was the aggressor in bringing on the fight resulting in McDaniel's death." The appellate court found no error in this instruction, given the plethora of evidence that permits a reasonable conclusion that Wood was the person looking for a fight with McDaniel, and not vice versa, and thus forfeited any self-defense claim.

The appellate court concluded that Wood was properly convicted of murder in the second degree and that he had no legal basis to mitigate this conviction to manslaughter.

Negligent Manslaughter

Many jurisdictions have responded to the prevalence of homicides involving motor vehicles by criminalizing negligent conduct that is less culpable than the reckless or gross negligence standard required for traditional involuntary manslaughter prosecutions. This "new" type of manslaughter (at least theoretically) requires that the criminal actor's conduct be more than a mere violation of the ordinary care standard employed in civil cases but less than gross negligence. **Negligent manslaughter** in some states is classified as a form of involuntary manslaughter and in other states exists as a separate statute often called "vehicular homicide," a lesser-included offense to involuntary manslaughter.

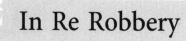

In Re Robbery

Robbery is a crime that many today consider to be a crime against persons because force is threatened or employed in the commission of the crime. It is actually a crime that straddles the traditional crimes against persons and crimes against property categories. Robbery is housed in this textbook in the crimes against property chapter because that is its traditional classification and because larceny is a lesser-included offense of robbery. Individuals interested in addressing this topic at this time can turn to the robbery discussion in Chapter 7.

Traditional Crimes of Assault and Battery

Although today the ancient crimes of **assault** and **battery** are sometimes merged into a single crime called assault, the *actus reus* of each is distinct.

Battery

A battery is committed when an offender who is acting without consent touches another person in an unlawful and harmful or offensive manner. Battery's *mens rea* is usually defined as requiring proof that the perpetrator intended to commit the *actus reus* (general intent) or acted negligently when committing the touching. A battery can be committed without the victim experiencing any physical injury or pain, and an offensive touching is a sufficient act. Thus, if a man intentionally and without consent, for example, touches a woman on her derriere as she walks by, a battery has been committed. Similarly, if one party to an argument spits on the other person, the spitter has committed a criminal battery.

TABLE 6.6	ELEMENTS OF BATTERY
Criminal act	Unlawful, harmful, or offensive touching of another person
Criminal intent	General intent—the actor intends the normal and probable consequences of his or her voluntary acts
Causation	Factual and proximate cause

In contact sports the physical contact that normally occurs within the rules of the game is classified as lawful and consensual. The players have implicitly consented to be battered. If, however, a player uses brutal and excessive force or goes into the stands and strikes an obnoxious fan, the player can be charged with battery.

Assault

Historically, assault prosecutions have targeted two scenarios. In *threatened battery assaults* (sometimes also called menacing), the prosecution proves that the offender has unlawfully and intentionally caused the victim reasonably to be in fear of an immediate harmful or offensive touching. Thus, if A is much larger and stronger than B and verbally threatens to "knock B's block off," moves toward B and starts pounding one of his fists into his other hand, and B reasonably fears an immediate battery, an assault has occurred. It is important to emphasize that threatening words alone are insufficient to constitute an assault; for an assault to occur, the perpetrator has to be within striking distance of the intended victim.

TABLE 6.7	ELEMENTS OF ASSAULT
Attempted Battery Assault	
Criminal Act	Unsuccessful attempt to commit a battery
Criminal intent	Specific intent to commit a battery
Threatened Battery Assault	
Criminal act	Placing target reasonably in fear of an imminent battery
Criminal intent	Specific intent to cause target to fear imminent battery
Causation	Factual and proximate causation

In *attempted battery assaults*, the prosecution proves that the offender has attempted to commit a battery but has been unsuccessful. Thus, if A throws a punch at B and misses, A has not battered B because B was never touched. But A has nevertheless committed a crime because when B saw the punch coming in her direction and ducked, she was reasonably placed in fear of being hit. Had A, who was behind B, tried to punch B in the back but missed because B, who knew nothing of A's action, decided to bend over and tie his shoes, A would have also committed an assault.

Contemporary Assault Statutes

Many states have merged the crimes of assault and battery. The excerpt from the Maine assault statute in Figure 6.6 is illustrative because it defines what is actually a battery as an assault.

Modern assault statutes often differentiate between assaults and batteries that do not involve special aggravating circumstances and those that do. Assaults and batteries that target law-enforcement officers, that accompany an intent to commit specified crimes (often rape, murder, or robbery), or that involve the use of weapons, are often classified as aggravated assaults and batteries. The excerpt from Georgia's aggravated assault statute is illustrative. See Figure 6.7.

Figure 6.6. Maine Assault Statute

> Title 17-A Section 207. Assault
> 1. A person is guilty of assault if he intentionally, knowingly, or recklessly causes bodily injury or offensive physical contact to another. . . .

Figure 6.7. Excerpt from Official Code of Georgia

> (a) A person commits the offense of aggravated assault when he or she assaults:
> (1) With intent to murder, to rape, or to rob;
> (2) With a deadly weapon or with any object, device, or instrument which, when used offensively against a person, is likely to or actually does result in serious bodily injury; or
> (3) A person or persons without legal justification by discharging a firearm from within a motor vehicle toward a person or persons.
> (b) Except as provided in subsections (c), (d), (e), (f), (g), (h), and (i) of this Code section, a person convicted of the offense of aggravated assault shall be punished by imprisonment for not less than one nor more than 20 years.
> (c) A person who knowingly commits the offense of aggravated assault upon a peace officer while the peace officer is engaged in, or on account of the performance of, his or her official duties shall, upon conviction thereof, be punished by imprisonment for not less than five nor more than 20 years.
> (d) Any person who commits the offense of aggravated assault against a person who is 65 years of age or older shall, upon conviction thereof, be punished by imprisonment for not less than three nor more than 20 years. . . .

HOPKINS v. THE STATE
553 S.E.2d 173
Court of Appeals of Georgia, Third Division
July 27, 2001

AUTHOR'S INTRODUCTION

Lavacus Antwane Graham, Christopher D. Hopkins, and a third man were present on December 26, 1995, in the parking lot behind a Donalsonville, Georgia, grocery store. Between 6:00 and 6:30 P.M., a car occupied by a male driver and a female passenger drove up. The driver and passenger had come to this place in the hopes of purchasing crack cocaine. Graham, Hopkins, and the third man approached the driver and demanded money, after which Graham displayed a semi-automatic pistol and the three renewed their monetary demand. A struggle then occurred between Graham and the driver, who grabbed the barrel of the pistol and pointed it toward the windshield. During this struggle, Hopkins and the third man were striking the driver. Graham somehow managed to pull the pistol from the driver's grasp and fatally shot the passenger. The three men then fled the scene on foot. Hopkins, who was subsequently identified as one of the assailants by the surviving victim, was tried by a jury, which acquitted him of murder, felony murder, and aggravated assault of the passenger. Hopkins was, however, convicted of aggravated assault of the driver. Hopkins appealed his conviction to the court of appeals on the grounds that the evidence used to support his conviction for aggravated assault was legally insufficient.

EXCERPT FROM THE CASE

Judge ELLINGTON:

Hopkins argues . . . that there was no evidence that he was the gunman. He contends that the evidence was insufficient to support a conviction of aggravated assault of the male victim in that there was no evidence he assaulted the victim with the intent to rob . . . or that he was a party to Graham's assault with a deadly weapon. . . . At trial, Hopkins advanced the defense theory that he was not associated with Graham, the gunman, but that he was merely present at the time of the shooting as a competing drug dealer seeking to make a sale.

Hopkins contends that testimony of the eyewitness who drove the victims to the hospital supported his defense that he approached the car only with the intent to make a drug sale, not to commit a robbery. Specifically, the eyewitness testified that when Hopkins approached the male victim's side of the car, the victim asked to "see the stuff" and Hopkins asked to first "see the money." Hopkins further contends that the testimony of the male victim that the three assailants approached the car and immediately demanded all their money was "successfully impeached" by proof of the victim's pretrial testimony that, when Hopkins first came up to his window, he asked "What's up?" Hopkins contends this testimony supported his defense that he was merely hoping to make a drug sale and that there was no evidence he was a participant in Graham's attempted armed robbery and assault with a deadly weapon.

These conflicts in the evidence identified by Hopkins do not support his argument that the evidence was insufficient to convict him.

The weight and credibility of witnesses are questions for the triers of fact; that some evidence offered by a witness seems contradictory to his own or to some other's, or incomplete or uncertain, does not automatically discredit the evidence given by that witness, or others, for it is the function of the triers of fact to determine to what evidence it gives credence. It is not for us to determine or question how the jury resolved any apparent conflicts or uncertainties in the evidence. . . .

The jury's verdict demonstrates that it resolved the conflicts and found beyond a reasonable doubt that Hopkins was guilty of aggravated assault. As detailed above, the evidence showed that Hopkins approached the victims' car with Graham and that he demanded the victims' money. Further, the evidence that he did not flee when Graham drew his weapon but rather stayed to assist in the assault by hitting the victim as he struggled for control of the gun—undermined his defense that he was merely a bystander. The evidence was sufficient for a rational trier of fact to find Hopkins willingly participated in an attempted armed robbery in which Graham threatened the victim with a handgun; therefore, the evidence was sufficient to convict him of aggravated assault. . . .

Judgment affirmed.

CASE QUESTION

What evidence was presented at trial which, if believed, would support the appellant's conviction for aggravated assault under the Georgia statute?

AUTHOR'S COMMENTARY

Aggravated assault statutes specify various circumstances that, if found to accompany the commission of a crime, will significantly enhance the perpetrator's sentence. These factors may include knowingly or purposely causing serious bodily injury, assaults against specified statuses such as police officers, pregnant women, or firefighters, assaults to commit other crimes such as rape or murder, and assaults with a deadly or dangerous weapon.

One of the more interesting discussions in assault with a dangerous weapon cases has to do with the determination of what constitutes a deadly weapon. The question is much more complicated than determining whether a weapon is naturally capable of causing death. For example, a starter's pistol, at first glance, is not capable of discharging a bullet and might appear to be incapable of causing death. But a closer look would show that a starter's pistol could readily be used to bludgeon someone to death. Thus, an instrument that is neither designed nor constructed for use as a dangerous weapon, such as a fire poker or baseball bat, could be transformed into a dangerous weapon by someone who had decided to use the instrument in a manner unintended by those who manufactured it.

Criminal defendants in assault with dangerous weapons cases sometimes try to defend by arguing that their weapon was unloaded or otherwise inoperable and therefore incapable of causing serious bodily injury. The rationale for classifying an assault with an unloaded firearm as an aggravated assault was explained by the Wyoming Supreme Court as follows:

> The aggravated assault statute enhances the punishment if the defendant uses a deadly weapon because deadly weapons cause a greater degree of fear in the person being assaulted. The victim does not know that the firearm is not loaded, and his apprehension and consequent reactions will be the same as if the firearm were loaded. He may try to escape or defend himself, conceivably putting himself and others into a precarious and dangerous situation. . . . [7]

Jurisdictions vary in their approach to defining what constitutes a dangerous weapon. Many would agree with the U.S. Court of Appeals for the Fourth Circuit, which said in *United States v. Sturgis*, 48 F.3d 784 [4th Cir. 1994]:

> The test of whether a particular object was used as a dangerous weapon is not so mechanical that it can be readily reduced to a question of law. Rather, it must be left to the jury to determine whether, under the circumstances of each case, the defendant used some instrumentality, object, or (in some instances) a part of his body to cause death or serious injury. This test clearly invites a functional inquiry into the use of the instrument rather than a metaphysical reflection on its nature.

The Michigan Court of Appeals said essentially the same thing in *People v. Norris*, 600 N.W.2d 658 (1999). It ruled that the use of tear gas and pepper gas in the commission of a jewelry store robbery constituted the use of a dangerous weapon under Michigan law. The court interpreted Michigan's statute as favoring a "use oriented approach," saying:

> "whether an object is a dangerous weapon depends upon the object itself and how it is used." . . . Further, a dangerous weapon has been described as either (1) a weapon designed to be dangerous and capable of causing death or serious injury . . . (e.g., a loaded gun) or (2) any other object capable of causing death or serious injury that the defendant used as a weapon (e.g., a screwdriver used as a knife) . . . (a dangerous weapon within the meaning of the felonious assault statute . . . is one that is deadly

or capable of inflicting serious injury). Whether an object is a dangerous weapon under the circumstances of the case is a question for the fact finder. . . .

But some courts disagree. New York's highest court, for example, departed from the "use approach" in the case of *People v. Maxwell Owusu*, 712 N.E.2d 1228 (1999). Owusu, the defendant in the case, was charged with burglary in the first degree for using a dangerous instrument while burglarizing a dwelling. Owusu had used his teeth to bite the victim's finger to the bone during a struggle that took place during the commission of the crime. The New York Court of Appeals took a categorical approach and ruled that no unaugmented part of the human body could be classified as a "dangerous instrument" under New York law. Thus, no part of the human body, not even a professional boxer's bare fists, nor the bare feet and hands of a martial arts expert, could be classified as deadly weapons. The court referred to such specialists as "extraordinary men," as contrasted with "ordinary men," and explained its reasoning as follows:

> An "extraordinary man" rule would create increased criminal liability for use of a dangerous instrument where a heavyweight champion merely threatens a blow (*see* Penal Law §§ 10.00 [definition of dangerous instrument includes use or "threatened" use]), but not where an ordinary man beats another to death. *Vollmer*, [an earlier New York case in which an ordinary man did kill the victim with his bare hands] sensibly avoided such a strained interpretation by concluding fists are not dangerous instruments. This conclusion was reached not because the defendant's fists, as utilized under those circumstances, were not readily capable of causing death (they in fact did), but because they were simply his hands, nothing more.

Rape and Sexual Assault

Prior to the reforms of the 1970s, the crime of **rape** required proof that sexual intercourse had occurred between an accused male and a female victim because of the defendant's use, or threatened use, of force against the woman. Prosecutors had to prove that the accused male used or threatened the use of force against the otherwise nonconsenting victim and that sexual penetration of the victim's vagina had occurred. The crime was traditionally a general intent offense (with a few exceptions), meaning that although the government had to prove that the defendant intended to commit the *actus reus*, it did not have to prove any additional criminal intent.

Defendants in rape prosecutions often claim that the victim consented to sexual intercourse. In such "he says/she says" cases, the absence of other witnesses makes the relative credibility of the parties of critical importance. Prior to legislative reforms, the defense in a rape case would often attack the victim's credibility by including a wide-ranging exploration of her prior sexual history. The justification

TABLE 6.8	TRADITIONAL ELEMENTS OF RAPE	
Criminal act	Sexual penetration of a female	
Criminal intent	General intent	
Circumstances	Female did not consent and accused used or threatened use of force	

for this line of inquiry was that it was necessary to determine whether or not she was "chaste" (which generally meant determining whether she had engaged in sexual relations outside of marriage). The inference was that if she had been sexually active in the past, she was more likely to have consented to intercourse with the accused. Another view held by many was that a "true" victim of rape would have quickly notified authorities or told some other person about what had happened. Therefore, the "reasoning" went, a victim who kept knowledge of the crime to herself might not be telling the truth. Yet another example of this kind of anachronistic thinking requires mentioning. If a victim failed to show that she had fought her assailant and "resisted to the utmost," the defense would argue that there was a reasonable doubt as to whether the defendant had, in fact, used force to accomplish the penetration. But the logical rebuttal to this assertion is that the person proposing sex should have the legal burden of making certain that the other person was consenting to participate in sexual intercourse.

Rape victims have often said they felt it was they who had been put on trial as much as, or more so, than their attackers, and many rapes have not been reported to authorities. It is also important to remember, however, that persons claiming to be rape victims have not always been truthful. There have been well-publicized cases in which persons convicted of rape were released from prison after their accusers admitted to having committed perjury while testifying at trial.

The late 1970s saw the rise of a national movement to reform the rape laws in this country. It was often difficult for prosecutors to prove their cases beyond a reasonable doubt, and juries would often acquit. Reformers believed that too many rapists were getting away with the crime. Proponents of change argued that victims needed more protection than was afforded them by the crime of rape and advocated for a fundamental redefinition of the offense. Reformers urged that rape be made a gender neutral offense, and that the marital exemption that protected spouses from prosecution for unconsensual sexual contact within marriage be eliminated.

The result was that the conduct formerly prosecuted as rape (i.e., forcible sexual intercourse) became only one form of a new and more comprehensive crime, criminal sexual conduct. The *actus reus* of **sexual assault** statutes is generally defined very broadly. In Michigan, for example, criminal sexual conduct consists of six offenses which are divided between crimes in which the offender penetrates a

Figure 6.8. Excerpt from Michigan Sexual Conduct Statute

Michigan Criminal Sexual Conduct Statute 750.520(b)—Criminal Sexual Conduct in the First Degree

(I) A person is guilty of criminal sexual conduct in the first degree if he or she engages in sexual penetration with another person and if any of the following circumstances exists:

(a) That other person is under 13 years of age.

(b) That other person is at least 13 but less than 16 years of age and any of the following:

(i) The actor is a member of the same household as the victim.

(ii) The actor is related to the victim by blood or affinity to the fourth degree.

(iii) The actor is in a position of authority over the victim and used this authority to coerce the victim to submit.

(c) Sexual penetration occurs under circumstances involving the commission of any other felony.

(d) The actor is aided or abetted by 1 or more other persons and either of the following circumstances exists:

(i) The actor knows or has reason to know that the victim is mentally incapable, mentally incapacitated, or physically helpless.

(ii) The actor uses force or coercion to accomplish the sexual penetration. Force or coercion includes but is not limited to any of the circumstances listed in subdivision (f)(i) to (v).

(e) The actor is armed with a weapon or any article used or fashioned in a manner to lead the victim to reasonably believe it to be a weapon.

(f) The actor causes personal injury to the victim and force or coercion is used to accomplish sexual penetration. Force or coercion includes but is not limited to any of the following circumstances:

(i) When the actor overcomes the victim through the actual application of physical force or physical violence.

(ii) When the actor coerces the victim to submit by threatening to use force or violence on the victim, and the victim believes that the actor has the present ability to execute these threats.

(iii) When the actor coerces the victim to submit by threatening to retaliate in the future against the victim, or any other person, and the victim believes that the actor has the ability to execute this threat. As used in this subdivision, "to retaliate" includes threats of physical punishment, kidnapping, or extortion.

(iv) When the actor engages in the medical treatment or examination of the victim in a manner or for purposes which are medically recognized as unethical or unacceptable.

(v) When the actor, through concealment or by the element of surprise, is able to overcome the victim.

Figure 6.8. Excerpt from Michigan Sexual Conduct Statute (continued)

(g) The actor causes personal injury to the victim, and the actor knows or has reason to know that the victim is mentally incapable, mentally incapacitated, or physically helpless.

(h) That other person is mentally incapable, mentally disabled, mentally incapacitated, or physically helpless, and any of the following:

(i) The actor is related to the victim by blood or affinity to the fourth degree.

(ii) The actor is in a position of authority over the victim and used this authority to coerce the victim to submit.

(2) Criminal sexual conduct in the first degree is a felony punishable by imprisonment in the state prison for life or for any term of years.

body cavity and contact offenses in which prohibited bodily contact occurs between the offender and the victim. Five of the six offenses are classified as felonies, and one is a misdemeanor. There are four degrees of criminal sexual conduct and two degrees of assault with intent to commit criminal sexual conduct. See Figure 6.8.

Internet Tip

In the interest of saving space, only the statute defining sexual criminal conduct in the first degree is reprinted here in Figure 6.8. The entire Michigan Sexual Conduct Statute can be found on the textbook's website with the Chapter 6 materials.

STATE v. DOUGLAS GOODWIN
671 A.2d 554
New Hampshire Supreme Court
February 15, 1996

AUTHOR'S INTRODUCTION

Douglas Goodwin was prosecuted and convicted in New Hampshire of the felonious sexual assault of a 15-year-old female. The sexual assault statute does not specify what degree of intent must be proven for conviction of this crime, and Goodwin argued on appeal that the trial court incorrectly charged the jury regarding the *mens rea* element for this crime.

EXCERPT FROM THE CASE

PER CURIAM.

The defendant, Douglas Goodwin, was convicted in the Superior Court (Perkins, J.) of five counts of felonious sexual assault against a 15-year-old girl. . . . He argues that the trial court erred in holding that the *mens rea* for the offense charged was "knowingly," rather than "purposely." . . .

[The statute] . . . provides that "[a] person is guilty of a class B felony if he . . . [e]ngages in sexual penetration with a person other than his legal spouse who is 13 years of age or older and under 16 years of age. . . ." In spite of the fact that there is no *mens rea* expressed in a statute, one cannot be convicted of a crime without proof that the act was accompanied by a culpable mental state. *State v. Ayer* . . . (1986) ("A person is guilty of . . . a felony . . . only if he acts purposely, knowingly, recklessly, or negligently, as the law may require, with respect to each material element of the offense."). "Where a specific mental state is not provided for the offense, we read [the statute] as requiring proof of a culpable mental state which is appropriate in light of the nature of the offense and the policy considerations for punishing the conduct in question." . . .

[The statute] defines felonious sexual assault as any one of three distinct proscribed acts. Two of these acts involve sexual contact, . . . the other act, which is at issue here, involves sexual penetration. . . . The defendant argues that because the appropriate mental state for the offenses [involving sexual contact] . . . is "purposely," see *State v. Pond* . . . (1989), "purposely" should likewise be the *mens rea* for the offense [involving sexual penetration]. . . . His argument is based upon the premise that sexual penetration necessarily encompasses sexual contact.

We disagree. . . . In *Pond*, we held that [t]he *mens rea* required for felonious sexual assault . . . is found in the definition of sexual contact . . . : " 'Sexual contact' means the intentional touching of the victim's or actor's sexual or intimate parts . . . which can be reasonably construed as being for the purpose of sexual arousal or gratification." This court concluded in 1986 that "intentionally" was synonymous with "purposely." Therefore, purposely is the *mens rea* for felonious sexual assault. . . . This analysis applies only to the mental state required for sexual contact. . . . Unlike the definition of sexual contact . . . there is no language in the definition of sexual penetration describing a requisite state of mind. . . .

Second, when a statute defining an offense is silent with respect to the *mens rea*, we will look to the common law origins of the crime, which in this case is rape. . . . Rape is generally considered to be a general intent, rather than a specific intent, crime. . . . "Whereas specific intent commonly refers to a special mental element above and beyond that required with respect to the criminal act itself, the general intent requirement for rape means that no intent is requisite other than that evidenced by the doing of the acts constituting the offense." . . .

The Criminal Code generally uses the terms "purposely" and "knowingly" in place of specific intent and general intent, respectively. . . . "A person acts purposely with respect to a material element of an offense when his conscious object is to cause the result or engage in the conduct that comprises the element." . . . On the other hand, "[a] person acts knowingly with respect to conduct or to a circumstance that is a material element of an offense when he is aware that his conduct is of such nature or that such circumstances exist." . . . We have stated that "[e]ngaging in sexual penetration in any of the statutorily prohibited circumstances is criminal when the actor is aware that his conduct is of such a nature or that such circumstances exist, that is, when he acts knowingly." . . .

We therefore conclude that "knowingly" is the appropriate *mens rea* for felonious sexual assault involving sexual penetration.

Affirmed.

CASE QUESTIONS

1. Why did the court rule that *knowingly* was the proper *mens rea* for felonious sexual assault by penetration?

2. Paragraph "m" of New Hampshire's Aggravated Felonious Sexual Assault statute makes it a crime for a person to continue with sexual intercourse) ". . . [if] at the time of the sexual assault, the victim indicates by speech or conduct that there is not freely given consent to performance of the sexual act." In your opinion, which party should have the responsibility of making sure that mutual consent exists for sexual intercourse where there is ambiguity because of silence or lack of physical opposition?

AUTHOR'S COMMENTARY

The Michigan criminal sexual conduct statute is comprehensive, gender neutral, and expansive in scope. While it includes the traditional *actus reus* for rape, it goes far beyond the conduct prohibited under traditional rape laws. The statute eliminates the old common law requirement that the victim prove that he or she resisted the attacker. The sexual penetration definition's inclusiveness is another departure from the common law. The statute clarifies for both criminal justice practitioners and the general public the broad range of prohibited conduct that is forbidden. It specifically addresses special relationships involving authority figures, such as teachers, who are prohibited from engaging in sexual conduct with their pupils, patients or charges, and it protects persons from exploitation who, due to other specified special circumstances and conditions, such as mental illness, are statutorily disqualified from giving consent. A person not wishing to commit sexual assault has an affirmative legal duty to ensure that none of the special considerations and circumstances apply that would make the contemplated sexual conduct criminal.

Rape Shield Laws

Michigan was the first state to adopt what we commonly refer to as a **"rape shield law"** in 1971. This type of legislation is often both a statute and an evidentiary rule. Rape shield laws vary from state to state, and there is no commonly accepted model. Some say that there are four different models operating in the country today, with such "laws" on the books in all states except Arizona.[8]

Internet Tip

Federal Rule of Evidence Rule 412, the federal "rape shield law," can be found on the textbook's website along with other materials relevant to Chapter 6.

STATE v. STEPHEN F.

188 P.3d 84
Supreme Court of New Mexico
June 23, 2008

AUTHOR'S INTRODUCTION

State v. Stephen F. is a "she said/he said" rape case involving two teenaged minors, Stephen F. (age 15) and B.G. (age 16).

Stephen, the accused, was a friend of the alleged victim B.G.'s brother and frequently stayed at B.G.'s house overnight, sleeping on a living room couch. Both Stephen and B.G. agree that on the night in question the two of them engaged in sexual intercourse. The following morning, B.G. told her mother that Stephen had raped her, and he was subsequently charged with that crime. Stephen maintained that B.G. had consented to sexual intercourse and was falsely accusing him to avoid parental punishment. He was aware that B.G. admitted in a deposition to having been disciplined previously by her parents for having consented to sexual intercourse with a previous boyfriend. Steven sought to cross-examine both B.G. and her parents at trial about the previous incident. He also wanted to show through cross-examination that B.G.'s parents were very religious and opposed to premarital sex.

New Mexico enacted both a rape shield law and an evidentiary rule to protect alleged rape victims from having to unnecessarily disclose their sexual histories in court. Pursuant to provisions in the statute and rule, Stephen requested a pre-trial hearing. At the hearing, Stephen argued that B.G.'s sexual history information should be admitted because it explained her motive for falsely claiming she had been raped. His entire defense depended on being able to impeach the credibility of his accuser by cross-examining her and her parents. He also argued that his fundamental due process rights under the state and federal constitutions to confront his accusers in court and cross-examine them should outweigh B.G.'s rights under the rape shield law and rule.

The state claimed that Stephen was seeking to introduce "propensity" evidence which was forbidden by the rapeshield law and rule. In a "propensity" defense, the defense hopes that admission by the alleged victim that she has consented to sex in the past will influence the jury to infer that the alleged victim was not "chaste" and therefore also likely to have consented to sex with the accused.

The trial judge ruled in favor of the state at the hearing, and Stephen was not permitted at trial to cross-examine the witnesses as he had proposed. He was subsequently convicted of rape and appealed to the state intermediate appellate court. The appellate court reversed his conviction, concluding that the cross-examinations should have been permitted. The state appealed to the New Mexico Supreme Court.

EXCERPT FROM THE CASE

Bosson, Justice.

This appeal implicates two competing interests—an accused's constitutional right to confront witnesses against him, and the State's interest, as expressed in our rape shield statute and corresponding rule of evidence, in protecting those witnesses from unwarranted intrusions on their privacy. . . .

DISCUSSION

This Court has previously acknowledged that "[i]f application of the rape shield law or rule would conflict with the accused's confrontation right, if it operates to preclude the defendant from presenting a full and fair defense, the statute and rule must yield." *State v. Johnson*, 944 P.2d 869 (1997). . . . *Rock v. Arkansas*, 483 U.S. 44, . . . (1987) ("[W]hen a state rule of evidence conflicts with the right [of the accused] to present witnesses, the rule may 'not be applied mechanistically to defeat the ends of justice,' but must meet the fundamental standards of due process." . . .) A defendant's "right to confront and to cross-examine is not absolute and may, in appropriate cases, bow to accommodate other legitimate interests in the criminal trial process." . . . . However, a court's decision to restrict a defendant's ability to confront a witness, even when based on legitimate state interests, "calls into question the ultimate integrity of the fact-finding process and requires that the competing interest be closely examined." . . .

Just as the Confrontation Clause does not give a defendant an absolute right to cross-examine a witness, rape shield laws do not act as absolute prohibitions to the admission of an alleged victim's sexual history. The goal of a rape shield statute is " 'to emphasize the general irrelevance of a victim's sexual history, not to remove relevant evidence from the jury's consideration.' " . . . Thus, "[a] defendant's right of confrontation—with its protection of the right to cross-examine, test credibility, detect bias, and otherwise challenge an opposing version of facts—is a *critical limitation* on the trial court's discretion to exclude evidence a defendant wishes to admit." . . . Under our statute and rule of evidence, "a defendant must show sufficient facts to support a particular theory of relevance" to enable the trial court to competently assess the constitutional significance of that theory. . . .

In *Johnson*, this Court suggested a five-factor framework to aid the court in determining whether the defendant has adequately established his theory of relevance. . . . The five factors are:

(1) whether there is a clear showing that the complainant committed the prior acts;
(2) whether the circumstances of the prior acts closely resemble those of the present case;
(3) whether the prior acts are clearly relevant to a material issue, such as identity, intent, or bias;
(4) whether the evidence is necessary to the defendant's case; and
(5) whether the probative value of the evidence outweighs its prejudicial effect. . . .

A district court's decision to exclude evidence of a victim's prior sexual conduct is reviewed for abuse of discretion. . . . We now evaluate the trial court's exercise of discretion in this case using the guidelines this Court set forth in *Johnson*.

STEPHEN ESTABLISHED A CONSTITUTIONAL RIGHT TO CROSS-EXAMINE B.G.

Stephen argues that his inability to cross-examine B.G. about her motive to lie "offend[ed][his] right to meaningful confrontation of the state's primary witness against him, as well as his right to due process," because the evidence he sought to introduce was relevant to Stephen's defense that he and B.G. had engaged in consensual sex. Relying appropriately on the *Johnson* factors, the Court of Appeals held that Stephen had a constitutional right to cross-examine B.G. . . .

The State suggests that Stephen could not meet the requirements of the second factor, . . . because he could not show that the circumstances of B.G.'s prior consensual sexual encounter closely resembled the sexual act between Stephen and B.G. . . .

We conclude that the Court of Appeals correctly held that the second factor does not apply in this case. . . . A comparison of the details of B.G.'s prior sexual encounter with the details of the alleged rape is simply not relevant to

Stephen's theory that B.G. fabricated the allegation because she feared being punished by her parents. Stephen's theory of the case is not that B.G. willingly engaged in a sex act with her boyfriend and therefore she willingly engaged in a similar sex act with Stephen. Instead, his theory is that she fabricated the rape charge because she did not want to be punished, and her fear of parental punishment arises from the mere fact of engaging in premarital sex, not from any purported similarity between the type of premarital sex. . . .

The State next argues that the Court of Appeals erred when it held that the third factor, . . . weighed in favor of allowing Stephen to cross-examine B.G. While the State agrees that "motive to lie" is a theory of relevance that may implicate a defendant's constitutional right, in this case Stephen failed to demonstrate facts upon which his theory was based. . . .

We are not persuaded. Stephen demonstrated that B.G.'s prior sexual encounter, and the resulting punishment, was relevant to bias, a material issue. . . . Not only was B.G.'s motive to lie relevant to show her possible bias, it was central to Stephen's defense that B.G. consented. The spontaneous nature of B.G.'s admission does not diminish the relevancy or the necessity of Stephen's theory that B.G. was motivated by her fear of punishment to lie to her mother. Instead, the conflicting meanings ascribed to B.G.'s admission present a classic jury question—evaluating the credibility of a witness. In denying Stephen the opportunity to cross-examine B.G., the trial court prohibited Stephen from "expos[ing] to the jury the facts from which jurors, as the sole triers of fact and credibility, could appropriately draw inferences relating to the reliability of the witness." *Davis v. Alaska*, 415 U.S. 308, . . . (1974).

The State further argues that Stephen did not adequately demonstrate that his ability to cross-examine B.G. was "necessary to [his] case," as required by the fourth *Johnson* factor. The State suggests that Stephen could have taken the stand in his defense and testified, giving the jury an alternate version of the facts to consider. Additionally, the trial court allowed Stephen the opportunity to attempt to cross-examine B.G. regarding her religious beliefs, subject to any objections about relevance. Therefore, the State contends that the trial court did not "strip [Stephen] of his only defense."

. . . By limiting Stephen's cross-examination to B.G.'s religious convictions, the trial court effectively foreclosed Stephen's ability to establish a motive for B.G. to fabricate the rape allegation. To establish that motive, Stephen needed to show that B.G. had a reason to fear punishment. To do so, it was necessary that Stephen have the ability to impeach B.G. with her deposition testimony that she had been punished previously. Without the aid of her deposition testimony, and because he was limited to questioning B.G. solely about her family's religious convictions, Stephen's argument that B.G. had a motive to lie became groundless and ineffective.

The trial court's refusal to allow Stephen to question B.G. about her motive to lie infringed on his right to effective cross-examination. Our conclusion is supported by *Davis v. Alaska*. . . . Just as in the instant appeal, the trial court allowed the defendant to question the witness about his bias toward the state, but without the benefit of backing up the defendant's theory of bias with the witness's juvenile record. . . . The U.S. Supreme Court concluded that the limited cross-examination that the court permitted ran afoul of the defendant's constitutional right to confront witnesses against him. . . .

. . . The Court concluded that "[o]n these facts it seems clear to us that *to make any such inquiry effective*, defense counsel should have been permitted to expose to the jury the facts from which jurors, as the sole triers of fact and credibility, could appropriately draw inferences relating to the reliability of the witness." . . .

. . . [T]to ensure that Stephen had the opportunity to *effectively* cross-examine B.G., he should have been allowed to challenge B.G.'s allegation that he raped her. He could only do so with her testimony and the testimony of her parents about the consequences that resulted from her prior consensual sexual experience. By prohibiting Stephen from so doing, the trial court deprived the jury of vital information and had the effect of stripping Stephen of his only defense.

Finally, the State contends that the Court of Appeals incorrectly concluded that the probative value of the evidence of B.G.'s motive to lie outweighed its prejudicial effect. . . .

We disagree. Although the trial court balanced the competing interests present in this case, it failed to accord proper weight to Stephen's constitutional right. During the pre-trial hearing Stephen expressed his concern that jurors, if left uninformed about B.G.'s past punishment, would wonder why B.G. would have lied to her parents in this instance. Stephen explained that the evidence he sought to admit would only be used to provide the jury with an explanation for B.G.'s actions, not as propensity evidence. The trial court expressed its concern that Stephen's proffered evidence might unintentionally have the effect of propensity evidence, stating: "I understand fully your statement that is not your intent, and you so state, but is that in fact the result? Is that not the . . . collateral damage that occurs?" The trial court refused to consider Stephen's Confrontation Clause claim stating, "I do not address [this claim] in terms suggested by counsel, that is, under the confrontation aspect but rather under the measure of prejudice versus probative value."

The trial court was appropriately concerned that cross-examining B.G. about her prior consensual sexual encounter may inflict "collateral damage." A trial court, however, must consider the effect of excluding such evidence on defendant's right to a fair trial and balance that effect against the potential prejudice to the truthfinding process itself . . . to determine whether the introduction of the victim's past sexual conduct may confuse the issues, mislead the jury, or cause the jury to decide the case on an improper or emotional basis. . . . While the trial court has the discretion to limit or even exclude such testimony, if the cross-examination is cumulative or only marginally relevant, or to protect against certain legitimate concerns, such as undue harassment, prejudice, or confusion of the issues, the trial court's decision to do so must not be "arbitrary or disproportionate to the purposes they are designed to serve." . . . The court's decision to exclude Stephen's proffered evidence must be closely examined because its decision to do so, even if based on legitimate state interests, "calls into question the ultimate integrity of the fact-finding process." . . . And, unless the State's interest in excluding the evidence in this case outweighs Stephen's constitutional right, the State's interest must give way. . . .

In this case, the State's interest in applying the rape shield statute to protect B.G.'s privacy, while important, is outweighed by Stephen's right of confrontation under the Sixth Amendment. Stephen's cross-examination of B.G. was simply not the type of evidence that the rape shield law was designed to prohibit. As previously explained, Stephen was not attempting to introduce the evidence for an improper motive; Stephen was not attempting to prove the "forbidden 'yes/yes inference' "— that because B.G. had consented before she must have consented now. . . . Further, because the evidence was limited to the *punishment* that resulted from the previous consensual sexual encounter, not the details about the sexual acts, it is less likely that the evidence would "confuse the issues, mislead the jury, or cause the jury to decide the case on an improper or emotional basis." . . .

In this case, the trial court could have protected B.G. from cross-examination designed only to unduly harass her or intrude unnecessarily on her personal life, while still allowing Stephen to question B.G. about her motive to lie. Our statute authorizes the trial court to impose limitations on the defendant's ability to cross-examine a witness and requires the court to "issue a written order stating what evidence may be introduced by the defendant and stating the specific questions to be permitted." . . . That the trial court could have tailored the cross-examination to protect B.G. undercuts the rationale for what we see as an overly broad and unnecessary ruling, which prohibited Stephen from questioning B.G. about her previous punishment.

Conversely, the effect that excluding the evidence had on Stephen's constitutional rights weighs in favor of admissibility. Stephen wanted to alert the jury to B.G.'s motive to lie, and impeach her credibility. It is just this type of evidence—motive, bias, and credibility—that the Confrontation Clause seeks to protect. . . . Further, the testimony that Stephen sought to elicit was central to his case. His sole defense was that B.G. consented to have sex with him, which hinged on the jury's evaluation of B.G.'s credibility. . . .

. . . [T]he trial court did not accord adequate weight to Stephen's Sixth Amendment claim. The trial court's concern about the collateral damage that B.G. might suffer does not "justify exclusion of cross-examination with such strong potential to demonstrate the falsity of [B.G.'s] testimony," and was, therefore, "beyond reason." . . .

Despite the adequacy of Stephen's showing that his constitutional rights were implicated by B.G.'s testimony, the trial court nevertheless concluded that the prejudicial effect of Stephen's proffered testimony outweighed its probative value. Because the trial court failed to accord the proper weight to Stephen's constitutional right when it balanced the probative value of admitting evidence of B.G.'s past sexual encounter against its prejudicial effect, we conclude that the trial court erred. . . .

CONCLUSION

We affirm the Court of Appeals and remand to the trial court for a new trial consistent with this Opinion. . . .

CASE QUESTIONS

1. Why was cross-examination particularly important in this case?

2. What could the trial judge have done at the pre-trial hearing to make sure that the interests of both parties were clearly and appropriately balanced?

3. What did you think of the state's suggestion that Stephen should have taken the witness stand and through his testimony explained his defense to the jury?

AUTHOR'S COMMENTARY

One of a federal or state supreme court's most important functions is to provide guideposts for the lower courts as to how to go about deciding difficult issues. The New Mexico Supreme Court's opinion in this case was a good example. It went far beyond merely affirming the intermediate appellate court's decision. It reviewed the decision-making process and made suggestions. It was aware of the difficult balancing of interests that trial judges must perform in cases like *State v. Stephen F.* Although determining the point at which competing interests are correctly balanced will vary from case to case, the issue presented in this case will reoccur. So, it sought to help trial judges avoid making mistakes in the future. The New Mexico Supreme Court in the *State v. Johnson* case, for example, identified the "five factors" judges should consider in rape shield cases. In future cases with facts similar to *Stephen F.*, trial judges will better understand how to weigh the right of cross-examination when balancing Sixth Amendment rights against an alleged victim's rights to protection under the rape shield act and rule.

Statutory Rape

Every state has established by statute an age at which individuals can lawfully consent to sexual relations. An individual who has sexual intercourse with an underage person is committing **statutory rape** and is strictly liable for his or her actions. As with other strict liability offenses, there is no *mens rea* element, and all the government need prove is commission of the *actus reus*. In most states, because intent is not an element of the crime, a statutory rape defendant cannot defend by claiming a mistake of fact about the individual's true age. Nor can an accused defend by claiming the underage person consented, even if this assertion is true, inasmuch as the rationale underlying the law to begin with is that such persons should not be participating in sexual intercourse.

Kidnapping and False Imprisonment

Kidnapping is an offense against an individual's right to self-determination of movement. A kidnapper is someone who, without lawful justification or excuse, seizes another person and moves that individual from one location to another place (**asportation**) or secretly confines the individual where it is unlikely others will find him or her. To satisfy the asportation requirement, the movement must be significant and not merely incidental to the other crime, must be distinctive and not inherent in the nature of the other crime, and must make the other crime easier to commit or significantly decrease the likelihood of detection.[9]

Kidnapping is a specific intent crime requiring proof that the offender was aware that his or her actions were unlawful. Traditionally, kidnapping statutes have required that the unlawful seizure of the victim be accomplished by force, the threat of force, or fraud (as in the case of a child by enticement).

TABLE 6.9	ELEMENTS OF KIDNAPPING
Criminal act	Seizing, detention, asportation and/or hiding
Criminal intent	Specific intent

A victim of **false imprisonment** is confined in a place of the offender's choosing and prevented from leaving. It is this unlawful restraint on freedom of movement that is the crux of the offense. False imprisonment is a specific intent offense, and the government must prove that the accused was aware of the unlawfulness of the confinement when the *actus reus* was committed.

TABLE 6.10	ELEMENTS OF FALSE IMPRISONMENT
Criminal act	Unlawful confinement and/or hiding
Criminal intent	Specific intent

ALLEN GARZA v. STATE
670 S.E.2d 73
Supreme Court of Georgia
November 3, 2008

AUTHOR'S INTRODUCTION

Allen Garza was convicted by a jury of two counts of kidnapping, four counts of false imprisonment, and one count of aggravated assault. He appealed to the intermediate court of appeals claiming that the state's evidence as to asportation was insufficient to support the kidnapping convictions. Garza also claimed that the false imprisonment and kidnapping counts related to the detention of the nine-year-old child, J.M., should have merged because they were not separate and distinct offenses as required by *Blockburger v. United States* (readers learned about *Blockburger* in Chapter 3's case of *Brown v. Ohio*). The intermediate appellate court rejected Garza's claims and affirmed all of his convictions. The lower appellate court's decision was subsequently appealed to the Georgia Supreme Court, which agreed to review the question as to whether the evidence of asportation was sufficient to support the kidnapping convictions.

EXCERPT FROM THE CASE

Hunstein, Presiding Justice.

... As recited in the opinion below, the evidence at trial established that on the evening of October 16, 2001, Garza gained entry into Angela Mendoza's residence on the pretext that he had left his wallet in her van. Once inside and while Mendoza's three children slept, he locked the door, drew a handgun from his pants, placed the weapon against Mendoza's head, and threatened to shoot her if she failed to follow his instructions. Garza struck Mendoza in the head with the handgun as she attempted to push it aside, causing her to fall to the floor. Garza then bound Mendoza's wrists with electrician's tape, tied her ankles with a torn sheet, and helped her up, made her sit in a chair, and instructed her not to move. Later, Garza allowed Mendoza to move to the floor where she joined her infant daughter and feigned sleep. When Garza fell asleep, Mendoza and her two-year-old son escaped out of a window, and Mendoza called the police.

Upon their arrival, the police forcibly entered the locked residence, removed Mendoza's infant daughter from the premises, and negotiated the release of Mendoza's nine-year-old son, J.M., for a six-pack of beer. . . . [A]s the police entered the residence, Garza awoke J.M., asked him if he wanted to play cops and robbers, and, while holding his shirt, ordered him to move to the back bedroom of the residence.

Once there, Garza continued to restrain J.M. by his shirt while openly holding his handgun. Although Garza did not point the weapon at him, J.M. was "scared" because he believed the weapon had been used to kill his mother. . . .

The issue presented is whether any of the movements of either Mendoza or J.M. during the course of the incident—Mendoza's falling to the floor from a standing position or being forced from the floor to a chair, . . . or J.M.'s being forced from the room where he slept into an adjacent bedroom—constituted asportation within the meaning of the Georgia kidnapping statute.

1. "A person commits the offense of kidnapping when he abducts or steals away any person without lawful authority or warrant and holds such person against his will." . . . Under current Georgia jurisprudence, the element of "abduct[ing] or steal[ing] away" the victim, known in legal parlance as "asportation," may be established by proof of "movement of the victim, however slight." . . . Thus, in addition to the more traditional scenarios involving child abduction or kidnapping for ransom, situations involving some other form of criminal activity have been found to support kidnapping charges even though the movement of the victim was merely a minor incident to the primary offense . . . (evidence of asportation sufficient where victim forced from one room to another in course of attempted rape); . . . (evidence of asportation sufficient where victim dragged ten feet from bus stop to bushes in course of robbery); . . . (evidence of asportation sufficient where victim grabbed and forced six to eight feet into store in course of armed robbery). . . .

In this Court's most recent pronouncement on the subject of asportation, we reaffirmed that "[t]he requirement of asportation to prove kidnapping is satisfied if there is movement of the victim, however slight that movement is. *Lyons v. State*, 652 S.E.2d 525 (2007). . . . The distance that a kidnapper transports the victim is not of legal significance. . . . We went on to state, however, that where the movement involved is minimal, and the alleged kidnapping occurs in furtherance of some other criminal enterprise, in order to constitute "asportation" the movement must be more than a mere positional change of the victim incidental to the other criminal act; it must be movement, even if a positional change, designed to better carry out the criminal activity. . . . Thus, we held that asportation was established where the defendants had forced the victim at gunpoint from a standing to a supine position, because this positional change "materially facilitated" the defendants in suffocating and robbing the victim. . . .

From our current vantage point, while the line drawn in *Lyons*—inconsequential movement versus movement "materially facilitating" another crime—may be analytically satisfying in harmonizing our courts' history of "hair-splitting decisions as to what is sufficient asportation," . . . this delineation does nothing to ameliorate the problems resulting from such a broad construction of the concept of asportation.

In its earliest incarnation, the common law crime of kidnapping required the asportation of the victim out of the country, the rationale being to prevent the victim's removal beyond law enforcement jurisdiction and isolation from the protection of the law. . . . Indeed, the earliest version of the Georgia kidnapping statute required removal of the victim across state or county lines. . . . Over time, however, as legislative attention turned increasingly to the subject in response to an increase in kidnappings correlating to more widespread use of the automobile as well as several high-profile abductions, the concept of asportation was broadened. . . . Following this trend, the Georgia Legislature in 1953 rewrote the kidnapping statute, removing the territorial component from the asportation requirement and thus eliminating therefrom any explicit distance threshold. . . .

The removal of the territorial component and failure to substitute any other explicit distance threshold has resulted in "it [being] left to the courts to determine in more specific terms the bases upon which the asportation in the particular case should be judged." . . . And it is thus how our courts have come to expand the concept of kidnapping so drastically from its origins as to encompass movements as "slight" as stepping from one room of an apartment into another. As other courts and commentators have noted, and as this Court has witnessed, this expansive construction of asportation poses a potential danger that the definition of kidnapping will sweep within its scope conduct that is decidedly wrongful but that should be punished as some other crime. Thus, for example, the robber who forces his victim to move from one room to another in order to find a cashbox or open a safe technically may commit kidnapping as well as robbery. This reasoning raises the possibility of cumulative penalties or of higher sanctions for kidnapping, even though the "removal" of the victim to another place was part and parcel of the robbery and not an independent wrong. . . . In other words, the appending of a kidnapping charge bears the potential to subject a defendant to greatly enhanced punishment—ranging in Georgia from a minimum ten-year sentence to life imprisonment, . . . for conduct that would be treated less harshly but for the occurrence of victim movement in the course thereof. Because "[u]nder the present holdings, almost any crime in which a victim moves from the point of initial contact with the defendant would authorize a kidnapping charge," . . . the expansive construction of asportation distorts the purpose of the kidnapping statute and raises serious constitutional issues.

First, by creating the potential for cumulative punishment under more than one criminal statute for a single course of conduct, such a construction implicates the principle of substantive double jeopardy, which "prevent[s] the sentencing court from prescribing greater punishment than the legislature intended." *Missouri v. Hunter*, 459 U.S. 359 . . . (1983). . . . Thus, using the armed robbery example cited above, is it reasonable to believe that the Legislature intended the mere fact of a victim's movement from one point to another within the situs of the robbery to justify another ten-years-to-life sentence in addition to the ten years to life prescribed for armed robbery? . . .

Second, convicting a person of kidnapping in a situation such as that in the armed robbery example or that presented herein poses a potential procedural due process problem. "[I]t is beyond question that the Due Process Clause requires that the law give a person of ordinary intelligence fair warning that [his] specific contemplated conduct is forbidden." . . . Though a person of ordinary intelligence would readily know that confining others against their will or committing armed robbery are acts which the law forbids, we are concerned that the plain language of the kidnapping statute may fail to provide fair warning that forcing the victims to move, however slightly, within the situs of the crime would justify prosecution for kidnapping. . . . The constitutional prohibition on vague laws is grounded not only in the principle of fair notice to the individual but also in the desirability of avoiding arbitrary and selective enforcement of criminal laws. . . . The relevance of the latter rationale in this context is clear: "[e]xperience reveals numerous instances of abusive prosecution under expansive kidnapping statutes for conduct that a rational and mature penal law would have treated as another crime." . . .

In addition to our constitutional concerns, we also note that, as is amply illustrated in the instant case, an expansive construction of asportation also effectively eviscerates the distinction between kidnapping and false imprisonment, the latter of which is treated by our statutory code as a serious crime but one that is far less serious than the crime of kidnapping. . . . (penalties for false imprisonment range from one to ten years imprisonment). Given that "[t]he only difference between the two offenses is asportation," . . . an asportation requirement so easily satisfied fails to justify the dramatic distinction in penalties between the two offenses, and simply cannot represent what the Legislature intended in enacting the current kidnapping statute.

In recognition of these problems, "the great majority of jurisdictions have accepted the view that kidnapping should not be recognized as a separate offense whenever the asportation relied upon to establish the kidnapping is merely incidental to another offense." . . . Though we stated in *Lyons*, . . . that "a mere positional change . . . incidental to [an]other criminal act" is not sufficient to sustain a kidnapping conviction, the effect of the rule we adopted, which requires only that the movement be "designed to better carry out the criminal activity . . . was in actuality to recognize as sufficient the use of movements that many other jurisdictions would view as "incidental" and thus not sufficient to sustain a kidnapping conviction. . . . *Kansas v. Kemp*, . . . (kidnapping convictions reversed where victim forced from one room to another and other victims forced from doorway to bedroom in course of aggravated robbery); *Walker v. Florida*, . . . (kidnapping convictions vacated where defendant forced victims to back of store in course of armed robbery); *Tennessee v. Sanders*, . . . (kidnapping conviction reversed where victim forced from parked car across street into restaurant and, along with other victims, forced into office and bound with duct tape in course of armed robbery). . . .

Accordingly, we find it necessary to adopt a more cogent standard for determining the sufficiency of evidence of asportation. Having surveyed the approaches of other jurisdictions in determining what movements are more than merely incidental to other criminal activity, we hereby adopt the test first articulated in *Govt. of Virgin Islands v. Berry*, 604 F.2d 221 (3d Cir. 1979), and since adopted by various of our sister states . . . as well as the Eleventh Circuit in its construction of the federal kidnapping statute. . . . The *Berry* test, formulated in an effort to synthesize the various standards adopted by those jurisdictions embracing the modern approach with respect to asportation, assesses four factors in determining whether the movement at issue constitutes asportation: (1) the duration of the movement; (2) whether the movement occurred during the commission of a separate offense; (3) whether such movement was an inherent part of that separate offense; and (4) whether the movement itself presented a significant danger to the victim independent of the danger posed by the separate offense. . . . Assessment of these factors will assist Georgia prosecutors and courts alike in determining whether the movement in question is in the nature of the evil the kidnapping statute was originally intended to address—i.e., movement serving to substantially isolate the victim from protection or rescue—or merely a "criminologically insignificant circumstance" attendant to some other crime. . . . To the extent prior case law and, specifically, the "slight movement" standard are inconsistent with this approach, those cases and that standard are hereby overruled. . . .

2. Applying the *Berry* factors to the evidence in this case, it is clear that neither of the two distinct movements of Mendoza during Garza's false imprisonment of her constitute the necessary asportation to support a kidnapping conviction. Both the act of falling to the floor and the act of rising to sit in the chair where Mendoza was bound were of minimal duration and occurred during the course of and incidental to Garza's false imprisonment of Mendoza and her children. Additionally, the blow that caused Mendoza's fall was an inherent part of the aggravated assault of which Garza was convicted. Moreover, Mendoza's movements did not significantly increase the dangers to her over those she faced as a victim of false imprisonment or aggravated assault. Application of the Berry factors thus clearly supports the reversal of Garza's conviction of the kidnapping of Mendoza.

3. The kidnapping charge as to J.M., while involving a slightly greater quantum of movement than that as to Mendoza, nonetheless meets a similar fate under the *Berry* test. The record reflects that, when police attempted to enter the apartment, Garza jumped onto the couch where J.M. had been sleeping, asked if he wanted to

play cops and robbers, and grabbed J.M.'s shirt, forcing him into an adjoining bedroom where the two stayed for the next approximately two to three hours while police attempted to negotiate J.M.'s release from outside via cell phone. On one or more occasions when Garza's cell phone battery ran out, Garza forced J.M. to walk with him down the hallway to retrieve replacement cell phones thrown into the front room by police. As with Mendoza, the movements themselves were of short duration and occurred as minor incidents in the course of Garza's false imprisonment of J.M. There was no evidence that the movements served to conceal J.M. from police, who were already aware he was being detained, to thwart in any appreciable way the efforts of police to free J.M., or to enhance significantly the risk J.M. already faced as the victim of false imprisonment. Accordingly, Garza's conviction for the kidnapping of J.M. must also be reversed. . . .

By adopting the above mode of analysis, we join in the "modern approach" and construe OCGA § 16-5-40(a) so as " 'to prevent gross distortion of lesser crimes into a much more serious crime. . . .'" In accordance with such mode of analysis, we hereby reverse the judgment below as to Counts 1 and 2. In all other respects, including Garza's convictions on four counts of false imprisonment and one count of aggravated assault, the judgment below is affirmed.

Judgment affirmed in part and reversed in part.

CASE QUESTIONS

1. Why was the asportation element so critical in this case?

2. The Georgia Supreme Court identified two constitutional problems with the existing asportation requirement in Georgia. What were they?

3. What non-constitutional reasons did the Georgia Supreme Court give for redefining the asportation requirement?

AUTHOR'S COMMENTARY

You may have noticed in the discussion in part 3 of this opinion the court's observation that Garza had not moved J.M. in order to hide him from police or to make it more difficult for the police to rescue this boy. Judge Hunstein also noted that from J.M.'s perspective the new location did not put him at greater risk of harm. These factors are often taken into consideration in determining whether there is sufficient evidence of asportation to sustain a kidnapping conviction.

False imprisonment is a lesser-included offense of kidnapping; the basic difference being the asportation/hiding element in kidnapping. Some jurisdictions, such as Arkansas, classify false imprisonment by degrees as can be seen in Figure 6.9.

Figure 6.9. Arkansas Code—False Imprisonment

Section 5-1 1-103 False Imprisonment in the first degree

(a) A person commits false imprisonment in the first degree, if without consent and without lawful authority, he knowingly restrains another person so as to interfere with his liberty in a manner that exposes that person to a substantial risk of serious injury.

(b) False imprisonment in the first degree is a Class C felony.

Section 5-1 1-104 False Imprisonment in the second degree

(a) A person commits false imprisonment in the second degree, if without consent and without lawful authority, he knowingly restrains another person so as to interfere with his liberty.

(b) False imprisonment in the second degree is a Class A misdemeanor.

Figure 6.10. Florida Code—False Imprisonment

787.02 False imprisonment; false imprisonment of child under age 13, aggravating circumstances

(1) (a) The term "false imprisonment" means forcibly, by threat, or secretly confining, abducting, imprisoning, or restraining another person without lawful authority and against her or his will.

(b) Confinement of a child under the age of 13 is against her or his will within the meaning of this section if such confinement is without the consent of her or his parent or legal guardian.

(2) A person who commits the offense of false imprisonment is guilty of a felony of the third degree, punishable as provided in s. 775.082, s. 775.083, or s. 775.084.

(3) (a) A person who commits the offense of false imprisonment upon a child under the age of 13 and who, in the course of committing the offense, commits any offense enumerated in subparagraphs 1.–5., commits a felony of the first degree, punishable by imprisonment for a term of years not exceeding life or as provided in s. 775.082, s. 775.083, or s. 775.084.

1. Aggravated child abuse, as defined in s. 827.03;

2. Sexual battery, as defined in chapter 794, against the child;

3. Lewd or lascivious battery, lewd or lascivious molestation, lewd or lascivious conduct, or lewd or lascivious exhibition, in violation of s. 800.04;

4. A violation of s. 796.03 or s. 796.04, relating to prostitution, upon the child; or

5. Exploitation of the child or allowing the child to be exploited, in violation of s. 450.151.

Figure 6.11. Oregon's Custodial Interference Statutes

> Excerpt from Oregon Revised Statute 163.257—Custodial interference in the first degree
>
> A person commits the crime of custodial interference in the first degree if the person violates ORS 163.245 and:
>
> (a) Causes the person taken, enticed or kept from the lawful custodian or in violation of a valid joint custody order to be removed from the state; or
>
> (b) Exposes that person to a substantial risk of illness or physical injury.
>
> Excerpt from Oregon Revised Statute 163.245—Custodial interference in the second degree
>
> A person commits the crime of custodial interference in the second degree if, knowing or having reason to know that the person has no legal right to do so, the person takes, entices or keeps another person from the other person's lawful custodian or in violation of a valid joint custody order with intent to hold the other person permanently or for a protracted period.

In Arkansas, if the accused's conduct puts the victim in great jeopardy of serious bodily harm, the accused is charged with a felony, false imprisonment in the first degree. If the perpetrator's conduct did not seriously jeopardize the victim's physical safety, the charge would be second-degree false imprisonment (a misdemeanor).

Other states, such as Florida, define specified conduct to be an aggravating circumstance, which on conviction will augment the length of the sentence that can lawfully be imposed, as can be seen in Figure 6.10.

Custodial Interference Statutes

Although all states have general kidnapping statutes, many states have enacted supplemental legislation, such as the Oregon Custodial Interference statutes excerpted in Figure 6.11. This particular supplemental statute is intended to help deter parents who are parties to bitter custody battles in conjunction with divorce actions from engaging in child stealing.

Chapter Summary

Concern about being personally attacked and physically harmed by a criminal offender is probably near the top of everyone's list of fundamental fears. People go to great lengths to protecting themselves and their loved ones especially from assaultive crimes (manslaughter, rape and sexual assault, battery, and simple assault). The fear of physical attack influences many lifestyle decisions, such as where to live, work, play, go to school, worship, and vacation.

Homicide

The common law recognized two homicide offenses, murder and manslaughter (which consisted of voluntary manslaughter and involuntary manslaughter). Manslaughter was thought of as a mitigated murder. What distinguished one offense from the other was the requirement in murder prosecutions that malice be proven. Murderers were executed under the common law.

Readers were invited to compare the murder statutes of Hawaii, Nebraska, and Virginia and to notice the differences in lists of enumerated crimes. All three states limited first-degree murder prosecutions to killings occurring under specified circumstances. Both Nebraska and Virginia retained the common law premeditation requirement (proof that the accused reflected on what he/she was going to do before), but only one of the three states included malice (a term defined in Figure 6.1) as an element of proof. Readers should also notice how much easier it is to read the Hawaiian statute. Hawaii has followed the Model Penal Code approach and eliminated all common law concepts and archaic language from its statute. Which statute was most clear to you? Would you prefer the Hawaiian definition over Michigan's common law definition from 1854, which is still the law today in that state: "Murder is where a person of sound memory and discretion unlawfully kills any reasonable creature in being, in the peace of the state, with malice prepense or aforethought, either express or implied."

Second-degree murder consists of unlawful killings not amounting to first-degree murder. Jurors often compromise on this verdict if they disagree about whether first-degree murder has been proven.

The crime of voluntary manslaughter was created in England so that persons would not have to be executed for first-degree murder who intentionally killed after extreme provocation. Involuntary murder was also established as a lesser offense to murder so that offenders who unintentionally killed as a consequence of reckless or grossly negligent conduct could receive a mitigated sentence.

Assault and Battery

Although assault and battery were distinct offenses under the common law, they are often merged today into a single statute. Assaults and batteries on police officers, that involve the use of deadly weapons, and occur in conjunction with the commission of other specified offenses are generally prosecuted for aggravated assault and if convicted receive enhanced sentences.

Rape and Sexual Assault

The reforms of the 1970s have drastically increased the prosecutor's arsenal and facilitated the prosecution of offenders for conduct falling short of the traditional requirements for a rape action. Modern statutes are gender neutral and protect spouses. Today, victims are no longer required to forcibly resist the offender, and evidence of a victim's sexual past is inadmissible unless declared relevant by a judge.

Sexual assault laws have evolved in a manner similar to murder statutes. The common law crime of rape has been replaced in many states with detailed lists of prohibited conduct and circumstances which affect what becomes classified as first-degree sexual assault and what becomes fourth-degree sexual contact. Some states define sexual assault in terms of outcomes. For example, in one state it is first-degree sexual assault for an offender to have sexual conduct or sexual intercourse which causes the victim great bodily harm or causes a victim to become pregnant. The use or threatened use of a dangerous weapon in the commission of a sexual assault is also prosecuted in many states as first-degree sexual assault.

Modern statutes generally address both types of sexual assaults; bodily contacts that involve the penetration of body cavities and bodily contacts limited to the surface of the skin. Sexual assault laws vary in length and scope. Some laws are written so generally as to presumably require prior consent before forcibly kissing another person. Perhaps an appellate court will have to decide whether an accused who admittedly did not having express consent could have reasonably believed that the recipient of a forcible kiss had implied consent to engage in that act.

Kidnapping and False Imprisonment

Kidnapping is essentially a false imprisonment accompanied by either an asportation or hiding. Both crimes subject the victim to a deprivation of liberty, and both require proof of specific intent. Kidnapping is punished more severely than false imprisonment because a person who is transported from a place of relative safety to a place of the offender's choosing will often be in a place of greater danger than someone detained where he or she was found and falsely imprisoned. Loved ones and police who are searching for a kidnap victim will normally look for the victim in places routinely traversed and frequently visited by the victim. A substantial change in environment makes it less likely that the victim will be found.

Discussion Questions

1. Thomas LaCava was estranged from his wife after they were unable to reconcile their differences. He did not handle the demise of the marriage well and began spying on his wife. She sued for divorce and began to see another man, events

that stressed LaCava considerably. He began to formulate a plan to kill her. He bought a gun; assembled knives, handcuffs, duct tape, a mask, rope, and other equipment; and lay in wait for his wife to come home. When she backed her car into a parking place, La Cava blocked her vehicle with his own. He approached his wife, and when she made a move that he interpreted as an attempt to drive the car, he fired five bullets into the car, killing her. He attempted to shoot himself but could not because he was out of bullets. Over the course of the next 12 hours, he drove around, occasionally pausing to stab himself in the neck and abdomen. He was subsequently apprehended and admitted to having shot and killed his wife as she sat in her car outside the apartment building where she lived with one of her daughters.

After consulting with a forensic psychologist, LaCava's attorney concluded there was insufficient evidence of insanity to pursue that defense. Given the facts of this case, do you see any other theories the attorney could have used to defend against the charge of murder in the first degree?

Commonwealth v. Thomas N. LaCava, SJC-06923, Supreme Judicial Court of Massachusetts (2003)

2. Terry Johnson went to Terry Baugh's house and challenged her boyfriend, Harold Hopson, to fight. Hopson's response was to get a .22 caliber rifle and fire two shots out of a window at the fleeing Johnson. Johnson shouted out that he would soon return. Baugh, believing that her children were in danger, hid them in an abandoned car in a field across the street from her house. Shortly after they took refuge in the abandoned car, the children noticed that the bushes at the edge of the field were moving. Simultaneously, Baugh's brother, Dennis Rogers, who was carrying a BB rifle, came running toward the abandoned car from his neighboring house. As Rogers approached, Baugh told him to look toward the bushes. As he pivoted to look in that direction, Johnson stood up and fired a shotgun at Rogers from a distance of 30 to 40 feet. Rogers was fatally injured from this shotgun blast and died. Eyewitnesses testified that Rogers did not point the BB rifle at the bushes or at Johnson at any point in this series of events.

Johnson was charged with murder in the second degree, and with possession of a firearm during the commission of a felony. He was convicted of both charges after a bench trial. The trial judge ruled that Johnson was not legally entitled either to perfect self-defense or imperfect self-defense given the facts of this case and refused to mitigate the murder to voluntary manslaughter. Did the trial judge commit any error in these rulings?

People v. Terry L. Johnson, No. 238202, Michigan Court of Appeals (2003)

3. Antonio Hallsell became enraged when his truck barely averted a collision with a passenger car containing a husband and wife. Hallsell subsequently used a metal

bar that he obtained from within his truck to break the passenger window of the car. The female sitting in the passenger side of the car would have been hit in the head had she not quickly moved to her right. When the passenger's husband attempted to open the car's trunk, Hallsell threw a portable radio at the husband, striking him in the back. Hallsell next took a motor vehicle battery out of the back of his truck and threw it through the passenger car's open back window, nearly missing a small boy. With what assaultive crimes should Hallsell be charged?

People v. Antonio Halsell, No. 238192, Michigan Court of Appeals (2003)

4. Police officers responded to a domestic disturbance resulting from a telephone call placed by Melvin J. Schroeder to the police department. He had reported that his wife had been shot in conjunction with a struggle they had been having over a firearm. When officers arrived, they discovered that Schroeder's wife was dead, and the house looked like it had been the scene of a struggle. Schroeder maintained that he had not intended to shoot his wife.

Evidence was introduced that the prosecution contended was inconsistent with a struggle involving a gun. The weapon used to inflict these injuries was at least 20 inches away from the victim when the shots were fired, and Mrs. Schroeder had been shot three times, with two shots entering her side and one entering her back. The coroner testified that the shot to the back was consistent with the victim trying to run away.

The victim's sister and mother testified that the victim always carried a .357 Magnum pistol in her purse and that the pistol looked like the weapon found at the scene of the crime, which had shot the victim. They also testified that the victim had a "mean streak" and would stand up for herself. The Schroeders were not known to fight each other. Schroeder testified that the dispute precipitating the shooting evolved from an argument about their financial problems. He indicated that his wife had pointed her gun at him and threatened to kill him when he left their bedroom, where he had been changing his pants, and he had attempted to take the pistol away from her. They struggled over control of the gun (she was 5-feet 8-inches tall and weighed 200 pounds) and in the process fell to the floor, rolling over and over. At some point in this struggle Mrs. Schroeder was shot.

The judge gave jury instructions on accident and self-defense but refused to instruct the jury on manslaughter. The jury convicted Schroeder of murder, and he appealed. Was Schroeder entitled to a manslaughter instruction?

Melvin J. Schroeder v. State, 13-01-333-CR, Texas Court of Appeals (2003)

NOTES

1. The Model Penal Code does not provide for multiple degrees of murder. It classifies criminal homicides as murder, manslaughter, and negligent homicide. It eliminates malice from its definition of first-degree murder.

2. See Justice Stewart's opinion in *Woodson v. California*, 428 U.S. 280 (1976), and Judge Henley's opinion in *Rothgeb v. United States*, 789 F.2d 647 (1986), which has within it the preamble to that 1794 Pennsylvania statute:

   "And whereas the several offenses which are included under the general denomination of murder, differ so greatly from each other in the degree of their atrociousness, that it is unjust to involve them in the same punishment." Pa. Laws of 1794 Ch. 257, Secs. 1, 2 (1794).

3. *Peterson v. Commonwealth*, 302 S.E.2d 520 (1983).

4. My source for this number is D. Van Zanten, "Felony Murder, The Merger Limitation, and Legislative Intent in *State v. Heemstra*: Deciphering the Proper Role of the Iowa Supreme Court in Interpreting Iowa's Felony-Murder Statute," 93 Iowa L. Rev. 1565 (2007), which in footnotes 23 and 39 credits A. Malani, "Does the Felony-Murder Rule Deter? Evidence from FBI Crime Data" (Dec. 3 2007), available at http://graphics8.nytimes.com/packages/pdf/natiional/malani.pdf, as his source.

5. Readers may recall that causation and "reasonable foreseeability" were previously discussed in Chapter 3.

6. *People v. Potter*, 5 Mich. 1 (1858), cited in *People v. Aaron*, 299 N.W.2d 304 (1980).

7. *Dike v. State*, 990 P.2d 1012 (1999).

8. J. McDonough, "Consent v. Credibility: The Complications of Evidentiary Purpose Rape Shield Statutes," Law and Society Journal at UCSB, Vol. V (2006).

9. *State v. Buggs*, 547 P.2d 720 (1976).

Crimes Against Property and Habitation

In Chapter 1, we learned that judges played the leading role in defining criminal offenses during the formative stages of the common law legal system which we inherited from England. Under the common law one of the highest priorities was protecting property rights. The crime known as **larceny** was the first common law property crime. Other crimes had to be created (some by the Parliament) in response to new schemes offenders developed (that for technical reasons did not constitute larceny) for acquiring other people's property. These new crimes included offenses such as **false pretenses**, **embezzlement**, **extortion**, **robbery**, and **forgery**. We begin this chapter with larceny.

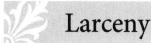 # Larceny

For conviction of common law larceny, the proof has to show that the offender has specific intent to steal **tangible personal property** from some other person who was rightfully in possession of the property item. Larceny is a specific intent crime because the prosecution has to prove that the defendant not only intended to commit the *actus reus* but had in addition the intent to permanently deprive the owner of the property. Readers might want to revisit the case of *State v. Gordon* in Chapter 3, which includes a good discussion of what it means to have intended to permanently deprive an owner of property.

At common law the property in question had to be tangible personal property. This means it had to consist of physical objects such as books, cars, tables, clothes, etc. It did not include the **theft** of fruit unlawfully picked from trees or crops growing in the fields because criminal conduct involving the right to possess land or the taking of things growing on land or permanently attached to land was prosecuted as a trespass to **real property**. The theft of fruit or crops after it had been harvested, however, would have been classified as tangible personal property.[1] Criminal conduct which was directed at **intangible property** rights was also excluded from prosecution as a larceny. Thus, alleged criminal conduct involving

TABLE 7.1	ELEMENTS OF COMMON LARCENY
Criminal act	Unlawful (trespassory) taking (**caption**) and **carrying away** (**asportation**)
Criminal intent	Specific intent to permanently deprive rightful possessor of possession
Circumstances	Tangible (physical, not an intellectual right to property) personal property (personalty) of another

the rights to non-physical property, such as the theft of documents that represent rights of ownership such as bank passbooks, deeds, patents, trademarks, stock certificates, could not be prosecuted as a larceny.[2]

Lastly, the proof also had to show that the offender had, without any lawful right to do so, exercised control over the rightful possessor's property and moved it, at least slightly, from the place where initially it had been found.

STEPHANIE M. HUNT v. VIRGINIA
614 S.E.2d 668
Court of Appeals of Virginia
June 21, 2005

AUTHOR'S INTRODUCTION

Many jurisdictions classify larcenies based on the value of the property that was taken. Thus, larcenies above a specified value are considered felonies and may be prosecuted as grand larceny while larcenies below the specified figure are misdemeanors and classified as petit (pronounced "petty") larceny.

The primary dispute in *Hunt v. Virginia*, the larceny case you are about to read, involves the valuation issue, an obsolete medieval common law rule and a botched prosecution. The defendant, Stephanie Hunt, was convicted of grand larceny for having stolen Thomas Motley's winning lottery ticket.

The prosecution could have charged the defendant with violating Virginia's larceny statute, but due to a prosecutorial error the defendant was only charged with common law larceny.

Hunt appealed claiming that she should not have been convicted of grand larceny because the value of the lottery ticket had been incorrectly calculated. To be convicted of grand larceny, the state had to prove that the stolen ticket had a value exceeding $200.

Hunt argued that under then existing Virginia law, the winning ticket at issue in this case should have been valued at fifty cents, the amount Motley spent on the ticket, and not the $2,500 that Motley was entitled to collect by presenting the winning ticket. She based her claim on archaic common law cases with origins in medieval England, which were still recognized in Virginia as authoritative at the time when this incident occurred (2003). According to these cases, the ticket would be classified as a "chose in action."

A chose in action under the common law was a paper containing writing that provided evidence of the existence of contractual rights to intangible, **personal property**. Under the common law, the monetary worth of a paper classified as a chose in action was based on the value of the paper itself and not on the value of the contractual rights contained in the writing appearing on the document.[3]

EXCERPT FROM THE CASE

James W. Benton, Jr., Judge.

. . . Hunt contends the trial judge erred in convicting her of grand larceny because the indictment, which charged a violation only under Code § 18.2-95, required proof of "value of $200 or more." She argues that at common law, a lottery ticket, like "credit cards, checks, and other papers," were "choses in action" and had no value beyond the paper on which they were written. She argues, therefore, she properly could have been convicted only of petit larceny. The Commonwealth responds that Code § 18.2-98 "has expanded the definition of larceny to include bank notes, checks, or other writings or paper with a value of $200 or more." Thus, the Commonwealth argues that the evidence proved a value in excess of $200 because Code § 18.2-98 is broad enough to include lottery tickets within its definition and provides that "the money due on or secured by the writing . . . shall be deemed to be the value of the article stolen."

"In Virginia, larceny is a common law crime." *Bryant v. Commonwealth*, . . . (1994). Larceny, a common law crime, is the wrongful or fraudulent taking of another's property without his permission and with the intent to deprive the owner of that property permanently. . . .

An indictment that charges grand larceny in violation of only Code § 18.2-95 alleges the common law crime. . . . Thus, unless violation of a specific statute other than Code § 18.2-95 is charged, a larceny indictment charges the common law offense.

"The value of the goods specified in [Code § 18.2-95] is an essential element of the crime, and the Commonwealth bears the burden of proving that element beyond a reasonable doubt." . . . "Proof that an article has some value is sufficient to warrant a conviction of petit larceny, but where the value of the thing stolen determines the grade of the offense, the value must be alleged and the Commonwealth must prove the value to be the statutory amount." . . .

We relied upon this principle in *Owolabi* [*v. Commonwealth* . . . (1993)], where we held that the taking of a paper or credit card could be the subject of larceny under the common law but that the value was simply of the paper or the plastic itself, not the value it represented. . . . Thus, the common law in Virginia still exempts choses in action from its coverage . . .

An accused is entitled to be clearly informed of the charge against him. Va. Const. art. I, § 8. Where, as here, the Commonwealth elects to prosecute a defendant for a specific category of larceny, and no other, its case must either prevail or fail upon that election. The Commonwealth cannot retrospectively argue that [the accused] should be convicted of a crime for which he was not prosecuted, and on which the jury was not instructed.

For reasons about which we may only speculate, the Commonwealth prosecuted Hunt for common law larceny and not for the statutory offense as provided in Code § 18.2-98. Under the common law, the value of the ticket is the value of the paper on which it is printed. Because the evidence failed to prove the value was $200 or more, it was insufficient to support a conviction for grand larceny under Code § 18.2-95 and was sufficient, at most, to prove petit larceny. Accordingly, we reverse the conviction and remand to the trial court for further proceedings consistent with this opinion.

Reversed and remanded.

CASE QUESTION

1. What was the prosecutions biggest mistake in this case?

2. Was there anything that the prosecutor could have done differently at trial to remedy this mistake?

AUTHOR'S COMMENTARY

In the aftermath of this decision, the Virginia legislature amended the statute as follows:

> Any person who steals or otherwise unlawfully converts to his own or another's use a lottery ticket, prize, share, or portion thereof shall be guilty of larceny. For purposes of this subsection, the face amount of a lottery ticket, prize, share, or portion thereof shall be deemed to be its value. Code § 58.1-4014, C.

States that still recognize common law crimes will occasionally encounter problems such as happened in this case when obsolete common law rules manage to resurface.

Common law rules evolved on a piecemeal basis in order to remedy a particular problem existing back "in days of yore." With the passage of decades and even centuries, they became established precedents and, unless repealed by statute or overturned by a subsequent court decision, manage to survive to the present. This can happen despite the fact that these relics of the past are totally unsuited to modern circumstances.

In part, to avoid the historical baggage that accompanies the continued use of the common law, many states have replaced it with **comprehensive theft statutes**. Modern statutes often eliminate many of the limitations and distinctions that existed under common law larceny. Today, larceny statutes generally include the taking and carrying away of intangible personal property as well as the theft of

Figure 7.1. Excerpt from Maine's Comprehensive Theft Statute

17-A Maine Revised Statutes Annotated Sec. 353 (1983). Class B Theft
    1. A person is guilty of theft if he obtains or exercises unauthorized control over the property of another with intent to deprive him thereof. . . .
    2. As used in this section, "exercises unauthorized control" includes but is not necessarily limited to conduct heretofore defined or known as common law larceny by trespassory taking, larceny by conversion, larceny by bailee and embezzlement.

---

services of various types (hotels, restaurants, equipment rentals, etc.) and utilities (electricity, cable and satellite TV, telephone, etc.).

Maine and Utah are examples of states that have enacted comprehensive theft statutes. Notice how the *actus reus* for theft in Maine's statute is broadly defined. It eliminates the tangible and personal property requirements of the common law and goes beyond the common law notion of a "taking" to prohibit the "unauthorized control" over property. (Figure 7.1) We will read a case involving Utah's comprehensive theft statute later on in this chapter.

Embezzlement

Assume that Bill is employed by Alice as a cashier in her convenience store. Assume further that Alice periodically entrusts Bill with sums of her cash so that he can carry out his duties as a cashier. Bill has agreed, as a condition of his employment, to use Alice's cash only as provided in the company rulebook. The rulebook specifies that cashiers can use their cash only to make change for customers who are making purchases at Alice's store. Assume that one day Bill discovers that he forgot his wallet and has no money with which to buy lunch. He takes $10 from the cash register and purchases lunch and then goes home and gets his wallet and puts $10 back in the cash register when he returns to work. Bill has committed embezzlement. Bill took money that belonged to Alice, and with which he was entrusted as Alice's employee and *converted* it (i.e., used it to his own advantage, without permission, and in a manner adverse to Alice's interests).

The above conduct could not be prosecuted as a larceny under common law because the *actus reus* for larceny requires a taking. Bill did not "take" the money from Alice, she handed him the money so that he could perform his work as her employee. The English Parliament enacted an anti-embezzlement statute in 1799 by making it criminal for a person who is entrusted with another's property to commit a **conversion**.

TABLE 7.2	ELEMENTS OF EMBEZZLEMENT
Criminal act	Entrustment and Conversion
Criminal intent	Specific intent (intent to defraud)

MAINE v. JOHN R. MOON
755 A.2d 527
Maine Supreme Judicial Court
July 21, 2000

AUTHOR'S INTRODUCTION

John Moon, while completing a graduate degree at the University of Maine, was employed as the director of fundraising for the purpose of attempting to revive the local chapter of the Sigma Chi fraternity. He also agreed to serve in a volunteer capacity as the local chapter's treasurer. He was alleged to have made numerous transfers of fraternity funds to his personal accounts, or to a company in which he was a prominent shareholder. He transferred approximately $123,000 of the fraternity's funds, $103,000 of which he had repaid. Moon's transfers of the fraternity's funds were unauthorized, and he used the funds to renovate a townhouse.

EXCERPT FROM THE CASE

Judge WATHEN:

Defendant John R. Moon appeals from a judgment entered in the Superior Court . . . following a jury verdict finding him guilty of theft (Class B), 17-A M.R.S.A. Sec 353 (1983). . . . Defendant contends that the court erred in limiting his expert's testimony, in instructing the jury concerning the charges of theft by unauthorized taking or transfer and theft by misapplication of property, in instructing the jury concerning the time at which an intention to deprive must exist, and in allowing overly remote evidence of the mental element. . . .

His defense at trial focused on demonstrating that he had no intent to deprive. He argued that he always intended to repay the money and that he believed he had $110,000.00 in equity in his Main Street property [the townhouse] to cover the money he had taken. To support his defense, defendant testified himself as to his intent and also introduced the testimony of Gregory Noonan, a certified fraud examiner, certified public accountant and attorney. Noonan testified before the jury as follows: Defendant kept a separate account entitled "accounts receivable other" in the journal and properly recorded each transaction in which defendant either took funds from the fraternity or returned funds. It was significant that defendant included no other receivables within the "accounts receivable—other" account, in accordance with generally accepted accounting principles, and important that he included none of these transfers in the general accounts receivable account, which would have been improper because he was an employee.

As a result, according to Noonan, defendant left a very good audit trail so that it was easy for an auditor to trace the transactions back to the check register and determine that the funds were made payable to John Moon or MIDCO. Noonan's review of the records confirmed that during the period from 1991 to 1994 the total amount that went to defendant was $123,477.86 and the amount repaid by defendant was approximately $103,505.00, leaving a balance of approximately $19,000.00.

Defendant was indicted in 1997 for theft by unauthorized taking or transfer in violation of 17-A M.R.S.A. Sec 353 (1983) and subsequently indicted for theft by misapplication of property in violation of 17-A M.R.S.A. Sec 358 (1983). In a trial on the consolidated counts, defendant was found guilty of theft in violation of 17-A M.R.S.A. Sec 353 and now appeals.

I. EXCLUSION OF EXPERT TESTIMONY

Despite the fact that Noonan testified at length, defendant now argues that the court erred by refusing to let him introduce the expert testimony of Noonan that would explain to the lay person how the financial records were kept, how the records created an audit trail, and how the audit trail was inconsistent with all methods of obscuring theft in the books of a business. In fact, the court excluded only the last element of Noonan's testimony. In *voir dire*, Noonan testified that there are four basic "embezzlement schemes," i.e., lapping a/k/a kiting, fictitious receivables, diverting payments in old written off receivables, and borrowing against receivables; that in fourteen years of experience he has not seen a situation of account receivable or cash fraud that fell outside of these four categories; and this case is distinguished because "every transaction was documented right to the T."

The court refused to allow this portion of Noonan's testimony on the basis of relevancy . . . and jury confusion. . . . The court determined that the expert's testimony dealt with embezzlement schemes, that defendant was charged with theft, and that embezzlement and theft are not necessarily co-extensive. It further found that the testimony could confuse the jurors because Noonan's audit standards for the embezzlement schemes differ from the statutory elements of theft. . . .

The jury had the expert's testimony . . . that explained how the financial records were kept and how the records created an audit trail. This evidence, without the proffered evidence, supported defendant's argument that because of his meticulous recordkeeping and because he returned a substantial portion of the funds, he did not intend to deprive the fraternity of the funds permanently, but instead intended to repay the debt. Moreover, whether defendant's conduct conforms with historical patterns of embezzlement is irrelevant to whether defendant committed theft by unauthorized taking or by misapplication of funds as defined by the statute. The court correctly found that the embezzlement schemes to which the expert would have testified and the crime of theft as defined by the statute are not co-extensive. . . .

Simply because a person is clever enough to devise a new method of committing a theft that does not conform with a known existing embezzlement scheme, or foolhardy enough to document his activity, does not make it less probable that the crime of theft was committed. Although defendant and his expert witness focused on his intent to repay the money to support his contention that he did not intend to deprive the fraternity of the funds permanently, . . . they ignored the . . . possibility that he committed theft in violation of the statute by using the fraternity's money "under circumstances that make it unlikely that the owner will recover it." . . . Accordingly, the expert's testimony concerning embezzlement schemes is not relevant and does not tend to prove that defendant lacked the intent to deprive based on the complete statutory definition of theft.

II. JURY INSTRUCTIONS

. . . Defendant argues that the court erred in consolidating the two indictments for theft, theft by unauthorized taking, 17-A M.R.S.A. Sec. 353, and theft by misapplication, 17-A M.R.S.A. Sec. 358, before the verdict because it confused the jury. . . .

Reviewed as a whole, the jury instructions were both complete and accurate and not confusing to the jury. At the beginning of the trial, the court instructed the jury as follows: "I do want to alert you at this point that those charges will be consolidated for your purposes of deliberation; in other words, when you deliberate and reach a verdict, you will be reaching one verdict, whether it's guilty or not guilty, rather than two separate verdicts on two separate charges." In its jury instructions at the end of the trial, the court separately described the elements of theft by unauthorized taking and the elements of theft by misapplication and defined the meaning of the various terms therein. The court explained that the jury could find defendant guilty if the jury found that the State had proven beyond a reasonable doubt that the defendant committed the crime of theft, either theft by unauthorized taking . . . or theft by misapplication of property. Therefore, the jury instructions relating to the two alternatives for finding theft were not erroneous.

Defendant also argues that the court erred because it refused to provide his proposed jury instructions which emphasized that the necessary mental element of intent to deprive must exist "at the time of the taking." Defendant's proposed instruction stated in relevant part:

> This intent to deprive the true owner of the property must have existed at the time that the unauthorized control first took place. . . . [I]f you find that the Defendant exercised unauthorized control over the fraternity's money, you must then examine the evidence whether, at the time Defendant began exercising unauthorized control, he then and there had the intent to deprive the fraternity of that money.

The court instructed the jury as follows:

> A person commits the crime of theft . . . if that person obtains or exercises unauthorized control over the property of another with the intent, at the time he obtains or exercises unauthorized control over the property, to deprive the owner thereof.

The difference between the instructions is that defendant sought to limit the criminal act to a single point in time, namely, "the time Defendant began exercising unauthorized control," for the purpose of determining the presence of the required mental element. The distinction, however, if any, is not relevant in this case. Even if defendant intended to repay the funds at the precise moment he took them, he nonetheless consciously used the money in a way which the jury could find made it unlikely that the fraternity would recover it, in violation of section 352(3) c. . . .

Judgment affirmed.

CASE QUESTIONS

1. John R. Moon challenged his conviction for theft (by embezzlement) for what reason?

2. How did Moon's conduct differ from that required for conviction of common law larceny?

AUTHOR'S COMMENTARY

For purposes of the following example, assume that a retailer of motorcycles has obtained a bank loan to purchase inventory to sell at his dealership. Assume further that the retailer used the loan proceeds to purchase 20 motorcycles and displayed them for sale on his showroom floor. Because the motorcycles constitute the bank's collateral for this loan, a loan officer visits the dealership every month and verifies that the bank has been repaid for each motorcycle that the dealer has sold and that the remaining collateral is still on display at the dealership. Assume that when the loan officer made her most recent visit she noticed that one motorcycle was missing from the inventory and that no payment had been made to the bank, as should have occurred had that vehicle been sold. The loan officer, believing that an embezzlement may have occurred, demanded that the dealer explain what happened to the missing motorcycle. Assume that the dealer failed to provide an acceptable explanation and the bank wanted to report its embezzlement concerns to the local prosecutor.

If an investigation does not disclose what happened to the motorcycle, the prosecutor in many states can establish a prima facie case of conversion by serving the defendant with notice of a demand and refusal. See Figure 7.2 for Wisconsin's statute.

Figure 7.2. Excerpt from Wisconsin Fraudulent Conversion Statute 943.25(3)

> It is *prima facie* evidence of an intent to defraud . . . if a person, with knowledge that the security interest exists, removes or sells the property without either the consent of the secured party or authorization by the security agreement and fails within 72 hours after service of written demand for the return of the property either to return it or, in the event that return is not possible, to make full disclosure to the secured party of all the information the person has concerning its disposition, location and possession.
>   943.25(4)

In this section "security interest" means an interest in property which secures payment or other performance of an obligation; "security agreement" means the agreement creating the security interest; "secured party" means the person designated in the security agreement as the person in whose favor there is a security interest or, in the case of an assignment of which the debtor has been notified, the assignee.

Thus, where the facts suggest that there has been an embezzlement of property that constitutes collateral, as in the above example, the refusal of the defendant to comply with the terms of the demand will create a rebuttable presumption of a fraudulent conversion. If the defendant fails to rebut the presumption at trial, the fact finder will be permitted, but not required, to find that embezzlement has been proven.

Larceny by False Pretenses (Theft by Deceit)

False pretenses, like embezzlement, traces its roots to a 1757 act of the English Parliament (during the reign of King George II). It was created to address one of the many loopholes in common law larceny.

The key conduct in false pretenses is the misrepresentation of at least one past or present material (important) fact that is indispensable to the transaction between the perpetrator and the victim. The factual misrepresentation is intended to both deceive and induce the victim into relying on the false facts. The perpetrator of this crime must know that a material fact is being misrepresented and must intend to defraud the victim. In a "successful" false pretense, the victim voluntarily transfers both possession and title of his or her property (often money) to the perpetrator.

TABLE 7.3   ELEMENTS OF FALSE PRETENSES

Criminal act	Accused misrepresented material facts
Criminal intent	Accused had intent to defraud and knew that material facts were misrepresented
Circumstances	Victim relied on misrepresented facts and voluntary transferred title

DARRELL S. LEWIS v. VIRGINIA
503 S.E.2d 222
Virginia Court of Appeals
August 18, 1998

AUTHOR'S INTRODUCTION

Darrell Lewis had entered into preliminary negotiations to purchase a Sir Speedy printing franchise that never came to fruition. However, when he was attempting to purchase a Mazda automobile, he knowingly misrepresented himself to the car dealership's finance manager as the owner of a Sir Speedy print shop. Lewis informed the dealer that his franchise was going to buy a truck for the company, and he completed all of the necessary paperwork, including a credit application form, application for title, the application for temporary 30-day tags, and a promissory note and security agreement. The dealer relied on Lewis's representations that he owned the printing franchise instead of checking on Lewis's credit and handed over the keys to the truck.

Lewis never paid the dealer, the truck was repossessed, and Lewis was prosecuted and convicted of obtaining title to a truck by false pretenses. He appealed on the ground that he had never obtained full title to the truck and that he believed that the trial court had incorrectly instructed the jury on *mens rea*.

EXCERPT FROM THE CASE

Judge CHARLES H. DUFF:

Appellant argues that the evidence was insufficient to prove he committed larceny by false pretenses because he obtained only temporary title to the truck and did not obtain actual title to, or ownership of, the truck. Appellant also contends the dealership remained the owner of the truck at all times based on the fact that several documents completed by appellant specified that the dealership retained the right to repossess the truck in the event appellant failed to pay for the vehicle. "An essential element of larceny by false pretenses is that both title to and possession of property must pass from the victim to the defendant (or his nominee). 'The gravamen of the offense . . . is the obtainment of ownership of property' . . ."

This case presents an issue of first impression in Virginia. However, other jurisdictions have sustained convictions for theft by false pretenses when the thief took property under a conditional sales contract, and the victim retained legal title to secure the unpaid balance of the purchase price. . . . [T]he doctrine that one must obtain title and possession in order to be guilty of the crime of false pretenses cannot mean an absolute title because any title obtained by fraud is voidable and the requirement would make it impossible for the crime to be consummated. . . .

We agree. . . . Although appellant signed a Promissory Note and Security Agreement that stated Brown's Mazda had the right to repossess the truck in the event of non-payment, Brown's Mazda retained legal title to the truck only for purposes of security. Brown's Mazda did not retain absolute ownership of the truck once appellant completed the paperwork and obtained delivery of the truck. To adopt appellant's argument "would reward the industrious and designing thief who, having perpetrated the proper fraud by making false representations, could escape criminal liability as long as the official title remained with the owner as security." . . .

Therefore, we conclude that the property interest conveyed by both the delivery of possession to appellant and the completion of the temporary certificate of ownership in appellant's name was sufficient to support a conviction for larceny by false pretenses. . . . Accordingly, the trial court did not err in ruling that the temporary certificate of ownership was sufficient to transfer ownership interest to appellant for purposes of this statute; for this reason, the trial court did not err in denying appellant's motion to strike the evidence. . . .

Appellant further argues that the trial court erred in refusing to grant several of his proffered jury instructions. The court refused to give appellant's proffered Instruction H, which contained the elements of the offense of obtaining property by false pretenses. The trial court granted the Commonwealth's Instruction 2 . . . [which] . . . provided:

> The Court instructs the jury that the defendant is charged with the crime of obtaining property by false pretense. The Commonwealth must prove beyond a reasonable doubt each of the following elements of that crime:
>
> (1) That the defendant made a false representation of a past event or existing fact; and
>
> (2) That the defendant had an intent to defraud Brown's Mazda; and
>
> (3) That because of the false representation, Brown's Mazda gave the defendant possession and title to the property; and
>
> (4) That the value of the property was over $200.00. If you find from the evidence that the Commonwealth has proved beyond a reasonable doubt each of the above elements of the offense as charged, then you shall find the defendant guilty and not fix his punishment until further instruction is heard by you. If you find that the Commonwealth has failed to prove beyond a reasonable doubt any one or more of the elements of the offense, then you shall find the defendant not guilty.

. . . Here, the granted Instruction 2 adequately covered the applicable principles of law. . . . However, the trial court also refused to give the jury appellant's proffered Instruction J, which provided:

> Fraudulent intent must be proved by more than a mere showing that Mr. Lewis knowingly provided a false statement to Brown's Mazda. In addition, the fraudulent intent must have existed at the time the false pretenses were made.

For more than a century, the law has required proof that the intent and the representation occur simultaneously. . . . The Supreme Court has unambiguously held that in a prosecution for larceny by false pretenses, the Commonwealth must prove "the fraudulent intent . . . existed at the time the false pretenses were made, by which the property was obtained." . . . Thus, in assessing whether Lewis was guilty of larceny by false pretenses, the jury had to determine whether "the intent to defraud existed at the time the act was committed." . . . The jury was not so instructed. . . . Because the jury should have been instructed that the intent to defraud must have existed at the time the false representations were made and because no other instruction addressed this element, we reverse the conviction and remand for further proceedings. . . .

CASE QUESTIONS

1. What was Lewis's argument regarding the government's proof of the *actus reus* in this case?

2. Why did the trial court reject Lewis's argument.

3. What error did the trial court make regarding the *mens rea* requirement of false pretenses?

AUTHOR'S COMMENTARY

Larceny by false pretense does not occur in situations where a seller suggests that a given item is worth a ridiculously inflated sum of money, because what something is worth is a matter of opinion, not fact. An item's value is determined in the marketplace by buyers and sellers—one person's junk is another person's treasure.

The following hypothetical example may help readers to better understand what constitutes larceny by false pretense.

Assume that a seller advertises an expensive watch of Swiss manufacture. Assume further that the seller knows full well that the watch she is selling is actually a U.S.-made, cheap, unauthorized imitation of the advertised Swiss watch. The place of manufacture is a material fact. If a person buys the imitation watch at an inflated price while relying on the knowingly false factual misrepresentations of the seller, the buyer would be a victim of a larceny by false pretenses.

Consolidated Theft

Many states have enacted comprehensive statutes to replace the traditional property acquisition offenses such as larceny, embezzlement, extortion, receiving stolen property, and false pretenses. They have defined these formerly separate offenses as alternative means of accomplishing theft.

The consolidated theft statutes simplify the prosecution's pleading and proof problems and avoid technical defenses such as occur when the prosecution discovers a discrepancy between its underlying theory of the case and the testimonial and physical evidence. The appellant in the following case challenged the government's right to change its prosecutorial theory of the case and amend its charges against the defendant after the conclusion of the preliminary hearing. The government argued that it was entitled to amend the information so that the charges in the information would conform to the evidence produced at the preliminary hearing.[4]

American states differ in the procedures they use to charge accused persons with felonies. In some states a grand jury issues a charging document called a "true bill of indictment." In non-grand jury states, an accused is charged in a document prepared by the prosecutor called the "information."

UTAH v. JOHN J. BUSH
47 P.3d 69
Utah Court of Appeals
January 11, 2001

AUTHOR'S INTRODUCTION

John Bush was charged with four counts of "theft by deception" because he "obtained or exercised control over the property of MBCl and DBCl by deception, with the purpose to deprive the owner thereof, and that the value of said property is or exceeds $5,000."

EXCERPT FROM THE CASE

Judge GREENWOOD:

... Defendant presents three questions: (1) did the trial court err in allowing the State to amend the information, changing the charge from theft by deception to theft of lost, mislaid, or mistakenly delivered property; (2) [omitted] ... and (3) [omitted]. ...

ANALYSIS

1. DOES AMENDING AN INFORMATION TO CHARGE A DIFFERENT THEFT THEORY CONSTITUTE A NEW AND DISTINCT OFFENSE UNDER RULE 4?

Defendant claims the trial court erred in allowing the State to amend the information after the preliminary hearing to charge theft of lost, mislaid, or mistakenly delivered property instead of theft by deception. ...

It is clear that the two theft crimes charged in this case involve different elements of proof. ... Notwithstanding the different elements required to prove these two crimes, Utah's consolidated theft statute provides:

Conduct denominated theft in this part constitutes a single offense embracing the separate offenses such as those heretofore known as larceny, larceny by trick, larceny by bailees, embezzlement, false pretense, extortion, blackmail, receiving stolen property. An accusation of theft may be supported by evidence that it was committed in any manner specified in Sections 76-6-404 through 76-6-410, subject to the power of the court to ensure a fair trial by granting a continuance or other appropriate relief where the conduct of the defense would be prejudiced by lack of fair notice or by surprise. ...

Thus, "[a]ll that is now required is to simply plead the general offense of theft and the accusation may be supported by evidence that it was committed in any manner specified in sections 404 through 410 of the Code. . . ." Specifically, the consolidated theft statute is designed to "eliminate the distinctions and technicalities previously existing, recognizing one crime of theft and incorporating therein all crimes involving the taking or obtaining of personal property without force." . . .

Therefore, the State argues that merely switching from one theory of theft to another does not constitute charging a new or different offense for purposes of Rule 4. We agree. The fundamental purposes of Rule 4 and section 76-6-403 are to provide a framework allowing the State to properly charge a defendant and to provide a defendant with notice of the crime charged and the evidence supporting the charge.

It is a fundamental principle of criminal law that a defendant is entitled to know "the nature and cause of the accusation against him," . . . and "to sufficient time to prepare adequately for trial." . . . Rule 4 protects a defendant's rights by requiring an indictment or information setting forth the offense and supporting facts and allowing a defendant to request a bill of particulars if desired. . . .

Section 76-6-403 is modeled after the Model Penal Code's consolidated theft statute. . . . The commentary to the Model Penal Code states: "[t]he purpose of consolidation . . . is not to avoid the need to confront the substantive difficulties in the definition of theft offenses. The appropriate objective is to avoid procedural problems." . . . As the commentary suggests, the purpose of the consolidated theft statute is not to allow the State to avoid the substantive safeguards contained in Rule 4. Rather, the consolidated theft statute is designed to prevent a defendant from escaping an otherwise valid theft charge on a mere technicality in the pleadings. . . . ("[I]n order to prevent a charge based on one method of unlawfully obtaining property from being defeated by the defense that the property was acquired by a different unlawful method, the statute allows the Commonwealth to introduce evidence at trial of any form of theft regardless of the form of theft charged, but always subject to the defendant's right to fair notice and an opportunity to defend").

In order to protect a defendant's right to know the nature of the accusation, several courts have stressed the importance of providing defendants with sufficient notice and time to adequately prepare a defense. . . . Thus, allowing the State to amend the information to charge a different theory of theft does not offend the procedural safeguards in the criminal process, so long as defendant is adequately notified of the theory being used and given ample time to prepare a defense to the charge.

Finally, defendant argues that if Utah's consolidated theft statute allows the State to amend the information, the State failed to properly plead the theft offense. Defendant argues that in order to charge under the consolidated theft statute, the State must charge the general provision contained in sections 76-6-403 and -404. Because the first information charged defendant under a specific theft provision, section 76-6-405, defendant claims the State lost the ability to change the charge to a different theft theory under a separate section of the theft statute. . . .

. . . [W]e must determine whether the State must plead under the general theft provision in order to have the ability to change its theory as to the specific type of theft charged. The State argues that by charging under the specific section, rather than the general, it is attempting to provide defendant with more information about the nature of the charge. Under this theory, the State believes it should not be foreclosed from changing the theft theory simply because its initial theory was incorrect. The State claims that Utah's theft statute is designed to avoid exactly this circumstance; procedural problems arising from difficulties of proof involving the specific means of theft. . . .

Although neither Utah nor any other state has specifically addressed whether the general provision must be pleaded in order to be advantaged by the consolidated theft statute, it is clear that other states have allowed an information to be amended from one specific theft provision to another. For example . . . the Idaho Court of Appeals allowed the State to amend the information from one specific theft crime to another, stating: "theft and theft by obtaining control over stolen property are simply alternate 'circumstances' under which the crime of theft may be charged." . . . In other words, under Idaho's theft statute, the different crimes are not separate offenses for purposes of amending an information, rather they are merely different circumstances of the single crime of theft. . . .

Similarly . . . the Supreme Court of New Hampshire allowed a bill of particulars to be amended, changing the crime from theft by unauthorized taking to theft by deception. . . . [T]he court stated:

> An accusation of theft may be supported by evidence that it was committed in any manner that would be theft under this chapter, notwithstanding the specification of a different manner in the indictment or information. . . .

Contrary to defendant's assertion that the general provision must be pleaded to invoke the consolidated theft statute's provisions, these other states have uniformly allowed the information to be amended from one specific theft provision to another. . . .

In light of the underlying purpose of consolidated theft statutes, we believe the more sound approach is that followed by jurisdictions that allow the State to amend an information from one specific theft theory to another. As the State points out, charging under a specific theft theory provides a defendant with more information about the nature of the charge than charging under the general section. If it turns out, as is the case here, that the State's initial theory of theft is not supported by the evidence and a different theory is warranted, the State should not be foreclosed from changing the theory of theft simply because it attempted to provide more information in the initial charge. The purpose of the consolidated theft statute is to allow the State to change its theory of the crime when it later determines the evidence supports a different theory. In so holding, however, we reiterate that allowing the State to amend the charge is always subject to a defendant's right to fair notice. . . .

CASE QUESTION

Why did the Utah Court of Appeals permit the prosecution to amend its information to charge a different theft theory?

AUTHOR'S COMMENTARY

Consolidated theft statutes eliminate technical defenses by allowing prosecutors to charge defendants with theft rather than false pretenses, embezzlement, or larceny. Jurors who agree that a theft has occurred, but who disagree as to whether the prosecution's evidence proved a larceny by trick, or false pretenses, would be able to reach a verdict if the defendant is charged under a consolidated statute. Utah's consolidated theft statute was quoted in the text of the last case. A second example of such a statute, Oregon's, is seen in Figure 7.3.

Internet Tip

Two additional larceny/theft cases, *State v. Alvin Walter West* and *State v. Kevin Anthony Cox*, can be found in the Chapter 7 materials found on the textbook's website.

Figure 7.3. Oregon Consolidated Theft Statute

Revised Statutes 164.015 Theft described

A person commits theft when, with intent to deprive another of property or to appropriate property to the person or to a third person, the person:

    (1) Takes, appropriates, obtains or withholds such property from an owner thereof; or

    (2) Commits theft of property lost, mislaid or delivered by mistake as provided in ORS 164.065; or

    (3) Commits theft by extortion as provided in ORS 164.075; or

    (4) Commits theft by deception as provided in ORS 164.085; or

    (5) Commits theft by receiving as provided in ORS 164.095.

Identity Theft

People have many reasons for wanting to expose themselves to criminal prosecution for assuming the personal identity of someone else or that of a fictitious person. Sometimes it's a parent who takes on a new identity in an attempt to avoid paying child support, or an illegal immigrant who assumes a false identification in an attempt to obtain a registration card and avoid deportation. Persons who do not qualify for assistance under the Social Security Act create fictitious identities to obtain benefits, convicted sexual predators seek to avoid the registration requirements that accompany such classifications, and both amateur criminals and sophisticated organized criminal syndicates use phony identifications to commit a wide array of financial crimes involving the internet, credit cards, and bank accounts.

Falsifying one's identity is in some instances primarily an end in itself. Thus, a person who illegally assumes a new and fictitious identity to avoid a criminal past in the hopes of making a fresh start in life may in fact thereafter be an otherwise exemplary citizen. But the creation and use of a false identity is often just the means to an end—a tool to be used in the commission of other crimes.

According to one source, reported **identity theft** in this country increased 22 percent from 2007 to 2008, resulting in the victimization of almost 10 million people.[5]

Arizona, in 1996, was the first American jurisdiction to enact a criminal statute exclusively focusing on identity theft. Congress, in 1998, enacted the first such federal statute, the Identity Theft Assumption Deterrence Act of 1998 (18 U.S.C. § 1028(a)(7)). The federal statute made it illegal to:

> knowingly transfer . . . , possess . . . , or use . . . , without lawful authority, a means of identification of another person with the intent to commit, or to aid or abet, or in connection with, any unlawful activity that constitutes a violation of Federal law, or that constitutes a felony under any applicable State or local law.

Today, all 50 states have identity theft statutes. Many state statutes punish financial identity fraud more severely than non-financial identity fraud. Other states have a punishment scheme with three categories—identity theft, trafficking, and obstructing justice. A third approach is also popular, which looks somewhat like common law larceny in that it imposes punishment based on the monetary value of the property fraudulently obtained and the amount of financial injury inflicted on victims. Congress has established two categories of offenses, basic identity theft and aggravated identity theft. This latter category provides for an additional two-five years of imprisonment for offenders who use identity theft as a tool in the commission of various specified federal offenses.

Because identity theft statutes differ, it is hard to generalize as to the elements required for conviction of this offense. The elements listed in Table 7.4 are generally found in most of the statutes. The *mens rea* requirement, however, varies between states that require purposeful intent, those that require that the offender act knowingly, and those that permit conviction under either theory.[6] Statutes also differ as to whether they specifically apply to identity thefts in which the offender assumes the identity of a fictitious person.

TABLE 7.4	TYPICAL ELEMENTS OF IDENTITY THEFT
Criminal acts	Obtaining and using another's personal identifying information
Criminal intent	With knowledge that the personal identifying information obtained and used belonged to a real or fictitious person
Circumstances	The personal identifying information was obtained and used without authority

STATE v. MICHAEL WOODFALL
206 P.3d 841
Supreme Court of Hawaii
April 29, 2009

AUTHOR'S INTRODUCTION

Michael Woodfall was accused of identity theft for assuming the identity of a fictitious person named Christopher B. Bailey and attempting to cash a check made payable to Bailey. Woodfall allegedly presented a check to a bank teller for payment which was purportedly issued by Design Build Inc. and was to be paid from a bank account assigned to that company. Woodfall presented the teller with an allegedly forged Idaho operator's license in the name of Bailey as supporting evidence of his identity. The teller became suspicious, called Design Build Inc., learned that the check was bogus, and called police.

Woodfall was charged with identity theft, forgery, and attempted theft. Woodfall was convicted of all charges by the trial court, and the judgment was affirmed by the intermediate court of appeal.

Woodfall appealed his identity theft conviction to the Hawaii Supreme Court. He acknowledged that while it is a crime to steal the identity of a real person the identity theft statute did not apply to someone who has falsely used the identity of a fictitious person.

Opinion of the Court by NAKAYAMA, J.

I. BACKGROUND

. . . Woodfall filed a motion to dismiss count I of the complaint, identity theft in the second degree ("motion to dismiss"). . . . Woodfall argued that, based on Hawaii case law and the HRS § 701-118(8) (Supp. 2006) definition of "another," the statutory language of HRS § 708-839.7 prohibiting "a transmission of any personal information of another," refers to the "transmission of any personal information" of an actual person. Woodfall reasoned that he attempted to assume a fictitious identity but did not attempt to transmit the "personal information of another." Therefore, he urged the court to dismiss this count.

The prosecution filed an objection to this motion . . . highlighting HRS § 708-839.7's phrase "personal information." The prosecution pointed out that for purposes of Chapter 708, "personal information" is defined as "information associated with an actual or a fictitious person . . . that is used . . . to confirm the identity of an actual or a fictitious person." HRS § 708-800. It concluded that the elements "a transmission of any personal information of another" include "a transmission of personal information of a fictitious person." (Emphasis added.)

At the . . . hearing on this motion, Woodfall argued that "the 'personal information' [of HRS § 708-839.7] is now qualified by the words 'of another.' The definition 'of another' by statute or by case law is a human being who was born and alive." Woodfall's counsel reiterated that under the plain language of the statute, Woodfall cannot "legally be found guilty of identity theft when he did not use the identity of an actual real person." The prosecution countered that the statute and the statutory definitions of "personal information" and "another" provide adequate notice that the conduct requirement of HRS § 708-839.7 prohibits the transmission of personal information of an actual or fictitious person.

. . . [T]he circuit court denied Woodfall's motion, concluding that the phrase in question prohibits the transmission of any personal information of an actual or fictitious person. The court rejected Woodfall's narrow interpretation of HRS § 708-839.7, noting that it would be "directly at odds" with the HRS § 708-800 definition of "personal information." It further held that "it certainly is not clear—especially in light of [HRS §] 708-800's definition of 'personal information'—that the legislature's use of 'another' was meant to exclude fictitious persons." In denying Woodfall's motion, the court [construed] . . . "another" as follows:

> . . . [HRS §] 708-800's definition of "personal information" is simply—"any real or fictitious person other than the person transmitting the information."

... Woodfall pled no contest to forgery in the second degree and attempted theft in the second degree. After the court denied Woodfall's motion to dismiss, ... Woodfall pled guilty to the charge of identity theft in the second degree. ...

C. ICA AFFIRMED THE CIRCUIT COURT'S RULING

On appeal, Woodfall argued that the plain language of the HRS § 708-839.7 phrase "transmission of any personal information of another" prohibits the transmission of personal information from a real person, but not a fictitious person. Woodfall also maintained that, even assuming that the statute is ambiguous and the court is required to resort to the statute's legislative history, extrinsic documents verify that the statute intended to "provide criminal penalties for those who steal the identity of another." ...

The prosecution argued that the circuit court's construction of HRS § 708-839.7 was correct under the plain language of the statute and the statute's legislative history. It pointed out that the legislature indicated that the bill that enacted this statute served to "provide criminal penalties for persons: (1) Committing identity theft of another individual; and (2) Obtaining identity documents under false pretenses or using a false or fictitious identity." ...

The ICA [Intermediate Court of Appeals] issued a summary disposition order that affirmed the circuit court's judgment. The ICA determined that the circuit court's interpretation of HRS § 708-839.7 was correct. ...

II. STANDARDS OF REVIEW

A. CERTIORARI [OMITTED TO CONSERVE SPACE]

B. STATUTORY INTERPRETATION [OMITTED TO CONSERVE SPACE]

III. DISCUSSION

As previously stated, Woodfall challenges the ICA's interpretation of HRS § 708-839.7, arguing that the term "of another" is a crucial and plain element of the statutory phrase "transmission of any personal information of another." He further maintains, in the alternative, that this interpretation is supported by the statute's legislative history: the statute's purpose "is to provide criminal penalties for those who steal the identity of another...." Woodfall contends that his use of a fictitious identity did not satisfy the conduct element of identity theft in the second degree, and he urges this court to vacate the circuit court's order denying his motion to dismiss this charge.

A. PLAIN LANGUAGE OF HRS § 708-839.7

To analyze HRS § 708-839.7, we begin with the language of the statute itself. HRS § 708-839.7 provides, in relevant part:

> A person commits the offense of identity theft in the second degree if that person makes or causes to be made, either directly or indirectly, a transmission of any personal information of another by any oral statement, any written statement, or any statement conveyed by any electronic means, with the intent to commit the offense of theft in the second degree from any person or entity. . . .

Specifically, we focus on the phrase "a transmission of any personal information of another."

"[P]ersonal information" is defined in HRS § 708-800, for purposes of Chapter 708, as follows:

> information associated with an actual person or a fictitious person that is a name, an address, a telephone number, an electronic mail address, a driver's license number, a social security number, an employer, a place of employment, information related to employment, an employee identification number, a mother's maiden name, an identifying number of a depository account, a bank account number, a password used for accessing information, or any other name, number, or code that is used, alone or in conjunction with other information, to confirm the identity of an actual or a fictitious person. . . .

The terms of HRS § 708-839.7 . . . conflict: "another" is defined as a "natural person," but "personal information" includes "information associated with . . . a fictitious person." Based on these differences, Woodfall and the prosecution dispute the plain meaning of HRS § 708-839.7.

According to Woodfall, the words "of another" is a "modifying term" of "personal information," and "limit the prohibitions of the statute only to information from a natural, actual person." Therefore, HRS § 708-839.7 requires the transmission of any other natural person's personal information. In our view, Woodfall presents a strong argument. The words "of another" appear to qualify the phrase "personal information." Woodfall's interpretation of HRS § 808-839.7, therefore, may be valid under the plain language of the statute.

The prosecution's interpretation of HRS § 708-839.7 is also persuasive. As the circuit court reasoned, if the phrase "personal information of another" "refers only to personal information of a real person, not a fictitious person," it would directly contradict the statutory definition of "personal information." See HRS § 708-800 (defining personal information as "information associated with an actual person or a fictitious person). Presented with these conflicting terms, the circuit court determined that the word "another must refer to "any real or fictitious person other than the person transmitting the information.

... [B]oth parties' construction of the identity theft in the second degree statute are plausible based on the statute's plain language. ...

B. EXTRINSIC AIDS [OMITTED TO CONSERVE SPACE]

C. THE RULE OF LENITY

When a statute is ambiguous, and the legislative history does not provide sufficient guidance, we follow the rule of lenity. ... This "means that the court will not interpret a state criminal statute so as to increase the penalty that it places on an individual when such an interpretation can be based on no more than a guess as to what the legislature intended. ... Accordingly, "[u]nder the rule of lenity, the statute must be strictly construed against the government and in favor of the accused. ...

Because HRS § 708-839.7 is ambiguous and the legislative history does not provide sufficient guidance, we must apply the rule of lenity and adopt a less expansive meaning of the phrase "personal information of another. We hold that the HRS § 708-839.7 phrase "transmission of any personal information of another prohibits the transmission of personal information of an actual person, but not the transmission of information associated with a fictitious person. Because Woodfall did not transmit the personal information of an actual person, he did not satisfy the conduct element of HRS § 708-839.7 and cannot be convicted of identity theft in the second degree. Therefore, the circuit court erred when it denied Woodfall's "Motion to Dismiss [Identity Theft In The Second Degree].

IV. CONCLUSION

Accordingly, we (1) vacate the ICA's November 18, 2008 judgment, the circuit court's October 10, 2007 final judgment, and the circuit court's February 23, 2007 order denying Woodfall's motion to dismiss, and (2) remand this case to the circuit court for further proceedings consistent with this opinion.

CASE QUESTIONS

1. Do you agree with the Hawaii Supreme Court that the legislature's failure to specifically prohibit the use of fictitious identities required reversal of Woodfall's convictions? Might another state's supreme court reasonably reach a different conclusion?

2. Did the Hawaii Supreme Court's decision require that Woodfall's other convictions also be overturned?

A copy of Arizona's identity theft statute can be found included in the Chapter 7 materials on the textbook's website.

AUTHOR'S COMMENTARY

In May of 2009, the U.S. Supreme Court decided the case of *Flores-Figueroa v. United States*, 129 S. Ct. 1186 (2009). Ignacio Carlos Flores-Figueroa, a Mexican citizen, sought to prove to his employer that he was a legal resident of the United States. He offered as proof fake alien registration and social security cards containing his correct name and identification numbers that had been issued to other people. Flores-Figueroa was charged in U.S. District Court with aggravated identity theft and convicted after a trial to the court. The federal statute required that the government prove that Flores-Figueroa had "knowingly . . . use[d], without lawful authority, a means of identification of another person." 18 U.S. Code 1028A(a)(1).

Flores-Figueroa argued at trial that he could not be convicted because the government had not proven that he knew that the false numbers he supplied to his employer had been assigned to persons other than himself. The trial court ruled in favor of the government and the court of appeals affirmed. Flores-Figueroa then successfully petitioned for certiorari to the U.S. Supreme Court. The government argued that Flores-Figueroa had to know that the numbers on the documents he submitted to his employer were fake and that these numbers had been assigned either to another person or were fictitious. A unanimous Supreme Court ruled against the government and held that the statute required the government to prove that the accused knew that the numbers belonged to another person.

Interested readers can read the Supreme Court's reasoning in the case of *Figueroa v. United States*, 129 S. Ct. 1186 (2009) by resorting to Loislaw online.

Internet Tip

The complete text of Arizona's identity theft statute can be found included in the Chapter 7 materials found on the textbook's website.

Robbery

Robbery has traditionally been viewed as an aggravated larceny. The aggravating element is the use of force or intimidation that accompanies the taking of property. In a robbery, the property must be taken from the victim's person or must be property that is under the victim's control (i.e., in the victim's presence). If the perpetrator threatens the victim or the victim's family with imminent death or bodily injury (i.e., intimidation), the crime is robbery. If, however, the threat is of future harm, the crime is not robbery, but rather extortion.

TABLE 7.5	ELEMENTS OF ROBBERY
Criminal act	Larceny by means of present force or intimidation
Criminal intent	Specific intent/intent to permanently deprive rightful possessor of possession of property
Circumstances	From the victim or victim's presence

TENNESSEE v. DAVID L. OWENS
20 S.W.3d 634
Supreme Court of Tennessee
June 20, 2000

AUTHOR'S INTRODUCTION

One of the enduring debates in robbery cases has been the extent to which the use or threatened use of immediate force must precede or coincide with the taking of property. This was the issue before the Tennessee Supreme Court in the *Owens* case.

David Owens was pursued by a store security guard and a supervisor after he was observed stealing an article of clothing from a Dollar General Store. At one point during the chase the supervisor closed in on Owens, and Owens dropped the item he had taken from the store and turned toward the supervisor while "brandishing" a box cutter. He was subsequently arrested, charged, and convicted of robbery, for which he received a sentence of imprisonment for nine years. He appealed from the Court of Appeals' affirmation of his conviction, contending that the evidence used at trial was legally insufficient.

EXCERPT FROM THE CASE

Judge BIRCH:

... We accepted review of this case in order to determine the temporal relationship required between the taking and the act of violence or putting a person in fear as they together constitute the offense of robbery. ... This is an issue we address for the first time. ...

... Owens contends that his confrontation with Mims [the supervisor] occurred after the taking had occurred; thus, the taking had not been accomplished by violence or fear. He insists, therefore, that this conduct does not constitute robbery. ... The State, on the other hand, contends that the act of theft continues for as long as the thief exercises control over the property. The State insists, therefore, that Owens was properly convicted of robbery ... because he used violence or fear while exercising control over the clothing he took from Dollar General Store. ...

... Our first question is how closely connected in time must the taking and the violence be? ...

In Tennessee, a "[r]obbery is the intentional or knowing theft of property from the person of another by violence or putting the person in fear." ... "A person commits a theft of property if, with the intent to deprive the owner of property, the person knowingly obtains or exercises control over the property without the owner's effective consent." ... The element which distinguishes theft from robbery is the use of violence or fear. If an individual uses violence or puts another in fear to obtain or exercise control over another's property, he or she has committed a robbery. Therefore, whether a taking is properly characterized as a theft or a robbery is contingent upon whether and when violence or fear is imposed. ... For common law robbery, the force used in the taking of property must "precede or be concomitant or contemporaneous with the taking. Violence or intimidation by the thief subsequent to the taking will not render the act robbery." ... The theft of property, therefore, must be the result of the force or fear or must have been facilitated or made less difficult by the violence. ... Force used to retain property already unforcibly taken or force used to escape, however, is not the force essential to satisfy the element of force required for robbery. ... Thus, "subsequent violence or putting in fear will not make a precedent taking, effected clandestinely, or without either violence or putting in fear, amount to robbery." . . . Several jurisdictions currently adhere to the common law rule. Moreover, a number of these jurisdictions have statutes similar to our own.

Many jurisdictions, however, have rejected the common law rule in favor of the "continuous offense theory." These jurisdictions interpret robbery as a continuous offense "that is not complete until the perpetrator reaches a place of temporary safety." . . . Under this theory, "a robbery is committed, not only if the perpetrator uses force or intimidation to 'take' possession of the property, but also if force or intimidation is used to retain possession immediately after the taking, or to carry away the property, or to facilitate escape." . . .

Although a majority of jurisdictions have adopted the continuous offense theory, an overwhelming majority have done so with the help of statutes which specifically define robbery to include the use of force to retain property or to escape. For example, under many of these statutory provisions a person commits a robbery if he or she uses force "in the course of committing" a theft. . . . Force is used in the course of committing a theft "if it occurs in an attempt to commit theft or in flight after the attempt or commission." . . . Other statutory provisions define robbery to include the use of force or fear "either to obtain or retain possession of the property or to prevent or overcome resistance to the taking" or to "assist . . . the [perpetrator's] escape. . . ."

Reviewing Tenn. Code Ann. § 39-13-401 in light of these rules of statutory construction, we first note that we are required by the General Assembly to construe the statute by reference to the common law. Such a requirement suggests that the General Assembly intended to codify the common law definition of robbery. Indeed, the definition of robbery under Tenn. Code Ann. § 39-13-401 is similar to the common law definition.

We have also compared Tenn. Code Ann. § 39-13-401 to the statutes of other jurisdictions and find [it] . . . is substantially similar to the statutes of the jurisdictions which follow the common law rule requiring violence or fear to precede or be contemporaneous with a theft to constitute robbery. Of particular significance is that, like Tenn. Code Ann. § 39-13-401, none of these statutes define robbery to include the use of force in retaining property or in effecting escape. On the other hand, we have found that the statutes of the overwhelming majority of continuous offense jurisdictions are significantly distinct from Tenn. Code Ann. § 39-13-401. These statutes . . . specifically define robbery to include the use of force to retain property or to effect escape. The exclusion of such language in . . . § 39-13-401, and the statute's similarity with the statutes of other jurisdictions applying the common law rule, suggests that the General Assembly intended to require that the use of violence or fear precede or be contemporaneous with the theft to constitute robbery under the statute. Indeed, robbery is committed in Tennessee only if the "theft of property from the person of another" is accomplished "by violence or putting the person in fear." . . .

Because we are required by the General Assembly to construe . . . § 39-13-401 with reference to the common law . . . we hereby adopt the common law rule. Any other interpretation would unduly expand the coverage of the statute and impermissibly extend the meaning of its language. While we recognize that a majority of jurisdictions have defined robbery to extend to those situations in which a use of force occurs after a taking of the property, it is up to the General Assembly, not this Court, to promulgate the parameters of the offense. . . . We hold, therefore, that the use of violence or fear must precede or be contemporaneous with the taking of property from the person to constitute the offense of robbery under Tenn. Code Ann. § 39-13-401.

Having determined the proper rule of law, we must next determine whether the evidence is sufficient to support Owens's conviction of robbery. . . .

Here, Owens took an article of clothing from Dollar General Store without paying and fled. After having run for at least five blocks, he stopped, dropped the clothes, turned towards Mims (who had given chase), and brandished a box cutter. This evidence is not sufficient to establish violence or fear preceding or contemporaneous with the taking of property. Indeed, in this case, the use of violence or fear was subsequent to the taking and temporally remote. Accordingly, there is insufficient evidence in the record to support Owens's conviction of robbery. There is, however, ample evidence in the record to support a conviction for theft under Tenn. Code Ann. § 39-14-103. Thus, in reversing Owens's conviction for robbery, we modify the trial court's judgment to show a conviction of theft and remand the case to the trial court for resentencing. . . .

For the reasons articulated above, Owens's conviction for robbery . . . is reversed, and the judgment of the trial court is modified to impose a conviction of theft. . . . The cause is remanded to the trial court for resentencing.

CASE QUESTION

How do states which have adopted the "continuous offense" approach differ with respect to the definition of robbery from states that continue to follow the common law theory of robbery?

AUTHOR'S COMMENTARY

Larceny and robbery are crimes with a long history, and courts have had to determine as a practical matter the boundaries separating these offenses. If a perpetrator is able to snatch a purse or wallet from the victim's hand without otherwise touching him or her, the criminal actor will most often be charged with larceny. If, however, the victim is bumped, or the victim struggles with the perpetrator for control over the purse or wallet, the charge is robbery.[7]

Because robbery is such a serious and greatly feared offense, a person convicted of this offense is seriously punished. Robbery statutes generally link the severity of the sentence with the degree of harm and fear experienced by the victim. The most important aggravating factors include the use or display of dangerous weapons and the extent to which the victim was injured or threatened with death or bodily injury in the commission of the crime. Thus an armed robber will receive a more serious sentence than an unarmed robber, and an offender who physically injures the victim will be sentenced more severely than a robber who causes no physical harm.

Offenders often develop strategies in the hope of avoiding an armed/aggravated robbery conviction in the event they are apprehended. They may use an unloaded weapon, an inoperable weapon, or a toy gun that appears to be real, or they may use a simulated weapon (such as a finger pressed into the victim's back), or bluff their victims into believing that they have a weapon when they actually are unarmed.[8]

Many courts, including the U.S. Supreme Court, have taken the position that an unloaded gun can be classified as a dangerous weapon. Justice Stevens explained the Supreme Court's rationale for its decision in a federal bank robbery case, *McLaughlin v. U.S.*:[9]

> Three reasons, each independently sufficient, support the conclusion that an unloaded gun is a "dangerous weapon." First, a gun is an article that is typically and characteristically dangerous; the use for which it is manufactured and sold is a dangerous one, and the law reasonably may presume that such an article is always dangerous even though it may not be armed at a particular time or place. In addition, the display of a gun instills fear in the average citizen; as a consequence, it creates an immediate danger that a violent response will ensue. Finally, a gun can cause harm when used as a bludgeon.

A "starter's pistol" (a gun with a solid barrel that fires blanks and is used to start running events at track meets) used to commit a robbery has been found to be a dangerous weapon.[10] The underlying test in many of these cases is whether the victim was reasonable in believing that the displayed device was a firearm.

However, a New Jersey court ruled in a robbery case that an accused who was bluffing when he threatened to use a gun in conjunction with a demand for money (and who was found to be armed with only a newspaper) could not be convicted of armed robbery. The court found that there was no evidence that the newspaper concealed a weapon or bore a sufficient resemblance to a weapon to be considered a deadly weapon. The court explained:

> . . . if a defendant does not actually possess a firearm or other object "known to be capable of producing death or bodily injury" in the course of a robbery, the State must prove that there was "some tangible object possessed by the defendant that the victim believed to be a deadly weapon. . . . A threat or reference to a gun alone is not enough." Moreover, the victim's subjective belief that the tangible object was a deadly weapon must have been "a reasonable one under the circumstances."[11]

Internet Tip

An additional case involving armed robbery, *People v. Walter Bridges,* can be found included in the Chapter 7 materials found on the textbook's website.

Extortion/Blackmail

TABLE 7.6	ELEMENTS OF EXTORTION
Criminal act	Offender intimidates victim by making present threat of future harm to victim's person, family, reputation, or property unless victim submits to a demand for money/property
Criminal intent	Specific intent/intent to permanently deprive rightful possessor of possession of property
Circumstances	Some jurisdictions require that the offender obtain the demanded money from the victim

Extortion is, like robbery, a close relation of larceny. In extortion, the perpetrator attempts to intimidate and thereby overcome the victim's ability to exercise free will by threatening future harm to the victim's person, family, reputation, or property in order to obtain possession of the victim's property. Although the Michigan extortion statute, which can be seen in Figure 7.4, permits prosecution for extortion without requiring that the offender actually obtain the demanded property, some states do have such a requirement.

The following example will help readers understand the *actus reus* of extortion. Assume that Arnold informed Carol, a woman with whom he had been having an adulterous affair, that he was ending their relationship and going back to his wife. Assume further that Carol, angry and seeking revenge, demanded that Arnold pay her $1,000 per month for the next six months or she would destroy Arnold's budding political career by revealing the details of their life together.

In threatening to do harm to Arnold's reputation unless he accedes to her demand for money, Carol has committed extortion. Carol is trying to force Arnold, against his will, into engaging in conduct that benefits her. Her intent is clear. At the time she made the threat and demand, she had a specific intent to damage his good name and permanently deprive Arnold of his property (money).

If Arnold succumbs to the intimidation and complies with the demand, the crime of extortion has been committed. If Arnold does not succumb to intimidation and refuses to comply with the demand, some states would prosecute Carol for extortion, while others would prosecute her for attempted extortion.

As can be seen in Figure 7.5, Congress has also enacted legislation intended to deter and punish persons who engage in extortion in ways that affect interstate commerce.

Figure 7.4. Michigan Extortion Statute

> **MCL 750.213 Malicious threats to extort money**
> Any person who shall, either orally or by a written or printed communication, maliciously threaten to accuse another of any crime or offense, or shall orally or by any written or printed communication maliciously threaten any injury to the person or property or mother, father, husband, wife, or child of another with intent thereby to extort money or any pecuniary advantage whatever, or with intent to compel the person so threatened to do or refrain from doing any act against his will, shall be guilty of a felony, punishable by imprisonment in the state prison not more than twenty years or by a fine of not more than ten thousand dollars.

Figure 7.5. Excerpt from the Hobbs Act 18 U.S.C. 1951

> (a) Whoever in any way or degree obstructs, delays, or affects commerce or the movement of any article or commodity in commerce, by robbery or extortion or attempts or conspires so to do . . . shall be fined not more than $10,000 or imprisoned not more than twenty years, or both.

UNITED STATES v. CHARLES G. STEPHENS, SR.

964 F.2d 424
United States Court of Appeals for the Fifth Circuit
June 19, 1992

AUTHOR'S INTRODUCTION

In this case, federal prosecutors relied on the federal statute excerpted in Figure 7.5 as the jurisdictional basis for a prosecution of corrupt local municipal police officers and others who had committed extortion. The case involved charges of conspiracy to commit extortion and alleged that various arrested drivers and a tow-truck company had been extorted. Stephens was charged with and convicted of extortion by a jury and appealed to the Fifth Circuit U.S. Court of Appeals. Readers can read excerpts from the indictment against Charles G. Stephens in Figure 7.6, which follows the Author's Commentary to the case.

EXCERPT FROM THE CASE

Judge GARZA:

. . . From 1982 through 1988, Stephens was employed by Guillory Bonding Company as a bail bondsman in the Vernon Parish area of Louisiana. He was also a town alderman in New Llano, Louisiana from June 1986 through May 1988. According to the Indictment, Stephens conspired with members of the New Llano police department to extort money from travelers passing through the town, in exchange for the dismissal or reduction of driving while intoxicated ("DWI") or operating under the influence ("OWI") charges, the return of the travelers' driver's licenses and the release of their vehicles from impoundment, and obtaining bond without being jailed. This conspiracy centered around the New Llano police department's traffic stops—the New Llano Chief of Police required each police officer to make at least sixty stops a month resulting in arrest for DWI or OWI.

The stops occurred mainly on six-tenths of a one-mile stretch of Highway 171, which runs through the town of New Llano. Local residents were rarely stopped—truck drivers, transients and military personnel were stopped most often. After the individuals were stopped, they were given a field sobriety test. If the individual failed the test, he was arrested for DWI/OWI and other traffic offenses.

When the vehicles were towed, they were almost always towed by B & B Towing. Other towing companies were allowed little opportunity to tow such vehicles. For every vehicle that B & B Towing towed, it made a "kickback" of $10.00 to the New Llano Chief of Police. Once at the police station, most of the individuals arrested had only the option of using Stephens of Guillory Bonding Company to make bond arrangements. They were "booked" and remained in the jail until bond arrangements were completed. B & B Towing did not release any of the individuals' cars until Stephens notified Bill Metlin, one of the owners of B & B Towing, that Stephens had been paid for his bail bonding services.

The individuals apparently would pay the amount requested by Stephens, and then they were permitted to leave. The standard fee charged was $150.00 for three offenses. The total of the bonds for three offenses was usually $1,000.00 ($500.00 for the DWI/ OWI, and $250.00 per other offense).The Government established that each surety bond was represented by a power of attorney. The New Llano Chief of Police required a separate power of attorney on each offense, resulting in a total fee of $150.00 for the three bonds. Stephens, however, did not adhere to this policy, but usually only attached one power of attorney aggregating all three offenses, which meant that he should have only charged ten percent—$100.00—of the total bond. Stephens would not account for this cash, or report less than the amount he actually received. . . .

Stephens argues that his convictions for conspiracy to commit extortion in violation of the Hobbs Act, as well as his convictions for the substantive violations under the Hobbs Act, were not supported by sufficient evidence. . . .

To convict for criminal conspiracy under 18 U.S.C. 1951, the jury must find an agreement between two or more persons to commit a crime, and an overt act by one of the conspirators to further the conspiracy. . . . The evidence in this case amply indicates the existence of a conspiracy. The New Llano Chief of Police had his officers make a minimum of sixty stops per month for DWI/ OWI offenses and other traffic violations. B & B Towing did the majority of the towing of these vehicles, despite the existence of other local towing companies and a local ordinance that required the rotation of wrecker services. For being allowed to do the towing, B & B Wrecking Service paid the New Llano Chief of Police $10.00 per vehicle, which was later increased to $15.00 per vehicle.

Stephens was good friends with the New Llano Chief of Police. When the New Llano Chief of Police was not in the office, the police officers were told to contact Stephens if they had any problems. When one of the individuals was in jail for a traffic offense, Stephens was almost always used as the bondsman. For each person bonded by Stephens, a charge was made which exceeded the amount Stephens reported to his employer, Guillory Bonding Company. A reasonable trier of fact could find from the circumstantial evidence that the New Llano Chief of Police and Stephens split the unreported amount of money in some manner. In addition, Stephens knew that B & B Towing was paying money to the Chief of Police and, when B & B Towing collected bond money for Stephens, Stephens' secretary would come and pick it up.

Stephens does not deny the existence of the conspiracy so much as he argues that he was not a part of it and had no knowledge of it. Specifically, he claims that he was not a participant in the conspiracy between the Chief of Police and the B & B Towing, and he contends that he did nothing wrong by collecting the money for bond services. We disagree because the totality of the circumstances involving Stephens indicates a common plan and purpose. . . . ([P]articipation in a criminal conspiracy may be inferred from a development and a collocation of circumstances). . . . [W]e find that the evidence is sufficient to support the jury's finding of a conspiracy between Stephens and members of the New Llano police department. . . .

Stephens argues that the Government failed to establish that the conspiracy and acts of extortion affected interstate commerce. He contends that the payment of kickbacks between the towing company and the New Llano Chief of Police did not have any effect on interstate commerce, and that a tenuous connection exists between the payment of bonds for release from jail in New Llano, Louisiana and interstate commerce.

"By statutory definition, in order for the extortion to constitute a federal crime under the Hobbs Act, some connection must be established between the extortionate conduct itself and interstate commerce." . . . The interstate commerce connection is determined on a case-by-case basis. . . . The impact on interstate commerce need not be substantial to meet the statutory requirement; all that is required is that commerce be affected by the extortion. . . . (Hobbs Act requires only minimal impact on interstate commerce). . . .

Stephens' arguments are unconvincing. The highway on which the cars were stopped and towed was six-tenths of a mile of U.S. Highway 171, a major four-lane highway that runs north and south through the western corridor of Louisiana. This highway provides access to other highways that lead to Texas if one travels west, and to Arkansas if one travels north. Testimony introduced at trial indicates that most of the people who were stopped and had their cars towed were not local residents, but individuals traveling to other states. Accordingly, we find Stephens' argument that interstate commerce was not affected to be without merit. . . .

Stephens contends his convictions for the substantive violations under the Hobbs Act were not supported by sufficient evidence. To establish an offense under the Hobbs Act, the Government must prove beyond a reasonable doubt that: (1) the defendant induced a person to part with property; (2) the defendant acted knowingly and willfully by means of extortion; and (3) that the extortionate transaction delayed, interrupted, or adversely affected interstate commerce. . . . "[T]he Government need only show that a public official has obtained a payment to which he was not entitled, knowing that the payment was made in return for official acts." . . .

Stephens contests his conviction on Count II of the indictment on the grounds that Adams never had any knowledge of Stephens' official capacity as a New Llano town alderman. Furthermore, Stephens argues that he did not indicate that he could have Adams' driver's license returned to him until after Adams agreed to make a payment.

Adams' testimony, however, indicates that Stephens indicated to him that, through his contacts, Stephens would get Adams' charges reduced or dismissed if Stephens was paid $1,040.00. Whether or not Adams knew what Stephens' official position was, Adams believed that Stephens had the power to fix Adams' ticket. Thus, Stephens was acting under color of official right and committed extortion . . . ("The official need not control the function in question if the extorted party possesses a reasonable belief in the official's powers.") . . .

Stephens contests his conviction on Count III of the Indictment, asserting that Hill did not bargain for anything which would result in having her charges reduced or dismissed. Stephens argues that Hill thought she was paying the money as a fine for her OWI offense. In the alternative, Stephens argues that the payment was nothing more than a cash bond. Stephens also asserts that Hill did not believe Stephens was acting under color of official right.

We do not agree with Stephens. As the parties agree, Hill's testimony at trial does indeed indicate some inconsistencies and confusion regarding the exact purpose of the money she paid to Stephens. But rather than indicating that the transaction was on the "up and up" as Stephens asserts, Hill's testimony indicates that she was unfamiliar with the court system and the purpose of and procedure for obtaining bonds.

Contrary to Stephens' assertions, the record indicates that Hill paid the money to Stephens because she thought Stephens could take care of the charges against her. That is why she paid Stephens the money—because of his "good relationship" with the police department and because he could "take care" of Hill's problems.

Such actions indicate Hill paid Stephens the money because of his public office. . . . Thus, we find a reasonable trier of fact could find beyond a reasonable doubt that Stephens extorted money from Hill under color of official right.

Stephens contests his conviction on Count IV of the Indictment, arguing that neither Metlin or James P. Bigley, the other owner of B & B Towing, were induced to hold vehicles until bonds were paid to Stephens. Stephens also contends that Count IV of the indictment alleges events taking place in 1984, and that because he was not an alderman until 1986, he was not acting under color of official right. . . .

Clearly, Count IV charges that Stephens' extortion of B & B—although initiated in the latter part of 1984 when B & B obtained exclusive rights to tow and impound vehicles for the town of New Llano—continued and was legally consummated for the purpose of 18 U.S.C. 1951 during the period of 1986 through 1987 when Stephens served as an alderman.

And this is exactly what the Government proved. Stephens knew that Metlin was paying money to the New Llano Chief of Police, and he knew that Metlin would not release vehicles that had been towed until he had Stephens' approval, which was given after the person whose car was towed had paid Stephens. Metlin knew that Stephens and the Chief of Police were "real good friends" and Metlin believed that Stephens could stop him from towing cars. A reasonable trier of fact could find that, because Metlin was afraid that he would not get any towing business if he did not, Metlin paid the money to the Chief of Police and collected money for the bond payment to Stephens; Metlin may also have believed that some of the money he was paying to the Chief of Police was for Stephens. Furthermore, Metlin could believe that Stephens might stop him from getting towing business from the town, so Metlin acceded to Stephens' demands not to release the vehicles until Stephens was paid. . . .

Stephens contests his conviction on Count V of the Indictment, asserting that the evidence does not show that he acted under color of official right, and that the evidence does not show that the payment was made to prevent prosecution of a DWI charge.

Again, Stephens mischaracterizes the evidence. The evidence shows that Cupit was stopped on a DWI/OWI charge, and, after paying Stephens $150.00 for bond, Cupit paid Stephens another $1,000.00. Cupit testified that the $1,000.00 was paid to Stephens to "take care" of these charges. Cupit asked for reassurance that nothing would happen to him, and Stephens said he did not "have to worry about nothing." Cupit understood that the $1,000 he paid to Stephens would "wipe everything clean like it never happened." Stephens then reassured Cupit that Stephens' "friend" would take care of Cupit's problem.

In addition, the records from Guillory Bonding Company for this period show that Stephens did not report the money. Cupit was not prosecuted on these charges, and the records from the clerk of the court of the City of Leesville indicate that no paperwork was received on Cupit. Thus, we conclude that a reasonable trier of fact could find beyond a reasonable doubt that Stephens extorted money from Cupit under color of official right. . . .

For the foregoing reasons, we AFFIRM.

CASE QUESTIONS

1. Should the federal government become involved in prosecuting extortion cases that can be readily addressed by state prosecutors?

2. Why was the discussion of the U.S. Constitution's Commerce Clause necessary in this case?

AUTHOR'S COMMENTARY

Extortion and **blackmail** were distinct crimes under the common law. Extortion was a specific intent crime and was committed when a governmental officer required the payment of an illegal fee (a bribe) before the officer would perform an official duty. Blackmail was the equivalent of extortion when committed by an ordinary citizen. Thus, in blackmail the offender, as a private person, makes a present threat of future harm to the victim's person, property, or reputation unless the victim agrees to meet the offender's demand for money or other valuable property.

Modern statutes generally have consolidated these offenses into a single offense called extortion.

Figure 7.6. Excerpts from the Indictment in *United States v. Charles G. Stephens, Sr.*[12]

Count 1 of the indictment, dealing with a conspiracy of the Hobbs Act, 18 U.S.C. 1951, alleges:

CHARLES G. STEPHENS, Sr., . . . and others . . . did knowingly, willfully and unlawfully conspire to commit extortion . . . in that . . . STEPHENS . . . (exercising authority and control over the actions of members of the New Llano Police Department), and others known and unknown . . . did wrongfully use their positions, defendant as a town Alderman, the co-conspirators as members of the New Llano Police Department, to unlawfully obtain, attempt to obtain, and cause to be obtained in connection with and in consideration for dismissal or reduction of DWI/OWI charges, towing contracts, returning of drivers' licenses, release of vehicles from impoundment and obtaining of bond without being jailed, payment of money not due to them or their office . . . from two owners of B & B Towing Company and approximately 72 individuals charged with DWI/OWI offenses, with their consent, said consent being induced under color of official right.

Count II states:

[O]n or about July 17, 1986 . . . STEPHENS . . . did knowingly, willfully and unlawfully commit extortion, which extortion obstructed, delayed and affected interstate commerce . . . in that . . . STEPHENS . . . did unlawfully seek, ask, solicit and receive a cash payment of . . . ($1,140.00) . . . from Richard A. Adams, which was not due . . . STEPHENS . . . or his office, with the consent of Richard A. Adams, said consent being obtained and induced through wrongful use of fear of economic loss and under color of official right . . . to prevent prosecution of Adams on a charge of Driving While Intoxicated. . . .

Count III of the Indictment charges:

[O]n . . . July 3, 1987 . . . STEPHENS . . . did knowingly, willfully and unlawfully commit extortion, which extortion obstructed, delayed and affected interstate commerce . . . in that . . . STEPHENS . . . did unlawfully seek, ask, solicit and receive a cash payment of . . . ($500.00) . . . from Debra Irene Hill, which was not due . . . STEPHENS . . . or his office, with the consent of Debra Irene Hill, said consent being obtained and induced through wrongful use of fear of economic loss and under color of official right, in that said . . . ($500.00) . . . was given by Debra Irene Hill in order to have the charge of Driving While Intoxicated and Illegal Lane Change reduced and/or dismissed when she appeared in Court. . . .

Count IV of the Indictment charges:

At a date unknown to the Grand Jury but sometime during the latter part of 1984 . . . STEPHENS . . . did knowingly, willfully and unlawfully commit extortion . . . in that . . . STEPHENS . . . did unlawfully seek, demand, ask, solicit and receive a promise and assurance from William Metlin, owner and

Figure 7.6. Excerpts from the Indictment in *United States v. Charles G. Stephens, Sr.*[12] (continued)

> operator of B & B that William Metlin would not release impounded vehicles in his care and custody until such time as the owners of said vehicles paid . . . STEPHENS . . . money that . . . STEPHENS had charged those individuals in regard to bonds, which promise and assurance was not due to . . . STEPHENS . . . or his office, with the consent of . . . Metlin, said consent being obtained and induced through wrongful use of fear of economic loss and under color of official right, in that said promise and assurance was given by . . . Metlin in order to continue towing vehicles for the town of New Llano. . . .

Forgery

A forger is someone who by hand or by computer creates, alters, falsifies, signs, or reproduces a credit card, check, passport, driver's license, or any other writing or document in order to perpetrate a fraud by deceiving others into believing that a writing is authentic. Forgery is a specific intent offense. If a person goes to the bank with a forged check that he or she knows is not authentic, intending to fraudulently obtain cash, the person has committed the crime called uttering a false instrument. Some states continue to follow the common law approach and recognize forgery and uttering as separate offenses. Other states have merged these offenses into a consolidated offense called forgery. Readers will see an example of such a statute in the next case, *State v. Mikael Hampton*.

TABLE 7.7   ELEMENTS OF FORGERY

Criminal act	Making, altering, falsifying, signing, or reproducing any kind of writing
Criminal intent	Specific intent to defraud

STATE v. MIKAEL HAMPTON
756 N.W.2d 49
Court of Appeals of Iowa
July 16, 2008

AUTHOR'S INTRODUCTION

Mikael Hampton was a passenger in a motor vehicle stopped by police. The officer making the stop asked Hampton for identification. Hampton claimed to be Jeffrey

Kowalzek, and the birth certificate and social security card Hampton presented to the officer contained the name of Kowalzek. Hampton was charged in an information with forgery and successfully petitioned the court for dismissal of the charge. The State of Iowa appealed to the Iowa Court of Appeals.

EXCERPT FROM THE CASE

VAITHESWARAN, J.

. . . The State charged Hampton with forgery, in violation of Iowa Code sections 715A.2(1) and (2)(a)(4) (2005). The State asserted Hampton did

> unlawfully and willfully fraudulently use, possess or utter a writing, to wit: a social security card in the name of Jeffrey Kowalzek, deceased, . . . knowing that said writing was forged by altering, completing, authenticating, issuing or transferring to be the act of another without their permission.

Hampton moved to dismiss the trial information. He asserted, "The minutes do not indicate that the State is in possession of any information or evidence that would prove the documents in Defendant's possession were forged. . . ." The district court granted the motion to dismiss. . . .

On the State's appeal, the sole issue we must decide is whether the court erred in concluding that the facts alleged in the trial information and minutes of evidence amounted to forgery as a matter of law. . . .

ANALYSIS

Iowa Code section 715A.2 (1) states:

> 1. A person is guilty of forgery if, with intent to defraud or injure anyone, or with knowledge that the person is facilitating a fraud or injury to be perpetrated by anyone, the person does any of the following:
>
>   a. Alters a writing of another without the other's permission.
>
>   b. Makes, completes, executes, authenticates, issues, or transfers a writing so that it purports to be the act of another who did not authorize that act, or so that it purports to have been executed at a time or place or in a numbered sequence other than was in fact the case, or so that it purports to be a copy of an original when no such original existed.
>
>   c. Utters a writing which the person knows to be forged in a manner specified in paragraph "a" or "b".
>
>   d. Possesses a writing which the person knows to be forged in a manner specified in paragraph "a" or "b".

The State maintains that the district court only considered subsection (a) and did not consider subsections (b) and (c). . . .

A necessary predicate to a charge under any alternative of section 715A.2(1) is an altered writing. . . . Subsection (a) addresses the clear case of an alteration of a writing without someone's permission. Subsection (b), while broader and fraught with some ambiguity, refers to the transfer of "a writing so that it purports to be the act of another who does not authorize that act. . . ." The word "it" in this sentence can only refer to the term "writing" preceding it. Therefore, this subsection charges a crime where the writing purports to be the writing of another who did not authorize it. Subsection(c) criminalizes the uttering of "a writing which the person knows to be forged in a manner specified in paragraph 'a' or 'b'." Subsection (d) criminalizes the possession of a writing "which the person knows to be forged in a manner specified in paragraph 'a' or 'b'."

The history and interpretation of the statute support this reading. Iowa's statute is a verbatim adoption of the Model Penal Code, section 224.1. . . . As the explanatory note to the Model Penal Code states, "[T]he prohibited conduct is drafted so as to focus the offense upon falsity as to genuineness or authenticity, rather than upon the falsity of any statement contained in a legitimate document. The legislature is presumed to have intended the statute to have the same meaning as explained in the comments to the model law. . . .

The Iowa Supreme Court has emphasized that this is indeed the focus, stating forgery is a crime that "affects the genuineness of the instrument." *State v. Calhoun*, . . . (Iowa 2000).

Notably, the State appears to concede that forgery generally refers to "the false making or material alteration, with intent to defraud, of a writing." The State also appears to concede that the Social Security card Hampton used was a genuine card. It simply argues that Hampton "transfer[red]" the card within the meaning of subsection (b) and "utter[ed]" the card within the meaning of subsection (c). These arguments ignore the remaining language of those subsections, which focuses on the predicate act of altering a writing.

We agree with the district court that the facts stated in the final information and minutes do not implicate the genuineness or authenticity of a document. The minutes presume that the Social Security card used by Hampton was genuine. As the district court pointed out, the crux of the charge is that Hampton used this genuine card to misrepresent his identity. . . . Accordingly, the district court did not err in granting Hampton's motion to dismiss. AFFIRMED.

CASE QUESTION

Given that defendant clearly gave false information to the police officer during the traffic stop in an attempt to deceive the officer as to the defendant's true identity, why did the trial and appellate courts dismiss the charges?

Burglary, Arson, and Trespass to Land/Dwellings

Burglary

TABLE 7.8	ELEMENTS OF BURGLARY
Criminal acts	Use of force that facilitates entry (breaking), unconsented entry (trespass)
Criminal intent	Specific intent at the time of trespass to commit a felony within the structure
Circumstances	Of a structure (initially a dwelling house or out-buildings within the curtilage) of another at night

Historically, as in modern times, the law has been concerned with protecting the place where people sleep at night (residence) and any outbuildings that are nearby and used in daily life by the people living in the residence (called the **curtilage**). Two common law felonies, **burglary** and **arson**, were created to protect the people inside structures from harm. The crime of burglary has existed since the Middle Ages. It was originally an offense that protected people inside any structure from invasion by uninvited outsiders at any time and then evolved into an offense that protected people in their *homes* from those who would *break* and *enter* during the *nighttime*. Obviously, in earlier times most people lived in homes that were not castles, and their meager defenses were often easily overcome by invaders— especially at night when the inhabitants were sleeping.

The common law requirement that a *breaking* precede and facilitate a subsequent *entry* was intended to show that the perpetrator had used at least some force to gain entry. Thus, pushing a door that is only open a crack would suffice, as would turning a handle, lifting up a hook, or pushing on a doorknob to gain entry. Modern statutes often dispense with this requirement.

The *entry* requirement is satisfied if any part of the offender's body intrudes into the targeted structure. Thus, a person who reaches through an open window has committed an entry for purposes of burglary. Modern statutes often redefine burglary to apply to those who lawfully enter but unlawfully *remain* within a structure for the purpose of committing some other crime (after which the perpetrator would presumably break out of the structure).

Most states no longer require that burglaries be committed during the "*nighttime*" and expand on the types of structures that are protected by the burglary statute. California's burglary statute, for example, protects a broad spectrum of unoccupied structures in addition to inhabited structures, as can be seen in Figure 7.7.

Traditionally, the *mens rea* for burglary required that the perpetrator be proven to have had the *intent to commit a felony* within the dwelling into which he was breaking and entering. Blackstone wrote in his *Commentaries* that burglary "has always been looked upon as a very heinous offense; not only because of the abundant terror that it naturally carries with it, but also as it is a forcible invasion and disturbance of that right of habitation, which every individual might acquire even in a state of nature; an invasion, which in such a state would be sure to be punished with death, unless the assailant were the stronger. But in civil society the laws also come in to the assistance of the weaker party; and, besides that they leave him this natural right of killing the aggressor, if he can . . . , they also protect and avenge him, in case the might of the assailant is too powerful. And the law of England has so particular and tender a regard to the immunity of a man's house, that it styles it his castle, and will never suffer it to be violated with impunity . . ." (4 *Blackstone's Commentaries* 223).

Today, some states continue to follow the common law approach with respect to the *mens rea* necessary for burglary and require the offender to have intended to commit a felony while inside the structure. But many states have redefined burglary. Some provide that a burglar must, at the time of entry, intend to commit theft. Others require that the burglar intend to commit some crime within the structure.

Figure 7.7. California's Burglary Statute

> **Penal Code Section 459**
> Every person who enters any house, room, apartment, tenement, shop, warehouse, store, mill, barn, stable, outhouse or other building, tent, vessel, . . . floating home, . . . railroad car, locked or sealed cargo container, whether or not mounted on a vehicle, trailer coach, . . . any house car, . . . inhabited camper, . . . vehicle, when the doors are locked, aircraft, . . . or mine or any underground portion thereof, with intent to commit grand or petit larceny or any felony is guilty of burglary.

PEOPLE v. MICHAEL W. DAVIS
958 P.2d 1083
California Supreme Court
July 30, 1998

AUTHOR'S INTRODUCTION

According to the prosecution, Michael W. Davis went to the outside walk-up window of a check-cashing business, waiting to cash a check. When it was his turn, he placed a forged check, which he had stolen, into the chute, intending that the teller, who was on the inside of the building, would cash it. Davis was charged and convicted of forgery, receiving stolen property, and burglary. Davis appealed this conviction, contending that he could not be convicted of burglary because he never "entered" the premises of the check-cashing company.

EXCERPT FROM THE CASE

Judge GEORGE:

On May 27, 1995, defendant approached the walk-up window of a check-cashing business named the Cash Box and presented a check to the teller by placing the check in a chute in the window. The teller later described the chute as follows: "It has a handle, and it opens out like a flap. It opens out, and they put the check in. They pass the check through." The check was drawn on the account of Robert and Joan Tallman, whose names were imprinted on the check, and was payable in the amount of $274 to Mike Woody, a name the defendant sometimes used.

The check was signed with the name Robert Tallman.

The teller placed a small white oval sticker on the back of the check, passed the check back to defendant, and asked him to place his thumbprint on the sticker and endorse the check. Defendant placed his thumbprint on the sticker, signed the back of the check with the name Michael D. Woody, and passed the check back to the teller, using the chute. . . .

The teller telephoned Robert Tallman, who denied having written the check. Tallman later discovered that a group of checks, including this one, had been stolen from his automobile. The teller placed Tallman on hold and telephoned the police. An officer arrived within minutes and arrested defendant, who still was waiting at the window. At the police station, the police directed defendant to give several examples of his handwriting by repeatedly signing the name "Robert Tallman."

At trial, Tallman testified that neither the signature nor any of the other writing on the check was his. Defendant was convicted of forgery, . . . burglary, . . . and receiving stolen property. . . . Defendant was sentenced on the forgery count to . . . four years in prison. Defendant was sentenced on the burglary count to a concurrent term of three years in prison, and on the receiving stolen property count to a concurrent term of three years in prison. The Court of Appeal affirmed the judgment. We granted review to determine whether there was sufficient evidence to support the conviction for burglary.

II

Under section 459, a person is guilty of burglary if he or she enters any building (or other listed structure) with the intent to commit larceny or any felony. . . . We must determine whether the Legislature intended the term "enter," as used in the burglary statute, to encompass passing a forged check through a chute in a walk-up window of a check-cashing or similar facility. . . .

Although the California Penal Code does not define "entry" for the purpose of burglary, the California courts have found that a burglary is complete upon the slightest partial entry of any kind, with the requisite intent, even if the intended larceny is neither committed nor even attempted. . . .

The interest sought to be protected by the common law crime of burglary was clear. At common law, burglary was the breaking and entering of a dwelling in the nighttime. The law was intended to protect the sanctity of a person's home during the night hours when the resident was most vulnerable. As one commentator observed: "The predominant factor underlying common law burglary was the desire to protect the security of the home, and the person within his home. Burglary was not an offense against property, real or personal, but an offense against the habitation, for it could only be committed against the dwelling of another. . . . The dwelling was sacred, but a duty was imposed on the owner to protect himself as well as looking to the law for protection. The intruder had to break and enter; if the owner left the door open, his carelessness would allow the intruder to go unpunished. The offense had to occur at night; in the daytime home-owners were not asleep, and could detect the intruder and protect their homes." . . .

In California, as in other states, the scope of the burglary law has been greatly expanded. There is no requirement of a breaking; an entry alone is sufficient. The crime is not limited to dwellings, but includes entry into a wide variety of structures. The crime need not be committed at night. "Of all common law crimes, burglary today perhaps least resembles the prototype from which it sprang. In ancient times it was a crime of the most precise definition, under which only certain restricted acts were criminal; today it has become one of the most generalized forms of crime, developed by judicial accretion and legislative revision.

Most strikingly it is a creature of modern Anglo-American law only. The rationale of common law burglary, and of house-breaking provisions in foreign codes, is insufficient to explain it." . . .

More than a century ago, in *People v. Barry* (1892) . . . , this court addressed the subject of what constitutes an entry for purposes of burglary. The defendant in

Barry entered a grocery store during business hours and attempted to commit larceny. This court, rejecting the contention that a burglary had not occurred because the defendant had entered lawfully as part of the public invited to enter the store, stated: "[A] party who enters with the intention to commit a felony enters without an invitation. He is not one of the public invited, nor is he entitled to enter." . . . In *People v. Gauze* (1975), we clarified our holding in *Barry* and held that a person cannot burglarize his or her own home. . . . We observed that "[a] burglary remains an entry which invades a possessory right in a building." . . . We then discussed the interest protected by the burglary statute: " 'Burglary laws are based primarily upon a recognition of the dangers to personal safety created by the usual burglary situation—the danger that the intruder will harm the occupants in attempting to perpetrate the intended crime or to escape and the danger that the occupants will in anger or panic react violently to the invasion, thereby inviting more violence. The laws are primarily designed, then, not to deter the trespass and the intended crime, which are prohibited by other laws, so much as to forestall the germination of a situation dangerous to personal safety.' Section 459, in short, is aimed at the danger caused by the unauthorized entry itself." . . .

Inserting a stolen ATM card into an ATM, or placing a forged check in a chute in the window of a check-cashing facility, is not using an instrument to effect an entry within the meaning of the burglary statute. Neither act violates the occupant's possessory interest in the building as does using a tool to reach into a building and remove property. It is true that the intended result in each instance is larceny. But the use of a tool to enter a building, whether as a prelude to a physical entry or to remove property or commit a felony, breaches the occupant's possessory interest in the building. Inserting an ATM card or presenting a forged check does not. Such acts are no different, for purposes of the burglary statute, from mailing a forged check to a bank or check-cashing facility. . . .

By analogy, a person who returns books to a library by depositing them in a book drop, causing the books to slide down a chute into the library, has not entered the library. It would be unreasonable to characterize the books as "instruments" used to enter the library. But if a person reaches his or her hand into the book drop, or uses a tool, in an attempt to steal books, such an act would constitute burglary. . . .

Our conclusion that the limits of the burglary statute should not be stretched beyond recognition does not leave the public without reasonable protection from criminal conduct, for the Legislature has enacted a variety of penal statutes that apply to the criminal activity involved in cases such as *Ravenscroft* or the present case. The use of an ATM card with intent to defraud, for example, specifically is penalized by section 484g and the Legislature, of course, could enact a similar statute pertaining to check-cashing facilities. Unauthorized entry into a computer system is addressed by sections 502 and 502.01. And in the present case, our reversal of defendant's conviction of burglary does not affect his convictions for forgery and receiving stolen property, or his resulting sentence of four years in prison. . . .

For the reasons discussed above, we conclude that defendant's placement of a forged check in the chute of the walk-up window of the check-cashing facility at issue cannot reasonably be termed an entry into the building for purposes of the burglary statute. Accordingly, the judgment of the Court of Appeal is reversed to the extent it affirms defendant's conviction for burglary, and affirmed in all other respects. . . .

Dissenting: Judge BAXTER:

I respectfully dissent. Defendant's act of passing a forged check through the walk-up security window of the check-cashing facility met the statutory and common law requirement of an "entry" sufficient to sustain his conviction of burglary. Defendant used the forged check as an instrumentality to trick the teller into handing him money back through a chute designed to protect this very type of particularly vulnerable business—a check-cashing facility—and its employee-occupants, from persons with criminal designs such as his. Defendant's use of the forged check served both to breach the security system of the business, by tricking the teller into taking the check from him through the security chute, and to gain entry into the premises, insofar as the check was literally used as a paper "hook" to enter the air space of the check-cashing facility and effectuate theft of cash on the spot from the business. Such was no less an act of larceny, and no less a breach of the business owner's "possessory interest" in his business premises accomplished through a burglarious entry, than if defendant had reached through an open window or entered through an unlocked door and grabbed his loot.

I

On appeal defendant contended there was insufficient evidence to sustain his conviction of burglary because evidence that he passed a forged check through the walk-up window or security chute of the check-cashing facility could not establish the element of "entry." The Court of Appeal disagreed. Since 1892, the courts of this state have recognized that the codification of burglary in Penal Code section 459 (hereafter section 459) shares few elements with the early common law crime of burglary. . . . Presently, any person who "enters any . . . building, . . . with intent to commit . . . larceny or any felony is guilty of burglary." . . . And "[i]t is well settled that an entry occurs for purposes of the burglary statute if any part of the intruder's body, or a tool or instrument wielded by the intruder, is 'inside the premises.'" . . .

Under a straightforward application of the law to the facts of this case, defendant stood at the walkup window and handed or passed a forged check through the security chute into the check-cashing facility with the intent to steal money from the business. His larcenous intent was a felonious intent.

Forgery is also a felony. . . . To the extent defendant passed the check through the chute to perfect and realize gains from his act of forgery, either felonious intent (larceny or forgery) would serve to establish the requisite unlawful specific intent for burglary. As regards the element of "entry," in this case we are concerned specifically with an entry by "tool or instrument wielded by the [defendant]" . . . to wit, the forged check. When defendant gave the forged check to the teller through the security chute, at the very least, the paper document he "wielded" in his hand crossed through the outer boundary of the business premises as it was received by the teller. Respondent's misleading and imprudent suggestion at oral argument that mailing a forged check from New York to a bank in California would likewise constitute burglary . . . and the majority's own hypothetically stated concern that a defendant "who, for a fraudulent purpose, accesses a bank's computer from his or her home computer via a modem [and] has [thereby] electronically entered the bank building" should not be subject to prosecution for burglary . . . are red herrings. In neither hypothetical has a tool or instrument been wielded by a burglar to serve as an extension of his hand, arm, or body for the purpose of gaining entry into the premises. Simply put: no burglar at the crime scene, no burglary.

The crux of the matter is simply this: Can the forged check validly be deemed a "tool or instrument" wielded by defendant and placed or passed through the outer boundary of the business premises (the security chute) for the felonious purpose of burglarizing the establishment? . . .

. . . [I]t is of legal significance to note that defendant used the forged check both as a tool or instrument to breach the secured premises of the check-cashing facility (i.e., trick the teller into taking it from him through the air space of the security chute through which all of the business's transactions were conducted), and as the means for effectuating his felonious intent to steal (i.e., further trick the teller into cashing the forged check and passing money back out to him through the chute). As Rollin Perkins observes in his textbook on Criminal Law: "If the instrument is inserted in such a manner that it is calculated not only to make a breach but also to accomplish the completion of the felonious design, this constitutes both a breach and an entry." . . .

Although either purpose would alone suffice to establish a burglarious entry under California law, here, use of the forged check to gain access into the business premises through the security chute and to steal money from the teller within satisfied both. In short, the forged check in this instance served both as a crowbar and a paper "hook."

II

The most commonly recognized test for determining whether an entry sufficient to establish a burglary has occurred is to ascertain whether the defendant, or any tool or instrument wielded by the defendant, has crossed the outer boundary of the "air space" of the structure or premises. . . . *Ravenscroft* . . . (1988). . . .

The Court of Appeal in this case, in discussing and contrasting the holding of *Nible* with the general air space test formulated in *Ravenscroft*, correctly questioned the applicability of *Nible's* holding "except in cases where the boundaries of the building's air space are difficult to determine." The Court of Appeal went on to conclude that even under the *Nible* test, defendant's actions here constituted a burglarious "entry" because "protection of the cashier is precisely the reason why the structure has a walk-up window and chute, rather than a door, or open window. Although it is expected and authorized to use the chute to pass checks to the cashier, [defendant] passed the check through with felonious intent unknown and unendorsed by the occupants."

I agree with the . . . Court of Appeal that defendant's act of passing the forged check through the security chute plainly established the requisite entry for burglary under the applicable air space test of *Ravenscroft*. As the Court of Appeal aptly observed, "[t]he insertion of a forged check through the chute of a walk-up window is at least as intrusive as inserting an ATM card into a machine." Obviously, the check-cashing facility is a commercial establishment that extends only a conditional invitation to its patrons to transact lawful business through its security chute—i.e., the tendering of valid checks to the teller through the chute for cashing. The facility clearly does not extend an invitation to persons like defendant to pass forged checks through its security chute in an attempt to gain possession of, and thereby steal cash from, the business. . . .

III

Although it is unclear exactly what aspect of the *Ravenscroft* analysis and its bright line air space test the majority today disapprove . . . in its stead the majority appear to adopt a test strikingly similar to that announced in *Nible*, . . . a test expressly discussed and found inapplicable to the facts of this case by the Court of Appeal below. . . .

To summarize, . . . [the] defendant's act of placing the forged check through the security chute with felonious intent to steal money from the check-cashing facility constituted a burglarious entry. The forged check, an extension of defendant's arm or hand as it was placed in the chute, crossed into the air space of the business. . . . [T]he conclusion is inescapable that the owners or occupants of the check-cashing facility considered the air space within the security chute, through which they conducted all of their business, to be part and parcel of the air space of their business premises generally, as the chute was obviously purposefully designed to afford them "the protection the owners or inhabitants of a structure reasonably expect." . . . And . . . defendant's passing of the forged check through the air space of the targeted business constituted a burglarious entry regardless of whether his unlawful intent and actions posed any physical danger to the employee-occupants. . . .

The majority, in contrast, turn . . . three explanatory authorities on their heads in concluding defendant's passing of the forged check through the air space of the security chute was not a burglarious entry because such an act "is not using an instrument to effect an entry within the meaning of the burglary statute" and "[is] no different, for purposes of the burglary statute, than mailing a forged check to a bank or check-cashing facility." ... I fail to see how our trial courts will be able to quantify, much less apply, the majority's nebulous new "test."

IV

From a factual standpoint, defendant's passing of the forged check through the security chute posed an increased danger to the employee-occupants of the check-cashing facility as well as others in the vicinity. A check-cashing business is known by all to have a large amount of cash on hand; the nature of its business operation is to cash checks and hand cash out to its patrons. For this very reason its business is transacted through the walk-up window and security chute—in a sense, the only way for a patron to get "in" or "out" of the facility, i.e., transact business with it, is through the air space of the security chute. In this case, the alert teller sensed crime afoot and summoned police, who were able to arrest defendant at the crime scene without further incident. However, the potential for harm or violence always exists during a burglary and will vary with the circumstances. Although a walk-up window and security chute are specifically designed to discourage theft and robberies, there is no guarantee they will accomplish that end in every instance.

In any event, even assuming arguendo defendant's passing of the forged check through the security chute in actuality posed no direct threat of harm or violence to the business's employee-occupants, ... that factor was legally irrelevant to the determination of whether a burglarious entry occurred. ... [A] shoplifter who surreptitiously enters a store with the intent to steal commits burglary even though his or her clandestine effort to slip merchandise into a jacket does not necessarily threaten anyone's personal safety. ...

The majority's holding today will further lead to anomalous results. Under the majority's rationale, if a person inserts a stolen ATM card into an ATM machine affixed to the exterior wall of a bank and succeeds in unlawfully withdrawing money from the cardholder's account, such is not burglary because the passing of the ATM card through the ATM machine is not an unauthorized entry of the sort the burglary statute is designed to prevent. ... But if that same person walks into the bank building with the stolen ATM card in hand, intending to perpetrate the same unlawful transaction at an ATM machine located inside the bank lobby, he has committed burglary at the moment he crosses the threshold of the building, and he can be arrested for that crime once inside the bank even if he never approaches the ATM or attempts the fraudulent transaction. The same anomalous results would obtain in comparing a business that has a walk-up window or security chute affixed to an external wall of the building, and one that admits patrons into a lobby but then requires them to transact business with their employees through openings in a secured or windowed counter area. In the former type of business, under the majority's rationale, the tendering of a forged check or similar fraudulent document through the external security chute is not burglary even if the suspect makes off with the loot, whereas in the latter business setting, a burglary would be complete when the suspect physically enters the lobby premises with felonious intent, without any further action necessary on his part to perfect his burglarious entry.

Yet another anomalous result that will flow from the majority's holding is that an incomplete and unsuccessful attempt at a forcible entry (i.e., inserting a crowbar or other burglar tool into the air space of a window, security chute mechanism, or ATM) will suffice as a legally sufficient entry for burglary, whereas a completed and successful nonforcible entry with a "tool or instrument" such as a stolen ATM card or forged check, by which the suspect nets his loot and makes his getaway, will not. The irony here is that those very businesses which, by their nature, are particularly vulnerable to theft and burglary, and for that reason protect themselves with anti-crime devices such as walk-up windows, security chutes, or card access machines requiring passwords, will receive less protection in our courts if the burglar is caught and an attempt made to bring him to justice.

The majority find it significant that "in the present case, our reversal of defendant's conviction of burglary does not affect his convictions of forgery and receiving stolen property, or his resulting sentence [therefor]." . . . I fail to see the significance of this observation. The statutes proscribing check forgery and receiving stolen property have as their primary underlying purpose protection of the security interests of the original maker of the check and his bank. Defendant did not make the forged check out to himself, endorse it in his real name, or attempt to deposit it into his own bank account. Under such facts, forgery, and perhaps only forgery, would be his crime. Here, in contrast, defendant made the stolen check out to a fictitious payee and endorsed it with that fictitious name. From a practical standpoint, the forged check, as made out, had no value to defendant other than as a "tool or instrument" useable for the dual purpose of breaching the security system of the check-cashing facility (when it was accepted through the air space of the walk-up security chute) and as a paper "hook" to grab the loot (had the teller been tricked into cashing the forged check and handing money out to him through the chute).

Moreover, lest we forget, every burglary by definition has as an integral element the suspect's intent to commit a felony within the targeted premises. It would seem to beg the question to suggest, as do the majority, that conviction of burglary is unnecessary where conviction of the target felony (here forgery and receiving stolen property) is otherwise obtainable. Such circular reasoning would preclude the charging and conviction of burglary in many if not most burglary cases where the target felony (i.e., larceny) has been completed. In sum, defendant's use of the forged check was no different than if he had "put a hand or a hook in at a window to draw out goods" from the victimized business, a clearly "burglarious entr[y]" even at common law. . . .

I would affirm the judgment of the Court of Appeal in its entirety.

CASE QUESTIONS

1. On what ground did Davis appeal his conviction for burglary?

2. Why did the California Supreme Court conclude that no burglary had been committed?

3. Why did Judge Baxter dissent? With whom do you agree?

AUTHOR'S COMMENTARY

It is important to remember that the crime of burglary targets an offender who unlawfully enters or remains within a structure and who intends to commit some other crime. The offender does not have to follow through and commit the other crime. If the offender does engage in additional illegal conduct, the offender is subject to prosecution for burglary as well as the homicide, rape, robbery, theft, or other crime that is subsequently committed.

There is no double jeopardy problem, for example, in charging a burglar with burglary and theft, because each of these offenses contains an element not required for conviction of the other. Burglary requires proof of an entry (which is not required for conviction of the theft or the other mentioned offenses), and the other offenses all require proof—of homicides, sexual assaults, misappropriation of property, and so forth—which is not required for conviction of burglary.

Now, a final observation regarding burglary: It is clear that the reason burglary is such a feared crime is in large measure a reflection of the general public's fear of being victimized at home by an intruding stranger. But if you think about who actually enters your home and commits theft, destroys property, and assaults and batters the inhabitants, it is often not intruding strangers. It is often the people with whom we live and work and know—other family members, relatives, friends, neighbors, and significant others.

Internet Tip

Two additional burglary cases, *People v. John D. Williams*, a *mens rea* case and *People v. Staten D. Taylor*, a burglary of a motor vehicle case, can be found included in the Chapter 7 materials found on the textbook's website.

Arson

Arson is a crime against possession of property. At common law, **arson** was a general intent crime that made it unlawful to cause another person's dwelling to burn without lawful justification or excuse (i.e., maliciously). As we have learned, it is permissible for the factfinder at trial to conclude from the facts and circumstances of the case that the accused acted maliciously and intended the normal and probable consequences of his or her voluntary acts.

TABLE 7.9	ELEMENTS OF ARSON
Criminal act	Burning (charring)
Criminal intent	General intent/accused intends to commit the criminal act (i.e., burn a protected dwelling or other structure)
Causation	Factual and proximate causation
Circumstances	A dwelling or other structure

The term *burning* has a very specific meaning in arson prosecutions. It is not enough that a structure be aflame or that a structure has become scorched or discolored by having been set ablaze. In an arson prosecution some portion of the targeted structure must be shown to have become *charred* (i.e., the wood has been transformed by the fire into coal).

This narrow definition has been substantially modified by statute in many jurisdictions. Today, it is common for states to define arson as including causing an explosion or starting a fire that destroys or damages occupied or unoccupied buildings, structures, and/or personal property. Modern statutes also make it a crime to set a fire for the specific purpose of collecting insurance.

STATE v. HARRY W. LOLLIS

No. 25240
South Carolina Supreme Court
January 29, 2001

AUTHOR'S INTRODUCTION

Henry Lollis was prosecuted for the arson of a mobile home in which he lived with his common law wife, Tammy Burgess. An investigation by state investigators indicated that the fire originated in two places, the kitchen stove and a hallway. Investigators discovered that the stove had been turned on high and paper of some kind was found wedged in between a skillet and an electric coil on the stove. They also noted the absence of personal effects from the home, a condition consistent with an arson. Burgess gave a written confession to authorities in which she assumed sole responsibility for the crime.

Despite Burgess's assertions that her husband was uninvolved in the arson, the state charged Lollis with arson in the second degree because of the state's belief that he had aided and abetted and/or conspired with Burgess in the commission of this crime.

Lollis was tried and convicted of second-degree arson. He unsuccessfully appealed to the state court of appeals, but his petition for certiorari to the state supreme court was granted. In the South Carolina Supreme Court, Lollis argued that the trial court had wrongfully denied his motion for a directed verdict of acquittal.

EXCERPT FROM THE CASE

Chief Justice TOAL:

... On February 19, 1998, at 9:05 A.M., the Liberty Fire Department responded to a fire at Lollis' mobile home. Later that day, the South Carolina Law Enforcement Division ("SLED") Arson Hotline received an anonymous tip concerning the fire. David Tafaoa ("Agent Tafaoa"), a SLED arson investigator, investigated the tip and opined the fire was intentionally set.

Agent Tafaoa's investigation revealed there were two areas of fire origination, the kitchen stove and another unconnected fire in the hallway. At the kitchen stove origination site, some type of paper product was rolled and placed between the skillet and the electric coil of the stove, and the eye of the skillet was turned to "high." Agent Tafaoa was further convinced the fire was intentionally set because many personal items were missing from the mobile home. For example, there were nails and screws in the walls, but there was nothing hanging on them or located on the floor beneath them. Also, a gun rack and a soft gun case were found in the master bedroom, but neither contained a gun. Furthermore, there was nothing in the nightstand drawers, there was only one pair of shoes in the closet, and there was no VCR, even though a VCR cable and a few tapes were found in the mobile home.

On the day of the fire, Lollis' common law wife, Tammy Burgess ("Burgess"), confessed in a statement to Agent Tafaoa that she was depressed about her husband's financial condition and intentionally started the fire by leaving a pan of grease on a hot eye of the stove. Burgess admitted Lollis was unaware of her plans to burn their home. She further confessed she took most of their valuables and placed them in a storage room they rented five days prior to the fire. According to Agent Tafaoa, Burgess burned the mobile home so the insurance company would pay the mortgage, their largest debt.

Lollis denies he had any involvement with the fire. He claims he never asked, encouraged, or aided Burgess in the burning of their home. According to Lollis, he had no reason to burn his home because it was being extensively remodeled when the fire occurred. Lollis claims he placed his personal items in the storage room on the day of the fire because he did not want his valuables ruined by drywall dust while he remodeled his home.

The State offered no evidence of Lollis' alleged financial trouble. On cross examination, the State's witness from the finance company testified Lollis was current on his mortgage payment at the time of the fire. Lollis also testified he was current on his accounts to Commercial Credit, Friendly Loans, State Farm Insurance, and Macy's Credit.

Lollis had an outstanding mortgage at the time of the fire. In October 1997, Lollis financed his home in order to pay for carpeting, delinquent taxes, and other matters. Because Lollis did not have homeowner's insurance, the finance company required that insurance be placed on the home in order to cover its mortgage. After the fire, the insurance company fully paid Lollis' mortgage. However, Lollis did not receive any money for his personalty destroyed in the fire because the items were not insured.

Agent Tafaoa was convinced Lollis conspired with his wife to commit arson because Lollis possessed the key to the storage room, which contained many of their valuable personal items, when he accompanied Burgess to the law enforcement center. Lollis was arrested a week after the fire and charged with second degree arson. . . .

Lollis argues the Court of Appeals erred in affirming the trial court's denial of his directed verdict motion because the State did not present substantial circumstantial evidence Lollis was guilty of second degree arson. Second degree arson is defined as:

> A person who willfully and maliciously causes an explosion, sets fire to, burns, or causes to be burned or aids, counsels, or procures the burning of a dwelling house, church or place of worship, a public or private school facility, a manufacturing plant or warehouse, a building where business is conducted, an institutional facility, or any structure designed for human occupancy to include local and municipal buildings, whether the property of himself or another, is guilty of arson in the second degree and, upon conviction, must be imprisoned not less than five nor more than twenty-five years. . . .

No direct evidence was adduced at trial linking Lollis to the fire. The State's case depended entirely on circumstantial evidence. When a motion for a directed verdict is made in a criminal case where the State relies exclusively on circumstantial evidence, "[t]he trial judge is required to submit the case to the jury if there is any substantial evidence which reasonably tends to prove the guilt of the accused, or from which his guilt may be fairly and logically deduced. . . ." The trial court is concerned with the existence or nonexistence of the evidence, not with its weight. . . .

The circumstantial evidence relied upon by the State is not substantial and merely raises a suspicion of guilt. The key pieces of circumstantial evidence relied upon by the State are: (1) the marital relationship between Burgess and Lollis; (2) Lollis' alleged financial trouble; (3) his placement of valuables in the storage room; and (4) his possession of the storage key on the day of the fire.

According to the trial judge, Lollis' possession of the storage key is the most significant piece of circumstantial evidence:

> I think that there's some substantial circumstantial evidence or sufficient circumstantial evidence, taking everything in the light most favorable to the State, the things that you mentioned, the relationship, the fact that he owned the property. But I think one of the strongest things, facts, is that I think I heard testimony that Mr. Lollis had the keys to the storage locker in his pocket where all the stuff that was taken from the house was stored. And I think that there is sufficient circumstantial evidence. I'd be required to submit it to the jury for their determination. . . .

Even viewing the circumstantial evidence in the light most favorable to the State, the evidence presented does not reasonably tend to prove Lollis' guilt. First, Burgess admitted to starting the fire without assistance from Lollis, and without his knowledge. The State presented no evidence of an agreement between them. Second, the State presented no evidence of Lollis' alleged financial trouble. To the contrary, Lollis' testimony he was current on his debts at the time of the fire was uncontradicted. The State's witness from the finance company also testified Lollis was current on his mortgage payments. Furthermore, Lollis did not have insurance on his personal property lost in the fire. Finally, Lollis presented a plausible explanation for placing valuables in the storage room on the day of the fire—he was trying to protect them from drywall dust as he remodeled his home.

Lollis' mere possession of a storage key is not substantial circumstantial evidence he asked, aided, or procured Burgess to burn the dwelling. The possession of the key only indicates Lollis had access to the storage room on the day of the fire, it in no way demonstrates he aided Burgess with the fire. Lollis fully admits he was visiting the storage room when the fire occurred that morning. However, placing valuables in a storage room, without any other evidence linking him to the fire, does not indicate he aided his wife in destroying their home, especially when he offered a valid reason for placing the items in storage, and Burgess confessed she acted alone. Therefore, the possession of the key does nothing more than arouse suspicion of Lollis' guilt, and is an improper basis to deny a motion for directed verdict.

Finally, in similar arson cases relying on circumstantial evidence, appellate courts have affirmed denials of directed verdict motions when there is clear circumstantial evidence of financial trouble, such as a pending foreclosure proceeding or a significant change in an insurance policy prior to the fire. The instant case does not contain the same quantum of evidence because the State presented no evidence of Lollis' financial difficulty, and no evidence Lollis would receive some financial gain as a result of the fire. . . .

CONCLUSION

Based on the foregoing, we REVERSE the Court of Appeals' decision.

CASE QUESTIONS

1. Why was the defendant charged with arson in the second degree?

2. Why did the state supreme court conclude that the trial court should have entered a directed verdict of acquittal in favor of the defendant at the end of the prosecution's case in chief?

AUTHOR'S COMMENTARY

As we saw in the *Lollis* case, arson has been significantly redefined in many jurisdictions and is no longer limited to the burning of dwellings. The South Carolina arson statute, included in the *Lollis* opinion, expands the *actus reus* to include not only the act of burning but also setting fire to, or causing an explosion to, protected structures. It also expands the kinds of protected structures to include not only dwelling houses but also houses of worship, schools, manufacturing sites and warehouses, structures housing businesses, and governmental buildings.

South Carolina, like many states, also classifies arson into three degrees. First-degree arson is committed by one whose conduct causes death or serious bodily injury; second-degree arson consists of arson that does not result in death or serious bodily injury; and third-degree arson involves damage to structures that are not designed for human occupancy, personal property, and various forms of transportation.

Trespass to Land/Dwellings

Trespass laws assist owners and occupiers of land and regulate who is permitted to enter and remain on their land and within their premises. Such statutes target persons who ignore written or oral instructions to stay out/to leave, enter, or remain on an owner/occupier's premises without consent or lawful authority. Trespass is usually a general intent crime

TABLE 7.10	ELEMENTS OF TRESPASS TO LAND/PREMISES

Criminal act	Entry/remaining on land or into premises of another
Criminal intent	General intent
Circumstances	Entry/remaining is without consent and after receiving written or oral notice not to enter/remain owner/occupier's premises without consent or lawful authority. Trespass is normally a general intent crime. The Michigan trespass statute in Figure 7.8 is illustrative of such legislation.

Figure 7.8. Michigan Trespass Statute

> **Michigan Consolidated Laws 750.552 Trespass upon lands or premises of another**
>
> Any person who shall willfully enter upon the lands or premises of another without lawful authority, after having been forbidden so to do by the owner or occupant, agent or servant of the owner or occupant, or any person being upon the land or premises of another, upon being notified to depart therefrom by the owner or occupant, the agent or servant of either, who without lawful authority neglects or refuses to depart therefrom, shall be guilty of a misdemeanor and upon conviction thereof shall be punished by imprisonment in the county jail for not more than 30 days or by a fine of not more than $50.00, or both, in the discretion of the court.

STATE OF TENNESSEE v. JOSEPH VELLA

No. E2000-01149-CCA-R3-CD
Court of Criminal Appeals of Tennessee
March 12, 2001

AUTHOR'S INTRODUCTION

Joseph Vella and his nephew Gary were in a bar for the purpose of watching a floor show featuring a female impersonator. An incident involving the performer and the defendant attracted the attention of the bar's security personnel. The testimony was divided, but there were reciprocal allegations of assaults involving the defendant, his nephew, and members of the security force. The defendant was allegedly escorted out of the bar and told by security staff members not to re-enter, but he ignored these admonitions and re-entered the bar. Vella testified that his wrists and ribs were broken and his face scratched in conjunction with the altercation. Joseph Vella was found guilty of misdemeanor criminal trespass and appealed.

EXCERPT FROM THE CASE

Judge WELLES:

After hearing this proof, the trial court found the Defendant guilty of criminal trespass. The statute defining criminal trespass provides:

(a) A person commits criminal trespass who, knowing the person does not have the owner's effective consent to do so, enters or remains on property, or a portion thereof. Knowledge that the person did not have the owner's effective consent may be inferred where notice against entering or remaining is given by:

(1) Personal communication to the person by the owner or by someone with apparent authority to act for the owner; ...

(b) It is a defense to prosecution under this section that:

(1) The property was open to the public when the person entered and remained;

(2) The person's conduct did not substantially interfere with the owner's use of the property; and

(3) The person immediately left the premises upon request. ...

Looking at the evidence in the light most favorable to the State, we conclude that the evidence was sufficient to support the Defendant's conviction of criminal trespass. It is undisputed that the property was open to the public when the Defendant entered, but he was asked to leave by a person with the apparent authority to act for the owner. The trial court also specifically found that the Defendant's conduct on the dance floor did not substantially interfere with the owner's use of the property. The pivotal issue at trial and on appeal is whether the Defendant remained on the property after being informed that he no longer had the owner's effective consent to be there or whether he left immediately upon request. We conclude that the evidence is sufficient to support the trial court's conclusion that the Defendant remained on the property after being asked to leave. The proof established that Mr. Sandifer and the other security guards asked the Defendant to leave. The Defendant was escorted out, but according to Mr. Sandifer, he reentered the building three times, while yelling and screaming. According to the Defendant himself, he attempted to reenter the building two or three times. Thus, the Defendant did not leave the property immediately upon request.

Accordingly, the judgment of the trial court is affirmed.

CASE QUESTIONS

1. On what ground did Joseph Vella appeal his trespass conviction?

2. Why did the state court of appeals affirm the trial court?

AUTHOR'S COMMENTARY

It is common for trespass to land statutes to require owner/occupiers of land to post "no trespassing" signs around their property that are likely to be seen by passersby. Many states supplement general trespass to land or premises statutes with specific statutes that limit the right of individuals to enter or remain within schools, public housing facilities, military bases, and other places that have received special statutory protection.

Chapter Summary

This crimes against property chapter shows students, once again, about the strong influence the common law continues to have on American law. Most of the crimes discussed have historical roots, some back to the middle ages. Obviously, over the centuries they have changed. In this chapter readers learned about the original laws, as well and how they have been changed to meet contemporary circumstances.

Larceny-Theft

It is appropriate to begin this summary with larceny because it was the first common law property crime. The *actus reus* of common law larceny included proof that an offender has taken and carried away an item of tangible personal property from another person who had possessory rights to the item. Because larceny is a specific intent crime, a larcenist had to have intended to permanently deprive the owner of his/her property when the *actus reus* was committed. Larceny is a crime against the possessory rights to a property but not the ownership rights ("title") to an item of property. Although the thief has unlawful possession of the stolen item, the thief has no property rights and cannot lawfully transfer it to anyone else. In fact, it is a crime to knowingly receive and conceal stolen property. The true owner of the item is legally entitled to regain possession of the item if it is recovered. Larcenies were classified as either grand or petit larceny based on the value of the property taken.

Over time the English Parliament enacted laws to combat creative strategies criminal offenders used to exploit legal loopholes in the definition of larceny. Examples include the crimes known as embezzlement and false pretenses.

Embezzlement and False Pretenses and Consolidated Theft Statutes

Embezzlement is a crime against ownership rights. In an embezzlement, the lawful owner of an item of property entrusts (voluntary transfers) possession to another for a limited time with the expectation it will be returned. The true owner expects that the recipient (the embezzler) will care for the item while it is in the recipient's possession. Because the embezzler was entrusted with possession there is no "taking" as in a larceny. The criminal act occurs when the embezzler trespasses on the ownership rights of the true owner and sells the item or otherwise uses it for his/her own advantage (this is called a "conversion").

In false pretenses, the criminal offender, instead of stealing or converting property, uses deception to persuade the true owner to transfer both possession and title be deceit (i.e., under false pretenses).

Today, although some states, like Virginia, continue to enforce common law larceny, many have taken a more modern approach. States are increasingly replacing common laws crimes with comprehensive theft statutes. These theft statutes consolidate the once separate crimes of larceny, embezzlement and false pretenses into a single statute. The new theft statutes abolish many of the old-fashioned requirements such as the taking, carrying away, and tangible property elements of larceny The scope of theft laws have been greatly expanded and now prohibit the theft of services of various types (hotels, restaurants, equipment rentals, etc.) and utilities (electricity, cable and satellite TV, telephone, etc.). Prosecutors in states with comprehensive theft statutes (such as Maine) prove that the accused has "obtained or exercised unauthorized control over the property of another with intent to deprive him thereof. . . ." (Figure 7.1).

Identify Theft

Criminal offenders have been taking advantage of the growing popularity of the Internet and Internet banking. All over the country, people have had their lives turned upside down as a result of having had their identities stolen. Identity theft first became a crime in 1996, and today, governments are scrambling to enact legislation that addresses this threat. The degree of harm posed by identity theft varies greatly. On the low end of the scale are offenders who seek to pass themselves off as somebody else (who has a better resume) in order to get a job, or the offender may be underage and uses a borrowed or stolen ID to purchase alcoholic beverages. The second and more serious offense is often classified as aggravated identity theft. An offender committing that offense assumes a false identity to defraud insurance companies of all types, social security and other governmental agencies, as well as banks and other financial institutions, to commit forgery and in conjunction with racketeering schemes.

Robbery, Extortion, and Blackmail

Robbery is a crime that many today consider to be a crime against persons because force is threatened or employed to accomplish the "taking" of the victim's property. Robbery is treated as a crime against property in this text, however, because that is its traditional classification and because larceny is a lesser-included offense of robbery. Robbery is an aggravated larceny. If force is neither threatened nor used in the taking of property, the crime is a larceny.

Courts have generally been unsympathetic to arguments that an unloaded gun is not a dangerous weapon. They have also generally rejected contentions that a "non-weapon" lookalike that is so realistic that a reasonable victim could believe it to be "real" should not be classified as a dangerous weapon.

Extortion and robbery are similar. Both involve attempts to intimidate the victim and overcome any thoughts of resistance, and in both crimes the objective is to obtain possession of the victim's money/property. But the nature of the threats differ. A robber is in the victim's presence when the force is immediately employed or threatened. An extortionist, however, does not have to be near the victim and can commit the *actus reus* by text messaging his/her demands for money or valuable property to the victim. Another difference between robbery and extortions is that an extortionist threatens to cause future harm to the victim's person, property, or reputation. States differ as to whether an extortionist is required to actually receive the demanded payment.

Blackmail, a distinct crime under the common law, prohibited government officials from demanding payment of a bribe before performing an official duty. Today, blackmail is generally merged into a single offense called extortion. Extortion, like robbery, is a close relation of larceny. In extortion, the perpetrator attempts to intimidate and thereby overcome the victim's ability to exercise free will by threatening future harm to the victim's person, family, reputation, or property in order to obtain possession of the victim's property. Although the Michigan extortion statute, which can be seen in Figure 7.4, permits prosecution for extortion without requiring that the offender actually obtain the demanded property, some states do have such a requirement.

Forgery

A forger is someone who by hand or by computer creates, alters, falsifies, signs, or reproduces a credit card, check, passport, driver's license, or any other writing or document in order to perpetrate a fraud by deceiving others into believing that a writing is authentic. States which have enacted consolidated forgery statutes usually define as forgery conduct that used to constitute the separate crime called uttering. One who utters a forged check, for example, goes to a bank and presents a check for payment while knowing that the check is forged and with the intent that the bank be defrauded.

Burglary, Arson, and Trespass to Land/Dwellings

Historically, as in modern times, the law has been concerned with protecting the people from intruders. Common law burglary was created to punish nighttime intruders (persons acting without consent) who break into and enter residential places (sleeping people fear and are most vulnerable to nighttime attacks) and any nearby outbuildings used in daily life by the people living in the residence (called the curtilage) in order to commit a felony.

Modern statutes have significantly redefined burglary and expanded its original purpose and scope. Today's burglary statutes should be thought of as focusing on protecting many types of structures from intruders irrespective of whether it is that structure is inhabited.

Arson

Arson punished someone who had intruded on property of another and caused the other person's residence (or structure within the curtilage) to burn. Arson was a general intent crime against property, and therefore the offender had to have intended that the residence burn when starting the fire. The offender's conduct would not constitute arson if the accused had a lawful justification or excuse, such as the burning was caused accidently or as a result of carelessness. Modern statutes generally expand the common law definition to include starting a fire that causes an explosion, sets fire to, burns, or causes structures to be burned.

Trespass to Land/Dwellings

Trespass statutes today, as in medieval times, protect property owners and lawful occupiers from uninvited and properly warned intruders. Trespass laws allow owners/occupiers to determine who is permitted to enter and remain on their land and within their premises. Persons have no right to ignore written or oral instructions to stay out/to leave, enter or remain on an owner/occupier's premises without consent or lawful authority. Trespass is usually a general intent crime.

Discussion Questions

1. "Appellant was charged in a three-count amended information with: (1) forgery, (2) uttering a forgery, and (3) petit theft based upon a counterfeit check that had been tendered to a grocery store. . . . At trial, the grocery store clerk, Heather Sauls, testified that she remembered cashing three payroll checks for three . . . males from a 'McKinsley Construction' company, which turned out to be non-existent. One of the checks named the payee as 'Kurt Watkins.' According to

Sauls, she matched the man who tendered the 'Kurt Watkins' check with the photograph on his Florida identification card. All three checks were subsequently dishonored by Columbia County Bank and returned. . . . The State's final witness, the investigating officer, testified that he did not know . . . who actually counterfeited the check. The State then rested its case and appellant moved for judgment of acquittal."

How should the trial court rule on the motion as to the forgery and uttering charges?

Watkins v. State, 826 So. 2d 471 (2002)

2. "The proof at trial showed that on July 23, 1998, the Defendant telephoned Senator Fred Thompson's office in Blountville, Tennessee, and he spoke with Kathy Tipton, a case worker . . . regarding a grievance the Defendant had with the Department of Justice. The Defendant informed Ms. Tipton that he had been a postal worker in Colorado and that he was a whistle blower. . . . Ms. Tipton informed the Defendant that she would need him to sign a release so that she could get information about his letter from the federal agency. The Defendant responded that 'if he wrote anything else, he'd go to the commode and throw up. He was tired of letter writing.' The conversation took several turns, with the Defendant at times becoming 'intimidating' and telling Ms. Tipton that he did not care about her rules, regulations or procedures. . . . After she ended the telephone conversation with the Defendant, Ms. Tipton contacted Lieutenant Doug Brewer of the Tri-Cities Airport Public Safety Department [where Senator Thompson's office was located] because she was afraid the Defendant might show up at her office. . . . Ms. Tipton told Lt. Brewer that she was afraid of the Defendant and that she did not want to meet with him. As a result, Lt. Brewer waited with Ms. Tipton in her office to see if the Defendant would arrive. About 2:30 that afternoon, Ms. Tipton saw the Defendant coming down the escalator. Lt. Brewer left the office to intercept the Defendant, and Ms. Tipton locked the door. Lt. Brewer, who was dressed in a police uniform, approached the Defendant and asked him to identify himself, which he did. The Defendant was carrying a manilla envelope packet, and he told Lt. Brewer that he wanted to deliver the packet to Ms. Tipton. Lt. Brewer testified that he told the Defendant that Ms. Tipton did not want to meet him and that she was afraid of him, and he offered the Defendant two alternatives to meeting with Ms. Tipton. He said that he told the Defendant he would deliver the packet to Ms. Tipton and let the Defendant watch through the glass window, or the Defendant could mail the packet to Ms. Tipton. The Defendant refused to accept either option; he told Lt. Brewer that he wanted to exercise his constitutional right to speak to his representative. Lt. Brewer said that he informed the Defendant that a personal meeting 'was not going to happen because she was

afraid.' When the Defendant continued to assert his desire to meet Ms. Tipton, Lt. Brewer asked the Defendant to leave. Lt. Brewer testified that the Defendant then told him, 'I was violating his civil rights, [and] that he would have me arrested.' Lt. Brewer again asked the Defendant to leave, and the Defendant refused. At this point, Lt. Brewer arrested the Defendant. Lt. Brewer said that the Defendant made no attempt to leave prior to being arrested, and he did not believe that the Defendant had any intentions of leaving without personally delivering the packet to Ms. Tipton." Was the evidence sufficient to sustain the conviction?

State v. Byrd, E2000-00118-CCA-R3-CD, Tennessee Court of Criminal Appeals (2000)

3. The indictment alleged that "Drew Feldpausch . . . while in the course of committing theft of property and with intent to obtain or maintain control of said property, intentionally, knowingly, or recklessly caused bodily injury to [the complainant] by striking at [the complainant] with defendant's hand causing [the complainant] to fall to the ground. . . ." The victim, a pizza delivery man, testified that instead of paying for the $50 worth of food that had been ordered, Feldpausch swung at him with a closed fist. The delivery man ducked, but Feldpausch's fist grazed the top of the delivery man's head and he fell to the ground on the concrete parking lot, hurting his hand in the process of breaking his fall. His contact with the concrete left a two- to three-inch scratch on the palm of his right hand. On cross-examination, the complainant insisted that he reported the injury to the sheriff's deputy, who responded immediately after the offense.

Detective Ron Stubblefield, who took the victim's statement some seven weeks after the crime, did not mention the hand injury in his report. Stubblefield testified that the victim did relate having fallen down on the concrete.

Testifying on his own behalf, Feldpausch admitted that he took the two two-liter bottles of soda, then grabbed the three pizzas and ran away, but denied that he swung at the pizza delivery man before taking the merchandise and that the complainant had fallen down. The prosecution offered no additional evidence that would corroborate the victim's injury claim. Has the state produced sufficient evidence to support a robbery conviction?

Feldpausch v. State, NO. 09-02-299 CR, Texas Court of Appeals (2003)

4. Attorney William J. Wilkinson's client, David Oisten, was being prosecuted for receiving and concealing stolen property. Wilkinson allegedly tried to coerce Robert Lombardini into anonymously making financial contributions for the purpose of helping Oisten meet his restitution obligations.

The Michigan Extortion statute, MCL 750.213, provides:

> Any person who shall, either orally or by a written or printed communication, maliciously threaten to accuse another of any crime or offense, or shall orally or by any written or printed communication maliciously threaten any injury to the person or property or mother, father, husband, wife, or child of another with intent thereby to extort money or any pecuniary advantage whatever, or with intent to compel the person so threatened to do or refrain from doing any act against his will, shall be guilty of a felony, punishable by imprisonment in the state prison not more than twenty years or by a fine of not more than ten thousand (10,000) dollars.

"The evidence indicated that in defendant's telephone conversation with [Attorney] Tobias on May 23, 1996, defendant told Tobias that if Lombardini did not reimburse the insurance company, Oisten would inform the authorities of Lombardini's involvement in criminal fraud against the insurance company, but that if Lombardini paid the restitution amount, Oisten would keep quiet about Lombardini's activities." Is the above evidence, if believed by the factfinder, sufficient to sustain an extortion conviction?

People v. Wilkinson, No. 232695, Michigan Court of Appeals (2003)

NOTES

1. W. L. Clark, *A Treatise on the Law of Crimes*, 5th ed. (Chicago: Callaghan, 1952), 408-411.
2. Ibid 408-411.
3. Ibid 421-423.
4. In states that do not use grand juries, the prosecutor charges a person with a felony in a written document called an "information."
5. U.S. Congressional Research Service. *Identity Theft: Trends and Issues* (R40599; May 27, 2009), by Kristin M Finklea. This report is available online by searching the title.
6. A summary of every state's identity theft statutes can be found online at the National Conference of State Legislatures website: www.ncsl.org.
7. *State v. Rembert*, No. 79297, Ohio Court of Appeals (2001).
8. *State v. LaFrance*, 569 A.2d 1308 (1990). A New Jersey robber who created a bulge inside his jacket so that he looked as if he possessed a gun was properly found guilty of armed robbery.
9. 467 U.S. 16 (1986).
10. *Johnson v. Commonwealth*, 163 S.E.2d 687 (1968).
11. *State v. Hutson*, 526 A.2d 687 (1987).
12. *United States v. Charles G. Stephens, Sr.*, No. 91-4472, U.S. Court of Appeals for the Fifth Circuit, June 19, 1992.

Inchoate Crimes and Derivative Crime

CHAPTER OUTLINE

The crimes of solicitation, attempt, and conspiracy are classified as inchoate offenses. The term inchoate refers to the fact that each inchoate offense is a prelude to some other offense. For example, someone who commands, encourages, or requests someone else to assist in committing arson could be prosecuted for solicitation. And a person who decides at the last minute not to go through with a bank robbery because he notices that the intended getaway car parked at the curb outside the bank has a flat tire could be prosecuted for attempted robbery. Finally, if two or more individuals agree to traffic in narcotics, they may be subject to prosecution for conspiracy.

For conviction of an inchoate offense, it is not necessary that the **target crime** be completed (i.e., the *arson* in the solicitation example, the *robbery* in the attempt example, and *trafficking in narcotics* in the conspiracy example). Solicitation, attempt, and conspiracy are usually defined by statute and are classified as felonies.

Because of statutes criminalizing activities that occur prior to the completion of the offenders' ultimate criminal objective, authorities can intervene during the planning stages of an offense. Thus, asking another to help commit a criminal offense can constitute solicitation, agreeing with another can amount to a conspiracy, and taking a substantial preparatory step tending towards the commission of a crime can result in being prosecuted for attempt. See Table 8.1.

TABLE 8.1	*ACTUS REUS* TIMELINE
Solicitation	Urging, persuading, or instigating another to commit a crime
Conspiracy	Agreement or agreement & overt act leading toward completion of target crime
Attempt	**Substantial act leading toward completion of target crime**
Crime Perpetrated	Completed criminal act

 # Solicitation

Solicitation laws are designed to allow society to prosecute persons who instigate others to commit criminal offenses. The solicitation may be made through any form of communication.

There are two basic forms of solicitation statutes. William Jensen, the defendant in the next case, for example, was prosecuted under Washington's general criminal solicitation statute (see Figure 8.1).

Figure 8.1. Washington Solicitation Statute RCW 9A.28.030(1)

> A person is guilty of criminal solicitation when, with intent to promote or facilitate the commission of a crime, he offers to give or gives money or other thing of value to another to engage in specific conduct which would constitute such crime or which would establish complicity of such other person in its commission or attempted commission had such crime been attempted or committed.

This Washington statute prohibits commanding, imploring, or trying to persuade another person to commit a felony. But states often supplement their general criminal solicitation statutes with other laws that target particular acts of solicitation as shown in the Virginia statute in Figure 8.2.

Figure 8.2. Virginia Code 63.1-220.4: Solicitation in Connection with a Placement or Adoption

> [N]o person or child-placing agency shall charge, pay, give, or agree to give or accept any money, property, service or other thing of value in connection with a placement or adoption or any act undertaken pursuant to this chapter. . . . No person shall advertise or solicit to perform any activity prohibited by this section. Any person violating the provisions of this section shall be guilty of a Class 6 felony.

Actus Reus

Solicitation statutes make it a crime for one person to urge, persuade, or instigate another to commit a crime. (Many jurisdictions require that the solicited offense be a serious felony such as rape, robbery, arson, or murder.) The criminal act is completed when the solicitation is made. Jurisdictions differ as to whether it makes a difference if the person being solicited receives the communication or not. Although many jurisdictions view receiving the solicitation as irrelevant, some jurisdictions treat solicitations that are made but not received as *attempts*. It is generally irrelevant whether the solicited person acts on the request or ignores it.

Mens Rea

The usual *mens rea* requirement is that the accused solicitor must intend that the person solicited become a principal in the commission of a targeted substantive offense. Thus, the prosecution would have to prove that the accused, at the time the solicitation was made, specifically intended that the person or group of persons solicited commit a crime.

STATE OF WASHINGTON v. WILLIAM F. JENSEN

195 P.3d 512
Supreme Court of Washington, En Banc
November 6, 2008

AUTHOR'S INTRODUCTION

William Jensen, while jailed for threatening his wife's life, asked a fellow inmate who was about to be released, named Carpenter, to kill four people (Jensen's wife, minor son, adult daughter, and sister-in-law) in exchange for money. Carpenter agreed to kill the adult females but refused to kill the son because he was still a child. Jensen arranged for Carpenter to be paid earnest money. Upon release, Carpenter quickly spent the earnest money on drugs and alcohol and ended up back in jail. He then told police about his "agreement" with Jensen. The police arranged for an undercover female detective to pretend to be a co-conspirator with Carpenter in the commission of the crimes. The detective twice visited Jensen in jail while pretending to be Carpenter's sister, "Lisa." During the second visit Jensen offered the detective money to arrange for the killing of Jensen's son.

Jensen was charged and convicted by a jury of four counts of solicitation to commit murder and was sentenced to consecutive terms, which added up to 60 years in prison. Jensen subsequently appealed his convictions to the Washington Supreme Court, contending that three of the convictions should be reversed.

EXCERPT FROM THE CASE

MADSEN, J.

This case concerns the unit of prosecution for solicitation to commit murder. While in jail for threatening his wife, William Jensen solicited a fellow inmate to murder four members of his family. He repeated the solicitation to the inmate's purported crime partner and offered an additional sum of money to kill the youngest victim. A jury convicted Jensen of four counts of solicitation of first degree murder, one for each target victim. Jensen contends three of the convictions must be vacated under this court's recent decision. . . .

The double jeopardy clause protects a person from being convicted more than once under the same statute for committing a single "unit of prosecution." . . . To determine the unit of prosecution, this court first looks to the statute. . . . If the statute does not plainly define the unit of prosecution, we examine the legislative history to discern legislative intent. . . . Unless the legislature clearly and unambiguously intends to turn a single transaction into multiple offenses, the rule of lenity requires a court to resolve ambiguity in favor of one offense. . . . The remedy for a double jeopardy violation is to vacate any multiplicious convictions. . . .

In [*State v.*] *Varnell*, we analyzed the unit of prosecution for solicitation to determine whether a single conversation in which the defendant solicited the commission of four murders supported multiple convictions. . . . The defendant in that case had offered an employee $50,000 to kill his ex-wife. The employee refused and contacted the police. The police arranged for Varnell to meet an undercover officer posing as a hit man. During a single recorded conversation, Varnell asked the detective to kill four people, including his ex-wife, her parents, and her brother. He offered $100 as a down payment. The State charged him with five counts of solicitation to commit murder: one based on the conversation with the employee and four based on the conversation with the detective.

In determining the unit of prosecution, this court analogized the crime of solicitation to the crime of conspiracy. . . . Whereas the conspiracy statute punishes the act of agreeing to undertake a criminal scheme, the solicitation statute punishes the act of engaging another to commit a crime. Both are inchoate crimes that target preparatory conduct without regard to whether the contemplated crime actually occurs.

In *Varnell*, we held that just as a single agreement to violate multiple statutes is a single unit of prosecution for conspiracy, a single enticement to violate multiple statutes is a single offense under the solicitation statute. The evil the solicitation statute criminalizes is the enticement to commit a criminal act; "[t]he number of victims is secondary to the statutory aim." . . . The number of victims may be important, however, as evidence of the number of incitements. . . . In 1975, our legislature joined other jurisdictions in adopting a solicitation statute based on the Model Penal Code. The justification for penalizing solicitation is that the solicitor's conduct and state of mind is no less blameworthy than a conspirator's. Both crimes involve an effort to engage another person in joint criminal activity, with the specific intent to commit a crime, which gives rise to accomplice liability for any act attempted or actualized at the actor's request. Both present a special danger associated with group criminal activity. . . .

Solicitation is properly analyzed as an "attempt to conspire." . . . Whereas the actus reus of conspiracy is an *agreement* with another to commit a specific completed offense, that of solicitation is an *attempt* to persuade another to commit a specific offense. Viewed as attempted conspiracy, it would be anomalous to punish solicitation more severely than conspiracy. Imposing *greater* punishment based on the fortuity of the solicitant's response would "shock the common sense of justice" no less than imposing none.

Under the Model Penal Code, when the inchoate crime encompasses multiple criminal objectives, it should be punished more severely only to the extent punishment is fixed according to the grade of the most serious crime contemplated. Regarding the crime of conspiracy, the drafters' reason: "A rule treating the agreement as several crimes, equivalent in number and grade to the substantive crimes contemplated, might be unduly harsh in cases, uncommon though they may be, in which the conspirators are apprehended in the very early stages of preparation. The grandiose nature of the scheme might be more indicative of braggadocio or foolhardiness than of the conspirators' actual abilities, propensities, and dangerousness as criminals." . . .

This rationale applies as well to the crime of solicitation, which is the most inchoate of the three anticipatory offenses. In the crime of solicitation, criminal liability may attach to words alone. Solicitation involves no more than asking someone to commit a crime in exchange for something of value. Unlike conspiracy and attempt, it requires no overt act other than the offer itself. The risk of imposing an unduly harsh punishment is greater than in the crime of conspiracy because in the case of solicitation no steps to complete the potential crime are taken. If the solicitant agrees, the solicitor incurs criminal liability for conspiracy, and if the solicitant attempts to commit or accomplishes the crime, the solicitor is liable as an accomplice.

The State asks us to abandon our analysis in *Varnell* and adopt a "victim-centered" unit of prosecution analysis. In the State's view, we should overrule *Varnell* to the extent it holds the number of target victims is not the measure of the unit of prosecution for solicitation to commit murder. . . .

According to the State, *Varnell* leads to the "incongruous result" that four telephone calls to solicit four people to commit one murder will support four separate convictions, while a single telephone call to solicit four murders will support only one conviction "notwithstanding the far greater harm that will follow if the solicitation is accepted and carried out." . . .

The State conflates the harm resulting from the enticement with the harm that would result if the contemplated crimes were realized. As discussed above, solicitation is an inchoate crime that is separate and distinct from the target offense. . . . The purpose of criminalizing solicitation is not to deter a person from committing the contemplated crime: that purpose is served by the penalties fixed for the contemplated crime. Rather, the solicitation statute aims to deter a person from enticing another person to commit a crime. . . .

By offering something of value to another person to commit a crime, a solicitor supplies a motive that otherwise would not exist, thereby increasing the risk the greater harm will occur. The harm of solicitation is fully realized when the solicitor offers something of value to another person with the intent to promote or facilitate a target crime or crimes. If the greater harm of an attempted or completed crime occurs, the solicitor will be criminally liable for that greater harm under the principles of accomplice liability and will be punished accordingly. . . .

In view of the harm the solicitation statute punishes, it is not incongruous to punish more severely a person who entices four people in four separate conversations to commit a single murder than one who entices one person to commit four murders in a single transaction. Four separate enticements produce more of the harm the solicitation statute aims to prevent. Separate enticements are more blameworthy because they increase the risk a completed crime will occur by exposing several people rather than one to the corrupting influence of the enticement.

The State poses another purportedly anomalous result. The State hypothesizes a solicitation to murder one person and knee-cap another. According to the State, because the punishment for solicitation, like attempt, is tied to the nature of the underlying crime, such a person necessarily would be liable for two counts of solicitation; one for murder and one for assault, whereas a person who solicits two murders would be liable for only one. On the contrary, the State's hypothetical solicitor would be liable for a single solicitation, with the punishment fixed according to the greater offense. Anticipatory offenses are punished according to "the most serious offense which is attempted or solicited or is an object of the conspiracy." . . .

We reaffirm our holding in *Varnell* that the unit of prosecution for solicitation centers on the enticement, not the number of victims. . . .

It is clear from the record the solicitation of Carpenter was a "package deal" involving three victims. As in *Varnell*, the killings were to occur at approximately the same time and place, in the same manner, and based on a single overarching motive. It was understood the criminal objective would fail unless all the killings took place. Jensen's jailhouse solicitation of Carpenter involved a single enticement, supporting a single conviction, although it encompassed three potential victims. . . .

Like the conspiracy statute, the solicitation statute punishes a course of conduct, not a single act. . . . The prohibited course of conduct is attempting to engage another person to participate in a specific crime. This is an "inherently continuous offense." . . . The crime continues so long as the offer remains open, exposing another person to the corrupting influence of the enticement.

Unlike conspiracy, however, a new or separate and distinct request may constitute a fresh enticement that supports a separate conviction. . . . Thus, in *Varnell*, this court concluded the facts supported two convictions where the defendant solicited an undercover detective after his employee rejected a similar offer. The solicitation of the undercover detective was "separate and distinct" from the solicitation of the employee because it constituted a fresh enticement after the first attempt failed. . . .

We reaffirm our holding in *Varnell* that the unit of prosecution for solicitation centers on the enticement, regardless of the number of crimes or objects of the solicitation. The unit of prosecution does not multiply with the mere addition of purported crime partners. However, a separate unit of prosecution arises when the facts support the conclusion the defendant enticed a different person, at a different time and place, to commit a distinct crime.

We hold that the facts of this case support two convictions of solicitation to commit murder. The jailhouse conversations with Carpenter constitute a single solicitation that continued through the conversations with the undercover detective. The second conversation with the undercover detective supports a separate conviction because it constitutes a fresh enticement to solicit the murder of Jensen's son. We reverse and remand for vacation of two convictions and for resentencing.

CASE QUESTIONS

1. How did the prosecution establish the *actus reus* for solicitation in this case?

2. What was the appellant's argument on appeal?

3. What did the court conclude and why?

AUTHOR'S COMMENTARY

Carpenter, after agreeing to commit three murders for Jensen and accepting the payment of the earnest money, was subject to prosecution as a co-conspirator to murder.[1] However, Carpenter's decision to tell the police about Jensen's criminal intentions was timely and permitted authorities to prevent the commission of the intended crimes. His voluntary act was not a convenient switch of allegiance because the police "were knocking on his door." Carpenter's intention to abandon his criminal involvement with Jensen was clearly demonstrated and constituted an "abandonment" of criminal intent. This relieved Carpenter of criminal liability as a co-conspirator. **Abandonment** is a well-recognized defense in solicitation, attempt, and conspiracy prosecutions.

Attempt

A person whose intentional conduct goes beyond the preparation stage but does not actually lead to the commission of an intended substantive crime can be prosecuted for the crime of **attempt** (see Figure 8.3).

Figure 8.3. Oregon Attempt Statute

> **161.405 Attempt described.** (1) A person is guilty of an attempt to commit a crime when the person intentionally engages in conduct which constitutes a substantial step toward commission of the crime.

Actus Reus

For the crime of attempt, the offender must have engaged in one or more acts beyond the planning and preparatory stages that is a *substantial step* leading to the perpetration of the target offense.[2] Proof that an accused was figuring out the "who, what, when, where, and how" of committing a future offense or had begun collecting materials and equipment needed to perpetrate a crime is legally insufficient to sustain an attempt conviction. But persons preparing to commit a target crime may be in violation of other statutes that criminalize the possession of specified tools, weapons, and substances—such as burglar's tools, bomb-making components in luggage at airports, materials to be used in the manufacture of controlled substances, or machine guns—and the carrying of concealed weapons.

Thus, in every attempt case, the proof must show that the accused had proceeded far enough down the theoretical continuum leading from planning to perpetration to be held responsible for partially completing a target crime.

It is easiest to determine that conduct has gone far enough to warrant an attempt prosecution when the target crime is not perpetrated only because of some extraneous occurrence. For example, if A intends to kill B and shoots a revolver at B but misses, or if the weapon jams and doesn't fire, the crime is attempted murder (or in some jurisdictions, assault with intent to commit murder). Similarly, if A intends to set her house afire in order to fraudulently collect on an insurance policy but is apprehended at the scene trying to operate a defective butane lighter that is subsequently discovered to be incapable of producing a flame, she can be prosecuted for attempted arson. However, many cases are not so clear, as will become apparent in the following case.

UNITED STATES v. PEDRO HERNANDEZ-FRANCO

189 F.3d 1151
Ninth Circuit U.S. Court of Appeals
September 3, 1999

AUTHOR'S INTRODUCTION

Sheriff's deputies responded to a report from a local resident who had become suspicious of a semi-tractor-trailer and a sedan that had turned into the property of a neighbor, Evan Hewes, that night. Upon arrival, deputies discovered 47 individuals, later found to be undocumented aliens, hiding in the truck, in the sedan, in the house, and elsewhere on the property. Pedro Hernandez-Franco admitted to having driven the truck to that location. The government introduced testimony from several of the aliens. They testified that they were apprehended while in the process of being loaded into the truck and sedan, which were to take them to Los Angeles. Hernandez-Franco was indicted and convicted by a jury of five counts of attempting to transport the aliens, a violation of Title 21, Section 1324(a)(l)(A)(ii) of the United States Code.

EXCERPT FROM THE CASE

Judge HALL:

Pedro Hernandez-Franco appeals his . . . conviction and sentence for attempt to transport undocumented aliens. . . .

I

. . . Appellant . . . testified [at trial] in his own defense. He stated that on the night of January 10, 1998, he had gone in his truck to Milan Street Cooling in Brawley, California, to pick up a load of lettuce. He did not pick up the lettuce, however, because some of the tires on his truck needed air. As a result, he went to a Texaco station to check his tires and to get some gas. A clerk at the station, Felipe Vargas, testified that he had seen appellant at the gas station at approximately 10:30 P.M. on January 10, 1998.

After appellant got back into his truck, he testified that he started to pull out of the station when a man in the back of the truck's cabin suddenly appeared and put a gun to his head, directing him to follow a grey car that was in front of him. Appellant followed the car to the Evan Hewes house, where he was instructed to get out of the truck and lie face down on the ground. Appellant testified that he had no idea why he was at the house, and although he saw many people around, he did not know that they were illegal aliens. When sheriff's deputies arrived at the house, everyone began to run off, and the man holding appellant at gunpoint allegedly escaped after pushing appellant into the water of the cistern area.

Appellant testified that he told sheriff's deputies immediately after they detained him that he was the driver of the truck and that he had been forced at gunpoint to drive the truck to the house. This testimony was in apparent conflict with the testimony of Reserve Deputy Michaud, who testified that the three people he had arrested at the cistern were quiet and did not ask him for any help. According to Deputy Edward DeMorst, it was not until DeMorst asked the three individuals who had brought the truck that appellant responded that he had brought the truck, explaining after a brief pause that he had been forced to bring the truck to the Evan Hewes residence at gunpoint.

The jury rejected appellant's testimony, convicting him of all five counts in the indictment. . . .

II

Appellant first argues that the district court erred in denying his motion for acquittal . . . 8 U.S.C. § 1324(a)(1)(A)(ii) "requires that the defendant knew that the alien was illegal and intended to further the alien's illegal presence in the United States." ... In general, "[a]n attempt conviction requires evidence that the defendant intended to violate the statute, and that he took a substantial step toward completing the violation." ... Here, appellant alleges that the government has failed to present sufficient evidence of both requirements.

A

Appellant first contends that there is insufficient evidence that he intended to transport undocumented aliens in violation of section 1324. We disagree. ...

Here, appellant does not contest that he has a commercial trucking license and that he drove his truck to the Evan Hewes residence at night. At that house were at least forty-seven undocumented aliens waiting to be transported north. At the time sheriff's deputies arrived, twelve undocumented aliens had already been loaded into the truck's trailer and were hiding in produce containers. [One alien's] testimony, viewed in the light most favorable to the government, also indicated that a person matching appellant's description was seen at the door in the back of the truck, watching the aliens being loaded. Finally, testimony was introduced at trial that appellant had previously requested to have the night off from his employer.

Although appellant put forward a different version of events, the jury was not required to credit it. ... The fact that no witnesses could identify appellant as having been at the scene is of no moment because appellant did not contest that he had actually been at the Evan Hewes residence while the aliens had been boarding his truck. The jury was entitled to infer from these facts that appellant possessed the requisite intent to violate section 1324.

This situation is not similar to that in *United States v. Buffington*, ... (1987). In *Buffington*, we found that there was insufficient evidence that the defendants had intended to rob a particular bank. The defendants were in the parking lot of a mall that included the bank, and they had engaged in pre-robbery activities, such as wearing disguises and observing the area. But there was insufficient evidence to sustain a finding of intent to rob the bank because "[n]o defendant came within 50 yards of the bank," and "[t]he evidence [was] focused no more on [the bank in question] than on other nearby institutions." ... Here, appellant and his truck were at a house containing forty-seven undocumented aliens, with twelve of them already on the truck. There can be no doubt that the focus or location of the intended crime was certain, and *Buffington* is therefore distinguishable from the case at hand.

B

Appellant next argues that there is insufficient evidence that he had taken a substantial step in transporting the aliens.

Evidence of mere preparation will not support an attempt conviction, rather, there must be proof that appellant has taken "[a] substantial step ... strongly corroborative of the firmness of a defendant's criminal intent." . . . "[T]here must be some appreciable fragment of the crime committed, it must be in such progress that it will be consummated unless interrupted by circumstances independent of the will of the attempter." . . .

Appellant drove his truck to the Evan Hewes address late at night, and twelve undocumented aliens had boarded it by the time sheriff's deputies arrived. In addition, there is evidence that appellant was at the trailer door as at least some of the aliens were boarding. If law enforcement officials had not arrived at the time they did, there is every reason to believe that the doors to the truck would have been shut and the truck would have been driven north. The fact that appellant drove his truck to the Evan Hewes address, and that aliens began boarding it, therefore constitutes an "appreciable fragment" of a section 1324 violation.

Appellant relies on several cases where the court reversed attempt convictions of defendants that had extensively planned their bank robbery crimes, but had failed to take a substantial step towards completing them. In *Buffington*, the court held that no substantial step had been taken because the defendants did not make a move to enter the bank, displayed no weapons, and did not indicate that they were about to enter the building . . . the defendant was sitting in his van with the motor running 200 feet from a bank, wearing a blonde wig. Because the facts did "not establish either actual movement toward the bank or actions that are analytically similar to such movement," the court found that there was insufficient proof that the defendant had taken a substantial step towards robbing the bank. . . . In *United States v. Harper*, . . . (1994), one of the defendants had created a "bill trap" in an automated teller machine that would summon service personnel to fix the machine, at which time the defendants would presumably have been able to overpower the repairman and steal the cash inside the machine. Police at the scene found the defendants sitting in a car in the bank parking lot with duct tape, a stun gun, ammunition, and latex gloves. Two loaded handguns were found nearby. . . . The court held that there was insufficient evidence to support the defendants' convictions for attempted bank robbery because at the time of the arrest, "[t]he robbery was in the future," and would not happen for up to ninety minutes after the bill trap was created. . . . The act of creating the bill trap was deemed "equivocal in itself," and did not demonstrate "a true commitment toward the robbery." . . .

In contrast to these cases, where it was unclear whether the bank would actually be robbed, the crime here was in the process of being completed. To extend the bank analogy, appellant had already entered the bank and was filling bags with money. At the very least, appellant had delivered a truck that others were filling with illegal aliens, and, the jury could infer, waiting for the truck to be full in order to leave. This conduct constitutes a substantial step corroborating appellant's intent to violate section 1324.

. . . Here, . . . the aliens were being loaded on appellant's truck. All that remained was for the truck to be full and appellant to drive away. A reasonable observer, viewing appellant's conduct in context, "could conclude beyond a reasonable doubt that it was undertaken in accordance with a design to violate the statute." ... The district court properly denied appellant's motion for an acquittal. ...

For the foregoing reasons, appellant's conviction and sentence are AFFIRMED. ...

CASE QUESTION

How did the prosecution establish the substantial step requirement in this case?

AUTHOR'S COMMENTARY

In some circumstances the determination as to whether conduct is preparatory or an attempt appears to be essentially subjective. The court of appeals in the *Hernandez-Franco* case referred to one of its prior decisions, *United States v. Harper*. *Harper* was a case in which the accused were apprehended by police while waiting in a bank parking lot with deadly weapons, duct tape, and latex gloves within 200 yards of a bank's automated teller machine. The suspects were apparently waiting to overpower repair persons whom they expected would be coming to repair the ATM that the accused had disabled, and they then intended to take the money from the machine. The Ninth Circuit Court of Appeals ruled that the substantial step requirement was not met in *Harper* because the accused had not made any movement toward the ATM prior to their apprehension, and it was premature to consider this an attempt given that the robbery would not likely occur for another 90 minutes.

Other courts might well interpret these facts differently. These defendants had brought deadly weapons, duct tape (which could be used to tie up the repair personnel), and latex gloves (which would prevent the leaving of fingerprints) from some other location to a bank's parking lot and were within 200 yards of a bank's disabled ATM machine. The defendants were lying in wait for the repair people to open up the ATM, an action that would facilitate their completion of the target crime. At the time of their apprehension by police they were waiting until the opportunity was right to make their move toward the bank. The problem of where conduct crosses the line from preparation to perpetration can, in particular applications, prove to be very difficult to determine and is an inherent problem of criminal attempt law.

Mens Rea

To be convicted of attempt in most jurisdictions, an offender must have specifically intended to commit the target offense. Thus, criminal attempt prosecutions cannot be based on general intent, recklessness, or strict liability.

STATE v. FRANK REED NORDLUND

202 WA 1325
Court of Appeals of Washington, Division Two
September 13, 2002

AUTHOR'S INTRODUCTION

Requiring proof of specific intent is important in attempt prosecutions because the target crime is not actually perpetrated. Without a perpetrated crime, there will inevitably be some degree of doubt about what would have happened had events not come to what the prosecution would argue was a premature conclusion. Would the suspect have continued and committed the target crime? By requiring that the prosecution produce evidence of conduct that is consistent with specific intent to commit the target crime, there is less danger of a wrongful conviction of a person who's criminal thoughts would not have been followed by criminal deeds.

EXCERPT FROM THE CASE

Judge HOUGHTON:
    . . . On September 28, 1998, J.W. was at a car wash in Tacoma around 1 P.M. She noticed a man approach her from another car wash stall. He had brown, wet hair that was combed back. He wore glasses, blue jeans, a blue checkered shirt, and brown shoes. She described him as five-foot-ten or eleven and "kind of stocky" looking. . . . The man asked J.W. if she had any change. She replied, "No," and started to walk away because the man was making her nervous. . . .
    The man then grabbed her neck, knocked the water hose from her hand, and forced her to the ground. J.W. unsuccessfully tried to kick herself free and ended up on her back with the attacker straddling her, pinning her arms to the ground. He then released one of her arms and pulled her dress up to her hips. He also unbuckled his belt.
    J.W. . . . started screaming. The attacker placed his hand over her mouth and told her to stop screaming. She bit his hand and continued to scream. The attacker then stood up and walked away.
    J.W.'s screams caught the attention of several passersby. Beverly Wilcoxson and her 15-year-old son, Russell, were driving by the car wash and heard J.W.'s screams. They looked in her direction. They saw a man straddling a woman on the

ground of the car wash stall. Beverly circled around through an alley adjacent to the car wash and entered it from the rear. Beverly then saw the same man who had just attacked the woman waving his arms and saying, "Somebody call the cops, there's a lady being attacked." . . . Beverly thought that it was "really strange" and "odd" that the attacker was seeking help for his victim. . . .

Beverly described the attacker as having stringy hair and a square face with a 5-o'clock shadow. He was wearing a blue and white checkered shirt, jeans, brown shoes, and tinted eyeglasses with rims that had dark plastic on top and gold on the bottom. She also noticed that his belt was undone. She was about 10 to 15 feet from the man. She tried to hit the man with her car, but he jumped over the fence and ran away.

Russell described the attacker as five-foot-two, between 200 and 220 pounds, dark complexion, and dark scruffy hair with sideburns. He was wearing sunglasses, blue jeans, and a plaid shirt. . . . [A]t trial, Beverly positively identified Nordlund as the attacker she saw at the car wash. . . .

Lori Martin lived in the apartment complex next to the car wash and was at home the afternoon of September 28. She was in her apartment when she heard someone screaming from the direction of the car wash. She looked out her window and saw people gathering around. She went outside and stood next to the fence that separated the car wash from the apartment complex. She learned that a woman had been attacked in the car wash. A man in the crowd started yelling, "Somebody call 911, this woman's been attacked." . . . The victim then screamed, "That's him, that's him." . . . The man who told people to call 911 looked around, then jumped over the fence and fled. The man was initially about 15 feet from Martin, but when he jumped over the fence, he landed approximately 2 feet from her before he ran away.

Martin later testified that she got a good look at the man and watched him for about 5 to 10 minutes. She described him as average height, "kind of husky, broad shouldered," having stringy and wet brown hair, and wearing boxy tinted eyeglasses with a dark frame. . . . [A]t trial, she positively identified Nordlund as J.W.'s attacker. . . .

The jury convicted Nordlund of attempted second degree rape as charged. Because he had a 1985 attempted second degree rape conviction, the trial court imposed a sentence of life imprisonment without the possibility of early release as a two-time persistent sex offender. . . . Nordlund appeals his conviction and life sentence. . . .

SUFFICIENCY OF THE EVIDENCE

Nordlund contends *pro* se that the State failed to present sufficient evidence at trial to prove the elements of intent and a substantial step in the attempted second degree rape charge. We review a challenge to the sufficiency of the evidence by viewing the evidence in the light most favorable to the State to determine whether any rational trier of fact could have found the elements of the crime beyond a reasonable doubt. . . .

The State charged Nordlund with attempted second degree rape. Rape in the second degree is committed when "under circumstances not constituting rape in the first degree, the person engages in sexual intercourse with another person: (a) By forcible compulsion." . . . The criminal attempt statute provides in part: "A person is guilty of an attempt to commit a crime if, with intent to commit a specific crime, he or she does any act which is a substantial step toward the commission of that crime." . . . Hence, the crime of attempt contains two elements: intent to commit the substantive crime and taking a substantial step in the commission of that crime. . . . There must be unity of intent and the overt act. . . .

To convict Nordlund of attempted second degree rape, the State had to prove beyond a reasonable doubt that Nordlund intended to engage in sexual intercourse with J.W. by forcible compulsion and took a substantial step in committing that crime. The record provides the requisite evidence. J.W. testified that after her attacker knocked her to the ground, he sat straddling her, and pinned her arms to her sides. Then he pulled her dress up to her hips with one hand and unbuckled his belt. Beverly also testified that when she first arrived at the car wash, she saw the attacker with his belt undone. Both witnesses positively identified Nordlund as the attacker. The event that the victim described in this case is a clear example of attempted rape. Substantial evidence supports the jury verdict. Affirmed.

CASE QUESTIONS

1. How might Nordlund have argued that these facts do not constitute the required *actus reus* for attempted rape?

2. Might Nordlund have argued that the facts are consistent with his having changed his mind about raping the victim? After all, he did walk away. Couldn't this be an abandonment?

AUTHOR'S COMMENTARY

Most federal and state courts have rejected **legal impossibility** as a defense in attempt cases. Assume, for example, that a hunter is illegally caught hunting outside the hunting season after having intentionally shot what turns out to be a stuffed "decoy" deer. The Vermont Supreme Court ruled in 1991 that the hunter's mistake regarding the "deer" will not prevent a prosecution for attempting to hunt out of season.[3] Similarly, a person trafficking in narcotics who mistakenly believes he possess a controlled substance that subsequently turns out after testing to be talcum powder will not be able to rely on his mistake as a defense in an attempt prosecution. The underlying rationale is the same in both examples. The criminal actor's intent was to perpetrate a criminal act, and the mistake as to what was actually possessed in no way lessened the danger posed by the actor to the public.

Conspiracy

The crime called conspiracy evolved in response to a traditionally based fear of group criminality. Criminal enterprises involving many co-conspirators can commit more sophisticated crimes and pose special threats to society. Such enterprises often commit "white collar" offenses and other crimes less likely to be investigated than the common variety of "street crimes" committed by sole practitioners.

Actus Reus

Conspiracy is generally defined as "a combination of two or more persons, by some concerted action, to accomplish some criminal or unlawful purpose, or to accomplish some purpose, not in itself criminal or unlawful, by criminal or unlawful means."[4]

In all criminal conspiracy prosecutions, the existence of an agreement can be proven with direct or circumstantial evidence, and proof of a formal agreement is not required (see Figure 8.4).

Figure 8.4. Oregon Conspiracy Statute 161.450

> (1) A person is guilty of criminal conspiracy if with the intent that conduct constituting a crime punishable as a felony or a Class A misdemeanor be performed, the person agrees with one or more persons to engage in or cause the performance of such conduct. . . .

Some statutes provide that at least one of the co-conspirators must have performed some act of commission (or a failure to act), which tends to advance the co-conspirator's criminal objectives (called the *overt act*). The North Dakota statute shown in Figure 8.5 is an example.

Figure 8.5. The North Dakota Conspiracy Statute 12.1-06-04(1)

> A person commits conspiracy if he agrees with one or more persons to engage in or cause conduct which, in fact, constitutes an offense or offenses, and any one or more of such persons does an overt act to effect an objective of the conspiracy. The agreement need not be explicit, but may be implicit in the fact of collaboration or existence of other circumstances.

Because the *actus reus* for conspiracy focuses primarily on proof of an agreement to perpetrate crime, there is less concern with showing that the defendant's acts were closely proximate to the **target crime**'s perpetration. This makes it possible for authorities to prosecute persons earlier than would be the case if they had to wait for an offender to take a "substantial step" leading to the perpetration of the target crime required for conviction of attempt (see Table 8.1 on page 382).

Mens Rea

The accused in a criminal conspiracy case can be properly convicted only if the proof demonstrates that the accused specifically intended to work together with other people and to commit the target crime. This means that the co-conspirators actually intended the level of wrongful intent required for conviction of the target offense (i.e., purposefully, knowingly, recklessly, or negligently). One does not become a co-conspirator merely by having knowledge that others have agreed to commit a crime or by being present when others form a conspiracy, because mere knowledge and presence are not indicative of agreement.

In federal conspiracy cases and in states that follow the **Pinkerton doctrine**, one member of a conspiracy can be held vicariously liable for the criminal acts committed by any other co-conspirator. This "joint liability for the acts of one" is permissible where the act taken by the co-conspirator helps to implement the conspiratorial objectives and where it can reasonably be said that the members of the conspiracy either did foresee or should have foreseen that the act committed was a possible outcome of their agreement. The U.S. Supreme Court approved the constitutionality of the *Pinkerton* doctrine in the 1946 case of *Pinkerton v. United States* (328 U.S. 640), and it is a staple of federal conspiracy prosecutions. Some states reject this doctrine for reasons similar to those set forth in Justice Rutledge's dissent in *Pinkerton*. Justice Rutledge agreed that the defendant brothers in that case, Walter and Daniel Pinkerton, were appropriately convicted of conspiracy. But, he maintained that the court should not have instructed the jury "without more than the proof of Daniel's criminal agreement with Walter and the latter's overt acts, which were also the substantive offenses charged, ... [that] they could find Daniel guilty of those substantive offenses. They did so." Justice Rutledge thought it wrong for Daniel to be held criminally liable for Walter's conduct where the evidence contained no proof that Daniel had any knowledge of Walter's actions nor proof that Daniel had personal culpability as a principle or an accessory. The majority of U.S. Supreme Court justices, however, agreed with the trial judge. The following case involves the use of the *Pinkerton* doctrine.

STATE v. JEROME LEGGETT
892 A.2d 1000
Appellate Court of Connecticut
March 21, 2006

AUTHOR'S INTRODUCTION

Jerome Legget, the defendant in this case, was accused of participating with James Arnold and Reginald Sledge in the armed robbery of a 7-11 convenience store. The prosecution's evidence showed that the three alleged co-conspirators met one morning and decided to rob a yet-to-be-determined convenience store later that same day. As part of their preparations they obtained a fake weapon, which they intended to use in the commission of the crime. They subsequently assembled that evening at Sledge's car and Sledge drove them around so that they could procure heroin and cocaine and so Arnold could obtain the clothes he intended to wear when committing the crime. The three subsequently mixed the drugs and injected themselves. At Arnold's suggestion, the group agreed to rob a 7-11 store.

Sledge drove the group in his car to the vicinity of the store. Two people were inside the store at the time of the robbery, the clerk, Salaou, and a customer, Zuerblis. Legget was the first of the alleged robbers to enter the store, followed by Arnold. Arnold pointed the fake gun at the clerk and demanded the money in the cash register. Arnold obtained the loot, and ordered the clerk and customer to get down on the floor. As this was occurring, Legget, after stealing cigarette cartons, exited the store, and returned to Sledge who was waiting nearby in the get-away car. Sledge abandoned Arnold, who was still in the store at this time, and drove off when he observed a police cruiser. Arnold remained in the store until he had completed robbing the customer of her money and jewelry. He was subsequently arrested by police where the get-away car had previously been parked.

EXCERPT FROM THE CASE

GRUENDEL, J.

The defendant, Jerome Leggett, appeals from the judgment of conviction, rendered after a jury trial, of two counts of robbery in the second degree . . . and one count of conspiracy to commit robbery in the second degree. . . . On appeal, the defendant claims that . . . there was insufficient evidence to convict him of . . . conspiracy to commit robbery, . . . robbery of the store clerk and . . . the trial court improperly instructed the jury on . . . *Pinkerton* . . . liability. . . .

. . . The defendant entered a . . . plea of not guilty to all counts. Following trial, the jury returned a verdict of guilty on all three counts. The court rendered judgment of conviction in accordance with the jury's verdict and . . . sentenced the defendant to an effective term of twenty years of incarceration, suspended after eight years, followed by five years of probation. This appeal followed. . . .

The defendant first claims that there was insufficient evidence for the jury to find him guilty of conspiracy to commit robbery in the second degree. . . . Specifically, the defendant argues that the state failed to show that he had the intent to agree to commit the robbery and that even if he had the intent to enter the store with Arnold, the state failed to show that he had the intent to use force or threatened force to carry out a larceny. . . .

The essential elements of the crime of conspiracy are well established. "To sustain a conviction . . . the state needs to prove beyond a reasonable doubt (1) that a defendant intended that conduct constituting a crime be performed, (2) that he agreed with one or more persons to engage in or cause the performance of such conduct and (3) that he or any one of those persons committed an overt act in pursuance of such conspiracy. . . . While the state must prove an agreement, the existence of a formal agreement between the conspirators need not be proved because [i]t is only in rare instances that conspiracy may be established by proof of an express agreement to unite to accomplish an unlawful purpose. . . . [T]he requisite agreement or confederation may be inferred from proof of the separate acts of the individuals accused as coconspirators and from the circumstances surrounding the commission of these acts." . . .

The defendant argues that there is insufficient evidence that he intended to agree to the conspiracy to commit robbery because he expressly disavowed his intent to participate in a robbery. He relies on Arnold's testimony that it was made clear that the defendant "only steals, he don't do robberies" and that "[h]e wasn't there to do the robbery, he was going out to steal cigarettes." "[W]e must defer to the jury's assessment of the credibility of the witnesses based on its firsthand observation of their conduct, demeanor and attitude." . . . The jury reasonably could have discredited Arnold's testimony of the defendant's intent to commit only larceny. "This court cannot substitute its own judgment for that of the jury if there is sufficient evidence to support the jury's verdict." . . .

The defendant further argues that the state failed to prove that he intended to agree with Sledge and Arnold to the conspiracy to commit robbery. . . . The defendant supports his assertion with citations to the record suggesting that he may not have been present for certain conversations between Sledge and Arnold pertaining to plans for the robbery. "A conviction of the crime of conspiracy can be based on circumstantial evidence, for conspiracies, by their very nature, are formed in secret and only rarely can be proved otherwise than by circumstantial evidence." *State v. Smith*, . . . 860 A.2d 801 (2004). Here, the jury was presented with sufficient evidence to find that the defendant agreed to the conspiracy to commit robbery. First, the defendant began the evening with either Arnold or Sledge; . . . who had previously agreed to commit a robbery that night and provided a facsimile weapon to further that purpose. Second, once all three men were present, Arnold asked if

Sledge would drive "*them* to go do a score," and Sledge agreed to drive "*them* somewhere to do something." . . . Third, the defendant was present when Arnold returned with the clothes to disguise his appearance and was also present for a conversation about where to carry out the robbery. Fourth, the defendant exited from the same car as Arnold and Sledge, entered the store immediately before Arnold, and waited until Arnold displayed the facsimile weapon to take the cigarettes. Fifth, the defendant returned to the same car, driven by Sledge, to which Arnold intended to return after the robbery. . . .

The jury's conclusion that the defendant intended to agree to the conspiracy is reasonable and logical in light of the evidence before it and the inferences that may be drawn therefrom. . . .

The defendant next argues that even if there was sufficient evidence to demonstrate that he intended to agree to the conspiracy, the evidence was insufficient to prove that he intended to commit a robbery because he did not intend to use or threaten the use of physical force. "To sustain a conviction for conspiracy to commit a particular offense, the prosecution must show not only that the conspirators intended to agree but also that they intended to commit the elements of the offense." . . . Robbery requires that a larceny be committed by the use or threatened use of immediate physical force. . . . "A person commits larceny when, with intent to deprive another of property or to appropriate the same to himself or a third person, he wrongfully takes, obtains or withholds such property from an owner. . . ." The defendant correctly concedes that the evidence "may support a finding that [he] had the intent to commit larceny." We therefore must look only to whether the defendant carried out the larceny through the use or threatened use of physical force . . . "[I]f the use of force occurs during the continuous sequence of events surrounding the taking or attempted taking, even though some time immediately before or after, it is considered to be in the course of the robbery or the attempted robbery within the meaning of the statute." . . . The record includes evidence that the defendant entered the store first but waited until Arnold threatened the use of force to take the cigarettes. From this evidence, the jury reasonably could have determined that the defendant had the intent to commit a larceny and did so through the use or threatened use of immediate force. . . .

After examining the evidence presented in the light most favorable to sustaining the verdict, we cannot say that the jury's inferences leading to the defendant's conviction on the count of conspiracy to commit robbery were illogical or unreasonable. . . .

The defendant next claims that the court deprived him of his right to a fair trial because it improperly instructed the jury on *Pinkerton* liability. . . .

We begin by setting forth the scope of *Pinkerton* liability, which our Supreme Court expressly adopted. . . . Under the *Pinkerton* doctrine, "a conspirator may be held liable for criminal offenses committed by a coconspirator that are within the scope of the conspiracy, are in furtherance of it, and are reasonably foreseeable as a necessary or natural consequence of the conspiracy. . . . The rationale for the principle is that, when the conspirator [has] played a necessary part in setting in motion a discrete course of criminal conduct, he should be held responsible, within appropriate limits, for the crimes committed as a natural and probable result of that course of conduct." . . .

. . . The defendant . . . argues that the *Pinkerton* instruction deprived him of his right to a fair trial because it allowed the jury to convict him of robbery without finding that he had the specific intent to commit the offense. *Pinkerton* allows the jury to impute to the defendant certain conduct by a coconspirator reasonably foreseeable as a natural consequence of the conspiracy. . . . Our Supreme Court has noted that it "fail[s] to see why a constitutional flaw appears when *Pinkerton* applies to the *intent* that accompanies that conduct. Both the intent and the conduct are essential elements of the crime and are subject to the principles of *In re Winship*, 397 U.S. 358 (1970), that due process requires the state to prove every element of the offense charged beyond a reasonable doubt." . . . We conclude that the *Pinkerton* instruction, therefore, properly instructed the jury as to the element of intent and that the defendant's due process rights were not violated. The defendant's claim, therefore, fails. . . .

The judgment is affirmed.

In this opinion the other judges concurred.

CASE QUESTIONS

1. Given that there was evidence introduced tending to establish guilt and suggesting that Jensen didn't engage in robbery, how did the Connecticut Court of Appeals explain its ruling to affirm the trial court?

2. The Pinkerton Doctrine allows for the imposition of greatly enhanced punishment on persons convicted of conspiracy. How would you balance the concept that criminal punishment should be administered to offenders based on the extent of the accused's personal culpability against the need to protect society from the enhanced harm caused by offenders who combine their efforts and commit crimes?

AUTHOR'S COMMENTARY

Although conspiracy statutes generally require proof of both an agreement among the co-conspirators and evidence of some act that tends to implement the purposes of the conspiracy, it is not an ironclad rule. The federal statute that makes it a crime to conspire to distribute and to possess controlled substances with intent to distribute, 21 U.S.C. Sec. 846, permits convictions based solely on proof that the defendants agreed to distribute controlled substances. No proof of any overt act tending to implement the conspiratorial objectives is required.

Prosecutors often charge defendants with conspiracy in addition to charging the accused with the target crime in order to increase the sentencing options after a defendant's conviction. This practice poses no constitutional problem, because conspiracy and complicity are constitutionally distinct offenses. Each offense contains an element not contained in the other. To prove a conspiracy, for example, the prosecution must prove the existence of an agreement, whereas in complicity cases, the defendant's participation in the perpetration of the offense must be proven. Some states prohibit prosecuting an accused for both an inchoate offense and the target crime.[5]

Internet Tip

United States v. Thomas J. McCarthy, 97 F.3d 1562 (1996) is a case based on 21 U.S.C. Sec. 846 and explains that in federal drug prosecutions the conspiracy statute does not contain any overt act requirement. Interested readers can find this case opinion online with Loislaw.

The Racketeer Influenced and Corrupt Organizations Act—A Derivative Crime

Congress enacted the **Racketeer Influenced and Corrupt Organizations Act (RICO)** in 1970. This statute is a powerful tool for use against racketeers and other organized criminal enterprises. Federal prosecutors use this law against criminal enterprises engaged in activities within the scope of the law if such acts even slightly affect interstate or foreign commerce. RICO's scope is quite broad and applies to legally operating business through which money derived illegally can be "laundered" (made to appear to have been derived legally) as well as to illegal enterprises, whether public or private. The law makes it illegal to receive money derived from "**racketeering activity**" or from the collection "of an unlawful debt" (such as money derived from gambling or from the collection of a debt which required the debtor to pay an illegally high rate of interest in violation of state or federal law). It also prohibits the use of racketeering money to acquire a financial stake or control over an enterprise that operates in or has an affect on interstate commerce. People who are employed directly or indirectly by racketeers, or who associate with a racketeer-controlled enterprise, and who conduct or participate in any aspect of such the enterprise's activities that operate in or affect interstate commerce, are also subject to RICO prosecutions.

The RICO statute requires that defendants in substantive RICO prosecutions have committed two or more of what it calls "predicate acts" within a ten-year period. It defines the predicate acts as encompassing conduct amounting to generic state crimes (such as murder, kidnapping, gambling, arson, robbery, bribery, extortion, and distributing controlled substances) as well as racketeering activities such as money laundering, loan sharking, extortion, and drug trafficking. Section 1962 (d) of the Act makes it illegal to conspire to violate any of the previously described provisions.

People convicted under RICO can be sued civilly and punished through the forfeiture of real and personal property acquired with money obtained through racketeering, fines, and up to 20 years' incarceration. Civil Penalties are also severe. The Act provides that "Any person injured in his business or property by reason of a violation of section 1962 of this chapter may sue therefor in any appropriate United States district court and shall recover threefold the damages he sustains and the cost of the suit, including a reasonable attorney's fee."

UNITED STATES v. ALLEN C. LAWSON

No. 04-4480
U.S. Court of Appeals, Sixth Circuit
October 9, 2008

AUTHOR'S INTRODUCTION

Allen Lawson, the defendant in the following RICO case, was a member of the Outlaw Motorcycle Club. Federal prosecutors accused Lawson of being a major drug dealer of marijuana and valium and of operating a drug distribution enterprise through which he and other members of the Outlaw Motorcycle Club resold marijuana and valium. Lawson was charged under the RICO Act with "substantive RICO," conspiracy to violate RICO, and with two non-RICO offenses for conspiring and distributing controlled substances.

EXCERPT FROM THE CASE

ROGERS, Circuit Judge.

This case is part of a consolidated appeal involving thirteen defendants who were members of the Outlaw Motorcycle Club ("OMC"), an international motorcycle club with chapters across the country and around the world. In 1997, the Federal Bureau of Investigation and state law enforcement agencies began an investigation into the Green region of the OMC, which consists of chapters in Dayton, Ohio; Fort Wayne, Indiana; Louisville, Kentucky; Indianapolis, Indiana; and Oklahoma City, Oklahoma. As a result of the investigation, a grand jury in the Northern District of Ohio returned a 40-count indictment in 2003 charging the defendants with various offenses, including Racketeer Influenced and Corrupt Organizations Act ("RICO"), drug trafficking, and firearms offenses. The defendants were tried before an anonymous jury.

Defendant Allen C. Lawson, a member of the OMC chapter in Dayton, Ohio, was charged with four offenses: (1) substantive RICO in violation of 18 U.S.C. § 1962(c); (2) RICO conspiracy in violation of 18 U.S.C. § 1962(d); (3) conspiracy to distribute controlled substances in violation of 21 U.S.C. § 846; and (4) distribution and possession with intent to distribute marijuana in violation of 21 U.S.C. § 841(a)(1). In support of the RICO charge, the indictment alleged four RICO predicate acts against Lawson: (1) conspiracy to distribute controlled substances; (2) distribution of marijuana; (3) distribution of valium; and (4) the 2001 murder of Eric Coulter at a Dayton, Ohio, strip club named Spanky's Dollhouse.

The jury found Lawson guilty of all four offenses with which he was charged. In a special verdict, the jury also concluded that Lawson had committed each of the four RICO predicate acts alleged in the indictment.... [T]he district court sentenced Lawson to 235 months in prison....

On appeal, Lawson argues that his convictions and sentence should be reversed ... because his convictions were not supported by sufficient evidence; and ... because the district court erroneously sentenced him under a mandatory Guidelines regime....

III.

Lawson was not entitled to a directed verdict on any of the charges of which he was convicted. This court reviews de novo the sufficiency of the evidence to sustain a conviction.... Evidence is sufficient to sustain a conviction if "after viewing the evidence in the light most favorable to the prosecution, and after giving the government the benefit of all inferences that could reasonably be drawn from the testimony, any rational trier of fact could find the elements of the crime beyond a reasonable doubt."... Evaluating the evidence according to this standard, it is clear that a rational jury could be convinced beyond a reasonable doubt of Lawson's guilt on each offense.

A.

A substantive RICO charge requires the Government to prove: (1) the existence of an enterprise which affects interstate or foreign commerce; (2) the defendant's association with the enterprise; (3) the defendant's participation in the conduct of the enterprise's affairs; and (4) that the participation was through a pattern of racketeering activity. . . . Only the third and fourth elements are at issue here, and both were sufficiently proven by the Government.

The third element is established here because the evidence is sufficient to convince a rational jury beyond a reasonable doubt that Lawson participated in the operation or management of the criminal enterprise. . . . The evidence indicates that one of the activities of the OMC criminal enterprise was the distribution of controlled substances. In fact, one can gather from the evidence that this was a prime source of funding for the OMC. The evidence also indicates that Lawson supplied large quantities of drugs to other OMC members with the knowledge that the members would resell the drugs at a profit. Viewed in the light most favorable to the Government, this evidence—coupled with Lawson's membership in the OMC—was enough for a rational trier of fact to infer that Lawson's drug dealing was an implementation of the OMC's decisions and policies concerning drug distribution. As explained in the companion case of *United States v. Fowler*, . . . (6th Cir. 2008), this is sufficient to satisfy the . . . "operation or management" test.

The evidence is also sufficient to allow a rational trier of fact to find the fourth element of the RICO offense—participation through a pattern of racketeering activity—beyond a reasonable doubt. A pattern of racketeering activity requires at least two predicate acts. *See* 18 U.S.C. § 1961(5). Four predicate acts were alleged against Lawson—Racketeering Act 1A (conspiracy to distribute controlled substances among OMC members), Racketeering Act 3 (distribution of marijuana), Racketeering Act 4 (distribution of valium), and Racketeering Act 25 (the murder of Eric Coulter). The jury found that Lawson committed all four predicate acts. Lawson, however, argues that there are too few predicate acts to support a RICO conviction because there is not sufficient evidence to prove that he committed Act 25, and because Acts 1A, 3, and 4 are really just one predicate act.

With respect to Act 25, Lawson appears to be correct; the evidence does not appear to permit a finding that he murdered Eric Coulter. It is undisputed that Glen Carlisle shot Coulter, and there is no evidence that Lawson aided Carlisle in any way, much less that he had the intent to do so. A member of a different motorcycle gang delivered the fatal shot, and there is no evidence that Lawson aided that act either. Thus, while Lawson admits that there is evidence that he assaulted Coulter, there is essentially no evidence to support a finding that he murdered Coulter. However, this makes no difference in the ultimate outcome because there is sufficient evidence to support the jury's findings on the other three predicate acts, which, contrary to Lawson's argument, are three distinct predicate acts. Lawson alleges that the drug conspiracy predicate act (1A) and the two drug distribution predicate acts must be merged into one predicate act because they were all part of the same conspiracy alleged in Racketeering Act 1A. This is not correct though. Conspiracy to commit a substantive crime and the substantive offense itself may count as separate predicate acts for RICO purposes. . . . Therefore, even without Racketeering Act 25, there are still enough predicate acts to sustain a RICO conviction.

The Government has also met the fourth element's additional requirement of satisfying the "continuity plus relationship" test by demonstrating a relationship between the predicate acts as well as a threat of continued activity. . . . Based on the extensive evidence of the OMC's participation in the drug trade, a rational jury could easily conclude that Racketeering Acts 1A, 3, and 4 were related to the activities of the enterprise. This is sufficient to satisfy the relatedness prong of the "continuity plus relationship" test. . . . The Government need not prove that the predicate acts were directly interrelated. . . . Instead, the predicate acts must "be connected to the affairs and operations of the criminal enterprise." . . . This can be established "by proof that: (1) the defendant was enabled to commit the offense solely by virtue of his position in the enterprise; or (2) the offense was related to the activities of the enterprise." . . .

Finally, there is no real question that the racketeering acts presented a threat of continued activity. The evidence is ample that "the predicates can be attributed to a defendant operating as part of a long-term association that exists for criminal purposes." . . .

In short, the evidence belies that Racketeering Acts 1A, 3, and 4 were sporadic, unrelated activities. There was sufficient evidence that they constituted a pattern of racketeering activity.

B.

Lawson argues that his RICO conspiracy conviction must be overturned because there is no evidence that he entered into an agreement to violate RICO. Although there is no direct evidence that Lawson entered into such an agreement, his RICO conspiracy conviction must be affirmed nonetheless because the agreement can be inferred from his acts. . . . The OMC was an organization that encouraged its members to engage in the drug trade. One can infer from the evidence that it facilitated such endeavors so that the profits could be used to finance the OMC's activities. Although there is no direct evidence that Lawson's drug profits went to the OMC, it was reasonable to infer that he joined the OMC drug-distribution ring and thereby agreed to violate RICO. Lawson contends that his drug dealing was not connected to the OMC and therefore is not evidence of an agreement to be part of the OMC drug-distribution ring. This argument is contradicted by evidence showing that he supplied drugs to fellow OMC members, and by the evidence that he did so with the knowledge that the drugs would be resold to the general public. Thus, one can infer that he had entered into an agreement with other OMC members to violate RICO by operating a drug ring. And because the evidence shows that Lawson committed three RICO predicate acts, a rational jury could infer that Lawson agreed that either he or someone else would commit at least two RICO predicate acts. This is sufficient for a RICO conspiracy conviction because it shows that he "intended to further 'an endeavor which, if completed, would satisfy all of the elements of a substantive [RICO] criminal offense. . . . '"

C.

Lawson's narcotics conspiracy conviction could be supported solely by James Dilts's testimony that Lawson had told Dilts that Lawson "had three other individuals selling valium for him . . . [and] made a profit of $1,200 a month from those three." The evidence of his guilt is all the more convincing when combined with the facts that Lawson was a member of an organization that distributed drugs—i.e., the OMC—and that he supplied drugs to other members of that organization with knowledge that the drugs would be broken down into smaller quantities and resold. All of this evidence allows for a finding of guilt beyond a reasonable doubt because it permits a rational jury to conclude that Lawson (1) had entered into an agreement with two or more persons to violate the drug laws, (2) had knowledge and intent to join in the conspiracy, and (3) participated in the conspiracy. . . .

IV.

Finally, Lawson's sentence must be vacated because of our conclusion that there is no evidence to support the jury's finding that he committed Racketeering Act 25—i.e., the murder of Eric Coulter. . . .

For the foregoing reasons, Lawson's convictions are affirmed, his sentence is vacated, and the case is remanded for resentencing.

CASE QUESTIONS

1. Why does the act require proof that the predicate acts have some affect on interstate commerce?

2. Prosecuting the predicate crimes relating to organized crime was the responsibility of the states until the passage of the RICO Act. Do you see any federalism issues associated with the federal government assuming a greater role in prosecuting cases of this type?

AUTHOR'S COMMENTARY

It is interesting to see how the prosecution constructed its case against Lawson. The government produced evidence at Lawson's trial that he was a member of the OMC, that he had committed murder, conspired to distribute controlled substances, distributed marijuana and valium to other members of the OMC who derived income from a racketeering enterprise, and participated and operated a racketeering enterprise as part of a larger conspiracy involving the OMC and the distribution of controlled substances.

Lawson successfully argued on appeal that his murder conviction should be overturned. He wasn't successful with his argument that the predicate acts involving the distribution of valium and marijuana should merge into the conspiracy predicate act. Lawson pointed out that identical evidence was used to prove both the single conspiracy predicate act and the two distribution predicate acts. He argued that for RICO purposes these acts should merge into a single predicate act.

But the Court of Appeals disagreed ruling that there was no merger. The substantive drug offenses were entirely distinct from the conspiracy offense. Congress, which was responding to public concern about organized crime in the country, intentionally made it less difficult for federal prosecutors to prove RICO conspiracy offenses. Congress provided that in RICO conspiracy cases the government would only have to prove the existence of an agreement. It did not require proof of the commission of an overt act in furtherance of the conspiracy, a normal evidentiary requirement in most federal non-RICO conspiracy cases not involving the distribution of controlled substances.

Thus, Lawson's argument failed in part because each offense contained a proof of an element not required by the other. The conspiracy predicate offense required proof of an agreement to distribute controlled substances. The substantive valium and marijuana predicate offenses required proof that controlled substances were distributed. If this sounds familiar, it relates back to the *Blockburger* test discussion in Chapter 3.

Internet Tip

U.S. Supreme Court Justice Kennedy wrote extensively about RICO conspiracy in the case of *Mario Salinas v. United States*, 522 U.S. 52 (1997). Interested readers will find it included in the Chapter 8 materials posted on the textbook's website.

Chapter Summary

The crimes studied in Chapter 8, like most of the other crimes studied, originated in England and were part of the common law. Solicitation, attempt, and conspiracy are unique in that they are anticipatory offenses. They criminalize conduct that occurs prior to the commission of some other substantive crime. For conviction of an inchoate offense, it is not necessary that the *target crime* be completed. Solicitation, attempt, and conspiracy are usually defined by statute and are classified as felonies. Because of inchoate crimes, police officers can intervene during the planning stages of an offense and if probable cause exists, make arrests and prevent the commission of future crimes.

Solicitation is committed by someone who commands, encourages, or requests another person to assist in committing a crime. Thus, words alone can constitute the *actus reus*. Prosecutors in a solicitation case prove that the accused specifically intended that the solicited person commit a designated substantive offense. Jurisdictions differ as to whether it is essential that the solicited person actually received the communication. The solicited individual's response is irrelevant. Some jurisdictions have general solicitation statutes while other states enact laws that limit solicitation prosecutions to serious felonies.

The crime of *attempt* requires proof of three elements. First, the solicitor must have possessed specific intent to commit a substantive crime. Second, the accused must have finished the planning phase and taken a substantial step tending towards the implementation of the plan—the commission of a specified criminal offense. Third, the intended substantive crime must not have been committed. For example, if the accused has decided to murder someone, has stalked his intended target, and fired a shot that misses its mark. Fortunately, nobody was killed. But the shooter possessed specific intent to kill the intended victim and took a substantial step toward the completion of the substantive crime. The accused constitutes a dangerous threat to society and can receive a substantial sentence of incarceration once convicted for attempted murder.

The common law crime of *conspiracy* was created in response to the public's well-founded fear of group criminality. Criminal organizations can commit more sophisticated crimes than sole practitioners. Such enterprises often commit "white collar" offenses and other crimes less likely to be investigated than the common variety of "street crimes" committed by sole practitioners. Conspiracy is generally defined as a combination of two or more persons, by some concerted action, to accomplish some criminal or unlawful purpose, or to accomplish some purpose, not in itself criminal or unlawful, by criminal or unlawful means. The existence of an agreement can be proven expressly or by implication from the circumstances of the case.

In federal conspiracy cases and in states that follow the *Pinkerton* doctrine, one member of a conspiracy can be held vicariously liable for the criminal acts committed by any other co-conspirator.

Lastly, readers were introduced to the Racketeer Influenced and Corrupt Organizations Act (RICO). This federal statute is a powerful tool which prosecutors use against organized criminal enterprises which affect interstate or foreign commerce.

Discussion Questions

1. A solicited B to assist him in robbing C. B was an undercover police officer pretending to be interested in committing a felony. The state conspiracy statute provides as follows: "If any two or more persons conspire or agree together to commit a felony . . . they shall be deemed guilty of a conspiracy." Does the fact that B did not actually intend to agree to commit a felony preclude the conviction of A for conspiracy to commit a felony?

2. A solicited B to assist him in robbing C. B pretended to be interested, even though he wasn't serious about participating in the crime. He subsequently contacted police and told them about the planned robbery. The next day, police arrested A and B at C's home, and the robbery was prevented. The state conspiracy statute provides as follows: "A person commits conspiracy when, with intent that an offense be committed, he agrees with another to the commission of that offense." Does the fact that B did not actually intend to agree to commit the robbery preclude the conviction of A for conspiracy to commit a robbery?

3. A and B are prosecuted for conspiracy in a single trial, and the evidence produced against each is the same. A is convicted and B is acquitted of the charges. Can the conviction of A stand?

Smith v. State, 297 S.E.2d 273 (1982)

4. A and B agree to break into the local appliance store and steal DVD players, and they successfully execute their plan. The police, with the assistance of surveillance cameras, are able to identify the perpetrators and arrest A and B. Can A and B be charged with conspiracy in addition to burglary and larceny?

NOTES

1. Under Washington law "a person is guilty of criminal conspiracy when, with intent that conduct constituting a crime be performed, her or she agrees with one or more persons to engage in or cause the performance of such conduct, and any one of them takes a substantial step in pursuance of such an agreement." RCW 9A.28.040(1).
2. This text has adopted the substantial step approach because it is the approach used by the federal judiciary and most, but not all, of the states. The jurisdictions that reject the substantial step approach focus on the defendant's acts in relation to what remained to be done in order to complete the commission of the target crime, or on the probability that the defendant's actions could be related to noncriminal behavior.
3. *State v. Curtis*, 603 A.2d 356 (1991).
4. *Commonwealth v. Hunt*, 45 Mass. 111 (1842).
5. *U.S. v. Thomas J. McCarthy*, 97 F.3d 1562 (1966), is a case based on 21 U.S.C. Sec. 846. Readers can find this case on the textbook's website.

Appendix A: Reading and Understanding the *Lopez* Case

Author's Tips on Reading and Understanding the *Lopez* Case

Self-immersion in a case is the best way for students new to briefing to study a case. The case that has been selected to illustrate this is *U.S. v. Lopez*. Students wishing to learn how to brief should read this commentary, study the case report online, and read the sample brief of the *Lopez* case (see below).

The following discussion of *U.S. v. Lopez* is intended to help students better understand some of the fundamentals that persons reading appellate case reports need to know. The heading of the case consists of four items. The first line contains the names of the parties to the suit. The United States of America, the party filing the criminal charges, was the plaintiff in the U.S. District Court (the trial court in the federal system). Alfonso Lopez, the accused, was the defendant. Lopez became an appellant when he appealed his district court conviction to the United States Court of Appeals for the Fifth Circuit. The United States, as the other party to the case, became an appellee. After the Fifth Circuit's decision in favor of Lopez was announced, the United States sought review of that decision by the U.S. Supreme Court. A party seeking review by the Supreme Court is required to petition for a writ of certiorari and is classified as the petitioner. The other party, in this case Lopez, is the respondent. The petition for certiorari will be granted if four or more justices believe that one or more issues raised in the case are important enough to warrant high court review.

The next item in the heading is the case number. Every case has a unique identifying number, in this instance 93-1260 which is assigned by the Clerk of the Supreme Court. Cases can be located either by case number or by the volume number, case reporter series, and page number where the case is published in printed form. The *Lopez* case is reported in volume 514 of the U.S. Reports, on page 549 (this citation is written 514 U.S. 549). The name of the court that decided the dispute is next in the heading (in this instance the U.S. Supreme Court), followed by the date the decision was announced. The first item in the body of the court opinion is the name of the judge or justice who wrote the court opinion. Usually only one judge is selected to write the majority opinion, even though several judges may have participated in reaching the decision.

In *Lopez*, the United States charged the defendant with carrying a concealed .38 caliber handgun and five bullets into the Edison High School in San Antonio, Texas, on March 10, 1992, an alleged violation of the federal statute that was enacted in 1990 as the Gun-Free School Zones Act. This statute was published in Title 18 of the United States Code in Section 922(q).

A federal grand jury reviewed evidence presented to it by a federal prosecutor and indicted Lopez on one count of violating the statute. The defense attorney moved to dismiss the indictment, arguing that the law was unconstitutional because it punished conduct that was beyond the scope of Congress' legislative power under Article I, Section 8, Clause 3 of the U.S. Constitution. The trial court (called the U.S. District Court) denied the motion. Lopez waived his right to a jury trial (under the Sixth and Fourteenth Amendments), and the district court tried the case without a jury (this is called a bench trial). The district court found the defendant guilty as charged and sentenced him to six months imprisonment followed by supervised release. Lopez appealed his conviction to the U.S. Court of Appeals for the Fifth Circuit, which reversed the district court. The Fifth Circuit concluded that Congress did not have constitutional authority under the Commerce Clause to enact the Gun-Free School Zones Act. The Supreme Court granted the government's petition for a writ of certiorari and agreed to review the Fifth Circuit's decision regarding Congress' legislative authority in this case. As a matter of law, a duly enacted statute, such as the Gun-Free School Zones Act, is presumed to be constitutional and Alfonso Lopez had the burden of proving that Congress had exceeded its constitutional authority. Although the federal courts have the power to declare Congressional acts unconstitutional, it is a power that is rarely exercised.

The issue before the Supreme Court was "Does Congress have constitutional authority under the Commerce Clause to enact a statute that prohibits the possession of a gun within a school zone?"

In order to reap the benefits of the case study method, students must carefully read each case and concentrate on the details. After reading a case, a student needs to have a precise understanding of what the court did. It is not enough for a student to have a general sense of what the case says. It is important to figure out the holding of the case—what the court decided on the facts of the case. Opinions are often discursive. Judges often discuss issues they need not decide. Their statements on these issues are labeled dicta. Although these statements may be important, they lack the authority of the case's holding.

Finding *United States v. Lopez* Online

Edited versions of the majority and dissenting opinions reported in the case of *United States v. Lopez* have been included in the Chapter 1 materials found on the textbook's website. The unedited opinions can be found online via Loislaw and other web sources. Simply search for the case by its name (U.S. v. Lopez) or citation (514 U.S. 549).

Tips on How to Brief a Case

Many students find it helpful to brief the cases they read because briefing requires careful reading and analysis of the decision and increases understanding of the material.

The following brief of the Lopez case illustrates one way of briefing. The elements in the example are usually found in most briefs, though writing style is often a matter of individual preference. It is usually desirable to keep copying from the text of the case to a minimum; briefs are not exercises in stenography. This brief was written to help students who have not previously read a case report. It is intended to help these students understand what is important in the material they have read.

Sample Brief
United States v. Alfonso Lopez, Jr.,
514 U.S. 549 (1995)

Facts:
The United States charged Lopez with carrying a concealed .38 caliber handgun and five bullets into the Edison High School in San Antonio, Texas, on March 10, 1992, an alleged violation of the federal statute that was enacted in 1990 as the Gun-Free School Zones Act.

Prior Proceedings:

The evidence in the case was presented before a federal grand jury which indicted Lopez on one count of violating the statute. The defense attorney moved to dismiss the indictment, arguing that the law was unconstitutional because it punished conduct that was beyond the scope of Congress' legislative power under Article I, Section 8, Clause 3 of the U.S. Constitution. The U.S. District Court denied the motion. Lopez received a bench trial and was found guilty as charged and sentenced to six months imprisonment followed by supervised release. Lopez appealed his conviction to the U.S. Court of Appeals for the Fifth Circuit. A panel of the Fifth Circuit initially reversed the district court but after en banc review, affirmed the district court. The Fifth Circuit concluded that Congress did not have constitutional authority under the Commerce Clause to enact the Gun-Free School Zones Act. The Supreme Court granted the government's petition for a writ of certiorari and agreed to review the Fifth Circuit's decision regarding Congress' legislative authority in this case.

Issue Presented:

Does Congress have constitutional authority to enact a statute that prohibits possession of a gun within a school zone?

Arguments or Objectives of the Parties:

Lopez argued that Congress had exceeded its constitutional authority when it enacted a statute prohibiting the possession of a gun within a school zone.

The government argued that Congress had developed "institutional expertise" when it came to regulating interstate commerce and that the judiciary should defer to the legislative body's judgment. The "costs of violent crime" also had an impact on interstate commerce, according to the government, because people who are afraid of violent crime will not do business in places that are reputed to be dangerous. The government's third argument was that the presence of guns in school zones would hinder the educational process and thereby negatively impact our "national economic productivity."

Disposition or Order by the Court:

The U.S. Supreme Court affirmed the decision of the Fifth Circuit U.S. Court of Appeals.

Holding/Rule of Law:

Criminalizing the possession of a firearm within a school zone is beyond the scope of Congress' legislative power under the Commerce Clause.

Rationale:

1. The statute does not fit within any of the three recognized categories where Congress has authority to regulate under the Commerce Clause:
   a. it does not regulate the channels of interstate commerce or "prohibit the transportation of a commodity through interstate commerce."

     b. it does not protect any instrumentality of interstate commerce (mail, electronic communication, trucks, trains, planes etc.)

     c. it does not regulate an activity that has a substantial affect on interstate commerce.

2. Congress did not require that the firearm(s) illegally possessed have some connection to interstate commerce.

3. Congress did not "expressly" establish how, in its opinion, gun possession in a school zone adversely affected interstate commerce.

4. The government's arguments fail because they could be used to create a functional federal "police power" which is incompatible with the Constitution's mandate that the federal government be a limited government with enumerated powers.

Appendix B: Procedural Considerations

 ## Procedural Primer

A defendant in a criminal case has a constitutional right to a jury trial if he or she is facing the possibility of being sentenced to a term of incarceration for more than six months. This right can be waived by a defendant who would rather be tried by a judge sitting without a jury (this is called a bench trial). The form of trial greatly determines the judge's role in the proceedings.

In a jury trial, the jury determines the facts (such as, "is the accused guilty or not guilty of the charges?"), and the judge rules on motions and makes sure that the procedural and evidentiary rules are followed, that decorum is preserved, and that the defendant receives a fair trial. If a bench trial is conducted, the judge has the additional responsibility of determining the facts in lieu of the jury. The prosecutor and defense attorney, when trying a case to a jury, normally explain their theory of the case to the jury prior to presenting evidence. Such statements will generally not be made in a bench trial, because the trial judge can follow the evidence as it is presented and does not need the lawyers to explain the big picture to understand how it all comes together.

A third procedural difference relates to the enforcement of the rules of evidence. These rules control how the lawyers prove their cases. The trial judges enforce the rules relatively strictly in jury cases so that jurors are not swayed by proof that should not be relied on in reaching a verdict. In a bench trial, the rules of evidence are more relaxed because trial judges are expert in evaluating evidence and can distinguish probative evidence from that which is not.

A fourth difference involves the use of jury instructions. Because few nonlawyer jurors understand exactly what it is that jurors will have to decide, the pertinent burdens of proof, the applicable law in each case, and the jury's responsibilities, it is essential that trial judges explain these matters to the jurors so that they can properly conduct deliberations and reach a verdict. The judge's explanation takes the form of jury instructions that are read to the jurors in the courtroom (usually after both parties have concluded their evidentiary presentations). In bench trials, it doesn't make much sense for the court to instruct itself on the law, as the judge knows the law and procedures.

The Order of Trial

It is important that students in an introductory course understand some of the procedural contexts in which substantive criminal law issues arise. What follows is a brief discussion of the order of trial, the role of legal presumptions, and why so much emphasis is placed on evidentiary burdens of proof.

Jury Selection

Although the composition of a federal jury is normally 12 persons, the states are not required to follow the federal practice. The U.S. Supreme Court has ruled that juries composed of six persons satisfy the requirements of due process under the federal Constitution. Prospective jurors, generally chosen from persons who are registered to vote, are summoned to the courthouse to serve as jurors. Once there, they are organized into groups called panels and are questioned as to their qualifications to serve in a particular case. The attorneys in some jurisdictions, and the judge in others, will question the prospective jurors to identify persons who should be disqualified from service.

Challenges to the Panel

Prospective jurors who are unfit to sit because of bias or prejudice, who are related to or associated with one of the parties, who have prejudged the case, or who are ill will be challenged for cause and excused by the court. Attorneys can challenge the qualifications of any prospective juror for cause.

In addition to the challenges for cause, the lawyers for each side are entitled to exclude jurors without cause by exercising what are called peremptory challenges.

The attorneys for both sides can use their allotted peremptory challenges to excuse prospective jurors they do not want sitting in judgment in the case. Each party will be allocated an equal number of peremptory challenges in accordance with prevailing rules in that jurisdiction. In high-profile cases, jury-consulting firms are sometimes retained to help the lawyers decide how to exercise their peremptory challenges. Prosecutors are prohibited from excluding prospective jurors peremptorily solely because of the juror's race or gender.

After the jurors (and a couple of alternates) have been qualified and the jury is sworn, it is time for the lawyers to present their opening statements.

Opening Statements

The prosecutor makes the first opening statement. The prosecutor normally introduces the parties and explains how the government intends to prove that a crime was committed and that the defendant is the responsible person. This presentation should not be thought of as evidence, because the prosecutor is not under oath and is not subject to cross-examination. It is an outline of what the prosecutor expects the evidence will show when it is offered as part of the government's case.

The defense attorney also has an opportunity to make an opening statement at this time, but if the procedural rules permit it, the defense's opening may be reserved until just before the defense presents its case, later on in the trial.

The prosecution presents evidence first instead of the defense, because every criminal defendant is afforded a presumption of innocence; as a matter of law, the accused has no legal obligation to prove innocence. A legally presumed fact (the defendant's innocence) is substituted for real evidence of innocence. A legal presumption also has a second function—the party burdened by the presumption (in this case, the prosecution) has a legal duty to disprove the presumed fact (rebut the defendant's presumed innocence with proof of the defendant's guilt). Thus it can be said that the presumption of innocence is a surrogate for evidence in a criminal case, and the prosecution is allocated the burden of proof with respect to evidence of the defendant's guilt.

By way of contrast, the legal presumption of sanity works exactly in reverse. All persons are presumed to be sane. Thus the prosecution has no affirmative duty in a homicide case to prove the criminal defendant's sanity as part of the government's case in chief. The presumption of sanity is a surrogate for evidence of sanity. Second, because the prosecution is benefited by the presumption of sanity in a murder case, the defendant has the burden of proof with respect to evidence of the defendant's insanity. The defendant must introduce evidence tending to prove this defense as part of the defense's case in chief if the issue is to be considered by the factfinder (the judge or jury).

The Presentation of the Prosecution's Case in Chief

The prosecution proves its case against the defendant by introducing evidence and calling witnesses who give sworn testimony that tends to prove the defendant's guilt (the presentation of the prosecution's case in chief). When the prosecution believes that it has met its burden of production as to every element of the crime with which the defendant is charged, it rests its case in chief. At this point the defense attorney asks the court to acquit the defendant. The defense argues in support of its motion that the prosecution's case is legally insufficient and that no reasonable juror could be permitted to convict the defendant beyond a reasonable doubt based on the existing record of admissible evidence. The court, for purposes of this motion, resolves all factual issues in favor of the prosecution (in other words, assumes that the prosecution witnesses are truthful and credible), reviews the evidence, and makes a ruling. Normally, the prosecution's evidence is satisfactory and the motion to acquit is denied.

The Presentation of the Defendant's Case in Chief

The presentation of the defendant's case in chief is the point in the trial where the defense attorney has the opportunity to call witnesses and introduce evidence. This evidence may be offered to contradict the prosecution's case, to establish a legal defense to the charges (such as insanity, self-defense, or entrapment), or to impeach the credibility of prosecution witnesses. The defendant has a constitutional right not to take the witness stand and cannot be made to incriminate himself or herself. If the defendant does testify, the defendant is subject to cross-examination by the prosecutor just like any other witness. The defendant cannot use the privilege against self-incrimination to avoid answering tough questions that are relevant to the charges currently being tried. In some instances, the defense may decide not to present any witnesses or evidence. Should the defense follow that strategy and rest its case without presenting evidence, the evidentiary part of the trial will have concluded. When the defense has concluded its presentation, it rests its case in chief.

The Presentation of the Prosecution's Rebuttal Case

After both sides have rested their cases in chief, it is time for the prosecution's rebuttal case, in which the prosecution offers testimony and evidence that tends to disprove any defenses raised by the defendant. The government may also try to rehabilitate any prosecution witnesses who have been impeached by the defense and may call witnesses who will contradict the testimony offered by defense witnesses.

The Defense Motion for Acquittal

After the parties have rested their cases, the defense attorney will again ask the court to award a verdict of acquittal in favor of the defendant, arguing that no reasonable juror could convict the defendant beyond a reasonable doubt on the current state of the evidence presented during the trial. The motion is usually denied, and the trial proceeds to the lawyers' closing arguments.

Closing Arguments

The lawyers become advocates when making a closing argument. In a bench trial, the argument is brief and to the point. Judges know how to evaluate testimony and assess the strengths and weaknesses of the respective cases. Judges also understand the presumption of innocence and the government's duty to persuade the factfinder of the defendant's guilt beyond a reasonable doubt. The lawyers are considerably more expansive when making an argument to a jury. They review the evidence, for example, and point out the strengths of their evidence and the weaknesses they see in their opponent's evidence. The lawyers also try to persuade the jury to render a verdict in favor of their client—the defendant or the people.

Jury Instructions

Judges use the jury instructions phase to explain the relevant legal principles jurors will need to understand in order to reach a verdict. Part of this presentation will involve explaining the meaning of the presumption of innocence, the prosecution's obligation to prove the defendant's guilt beyond a reasonable doubt, and in some instances the defendant's burden of convincing the jury of the validity of an "affirmative defense."

The Jury's Verdict

After the jury has been instructed by the judge, it retires to weigh the evidence and reach a verdict of guilty or not guilty as to each charge for which the defendant has stood trial. Jurors normally deliberate until they reach a legally acceptable verdict. In many jurisdictions the jury must unanimously agree on the verdict. The U.S. Supreme Court, however, has ruled that unanimous verdicts are not constitutionally required. In some states a verdict in which 9 out of 12 jurors agree is acceptable, and in other states a vote of 10 to 2 will suffice. If jurors are unable to reach a legally acceptable verdict, a hung jury will be declared. If this situation occurs, the court discharges the current jury, declares a mistrial, and gives the prosecution a period of time to decide whether it wishes to schedule the case for retrial. Because the first trial did not produce a legally acceptable verdict, the retrial will not amount to a second prosecution against the defendant for the same offense and thus there is no double jeopardy.

If the jury returns with a verdict of not guilty, the court will enter a judgment in favor of the defendant. This means that the matter cannot be re-prosecuted in any court, because to do so would violate the double jeopardy protections of the Fifth and Fourteenth Amendments to the U.S. Constitution. If the jury returns with a verdict of guilty, the prosecution will ask the court to enter judgment in accordance with the verdict in favor of the government.

Motions After Verdict

If the defendant is convicted, the defense is entitled to make motions for a new trial and for judgment notwithstanding the verdict. These post-verdict motions are routinely made and rarely granted. They are granted in situations where significant errors compromised the trial or where the court is persuaded that the evidence was so weak that it would be a miscarriage of justice for the jury to find the defendant guilty beyond a reasonable doubt. If these motions are denied, a date is set for sentencing.

Most jurisdictions have a wide variety of legally authorized sentencing options. Offenders vary in terms of the amount of risk they pose to society, the extent to which they can be rehabilitated, the severity of their crimes, and their status as a first offender or a recidivist. The sentencing options typically include capital punishment, incarceration, fines for serious crimes, probation, community service, restitution, and deferred judgments (leading ultimately to dismissal after a stated term if certain conditions are met) for less serious offenses.

Glossary

Abandonment The voluntary exiting of a person from a conspiracy

Accessory after the fact A person who provides assistance to the criminal after the crime has been committed

Accessory before the fact A person who aids or abets the commission of a crime but is not present when it is perpetrated

Actual possession Physical possession of contraband

Actus reus One component of a crime; any overt act that accompanies the intent to commit a crime

Affirmative defense Response to a criminal charge where the defendant bears the burden of proof. Goes beyond the simple denial of facts and gives new facts in favor of the defendant, if facts in the original complaint are true

Aggravated assault An unlawful attack by one person on another for the purpose of inflicting severe injury, or the attempt, or threat thereof

Alibi Defense to a criminal allegation that places an accused individual at some place other than the crime scene at the time the crime occurred

Arson Intentional burning (charring) of a protected dwelling or structure

Asportation The carrying away of something. The carrying away of a victim during the commission of a kidnapping

425

Assault Any unlawful attempt, with force or violence, to harm or frighten another

Assumed duty An affirmative duty applying to someone who has assumed a non-contractual duty for someone else

Attempt An overt action associated with a crime and done with criminal intent that goes beyond preparation, but does not necessarily mean that the act has been completed

B

Battery Unlawful, harmful, or offensive touching of another person

Bench trial A trial, chosen by a defendant, where a verdict is determined by a sitting judge rather than a jury

Bill of attainder A law passed by a legislative body that declares a criminally accused person to be guilty and imposes capital punishment on them

Blackmail *See* Extortion

Burden of persuasion Defense where the government has failed to establish guilt beyond a reasonable doubt

Burden of production Defense where the prosecution's evidence is legally insufficient

Burglary Use of force facilitating entry with the intent, at the time of trespass, to commit a felony within

C

Capital punishment Imposition of the death penalty for the most serious crimes

Certiorari A writ issued by a higher court directing a lower court to prepare the record of a case for review

Challenge for cause Ability for defendant or prosecution to challenge a prospective juror for cause because the prospective juror may have prejudged the case or is ill, or because of preexisting bias, relation, or association with one of the parties

Charges in the alternative A prosecution where charges were authorized by more than one statute

Choice of evils defense *See* Necessity defense

Civil suits Suit usually involving a dispute between private parties

Closing arguments Arguments presented by prosecutor and defense at the end of the trial

Codes Collection of statutes that relate to a particular topic

Common law tradition Authority based on court decrees and judgments that recognize, affirm, and force certain usages and customs of the people based upon the English tradition

Consolidated theft statues Statutes providing for simplification of prosecution's pleadings and proof problems in order to avoid technical defenses

Conspiracy The crime of two or more persons agreeing or planning to commit a crime

Constructive possession Possession of contraband where the object is under the possessor's dominion, control, or authority

Contractual duty Affirmative duty imposed by contract, where inaction is prosecutable

Corpus delicti The body of the crime made up of the *actus reus* and *mens rea*. The fact that proves that a crime has been committed

Criminal case Case brought by the state or federal government alleging a violation of a criminal duty, usually contained in a statute

Criminal intent The *mens rea* or evil intention necessary to commit a crime

Curtilage Outbuildings or fields attached to a residence

D

Defense of others Defense where action is justified if the defender reasonably believes the attacker is unlawfully threatening use of force against a third person

Double jeopardy Fifth Amendment prohibition against subjecting persons to prosecution more than once in the same jurisdiction for the same offense

Dual sovereignty A government made up of two separate, fully functioning governments (i.e., state and federal) complete with a legislative, executive, and judicial branch

Due process Clause located in the Fifth Amendment of the U.S. Constitution providing that no person shall be "deprived of life, liberty or property without due process of the law."

Duress A complete defense where the accused honestly and reasonably believed that he or she would suffer imminent death or serious bodily harm unless he or she committed a criminal act

E

Embezzlement Crime involving withholding or withdrawing, converting, or misappropriating, without consent, funds entrusted to an agent

Entrapment Defense used to show otherwise criminal act would not have occurred without police intervention, assistance, and/or encouragement

Equal protection clause Clause of the Fourteenth Amendment guaranteeing equal protection of the law regardless of color, class, gender, national origin, race, or religion

Excuse defense Defense in which accused persons maintain they lacked the intent to commit the crime

Ex post facto law Retroactive criminalizing of conduct that occurred before conduct was made criminal

Extortion Intimidation of victim by making present threat of future harm to victim's person, family, or property

F

Factual causation Conduct that is determined to be the cause of a harmful event

False imprisonment Confinement in a place of an offender's choosing where victim is prevented from leaving

Felony A crime carrying penalties of incarceration for one year or more

First-degree murder Murder requiring specific intent, preceded by premeditation and deliberation

Forgery The fraudulent making, altering, falsifying, signing, or reproducing any kind of writing

G

General deterrence Imposition of punishment imposed to set an example for society as whole in order to prevent future crimes

General intent Intent, without any legal justification to commit the *actus reus* specified for that crime

Good character defense Defense that attempts to establish reasonable doubt as to whether the defendant's character would have allowed the commission of the crime

H

Habeas corpus Writ meaning "produce the body"; used by prisoners to challenge the nature and length of their confinement

Hung jury An instance where jurors are unable to reach a legally acceptable verdict

I

Impossibility as a defense A defense where the intent was to commit a crime but none was committed (a drug trafficker believing he was trafficking narcotics that turned out to be talcum powder)

Inchoate offenses An offense that is a prelude to some other offense (i.e., solicitation or conspiracy)

Incompetency Lack of fitness to give testimony or stand trial

Independent, intervening cause Consequences that an accused is not responsible for during an event

Insanity A defense claiming that defendant lacks the legal capacity to be criminally responsible for what would otherwise constitute criminal conduct

Involuntary manslaughter Unintentional killing by a person committing a misdemeanor or engaging in reckless or grossly negligent conduct

Irresistible impulse test A desire that cannot be resisted due to impairment of the will by mental disease or defect

J

Joinder Coupling of two or more criminal prosecutions

Jury instructions A set of instructions given by a judge to a jury explaining what they will need to decide, the pertinent burdens of proof, the applicable law, and the jury's responsibilities

Jury selection Process by which a jury is chosen on a particular trial

Jury trial Trial where the guilt or innocence of a defendant is determined by jury instead of by the judge

Justification defense Defense to a criminal charge in which defendants maintain that their actions were appropriate or noncriminal according to the circumstances

K

Kidnapping Seizure, detention, and asportation or hiding of a victim

L

Larceny Unlawful taking, carrying, leading, or riding away of property from the possession or constructive possession of another

Larceny by false pretenses Induction of victims to part with their property through trickery, deceit, or misrepresentation

M

Mala in se **offenses** Offenses requiring proof of criminal intent

Mala prohibita **offenses** Acts that are not intrinsically evil, defined as being criminal by legislative bodies in order to promote the public health, welfare, safety, or morals of a society

Malice aforethought The *mens rea* requirement for murder, consisting of the intention to kill with the awareness that there is no right to kill

Mens rea Evil intent necessary for the commission of a crime

Misdemeanor Crime punishable by fines and/or imprisonment for periods of less than one year

Misprision of felony Crime of concealing a felony committed by another

Mistake of law defense Defense claiming that the person mistakenly believed his conduct to be lawful at the time of commission

Mistrial A trial that cannot stand, that is declared invalid by a judge

M'Naghten **rule** A criminal defendant can be excused from criminal responsibility only if (1) he was not, because of mental illness, aware of the nature and quality of his actions, or (2) he did know what he was doing; he was unable, when he acted, to distinguish right from wrong

Model Penal Code Code developed by the American Law Institute clarifying crime and accompanying punishments

Motion An oral or written request to a judge that asks the court to make a specific ruling, finding, decision, or order

N

Necessity defense An affirmative defense where someone is compelled to act because of perceived needs

O

Obstruction of justice Impeding or preventing the administration of justice

Opening statements Remarks made by the prosecution and defense attorneys to the jury at the commencement of trial proceedings

Overbreadth Legislation infringing on constitutionally protected rights

P

Panels A set of jurors or prospective jurors

Peremptory challenges Each side's right to exclude an allotment of jurors without cause

Police power Influence of government to legislate to protect public health, safety, welfare, and morality

Post-verdict motions Motions made after the verdict has been reached

Presumption of innocence Legal presumption that a person is innocent until proven guilty stemming from the Fifth and Fourteenth Amendments

Presumption of sanity Legal presumption that a person is sane until proven otherwise

***Prima facie* case** A case for which there is as much evidence as would warrant the conviction of defendant if properly proved in court. A case that meets the evidentiary requirements for a grand jury indictment

Principal in the first degree Under common law, the person who committed the *actus reus* in the commission of a crime

Principal in the second degree Under common law, the person who aided or abetted the commission of a crime and was present when it was perpetrated

Protective custody law Statutes authorizing police officers to take intoxicated persons found in public places into custody

Proximate cause The factor closest to actually causing an event

Public welfare offenses *See* Strict liability offenses

R

Rape Sexual penetration of a female without consent and with use or threatened use of force

Rebuttal case The presentation of testimony and evidence offered in order to disprove any defenses raised by defendant during the presentation of his or her case

Rehabilitation A form of correction including probation, treatment, or parole

Retribution Punishment for the sake of revenge

Right to privacy The freedom of individuals to choose for themselves the time, circumstances, and extent to which their beliefs and behavior are to be shared or withheld from others

Robbery Larceny by means of present force or intimidation

Rules of evidence Rules governing how the prosecution and defense may prove their case

S

Second-degree murder Murder requiring the prosecution to prove intent to kill, death, and causation

Self defense Affirmative defense in which defendants explain otherwise criminal conduct by showing the necessity to defend themselves against aggressive victims

Sexual assault In modern statutes, the unlawful oral, anal, or vaginal penetration by or union with the sexual organ of another

Solicitation The inchoate offense of requesting or encouraging someone to engage in illegal conduct

Specific deterrence Punishment imposed to convince an existing offender not to commit future crimes

Specific intent The intent to accomplish a specific purpose as an element of a crime

Status duty Affirmative duty imposed by virtue of status, where inaction is prosecutable

Statutes Written laws enacted by legislatures

Statutory duty Affirmative duty imposed by statute, where inaction is prosecutable

Statutory rape The crime of having sexual relations with an underage person

Strict liability offenses Offenses where the law provides for convictions of offenders without regard to the existence, or lack, of a culpable mind

Substantive law The part of law that creates and defines legal rights and duties

Supremacy Clause Tenth Amendment clause declaring that state laws are invalid if they frustrate or are contrary to congressional objectives in a subject area that is appropriately within the federal domain

T

Theft by deceit *See* Larceny by false pretenses

Transferred intent doctrine If an illegal yet unintended act results from the intent to commit a crime, that act is also considered illegal

Trespass to land/dwellings Entry/remaining on land or into premises of another without consent and after receiving written or oral notice not to enter/remain

V

Verdict Decision by a judge or a jury concerning the guilt or innocence of a defendant

Vicarious liability Liability for criminal acts that were committed by others

Voluntary manslaughter Charge where the perpetrator intentionally kills the victim in response to extreme provocation causing the perpetrator to lose self-control

Table of Cases

Principal cases appear in italics

Index